World Surfing Champion Shaun Tomson/Jones

With special sections on:

Aruba, Australia, Bahamas, Bonaire, Cayman Islands, Curacao, the French West Indies, Hawaii, Puerto Rico, Saba, St. Vincent and the Turks & Caicos Islands

Travel & Sports Guide

South Pacific/Kelly

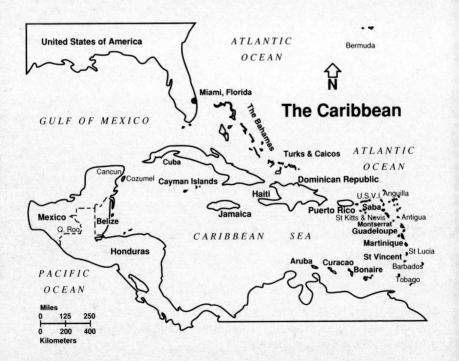

United States of America

ATLANTIC OCEAN

Bermuda

N

Miami, Florida

The Caribbean

GULF OF MEXICO

The Bahamas

Turks & Caicos

ATLANTIC OCEAN

Cuba

Cancun

Cozumel

Cayman Islands

Dominican Republic

Haiti

U.S.V.I. Anguilla

Saba

Puerto Rico

St Kitts & Nevis

Antigua

Mexico

Belize

Jamaica

Montserrat

Guadeloupe

Q. Roo

CARIBBEAN SEA

Martinique

St Lucia

Honduras

St Vincent

Aruba

Curacao

Bonaire

Barbados

Tobago

PACIFIC OCEAN

Miles
0   125   250

0   200   400
Kilometers

Travel & Sports Guide

Index

For maps of Aruba, Australia, Bahamas, Bonaire, Cayman Islands, Curacao, French West Indies, Hawaii, Puerto Rico, Saba, St. Vincent and the Turks & Caicos Islands: see the individual section.

Travel & Sports Guide

Interested in working with Travel & Sports?

At Travel & Sports we are privileged to work with some of the best photographers and journalists in the world. As we expand into new areas, we look for photojournalists with experience and insight into the areas and people covered. If you would like to become part of the Travel & Sports team, contact us at the address below.

Masthead

Travel & Sports Guide
300 Brannan St. #501
San Francisco, CA 94107
- **Publisher: John C. Dean**
- **Director of Marketing: Ron Pinkston**
- **Senior Editor: Karla Jacobs**
- **Final Edit: Dolly Huysman, Suzanne Maineri**
- **Consulting Editor: Jane Edmunds**
- **Writers:**
  Karla Jacobs: Australia, French West Indies, Saba, St. Vincent & the Grenadines, Turks & Caicos
  Irene Freidman: Puerto Rico
  Jan Steites: The Bahamas
  Joe Troise: Aruba, Bonaire, Caymans, Curacao
  Other writers: Nina Greenberg, Suzanne Maineri, Diane Tegmeyer
- **Photography:**
  Bruce Bassett, Tony Bell, Nick Fain, Dan Hobby, Karla Jacobs, Forest Johnson, Darrell Jones, Marty Kelly, Frazier Nivens, Carl Roessler, Jerry Schnabel, Sun Star, Chris Weisner. All the photographers may be contacted through Travel & Sports.
- **Design: Ray Dorn**
- **Copyright 1988, John C. Dean, All Rights Reserved**
- **Travel & Sports, and Travel & Sports Guide are trademarks of Travel & Sports.**
- **To order copies of this book:**
  Send a check for $9.95 per copy plus $2.75 shipping and handling to the address above (California residents add 6.5% sales tax), or call 415-546-0303.
- **Bookstores**
  Order directly from: Publishers Group West, 800-982-8319, 415-658-3453, 4065 Hollis, Emeryville, CA 94608.

Disclaimer

The Travel & Sports Guide is only a guide. Travel & Sports, its publisher, staff, writers, affiliated individuals and companies do not recommend any particular activity, operator, accommodation or destination. No one at Travel & Sports is authorized to make any such recommendation. Travel & Sports does not attest to the qualifications or competence of anyone listed in the Travel & Sports Guide: you must make that judgment for yourself.

All sports contain an element of risk. Always discuss the current local conditions with qualified and competent local sports professionals. Follow their recommendations.

Travel & Sports does not rate any sport or activity by level of difficulty: you must obtain that information locally. Travel & Sports disclaims any responsibility for injury that may occur to anyone through or by the use of the information in the Travel & Sports Guide.

Curacao Regatta/Jones

INTRODUCTION

The Travel & Sports Guide was written especially for today's active traveler. The kind of traveler who isn't content to lie on the beach. The kind who likes to get under the skin of a new place, meet the people, climb the mountains, check out the local golf course, try parasailing and take the plunge to see what's new under that beautiful turquoise water. You know the type. If you've read this far, you probably are the type.

So for all those who think a vacation should be an adventure, welcome to the new Travel & Sports Guide. Get ready for a fantasy tour of some of the world's best sports vacation destinations. We'll take you diving on Australia's Great Barrier Reef, wind surfing in the French West Indies, sailing in St. Vincent and the Grenadines and surfing in Puerto Rico. We'll guide you on a long, leisurely tour of every island in the Bahamas, explore the charming and as-yet undiscovered Turks and Caicos Islands and journey to the Dutch islands of Aruba, Bonaire and Curacao.

In addition to sports, we'll describe the other attractions each island has to offer: casinos, shops, museums, history, culture, ecology and lots, lots more. A choice of accommodations, ranging from thatched bures in Fiji to the unique and elegant resorts of Martinique to cozy guesthouses on Saba, await your consideration. And thousands of miles of beaches, hundreds of hours of sunshine and uncountable adventures will tempt you to do more than just daydream. Why not go! Everything you need to plan and book your trip is here in the Travel & Sports Guide.

Travel & Sports is constantly updating its research on the Caribbean, the Bahamas, Mexico, Hawaii, Australia and the South Pacific. We send teams of writers and photographers to capture the flavor of these tropical destinations and collect information on the sports operators and accommodations that cater to active travelers. We go to the beaches, the dive shops, the hotels, the cruise ships and the tennis courts (it's a tough job, but somebody has to do it).

The Sports sections of each chapter are the result of hundreds of on-site interviews with local sports professionals, hoteliers and tourist boards to discover the latest sports offerings available to visitors.

There is no other publication like Travel & Sports Guide for its comprehensive coverage of special events, sports offerings and up-to-date, factual information.

Travel & Sports Guide

Sports

There are two ways to go about selecting a sports-oriented vacation: you can pick a resort based upon what sports they offer, or, you can select the sports operator and then check out what resorts they have package deals with. Of course, you can always select the resort of your choice and use other sports operators, but there are advantages to using accommodations with built-in sports facilities: usually the resort and sports operator will have worked out all the mechanics, such as transportation and equipment.

A multitude of other sports and events are included in the Sports sections, especially spectator sports, that are particular to each area. The kinds of events you'll find include: surf championships, air shows, rugby, squash, rodeo, running, golf tournaments, kayaking, white-water rafting, bicycling, swimming, marathons, triathlons and sailing regattas -- to name a few. In fact, you'll find a sporting event for things you probably never even dreamed of, like the famous and wild Carole Kai Bed Race in Hawaii (yes, real beds), and Australia's Beer Can Regatta with boats made of... empties of course! And at most of these events there's always some sort of festivities going on, whether sponsored or not, that you can invite yourself to.

Diving

Opportunities and dive operators are available for the most advanced scuba diver to the beginner or snorkeler. Some dive areas are very developed, with lots of operators, sites, equipment and divers. Others, like the Turks and Caicos Islands are just getting word out about their underwater resources. When possible, we have listed each area's sites in detail, giving you an idea of the kind of diving you'll find there.

For a complete and critical review of dive areas and operators throughout the world, get the Undercurrents newsletter (800-521-7004 or 212-873-5900). If you are interested in striking dive videos, contact Sea Fans Videos (303-750-0055 or 800-622-8767).

Fishing

Fishing tournaments take place all over, perhaps the most outrageous being the Million Dollar Month Tournament in the Cayman Islands where, among various other prizes, one million dollars and a lifetime pass aboard Cayman Airways will be awarded to the skilled angler who breaks the Atlantic Blue Marlin record.

Fishing charters are usually arranged by the hotels. Charters range in price from $100 for a day of bonefishing to $500 - $1,000 for a large billfishing expedition for 6 to 8 people including tackle. If you're headed for a specific fishing-oriented resort, for example the resorts on Little Cayman, your choice of accommodations will be based on the operator you intend to fish with. Otherwise, since you won't be lugging around a lot of equipment, and it's as just as easy to get to one boat as another, your choice of accommodation may not be based on its sports facilities.

Golf

All these destinations offer beautiful greens, usually right on the water with spectacular views. Green fees are pretty reasonable and most of the courses throughout the Caribbean and Bahamas are PGA rated. They run an average of 6,500 to 7,000 yards, 18 holes, par 72. You can pick a resort situated right on the greens and catering especially to golfers, such as the Cotton Bay Beach and Golf Club in Eleuthera, Bahamas or The Divi South Ocean Beach in Nassau, Bahamas.

Hiking

Some of these areas are as flat as pancakes. Obviously they don't make for good, challenging hikes. But then there are destinations like the Yucatan in Mexico where, even though the terrain isn't that vigorous, you'll be stumbling across ancient ruins every 50 feet. Other areas, like Saba, have beautiful mountainous terrain with well-developed hiking trails taking you throughout the countryside and showing off some spectacular scenery.

South Pacific/Jacobs

Sailing

Almost all these destinations have facilities for larger yachts. Some areas, like St. Vincent and the Grenadines, are particularly well-known for their spectacular sailing and calm harbors. Some sports operators will actually come out to your boat and provide you with equipment and even lessons for diving and other watersports.

Tennis

Every place we visited had tennis courts, whether private clubs, public or resort courts. You can always find an available court somewhere. If you're interested in tournaments, check the tennis heading for a list of annual events.

Windsurfing

Windsurfing is the hot new sport, and boards are available at practically every resort and at 95% of the beach properties. Some of the equipment is a little beat-up and water-logged, but in areas with excellent windsurfing conditions, such as the French West Indies, Aruba, Bonaire and Curacao, you'll find quality up-to-date equipment managed by reputable people. The islands have 15 mile per hour trade winds that blow steadily throughout the year, making for any combination of wild wavesailing to flat calm waters, with on and offshore winds.

Other Watersports

Everything from jetskiing, waterskiing and parasailing to Hobie and Sunfish sailing to kayaking and surfing. Almost all the resorts offer some combination of watersports. Larger resorts are almost sure to offer jetskiing, a sport that's become popular world-wide. When planning your vacation, check to see whether or not the use and cost of the equipment is included in your package, and if it's not, what the cost will be, what condition it is in and who operates it. Remember that some resorts have very limited watersports, while others have a full line and range of equipment, so ask in advance.

For excellent surfing in the Caribbean, head to Puerto Rico. In the Pacific, of course, Hawaii is the number one destination, and in the South Pacific it has to be Australia.

Travel & Sports Guide

Useful Facts

• **Airline Connections**

You can easily fly into any of the major islands in the Caribbean and Bahamas. Others, with only infrequently scheduled flights, can be harder to reach.

Flying into Australia and Hawaii, with their many efficient airports and major carriers, is a breeze. Flying into other parts of the South Pacific, however, can be a little more difficult. Usually flights into the South Pacific depart from Australia, Japan or Hawaii.

Packages offer advantages: for instance, you are not charged for rooms if airline problems delay your arrival, and some packages also include round-trip private-plane service to remote cays or islets. Keep your toothbrush and essentials (including swimsuit) in your carry-ons in case of checked-luggage delay. Most areas insist on cash payment of an airport departure tax.

• **Banking**

Don't bring foreign currency back to the United States unless you want souvenirs. You'll get a much better exchange rate at the local airport. Credit cards are accepted by large resorts as well as some restaurants and shops in the more developed towns. Incidentally, if you run into severe problems, American Express (if you use their credit card) will honor reasonable stop-payment requests.

• **Courtesy & Dress**

Casual is the common description. A few swankier places prefer ties and heels (not necessarily on the same person). Attire in Australia, like any large country, varies from city to town to resort. Of course, if you plan to spend time in the major cities, include more formal attire. While casual applies to general attire and attitude in the South Pacific, know that short shorts and brief attire are considered inappropriate off the beach.

• **Customs & Immigrations**

Entering most nations is quite easy. A passport and onward or return ticket are usually enough. Occasionally, you can get by with a driver's license, voter's registration card or birth certificate -- but don't count on it. Typically your baggage will be subjected to a minimal search or none at all. Your cameras and sports gear will not be a problem. Miami Airport, the major port of entry from the Caribbean, can be a real bottleneck on your return.

To enter Australia, both a passport _and_ visa are necessary. For other destinations in the South Pacific, you'll need a passport and onward or return ticket. It's a good idea to get all the required paperwork done at least 4 to 6 weeks before departure.

You may bring back to the US $400 worth of articles duty-free, including one quart of liquor per person. For duty rates on additional purchases and information on special duty-free items and prohibited items, consult US Customs, or write for <u>Know Before You Go -- Customs Hints for Returning Residents</u>, or <u>US Customs Pocket Hints</u>. These and other specialized customs publications are available from US Customs, Box 7404, Washington DC, 20044, or call 202-556-8195.

• **Languages**

In any country, with a little effort, you can always communicate.

• **Medical**

Most islands have medical centers. Australian and Hawaiian facilities are numerous and excellent. In the South Pacific, good facilities are found in the major towns. If you plan on traveling to Central America or the remote areas of the South Pacific, make sure you are prepared against malaria.

• **Off-Season Dates & Rates**

The off-season begins mid-April and extends until mid-November or December. During this period, you can cash in on savings of up to 50%. Australia does not have an off-season.

• **Taxes & Tipping**

In the Caribbean and Bahamas, a 10-15% tip is customary. Check with the hotel before you tip as the charge is often part of the bill. Most governments charge hotel taxes. In Australia, tipping is up to you. In the South Pacific, tips aren't expected; in fact, they're considered rude.

Caribbean/Bell

• Taxi Fares
Most fares are fixed by destination. Determine the fare in advance and know if it's quoted in US or local currency (especially if the local currency is also called a "dollar"). Fixed-rate schedules are available at many airports.

• Telephone
Big cities in major areas offer efficient direct-dial telephoning. It's often cheaper to use your phone company credit card than to pay local rates. It is much easier (and cheaper) to call the islands, than it is to call the US from the islands.

• Time
All Caribbean countries are on either Eastern Standard Time (EST) or Atlantic Standard Time (AST). Atlantic Standard Time is one hour ahead of Eastern Standard Time. Some go on Daylight Savings Time; others do not. Australia and the South Pacific are on 10 and 11 Greenwich Mean Time (GMT). Generally, that adds up to one day <u>ahead</u> but 5 to 7 hours <u>behind</u> Pacific Standard Time.

• Weather
We've included tropical and sub-tropical islands. On the former, the coastal temperature averages 77 degrees year round. The sub-tropical islands can drop to the 60's in winter. Inland, the temperatures vary more depending on topography. The Caribbean rainy season lasts from May or June to October or November, but the rain tends to be concentrated in brief, heavy showers, with the rest of the day sunny.

Australia's weather varies greatly from coast to coast and season to season. Some areas are warm year round, while others are visited by seasonal heavy rains and chill. In the South Pacific, temperatures are generally warm and balmy, ranging from the 70's to 80's. Expect a daily tropical shower in the cooler and drier summer months (approximately May to Oct.) and heavy rainfall in the muggier winter months (Dec.- March).

Travel & Sports Guide

Directories:

The prices listed in the Directory were obtained directly from each property or business. All prices are in US dollars and reflect flat high-season rates. Package deals and low-season rates can reduce these figures by as much as 50%.

Sample Accommodations Listing:

BUSINESS NAME 800-000-0000   100 Units: $50-250 BDFGKOPRSTW

415-000-0000 415-000-0000FX Street Address City ST 00000. This is a sample listing for an accommodation. All the offerings are indicated by the letter code to the right of the name. The toll free 800 number, if available, is always shown first. The second and third numbers are usually not toll free and include local numbers, fax numbers and US numbers. In some instances the descriptions in the Travel & Sports Guide were provided by the listed business. See: Business Name.

Our price range is based on the high-season rate, double occupancy, not including meals (unless indicated in the text of the listing). The letter codes show the offerings (see Key explanation below). Looking at the combination of units, price and offerings, you get a good idea of what to expect at a property.

Phone numbers shown with the suffix "FX" indicate the direct line for a FAX machine. In most cases, a photograph of the resort has been included to go along with the descriptions. If any affiliated sports facility exists, it is cross-referenced at the end of the description.

What the Key codes mean:

Key: The accommodations price range is based on the high season rate per night, double occupancy. The Liveaboard price range is per berth, high season. The dive price range is based on the cost of a two tank dive. Letter codes: Beach (or on the water), Diving, Fishing, Golf, Other watersports, Pool, Restaurant & Bar, Sailing, Tennis, Windsurfing.

B = The property is located on the beach or on the water. Some resorts have miles of white sand beaches, others have "beaches" that would fit in a child's sandbox. If a beach is important to you, ask before booking.

D = Diving is offered.

F = Fishing. Deep-sea, big game, tarpon and/or bonefishing are available. Usually boats, guides and tackle are included. Arrangements are made directly with the resort or with their affiliated sports facility.

G = Golf. The resort has a course on the premises or has transportation to nearby greens.

K = Kitchens or Kitchenettes are available in all or some of the units.

O = Other watersports. This heading includes sports like jetskiing, water skiing, snorkeling and paddleboating.

P = Pool on the premises.

R = Restaurant and bar on the premises.

S = Sailing, from Hobie Cats to Yachts.

T = Tennis courts on the premises.

W = Windsurfing is offered.

Sea Fans Video Magazine on Location

South Pacific/Kelly

Whitsunday, Australia/Kelly

Caribbean/Bell

The Polynesia in Saba, Windjammer Barefoot Cruises/Fain

Polynesia, Windjammer Barefoot Cruises

Yankee Clipper, Windjammer Barefoot

Flying Cloud, Windjammer Barefoot Cruises

Bahamas/Bell

CRUISE TRAVEL

If you've never taken a cruise, you're in for a pleasant surprise. Many old truths about cruising simply don't hold water anymore. For example, no longer are cruise boats the exclusive domain of the rich, famous and retired. Nor is cruising necessarily a formal vacation requiring a wardrobe of tuxedos and evening gowns. And thanks to high-tech stabilizers, seasickness is, with few exceptions, a thing of the past. The entire cruising experience has expanded and changed, along with the American way of life.

Younger, more active and adventurous travelers have discovered that today's cruise travel provides exercise, excitement, romance and unlimited choices of activities at a price that's not necessarily expensive. Compared to a traditional vacation to a single destination, including airfare, transfers, hotels, food, entertainment, car rentals and side trips, a moderately priced, all-inclusive cruise can be a bargain.

Cruises offer certain advantages over traditional vacations, including the opportunity to visit a number of different destinations, the lack of travel frustrations, great service, gourmet food and the opportunity to see the world from a whole new perspective. There are cruises on sailing yachts, educational cruises, family-oriented ships, distinguished first-class vessels and rollicking love-boat style experiences. Theme cruises are available for special interest groups ranging from archaeologists to murder mystery fans, from tournament fishermen to computer fanatics.

It's no wonder that cruising is the fastest-growing travel market in the world. One-third of all passengers are now between 18 and 34. Another 25% are in the 35 to 54 bracket. When these passengers go ashore, they're looking for shopping, yes, but they're also looking for the nearest dive shop, the best surfing beach and the highest mountain to climb. Many ships make arrangements with sports operators and local tour companies for group rates on hikes, scuba expeditions and watersports rentals. Many of the sports operators listed in the Travel & Sports Guide work with the cruise lines to provide services to passengers on a regular basis.

To decide which of the many options is right for you, plan ahead. Decide where you'd like to go, for how long, what type of vessel you'd prefer, and what type of company you wish to keep. Consider your own personality, interests and style of traveling when deciding on a ship. The size of your budget will help you decide on the size of your cabin and the length of your trip.

In making your cruise travel decisions, use the Travel & Sports Guide to select your general destination. Then refer to the chart on pages 14 and 15 to learn which ships service the areas you wish to visit. With this information, you can call the cruise line (their 800 number is listed on page 15) for brochures, then consult your travel agent for the best booking.

Cruise Travel & Sports

Line	Nos. of Ships	Nos. of Berths	Anguilla	Antigua	Aruba	Bahamas	Barbados	Belize	Bermuda	Bonaire	British Vir. Isl	Cayman Islands	Curacao	Dominica	Dominican Republic	French West Indies	Grenada
ADMIRAL	3	2476			•					•							
AM-CANADIAN	2	148	•	•	•		•			•		•				•	•
AM-HAWAIIAN	2	1600															
ALOHA PACIFIC	1	598															
BERMUDA STAR	3	1630					•										
CARNIVAL	7	10718			•	•						•	•			•	
CLIPPER	3	342	•							•							
COSTA	6	4272	•		•	•					•	•				•	•
COMMODORE	1	1160								•	•			•			
CHANDRIS FANTASY	6	4609	•	•	•	•	•			•		•		•	•	•	•
CUNARD	7	4844	•	•	•	•	•	•		•	•	•		•	•	•	•
DOLPHIN	1	590			•												
EPIROTIKI	11	5126				•											
EXPLORATION	7	820				•											
EXPRINTER	3	1275	•							•					•	•	•
HOLLAND-AM	4	4820		•	•					•	•	•			•	•	
NORWEGIAN	6	6216	•		•	•	•				•	•			•	•	
OCEAN	3	1180	•	•	•						•				•	•	
PRINCESS	5	4012	•	•	•	•						•			•	•	
PREMIER	3	3800			•												
PAQUET FRENCH	1	530	•		•										•	•	
REGENCY	3	2490		•								•					
ROYAL	3	2318		•													
ROYAL CARIBBEAN	5	6426	•	•		•	•			•		•				•	
ROYAL VIKING	3	2160	•	•	•						•	•			•	•	
SALEM-LINDBLAD	6	600		•				•	•	•		•					
SEABOURN	2	424				•						•	•				
SEA ESCAPE	4	4052		•													
SITMAR	5	6500		•	•	•				•	•	•			•		
SUN LINE	3	1100	•		•	•				•	•	•		•	•		
WINDJAMMER BF	5	470	•	•	•	•				•				•	•		•

Cruise Travel & Sports

Line	Jamaica	Mexico	Montserrat	Puerto Rico	Saba	St. Eustatius	St. Kitts & Nevi	St. Lucia	St. Maarten	St. Vincent	Tobago	Turks & Caicos	USVI	Australia & Pacific	Hawaii
ADMIRAL		•													
AM-CANADIAN		•		•		•	•	•	•			•			
AM-HAWAIIAN														•	
ALOHA PACIFIC															•
BERMUDA STAR		•													
CARNIVAL	•	•	•					•				•			
CLIPPER			•		•	•	•	•				•			
COSTA	•	•	•					•	•			•			
COMMODORE	•	•	•									•			
CHANDRIS FANTASY	•	•	•				•	•	•	•	•	•			
CUNARD	•	•	•					•	•			•	•	•	
DOLPHIN															
EPIROTIKI									•	•					
EXPLORATION		•	•		•	•	•	•	•			•	•		
EXPRINTER	•									•	•		•		
HOLLAND-AM	•	•	•					•	•			•			
NORWEGIAN	•	•	•				•	•	•			•			
OCEAN	•							•		•	•	•	•		
PRINCESS		•	•						•	•		•	•		
PREMIER															
PAQUET FRENCH		•	•					•		•		•			
REGENCY	•	•													
ROYAL		•	•										•		
ROYAL CARIBBEAN	•	•	•					•				•			
ROYAL VIKING	•	•						•				•	•	•	
SALEM-LINDBLAD													•		
SEABOURN	•	•	•		•		•	•				•			
SEA ESCAPE		•													
SITMAR	•	•	•					•				•	•	•	
SUN LINE	•	•	•				•	•				•			
WINDJAMMER BF			•	•	•	•		•	•		•	•			

Cruise Travel & Sports

Cruise Line Directory

ADMIRAL CRUISES 800-327-0271
813-961-7949 800-327-2693 1220 Biscayne Bay Blvd. Miami FL 33132

AMERICAN CANADIAN 800-556-7450
401-247-0955 Box 368 Warren RI 02885

AMERICAN HAWAIIAN 800-227-3666
415-392-9400 550 Kearney St. San Francisco CA 94108

BERMUDA STAR CRUISE 800-237-5361
201-837-0400 1086 Teaneck Rd. Teaneck NJ 07666

CARNIVAL CRUISE LINES 800-327-9501
800-327-7276 5225 N.W. 87th Ave. Miami FL 33178

CHANDRIS FANTASY 800-223-0848
212-223-3003 212-697-5600 900 Third Avenue (10th Floor) New York NY 10022

CLIPPER CRUISE LINE 800-325-0010
314-727-2929 7711 Bonhome Ave. St. Louis MO 63105

COMMODORE CRUISE 800-327-5617
800-432-6793 800-832-1122 1007 North American Way Miami FL 33132

COSTA CRUISES 800-447-6877
FX:305-375-0676 Box 019614 Miami FL 33130

CUNARD CRUISE LINE 800-221-4770
212-880-7528 FX:212-949-0915 555 Fifth Avenue (5th Floor) New York NY 10017

DOLPHIN CRUISE LINE 800-222-1003
800-521-4299 FX:305-358-4807 1007 N. American Way Miami FL 33132

EPIROTIKI CRUISE LINES 800-221-2470
FX:212-687-0241 551 Fifth Ave., Suite 605 New York NY 10176

EXPLORATION CRUISE 800-426-0600
800-365-8184 TX:329636 1500 Metropolitan Park Building Seattle WA 98101

EXPRINTER CRUISES 800-221-1666
500 Fifth Avenue, Suite 510 New York NY 10110

HOLLAND AMERICA 800-426-0327
206-281-3535 800-445-3731 300 Elliott Ave., West Seattle WA 98119

NORWEGIAN CRUISE 800-327-7030
305-358-6670 800-327-3090 Two Alhambra Plaza Coral Gables FL 33134

OCEAN CRUISE LINES 800-556-8850
1510 S.E. 17th Street Ft. Lauderdale FL 33316

PAQUET FRENCH 800-999-0555
240 S. Conty Rd. Palm Beach FL 33480

PREMIER CRUISE LINES 800-327-7113
305-783-5061 P. O. Box 573 Cape Canaveral FL 32920

PRINCESS CRUISES 800-421-0522
800-354-4441 2029 Century Park East Los Angeles CA 90067

REGENCY CRUISES 800-457-5566
800-255-8984 260 Madison Avenue New York NY 10016

ROYAL CARIBBEAN 800-327-6700
305-379-2601 903 South American Way Miami FL 33132

ROYAL CRUISE LINES 415-956-7200
One Maritime Plaza San Francisco CA 94111

ROYAL VIKING 800-451-8572
415-398-8000 750 Battery San Francisco CA 94111

SALEM-LINDBLAD CRUISE 800-223-5688
133 E. 55th St. New York NY 10022

SEA ESCAPE 800-327-7400
305-377-9000 1080 Port Blvd. Miami FL 33132

SEABOURN CRUISE LINES 800-351-9595
415-397-9595 55 Francisco Street, Suite 710 San Francisco CA 94133

SITMAR CRUISES 800-421-0880
213-553-1666 800-527-6200 10100 Santa Monica Blvd. Los Angeles CA 90067

SUN LINE CRUISES 800-872-6400
212-397-6400 800-368-3888CAN One Rockefeller Plaza Suite 315 New York NY 10020

WINDJAMMER BAREFOOT CRUISES
800-327-2602 305-672-6453 FX:305-674-1219 P.O. Box 120 Miami Beach FL 33119. A Windjammer Caribbean holiday combines the adventure and romance of full- masted sailing with luxurious berths, gourmet food and exotic ports of call. Enjoy moonlight sails on 1 of 5 beautifully restored tall ships: the Fantome, Flying Cloud, Mandalay, Polynesia or Yankee Clipper. Or, cruise aboard the "Orient Express" of the Caribbean on the Amazing Grace, once the prestigious weekend host to Britan's Royal Family. With cruises of one to three weeks, there's plenty to do: snorkel, explore deserted beaches, shop or wander about town. Or you can do nothing at all, just sit back and enjoy.

Aruba

Windsurfer/Jones

Travel & Sports Guide

S.S. Antila/ Bailey & Rodriguez

Sand Crab/Bell

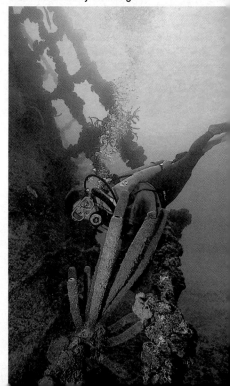

Aruba

Useful Facts

• Airline Connections   Direct daily flights from Miami on Eastern and from New York on American Airlines. Aeropostal and Avensa have daily flights from Venezuela. KLM offers regular flights from Europe. ALM is the sole provider of inter-island flights between Aruba, Bonaire, Curacao and Sint Maarten. Airport departure tax is Afl 13 / US $7.75.

• Banking   The unit of currency is the Aruba florin, or "guilder" as it is often referred to. Written as Afl, the guilder is divided into 100 cents and issued in many denominations up to 500 guilders. Banks offer the best exchange rate. Currency is tied to the US dollar and remains constant at Afl 1 = US $0.57. US currency is readily accepted on Aruba. Major credit cards, such as American Express, MasterCard and Visa, are honored at all major hotels, restaurants and bars. Banks are open from 8:30am to noon, and 1:30pm to 4pm, Mon. through Fri.

• Courtesy & Dress   Aruba is warm and arid; light cotton clothing seems to work best. Some casinos require jackets. Formal business dealings may require dressier clothing. As in most of the Caribbean, Arubans regard bathing suits as beach wear only, not proper attire for shopping and dining out.

• Customs & Immigration   Proof of citizenship, a completed immigration card and a return or onward ticket are required for entry into the country. The best proof of citizenship is always your passport, but a birth certificate or voter's registration card or affidavit of birth place will suffice. At the airport, the baggage claim area is close to the Immigration counters, and taxis are readily available to take you to your accommodations.

• Driving   Foreign and international licenses are accepted. Cars drive on the right, and the roads are in good condition.

• Electricity   US standards.

• Events & Holidays   New Year's Day; Flag Day (March 18); Carnival (weekend before Lent); Good Friday; Easter; Easter Monday; Queen's Day (April 30); Labor Day (May 1); Ascension Day; Christmas; Boxing Day (Dec.).

• Events, Bon Bini Festival   Each Tuesday evening from May to December, Aruba welcomes its visitors with the Bon Bini Festival. Held under the sunset skies on Fort Zoutman's patio in Oranjestad, local craftsmen, cooks and performers display their talents. This festival is the perfect way to become acquainted with the island's folklore. Wander about displays of local fabric, pottery and paintings and sample delicious cuisine like creole-style fish, stews and various sweets. Quench your thirst from freshly cut coconuts or with beverages prepared by the hosting hotels. Throughout the evening, the air is filled with Antillean music and folkloric dances, and a master of ceremonies explains the significance of the music, instruments and dances.

• Events, Carnival   Often a month-long celebration, Aruba's annual Carnival is an unforgettable experience. The main event, occurring the Sunday before Ash Wednesday, is the Grand Parade, a procession of outrageous and vividly decorated floats, colorfully costumed contestants accompanied by rhythmic steel and brass band music. During this joyous festival, the streets are filled with music, song and revelry. Contests are held for the best singers, musicians, floats, costumes and for the beautiful Carnival Queen. The week before the Grand Parade sees the spectacular Lighting Parade; marking the end of the merrymaking is the Old Mask Parade. To recover from the celebration, the following Monday is a national holiday.

• Events, New Year's Day   New Year's Day is more than just a celebration of the incoming year, it is an opportunity to ward off evil spirits with a dazzling display of fireworks. Throughout the night, a group of musicians

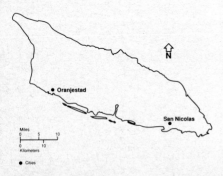

Charter Boats/Dean

called "Dandes" stroll from house to house singing greetings for the new year.

• Languages   Dutch and Papiamento are the native tongues, but English and Spanish are spoken widely.

• Medical   One modern well-equipped hospital. There is a physician trained in diving medicine on staff.

• Off-Season Dates & Rates   Dates may vary slightly at each hotel, but generally from April 15 through December 20. Expect to save 25 to 30%.

• Taxes & Tipping   Hotel charges include a 5% government tax. Many also add a 11% to 15% service charge onto the bill.

• Taxi Fares   Taxis are not metered, but drivers carry rate cards. Determine your fare before starting out. Most cabs are identified by roof signs and the TX or BUS suffix on license plates. Typically the fare from the airport to a hotel in or near Oranjestad is nominal. Up to four passengers may divide the fare. Extra large pieces of luggage may cost an extra US $1.00. Fares generally increase 25% after 11pm. Taxis may be hired for tours, for about US $12.00.

• Telephone   From the US dial direct: 011 + 297 + 8 + the 5-digit Aruba number. Pay phones are Afl $0.25.

• Time   Atlantic Standard (Eastern Standard + 1 hour) year round.

• Weather   A very pleasant climate year round, with an average temperature of 83 degrees and an annual rainfall of 22 inches. Rainiest months are November and December; humidity is typically 76%.

History

While closely allied to Bonaire and Curacao economically, and geographically, Aruba does not necessarily share a common history with its sister islands. Although it seems likely that Aruba was discovered at about the same time, around

Windmill/Dean

Aruba

1499, Spain did not choose to exploit it with the same vigor expended upon Curacao, and to a lesser extent, Bonaire. Consequently, the Indian population of Caiquetios (a tribe of the Arawaks) did not suffer total annihilation, and for this reason their influence on Aruban culture and racial makeup is much stronger than on the neighboring islands.

When the Dutch took over the island in 1634, settling in Savaneta as the Spanish had, they took to horse-breeding and made plans to develop agricultural industries for the benefit of Curacao. But colonization was not encouraged, nor was black slavery. In fact, aside from the local garrison, no whites lived on Aruba until 1754, when the first official colonist, Moses Levy Maduro, was admitted.

White colonization only became significant around 1790, and it took the discovery of gold in 1824 to stimulate interest in the island. In the 1860's various agricultural endeavors, such as aloe plantations, were undertaken. This period also marked the passing of the last of the full-blooded Indian population.

With the end of the gold rush in 1913, economic prospects looked a bit grim for Aruba, but this was remedied shortly by the construction of Standard Oil of New Jersey's huge Lago refinery in 1924. This facility brought prosperity to Aruba, employing over 8,000 at one point and, during World War II, supplying the Allied forces with 6% of their aviation fuel.

/Bailey & Rodriguez

Tourism became a serious enterprise for Aruba in the 1960's, with the opening of major hotels and the first visits by cruise ships. Diversifying the island's economy in this way proved to be an excellent decision, especially in light of the current crisis in the world's oil industries. While the phasing out of the Lago refinery (later owned by Exxon) in recent years has impacted the island's economy, Aruba's popularity with tourists has served to buffer this change.

Aruba is a separate entity within the Kingdom of the Netherlands, having secured for itself political autonomy within the "commonwealth." This does not give the island full independence from Holland, but rather allows the Aruban government to conduct its affairs without the ratification by the Central Government required of the other five Dutch Islands.

The Aruba of today is definitely an island in transition, loosening its economic dependence upon oil revenues and its political dependence upon Curacao. The place that calls itself "One Happy Island" is likely to become an even more appealing destination not only for cruise ship passengers, but sports enthusiasts as well.

Exploring

Aruba differs from its sister islands of Curacao and Bonaire in two noticeable respects--a varied and sophisticated nightlife, and long stretches of wide, white beaches. Aruba is a small island (only 70 square miles) and a place heavily influenced by both North and South America. Aruba's beaches are so remarkable that <u>Sports Illustrated</u> has featured them in its famous swimsuit editions.

Aruba's most interesting sites are to the east and south. You might want to spend one day touring by rental car, then choose one of the many specialized tours offered by Aruba's major tour services. These well-organized trips include general tours of the island, archeological and architectural expeditions, birdwatching, hiking treks to places accessible only on foot, botanical explorations and even a hands-on marine life tour.

If you strike out on your own, start your tour in Oranjestad, the island's capital and major shopping area. There is some very interesting history here as well as numerous shops and restaurants. The major road in and out of town is Lloyd G. Smith Boulevard, named after the first president of the Lago refinery. Approaching Oranjestad

Mt. Jamanota/Bell

Casino/Bell

from the major hotel area, you'll spot the waterfront Marketplace, which offers fresh produce from South America. A little farther down is the floating Fish Market, populated by boats coming over from Venezuela. They arrive about 8:30am every weekday.

To get a good look at Oranjestad, park somewhere near the Aruba Tourist Bureau, which is on Schuttestraat. Here you can pick up a copy of <u>Aruba Holiday</u>, a very handy and accurate tourist guide. Walking along Schuttestraat, turn right on Zoutmanstraat one block until you reach Fort Zoutman. This structure is the oldest standing building on Aruba, built in 1796 to protect the town from sea-borne invaders. In 1868, the Willem III Tower was added to serve as a lighthouse, although the clock at the top didn't start ticking until the 1920's. The Aruba Historical Museum, located right in the fort, is an interesting place and well worth the Afl $1.00 admission (half-price for kids). Hours are Monday to Friday, 9am to 4pm, and Saturday from 9am to 12 noon. Artifacts from pre-colonial times through the present day are displayed. The fort is also the site of the weekly "Bon Bini Festival," from May to December.

Walking back down Zoutmanstraat, this time on the other side of the street, stop by the Archaeological Museum located diagonally across from the police station. Admission is free, and the two-room exhibit provides a fascinating look at the very early history of Aruba, much of which is still being unearthed and studied. Museum hours are Monday through Friday from 9am until noon, and then again from 1:30pm until 4:30pm.

If you head toward Nassaustraat, in the direction opposite the waterfront, you'll pass the Protestant Church (1846), a nice example of Aruban architecture. At Nassáustraat is the greatest concentration of shops, with goods from all over the world.

At Hendrikstraat, walk along it until you come to the Roman Catholic Church. Just behind the church, in the Ministry of Culture at 2-A Irausquinplein, is the Numismatic Museum, which displays over 30,000 different kinds of currency. Some of the coins date from ancient Greece and Rome. Others are even more unusual. There is no entrance fee, but donations are accepted. Hours are Monday through Friday, 7:30am to noon, and from 1pm to 4:30pm.

When you're ready to leave Oranjestad, head east. On the left as you pass the airport, you'll spot Hooiberg, the "Haystack," a curious volcanic formation over 500 feet high. To the right, on the water side, is the harbor of Barcadera, which is home to one of the world's largest saltwater distillation plants. Electrical power is also generated here. At the drive-in theater, take a left and then a right at the first major intersection. This will take you through Frenchman's Pass, the site of a legendary battle between local Indians and French pirates. Parakeets frequent this area. Farther along on this road, to the right, are the ruins of a 19th

Aruba

century gold mill. Nearby are the ubiquitous watapana or divi-divi trees, permanently shaped by the wind into living weather vanes forever pointing southwest.

As this road heads back to the southern coast, you'll see fields of aloe under cultivation, still farmed as they were 100 years ago. Back on the coast road, you might want to stop at Spanish Lagoon for some snorkeling, a picnic or a snooze underneath the mangrove trees. This spot is often identified as an old pirate hideout, but as yet no one has tripped over a half-buried wooden chest. Farther down the coast is Savaneta, the former capital of the island and the site of the first white settlements. White man wasn't the first local, however; some of the oldest evidence of human habitation on Aruba has been unearthed in this area. If you'd care to stop for a seafood lunch, the Brisas del Mar is a nice place.

Following the coast road you'll come to San Nicolas, which was first an industrial center for phosphate mining in the late 1800's and later a commercial center for the nearby Lago refinery.

Geert van den Burg/Jones

With the closing down of the refinery in March 1985, the town has become much quieter. Things might liven up for you in Charlie's Bar, or browse around town and do some shopping.

East of San Nicolas is an area called Seroe Colorado, once the home of Americans working at Exxon, but now more of a hideaway for Arubans. Even though the refinery seems to dominate the landscape, a little exploration will reveal some excellent beaches. After going through the refinery guard gate, you can check out the residential section of Seroe Colorado as well as Baby Beach (calm and shallow) and Rodger's Beach, which is secluded, clean and good for snorkeling.

From Seroe Colorado drive along the north coast to the caves at Huliba, Guadirikiri and Fontein. The Guadirikiri site is particularly nice, with large caverns and natural skylights for illumination. These caves also contain some Indian inscriptions, but many of the designs are actually modern-day imitations. Other sites in this general area use fencing to protect inscriptions from being damaged or altered.

At Fontein you can see the sand dunes of Boca Prins and Dos Playa. Both areas are quite beautiful, but definitely not recommended for swimming.

Swinging inland, you'll see Yamanota, the highest point on Aruba. There's a paved road to the top in case you'd like to enjoy the panoramic view. Heading north, you'll come to Ayo, with more bizarre rock formations. There are marked trials winding through the boulders to an Indian cave and some interesting inscriptions. Farther along the road is Boca Andicouri, a private beach which is open to visitors for a small fee, payable at the house guarding the driveway. This is a pretty spot and worth a stop if you'd like to see the full fury of the surf's assault on the north coast.

On up the road is Bushiribana, another gold mill ruin (some say it was more of a storage facility than a full-fledged processing plant) that remained active for about 100 years.

Follow the road farther, and it will hook back to the east for a short distance and take you to the Natural Bridge. This graceful arch was carved by centuries of violent wave action. Nearby is a snack bar and gift shop. Ask them about the "Tingy-Lingy Box." It's a wonderful contraption, sort of a gargantuan, manually-operated music box, but with an unusual feature -- the operator can select

High Winds Regatta/Jones

one of ten songs by turning a little shaft on the side -- truly an amazing piece of work by a local artist. The bartender might also ask you to solve a few simple puzzles with pieces of paper. Don't make any bets unless you're smarter than we thought we were.

On the way back toward Oranjestad, is Casabari, another strange formation of volcanic rock surrounded by a landscape of local flora that would make a great outer space movie set.The Church of Santa Ana in Noord has a lovely hand-carved altar. It was commissioned sometime around 1870, and sent to Aruba in 1928 from Holland.

From Noord you can drive to the lighthouse at California Point. From this point south, toward Oranjestad, there are a number of wrecks offshore.

There's good snorkeling at a beach called Arashi. Farther down, at Malmok, you can actually see the mast of the German freighter Antila (or Antilla or Antilia-- everyone you meet seems to have their own personal spelling) exactly where she was scuttled in 1940. Just south of the Antila are the remains of the tanker Perdernales.

One last stop you may want to make before returning to Oranjestad or your hotel is the Bubali bird pond, which sits just south of the old red windmill, across the road from Palm Beach. It's a pleasant spot to end a day's touring.

Food

Aruban cuisine caters to tourists, so count on finding everything from Chinese to Indonesian fast-food to gourmet French.

Aruba

Kneel boarding/Bell

/Bailey & Rodriguez
Aruba 8 (24)

Aruba

/Bailey & Rodriguez

Bailey/Rodriguez

/Bailey & Rodriguez

Aruba

Nightlife

The varied nightlife is one of Aruba's main attractions. Virtually every hotel with more than 200 rooms has its own casino. In addition to a wide variety of bars and discos, Aruba also hosts special concerts and events in the summer.

The Aruba Jazz and Latin Music Festival in June attracts some of the best names in the business including: Yellowjackets, Michael Franks, Hiroshima, George Benson, Dianne Reeves, Tito Puente, Celia Cruz, Willie Colon, Jean-Luc Ponty, Kirk Whalum, Al Jarreau, Najee, Paquito D'Rivera, Mongo Santamaria, D'Javan, Ivan Lins, Koinonia, Tania Maria & The Wave, Ruben Blades, Jose Feliciano, Spyro Gyra, Al Dimeola, Count Basie's Orchestra, Diane Schuur and Henry Butler.

Shopping

Aruba is not a duty-free, bargain paradise; rather there are numbers of high-quality, exclusive shops with some luxury items at attractive prices.

Sports

Aruba offers a surprising variety of sports, and the list grows every year. The latest addition is the new De Palm Island. During the day it's a watersports center. At night there is live music, a restaurant and bar. You will find a good mix of locals and tourists on any given day. The island is reached by a short ferry ride from their dock south of the airport.

• Car Races

In April, Aruba hosts the International Drag Race Champions with drag racers from the US and the Caribbean. This event is rapidly growing in popularity, both with the participants and spectators. If you are interested in participating, get in touch with the Tourist Board; they make all the arrangements.

In November the Pan American Race of Champs is held at the Palo Marga Racetrack.

• Fishing

To start off the season, which lasts from October to January, the Aruba Nautical Club and the Bucuti Club each host annual fishing tournaments. Participants come from Curacao, Venezuela, Aruba and the US. Also novices and experienced sportsmen alike can take advantage of half and full day charters, arranged through your hotel or travel agent. Some of the prize quarry includes: sailfish, white and blue marlin, wahoo, shark, barracuda, kingfish, amberjack, black and yellowfin tuna.

On the lee side of the island, there are about 10 charter boats for hire. The current list of boats is available at the Tourist Board.

• Golf

Golf enthusiasts will find the unusual oiled sand greens at the Aruba Golf Club a challenge. Located north of Seroe Colorado in San Nicolas, this 9-hole course offers 20 sand and 5 water traps. The longest hole is 632 yards, par 5 and the shortest 160 yards, par 3. The clubhouse is complete with showers, lockers and bar. Equipment rentals are available.

• Hiking

There are a few spots, accessible only by foot, that are well worth the hike. The hike up Mount Jamanota is one possibility, with the spectacular panoramic view of Aruba as your reward.

• Running

Runners have many choices in Aruba, from challenging, competitive marathons to gentle, scenic jogs along the beaches and jogging tracks. In June, runners from around the world participate in the Annual Mini-Marathon 10km Run. Really serious runners lace up their shoes for the more rugged Aruba Annual Marathon later that month. Also, check with the Tourist Board for additional events as various clubs sponsor races throughout the year. If a race isn't what you had in mind, there's a good running path from Cattle Baron Restaurant circling up to Bubali Road and back down to the restaurant.

• Tennis

You'll find a number of well-surfaced courts all over the island, from hotels to private clubs welcoming visitors. The private clubs include: the Caribe, the Eagle, the San Nicolas Sportpark, the Tivoli and the POVA.

• Windsurfing

Besides rentals, Windsurfing Aruba offers instruction and guided windsurfing tours. De Palm Tours operating out of Aruba Palm Beach Hotel, and Pelican Tours offer rental as well as instruction. Sailboard Aruba is known for its design and fabrication of custom boards. Caribbe Windsurfing operates out of Best Western Manchebo Beach.

Aruba features very steady winds of approximately 15 knots. In June and July the winds

Aruba

pick up to 18 knots. In September through November they drop to 14 knots though the wind is not as consistent. The average wind direction is from the East: ESE in the morning, shifting to ENE in the afternoon. In the winter the winds are more northerly, and in the summer they tend to be more southerly. Some special packages combining accommodations with windsurfing are offered.

The Aruba Hi-Winds ProAm International Windsurfing Tournament in June attracts strong competitors from around the world to compete for over $40,000 in prize money.

• Diving

There are already a number of wrecks off Aruba to explore. In the future those wrecks may be augmented by four small boats (30-to-40 footers), one medium freighter and one large freighter awaiting disposition in the harbor. There have also been a few private planes seized in crackdowns on drug-smuggling that may end up deep-sixed as well.

You may also want to ask the local fisherman about wrecks known only to them. There is a 110-foot yacht somewhere on the south side as well as an old floating restaurant (now submerged, of course). We were not able to pin down the exact locations.

The leeward side of Aruba is where all the resorts and dive operators are located. The best visibility is at the south east corner of the island around Baby Beach. Due to the sandy bottom, the visibility drops off as you proceed up the south coast. The current runs east to west. The area north of Manchebo Beach to Arashi has very little current and some interesting dives. The strongest current is right off Manchebo Beach. The whole south coastline from Rodger's Beach to Manchebo Beach makes for good drift diving.

The windward (east) side of the island has a number of "bocas" or small bays. The ease of entry to each boca varies; current is the key and careful planning with an experienced guide is a must. All of the dives on the windward side are considered to be worthwhile and they are at their best when the wind is from the southeast in the early part of the day.

Fall is the best time to dive the windward side as the wind drops off significantly. Most windward-side diving requires excellent and experienced divers in very good shape, accompanied by an experienced dive guide.

/Bell

/Bell

• Leeward Dive Sites

Here is a partial list of dive sites, starting on the northern tip of the island and going down the leeward side:

· (1) The wreck of the <u>SS California</u>, usually a boat dive, is found at the northwest tip of the is-

Aruba

land, just off the dunes. The SS California (sunk about 1911), supposedly heard the distress call from the Titanic but failed to answer it. The ship sank in 15 to 30 feet of water nine years after the Titanic went down.

This whole area is part of a buffer zone that extends from Aruba to Venezuela, so you can expect to see a fair amount of marine life. There is a strong current which at times reaches 3 knots. Out past the wreck there is a gradual slope with gorgonians, fan coral and huge brain coral which almost break the surface at low tide. Sponges and large rocks are everywhere. Black coral may be found at 150 feet and deeper. You will probably see bull and hammerhead sharks at this site. Due to the location of the dive (on the northernmost point), visibility is 120 plus feet.

(2) Arashi is a shallow (20 to-40-foot deep) reef with lots of elkhorn coral on a sandy bottom. As this dive is on the northwest side of the island, the water may be very murky depending on the currents and the time of year. But it may be reached by snorkeling from the beach.

(3) Malmok is a boat or shore dive. You will not find strong current, but you will see small basket sponges, gorgonians and all sorts of coral formations in this snorkel/dive area 40 feet below the surface.

(4) The SS Antila is a huge wreck. The average visibility is about 50-60 feet but at times is a little murkier. The ship was used by the Germans early in World War II to supply submarines. At the time, Aruba was a neutral zone, and the ship tied up here between missions. Try as they might, the Allies were unable to locate and sink the ship outside of Aruban waters, and hence dubbed it the "ghost ship." On the day Aruba entered the war (on the side of the Allies) the Antila was moored where you will find her now. Accordingly, the local police demanded her surrender but agreed to give the captain until the next day to think it over. When the police arrived the next morning they found the entire crew lined up on the beach ready to surrender; during the night the captain had ordered the ship scuttled.

By the way, the locals swear that Aruba was the only of the Dutch Antilles attacked by Germany. A sub supposedly fired two torpedoes at an empty oil tanker; these passed under the tanker and landed on the beach where the DIVI properties now stand.

(5) Directly south of Malmok are 200 to 300 yards of reef incongruously known as the "Seventy Foot Reef." This reef is in a tanker anchorage and the anchors have severely damaged the reef in spots. Visibility is 50-60 feet, and watch for large, heavy, metal objects dropped from above. Don't be surprised to find Atlantic, manta, southern and eagle rays.

(6) Bula Dor ("flying fish") is a shallow reef about one mile from shore in 30-to-40 feet of water. It's about 800 yards long and makes for some great snorkeling or shallow diving.

(7) Pedernales is the center section of a torpedoed oil tanker. Apparently the tanker was hit at the refinery and made it to this spot. The fore and aft sections were sealed and the center section cut out and allowed to sink. The salvaged parts were towed to the US and incorporated into a ship later employed in the Normandy invasion.

This boat dive is in front of the Holiday Inn and is also used by snorkelers. Visibility is about 60 feet, and there is almost no current. The depth ranges from 25 to 40 feet. If you look closely you will see two torpedoes in the wreckage.

(8) Manchebo Beach Reef is a pleasant reef about 800 yards from shore, in 50 to 80 feet of water.

(9) Harbor Entrance Reef, or Harbor Reef, is a dive characteristic of the entire south coast of Aruba. This particular formation starts at the surface 600 yards from shore and goes down to 80 feet. You will find elkhorn, staghorn, fan corals and gorgonians. The reef is interrupted by a rock and sand bottom, and then a little farther out, a deeper reef starts at 110 feet. This double reef structure offers very good visibility in the 100 foot range most of the year, though in October and November the visibility may drop down to 40 or 50 feet.

(10) The Lagoon across from the airport is a sheltered spot for shallow snorkeling in 2 to 20 feet of water. There are a number of Christmas trees and small shells. This is either a beach or boat dive. When diving outside Harbor Entrance Reef and Lagoon, you will find the current running about 1.5 knots.

(11) To get to Mangel Haeto or Casa Cuna Reef, swim out 50 yards to the reef. The visibility ranges from 120 to 60 feet. You encounter a double reef structure, with the first reef dropping down to 110 feet, and a flat sand bottom just

before a deeper second reef. There are several deep underwater caves about 130 feet down.

This dive can also been done as a drift dive by walking out at the lagoon's southern end and then drifting back into the lagoon at its north entrance. There is a pretty steep drop-off here, making this almost a wall dive.

(12) Isla de Oro (Gold Island) is a mere 50 feet from shore. This dive starts with a walk through mangroves to a pier where you jump in. Quickly the depths go to 130 feet and you may find the occasional turtle that comes in to feed on the mangroves. There is a fair amount of fan and sheet coral around.

(13) Water Plant Reef or Scalahein is a 100-foot wall dive similar to the type of walls found in Bonaire.

(14) Lago Harbor is in front of the old abandoned oil refinery. Eight years ago a pilot boat sank here, but it's never been found. Expect a gentle current, a nice slope to 110 feet, good coral formations and lots of marine life.

(15) Barcadera Reef is essentially the west end of Water Plant, a two-mile-long reef.

(16) Indian Hat lies south of Aruba, off Rodger's Beach. This boat dive starts at an islet and gradually drops-off. An elkhorn coral community changes to staghorn, numerous basket sponges, fans and gorgonians. You are likely to see some big fish such as wahoo and barracuda, plus many windsurfers as this is a popular area for them too.

(17) Baby Beach is a primo dive. Due to its location at the tip of the island, there is consistent 80-to-120-foot visibility. In addition you will find a sunken coast liner which makes for an unusual dive. There is lots of marine life among the elkhorn, soft and pillar corals. The extensive second reef contains multiple patches of big rocks. The current is usually under 1 knot, allowing access from the beach.

(18) Santa di Cacho (Dog Cemetery) is similar to Indian Hat except that at 30 feet there is a jungle of fans, gorgonians and sponges, with a slope beginning at 45 feet. Depths soon attain 60 to 70 feet, and you can do an unusual, shore-to-shore drift dive, ending up at Baby Beach.

• **Windward Dive Sites**

Dives sites on the windward side, from the south east to north east include:

(1) Coral Point makes for an excellent drift dive. A boat is required due to the very turbulent

/Bell

/Bell

water. The current splits north and south at a point of impact on the island which changes, so you must have a boat to keep up with shifts in the current. This area has the best visibility on the island-- consistently over 100 feet. The first reef goes down to 60 feet and the second reef drops-off to a considerable depth.

(2) On a quiet day at Bachelor's Beach you can swim out, but expect to find a strong and

Aruba

/Jones

tricky current. A double reef starts 50 feet from shore. The first reef slopes to 60 feet, the second drops to 160 feet. You will find small holes filled will rock dwellers, and sharks and barracuda are seen often.

(3) Boca Grandi Reef is a shallow reef, 20 to 30 yards wide, that extends from Boca Grandi in the south to Rincon in the north. There is strong wave action and a nasty current outside the reef. This reef is fairly typical of the windward side

/Bell

DIVI DIVI Beach Resort

Aruba Concorde Hotel & Casino

reefs. Look for the reef to drop to 60 to 80 feet with some sand channels. The reef stops at large rocks or a sandy bottom. The visibility is a very good and consistent 80 to 100 feet. As expected, on the windward side of any island, you will occasionally run across a shark.

(4) The Pinnacle wall dive is 600 yards from shore, starting at around 40 feet and going down to depths of 180 or so. The current zips along at 2-3 knots, so your divemaster will probably set you up with a drift dive.

Underwater Photo Credits: S. Bailey & E. Rodriguez.

DIVI Tamarijn Beach Resort

Key: The accommodations price range is based on the high season rate per night, double occupancy. The Liveaboard price range is per berth, high season. The dive price range is based on the cost of a two tank dive. Letter codes: Beach (or on the water), Diving, Fishing, Golf, Other watersports, Pool, Restaurant & Bar, Sailing, Tennis, Windsurfing.

Accommodations

AMERICANA ARUBA HOTEL & CASINO 800-223-1588   204 Units: $140-190 BDPRTW
  011-297-824500 011-297-823191 Box 218, L.G. Smith Blvd. # 83 Aruba. See: De Palm Island & Tours.
ARUBA BEACH CLUB 212-563-6940   132 Units: $165-245 BDKOPRSTW
  011-297-824595 011-297-826557 Box 368, L.G. Smith Blvd #53 Aruba. See: Pelican Watersports.
ARUBA CONCORDE HOTEL & CASINO 800-223-7944 500 Units: $150-400 BDFOPRSTW
  305-358-3252 305-374-7201FX 848 Brickell Avenue, Suite 1200 Miami FL 33131. Friendly and excellent service. 18 stories of sleek luxury with gorgeous air conditioned terraced rooms and suites. Offering ocean views, closed circuit movies and amenities. An action-packed casino, six restaurants, sizzling night club, four cocktail lounges, beach, chaise lounges, swimming pool, laundry and valet service, two lighted tennis courts, game room, car rental, tours and watersports counter, ballroom with meeting and banquet rooms and shopping. See: De Palm Island & Tours.
ARUBA PALM BEACH HOTEL 800-345-2782   200 Units: $145-235 BDFOPRSTW
  305-427-7481FX TX:5033 240 Southwest 12th Avenue Deerfield Beach FL 33442. See: De Palm Island & Tours.
ASTORIA HOTEL 011-297-845132   10 Units: $25-25 R
  Box 173 San Nicolas, Aruba.
BEST WESTERN MANCHEBO BEACH RESORT 800-223-1108   134 Units: $130-210 BFOPRT
  800-334-7234 011-297-823444 L.G. Smith Blvd. #55 Aruba.

Aruba

BEST WESTERN TALK OF THE TOWN RESORT 800-223-1108   63 Units: $95-165 BOPR
011-297-823380 011-297-832446FX L.G. Smith Blvd. # 2 Aruba.
BUSHIRI BEACH RESORT 800-622-7836   154 Units: $115-220 BDFOPRSTW
011-297-825216 212-986-5988FX L. G. Smith Blvd. #35 Aruba.
CASA DEL MAR BEACH RESORT 212-563-6940   32 Units: $295-295 BDFOPRSTW
011-297-824595 011-297-826657FX Box 368, L G Smith Blvd. 53 Aruba. See: Pelican Watersports.
CENTRAL HOTEL 011-297-822260   18 Units: $27-27
011-297-822261 Elleboogstraat 23 Oranjestad, Aruba.

DIVI DIVI BEACH RESORT 800-367-3484   202 Units: $200-600 BDOPRSTW
607-277-3484 011-297-823300 L. G. Smith Blvd. #45 Aruba. Jeans, bikinis and black ties are compatible here. All rooms airconditioned & have a patio or balcony, radio, telephone and jacuzzi bath tub. Free-formed pool at Dividos with island tea house in the center, accessible by a bridge. Beach, swimming pool and restaurant, tennis courts and dancing. De Palm Tours office on premise for watersports and tours. Exchange privileges with Tamarijn and Papagayo. Plenty of restaurants and shopping and much more.

DIVI DUTCH VILLAGE APARTMENTS 800-367-3484   70 Units: $260-450 BDKOPRSTW
607-277-3484 011-297-823300 L. G. Smith Blvd. #39 Oranjestad, Aruba. Top quality spacious apartments in a private setting. They are luxurious and oversized, with kitchen facilities, tub and shower baths, private jacuzzi and patio or balcony. Radio, telephone, TV, beach, swimming pool, tennis courts, laundromat, baby sitting. Free transportation between the Tamarijn-Divi Divi Resorts & Alhambra casino & shopping bazaar. Full dine-around program with Tamarijn Beach Resort Divi Divi Beach Resort and Alhambra Casino & Bazaar.

DIVI TAMARIJN BEACH RESORT 800-367-3484   236 Units: $180-200 BDRSTW
607-277-3484 011-297-824150 54 Gunderman Rd. Ithaca NY 14850. Barefoot Elegance is our byword. Our spacious oceanfront and superior airconditioned rooms come with two double beds, tub & shower baths, patio or balcony, radio, and telephone. Beach, swimming pool and tennis courts shuffleboard, laundromat, free transportation between DIVI DIVI, Alhambra Entertainment Center & Tamarijn. Open-air dancing, restaurants and exchange privileges with Tamarijn and Papagayo. Group packages available.

GOLDEN TULIP CARIBBEAN HOTEL 800-223-6510   406 Units: $175-830 BGOPRTW
212-486-2996 212-759-9702FX 140 East 63rd, Suite 933A New York NY 10021.
HOLIDAY INN INT./ ARUBA BEACH RESORT 800-465-4329   388 Units: $74-191 BDFKOPRSTW
305-445-9505 305-448-9662FX 950 N.W. Le Jeune Rd. Miami FL 33126. See: Pelican Watersports.
PLAYA LINDA BEACH RESORT 212-594-5441   201 Units: $180-350 BDFKOPRSTW
011-297-831000 011-297-822256FX Box 253 Oranjestad, Aruba. See: Pelican Watersports.
VICTORIA HOTEL 011-297-823850   30 Units: $26-26
Nassaustraat 126 Oranjestad, Aruba.
VISTALMAR 011-297-828579   8 Units: $50-75 BK
Bucutiweg 28 Oranjestad, Aruba.

Information

ARUBA TOURIST BUREAU 800-TO-ARUBA
212-246-3030 011-297-823777 1270 Avenue of the Americas, Suite 2212 New York NY 10020.

Sports

CARIBE WINDSURFING 011-297-823444
c\o Best Western, L.G. Smith Bvd. #55 Aruba. See: Best Western Manchebo Beach Resort.

DE PALM ISLAND & TOURS 800-533-7256
212-864-0107 011-297-824400 L.G. Smith Blvd. #142, Box 656 Oranjestad, Aruba. At the pier of the Palm Beach Hotel, this is a complete watersports operation. Here you can sign up for cruises, glass-bottom boat trips, windsurfing and jetskiing. This group can also provide you with package tours of Aruba and trips to De Palm Island. See: Aruba Palm Beach Hotel.

PELICAN WATERSPORTS 011-297-823888   55 Divers: $40-40 DOW
TX:5038 Box 36 Oranjestad, Aruba. All new Scubapro and Sherwood equipment. Each setup comes with an octopus and pressure & depth gauge. All their guides are PADI certified. They communicate in Dutch, English & Spanish. New dock in use now. Shop is open 7 days a week from 9am to 6pm. Pickup at all major hotels. Pier and boat diving available. They also specialize in windsurfing instruction and training. All other watersports are arranged at or next to the shop. Ask for special packages. See: Holiday Inn Int./ Aruba Beach Resort.

SAILBOARDS ARUBA 011-297-827881
800-635-1155 011-297-822018FX Aruba. This small shop is located a few miles off the main beach area. Their primary focus is the design and production of custom sailboards. If you are interested in working up a special board, you might want to give them a call.

WINDSURFING ARUBA 011-297-821036
011-297-833472 Box 256 Aruba. This is the oldest windsurfing shop on Aruba. The director is an experienced diver and fisherman. His knowledge of the waters, winds and currents of Aruba is second to none. Among his other qualifications he is a Doctor at the hospital. Windsurfing Aruba can arrange complete windsurfing packages including lodging and equipment.

Bahamas

/Jones

Travel & Sports Guide

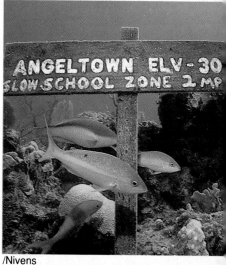

/Nivens

/Jones

Bahamas

Airline Connections

• General Information Nassau and Freeport are easily reached from the States on numerous carriers. Most Family Islands can only be reached from Nassau, some only once or twice a week. A few have regularly scheduled charter flights from Florida. Be advised that "regularly scheduled" doesn't necessarily guarantee regularly flying. Some charter airlines cancel inadequately booked flights. One reliable carrier that specializes in flights to the Family Islands and Freeport is Aero Coach Aviation. Aero Coach has over 70 daily flights from Ft. Lauderdale, Miami and West Palm Beach to The Bahamas. This airline prides itself on its extensive schedule and on its timely departure record. Check our Directory for their toll free booking numbers. Most smaller Family Islands offer reliable private flights as part of their accommodations packages. The airport departure tax is US $5.00 for adults, $2.50 for children 3-12 and free for children under 3. There's a $10.00 seaport departure tax from Freeport.

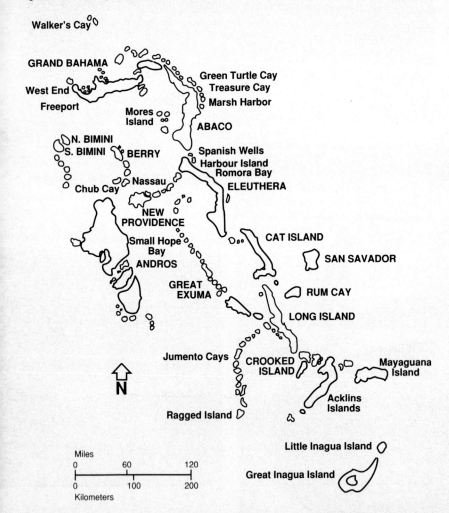

Bahamas

• **Abaco**   You can reach Marsh Harbour on direct flights from Ft. Lauderdale, Miami, Nassau and West Palm Beach. Carriers include Aero Coach, and Bahamasair. Aero Coach serves Treasure Cay. To reach Green Turtle Cay, fly to Treasure Cay and take a water taxi. To Walker's Cay you fly on the Walker's Cay Airline from from Ft. Lauderdale or take Taino Air to Walkers from Freeport.

• **Andros**   Bahamasair flies out of Nassau to both the northern San Andros and the more southern Andros. Town. Both facilities also offer private charters, the former from Miami and Ft. Lauderdale, the latter from most points in The Bahamas.

• **Berry Islands (Chub Cay)**   A private plane flies divers in from Miami and Fort Lauderdale. You can also catch a scheduled charter out of Nassau on Key Largo Air. To arrange private flights from the States, contact Chub Cay Club.

• **Bimini**   You can get scheduled flights on Chalk's Air out of Fort Lauderdale and Miami and Aero Coach from W. Palm Beach. The latter lands in South Bimini; catch a water taxi to Alice Town. The dive operation provides its own flights out of Miami and Ft. Lauderdale for package divers.

• **Cat Island**   Bahamasair services provides twice weekly from Nassau.

• **Crooked Islands**   Bahamasair services provides twice weekly from Nassau.

• **Eleuthera**   To get to Harbour Island or Spanish Wells, fly to North Eleuthera from Miami, Ft. Lauderdale and Nassau, then catch a water taxi. Scheduled carriers are Bahamasair, and Aero Coach. To get to the Cotton Bay Club you fly to the Rock Sound Airport using Aero Coach.

• **Exuma**   There are frequent flights to George Town from Ft. Lauderdale, Miami, W. Palm Beach, Nassau and Deadman's Cay. Scheduled carriers are Bahamasair, and Aero Coach.

• **Grand Bahama**   You can fly from most Florida centers, some major US cities and Nassau. Carriers include Aero Coach, Bahamasair, United, Eastern, TWA, Pan Am, and Air Canada.

• **Long Island**   Bahamasair flies out of Nassau once a week.

• **New Providence**   You can fly directly to Nassau or Paradise Island from many cities

including Miami, Ft. Lauderdale, Tampa, W. Palm Beach, Atlanta, Boston, Chicago, Cleveland, Dallas, Kansas City, Los Angeles, Montreal, New Orleans, New York, Pittsburgh, St. Louis, San Antonio and Toronto. Carriers include Bahamasair, Delta, Eastern, TWA, United, Air Canada and Chalk's.

• **Rum Cay**   Take any of the many flights to George Town in the Exumas, then catch a Harken Charter flight to Rum Cay. Private flights are available between Stella Maris on Long Island and Rum Cay.

• **San Salvador**   There are no regularly scheduled commercial flights from the US to San Salvador. Charters are arranged through the Riding Rock Inn's US office in Fort LauderdalE. Another possibility is to take Bahamasair from Nassau.

• **West End, Grand Bahama**   Aero Coach flys direct to the West End from West Palm Beach and Ft. Lauderdale.

Index:

Bahamas

Useful Facts

• Banking   The Bahamian dollar (B$1) is equal to the US dollar, and the currencies are used interchangeably throughout the islands. Major US credit cards are accepted almost everywhere, especially at major hotels, restaurants and shops. Banking hours for Nassau and Freeport are 9:30am-3pm Monday through Thursday, with banks open until 5pm on Friday. On the Family Islands, banks are usually open shorter hours and in some places are only open two or three days of the week.

• Courtesy & Dress   Usually casual. We advise light, comfortable warm weather clothes for most occasions, plus a sweater or jacket for chillier winter nights. On Grand Bahama and New Providence, some hotels and restaurants prefer a dressier look for evening meals.. On the Family Islands, dressing up means wearing shoes.

• Customs & Immigration   For stays of eight months or less, US and Commonwealth nation citizens simply require proof of citizenship: passport, voter's registration card or birth certificate. Non-citizens who are US residents need their Alien Registration Card. Other visitors must present a passport. Upon entering The Bahamas, each adult can bring in duty-free: 50 cigars or 200 cigarettes or one pound of tobacco, one quart of alcohol and their personal effects. Household items are dutiable. Do not bring drugs to or from The Bahamas. The Bahamas recently granted the US Drug Enforcement Agency powers of arrest.

• Driving   On the left. Streets in Nassau and Freeport are in fine shape. If you do rent a car for the Family Islands, we'd recommend something sturdy. Foreign and international licenses are accepted.

• Electricity   US standards.

• Events & Holidays   Want a tropical Mardi Gras? Visit The Bahamas for Junkanoo. It begins the morning of December 26 with drums, bells, horns and whistles. Costumed people dance and prance through the streets. There's a second parade in the early hours of New Years' Day to wrap up the intervening week's festivities. Nassau's celebration is the biggest, but many towns join in the fun. The origin of the word "junkanoo" is disputed, but the high-energy fun is unquestioned. Goombay is a series of festivities to attract visitors during the summer off-season and includes street festivals, music and various events. Goombay is the name for Bahamian music, similar to calypso, combining indigenous instruments and West African rhythms. Public holidays are: New Years Day; Good Friday; Easter Monday; Labour Day (first Friday in June); Whitmonday (June); Independence Day (July 10); Emancipation Day (Aug.); Discovery Day (Oct. 12); Christmas; and Boxing Day (Dec. 26).

• Languages   English is spoken, if not always understood by visitors. The blend of English words with Scottish, Irish, African and West Indian accents can produce some initial confusion. Fortunately, most ears attune quickly.

• Medical   There are hospitals, both public and private, in Nassau and Freeport. In the Family Islands there are 13 health centers plus three dozen scattered clinics. Emergency cases are flown to the 455 bed, government-operated Princess Margaret Hospital in Nassau. There's a double lock recompression chamber on Grand Bahama.

• Off-Season Rates   Starting and ending dates vary somewhat, but generally the off-season period is mid-April or early May to mid-December. Rates are generally 15-50% lower.

• Taxes & Tipping   Hotels charge a 15% food and beverage service plus a 6% room tax and nominal maid fee. Many restaurants add an automatic 15% service charge to your bill. Taxi drivers, tour guides and others also receive the standard 15% tip.

• Taxi Fares   Taxis are metered. Rates are fixed by law in major areas like Nassau and Freeport. Otherwise the rate is $14/hour, but some drivers will negotiate fares.

• Time   Eastern Standard; changes from Standard to Daylight Savings in April and October so it is always identical with EST. The Bahamas are a great place to slow down.

• Telephone   Direct Distance Dialing world wide.

• Weather   Subtropical, rarely below 70 or above 83 degrees on most islands. Can be slightly cooler in the northernmost Abacos in winter. Water temperatures are usually between 68 and 76 in the winter and 76 to the high 80's in the summer. It rains most in the summer, but even then the sun usually shines for at least seven hours.

/Bell

History

American woes have often proved to be Bahamian boons. This irony has been acknowledged by Bahamian stamps commemorating shipwrecking, privateering, Civil War blockade busting and rum running. The benefits have not been one-sided, however. For years, refreshed Americans have returned to their own sometimes snow-covered land with exciting tales of their adventures in paradise.

The early history of The Bahamas parallels much of the rest of the Caribbean: Columbus accidentally landed and the Spanish imprisoned Lucayan Indian inhabitants. Because the Lucayans were such amazing free divers, Spain forced them to work in its South American pearl fisheries, as well as its mines. The Lucayan people were exterminated in one tragic generation.

England became interested in the islands for geopolitical reasons and for years disputed title with Spain. Finally Britain gained control in the mid 1600's.

Among the first groups to discover the lure of The Bahamas were privateers and pirates. The former were government-licensed and only looted enemy ships; the latter plundered anyone. The Bahamas' strategic location amid New/Old World shipping lanes made pirating a lucrative, if risky, profession. It also offered unusual opportunity for women. Though Edward Teach, alias Blackbeard, was the most notorious pirate, Mary Reid and Anne Bonny enjoyed their share of ill fame.

Pirates weren't the only ones who profited from sinking ships; and they're not the only ones who sank them. Salvaging cargo from the ships that ran aground on treacherous reefs was considered a legitimate profession. Slightly more questionable was the practice of starting strategically placed fires to lure ships onto the reefs.

During the American Revolution, Loyalists fled here from threatened tar-and-feathering in the Colonies. Many brought their slaves and took up

Aero Coach Aviation

Bahamas

Family Islands/Bell

residence. Most initially attempted cotton planta-tions, but these eventually failed due to depleted soil and insect plagues. Slaves were freed in 1834, 31 years before their US counterparts.

The second influx of Americans came during the Civil War. Confederate blockade runners made Nassau their headquarters, spawning an economic boon such as The Bahamas had never seen.

When America officially closed its doors to liquor, rum runners searched for the cracks in The Bahamas' shores. They crowded Nassau, Grand Bahama and Bimini. Rival gangs peacefully shared the same hotels on the islands, reluctant to endanger their Bahamian sanctuary. Liquor duties not only wiped out the entire Bahama national debt -- they created a surplus as well!

Today Americans still swarm over Bahamian shores, albeit usually in more legal pursuits.

Tourism generates over 70% of the Gross Nation-al Product.

The Bahamas remained a British colony until 1973, when the struggle for independence finally succeeded. Incidentally, women had only won the right to vote 12 years prior.

Today the country's government consists of a two-chambered parliament. One chamber is elected, the other appointed by the Governor General, who in turn is appointed by the British Queen. The Bahamas is a stable democracy.

Half the current population of approximately 235,000 people is under 25. Most are of African or mixed African, Spanish and British descent. Over 60% of the entire population lives on New Providence, especially in and around Nassau.

For additional information, we recommend Paul Albury's delightful history, The Story of the Bahamas..

New Providence/Bell

The Colmbus Underwater Monument, San Salvador/Zamrog

Dive Abaco/Bell

Marsh Harbour

If a visitor first entered Marsh Harbour by boat and didn't know where he was, his immediate guess might be New England. There are more hardwood trees here than palms and hills unusual for the typically flat Bahamas. Yachts outnumber fishing boats. The pastel houses seem muted when

Great Abaco Beach

compared to the vivid sherbet colors found on other islands.

Marsh Harbour is one of the largest Bahamian towns. You'll find everything from good roads, excellent supermarkets, superb hotel and condominium accommodations featuring telephones in the rooms, and an abundance of watersports. And, among the other gourmet delights at popular Wally's Restaurant, Godiva chocolate cake flown in from San Francisco. You won't find many sightseeing landmarks other than Seaview Castle, a definitely Bahamian version of the genre. It was built by Dr. Cottman, known as the Out Island Doctor, though he was actually a science teacher. His aqua-green house sits on lovely garden grounds and surveys the harbor. Don't ask for tours, however. Dr. Cottman's widow still lives here.

For sightseeing, take a ferry or rent sail or motorboats to visit any of several scenic neighboring cays. Man 'O War Cay is one of the most popular. Settled in 1780 by descendants of Loyalists, this cay remains a shipbuilding and repair center. You can walk along its waterfront road and watch craftsmen working on boats of all descriptions. Gift shops dot the quiet streets. There are no cars on this island, and no liquor or cigarettes are sold here; the strong religious tradition prohibits both. Cap off your tour with a stroll along the waterfront, past the flower-covered clapboard houses selling ice cream, which seems to have replaced alcohol and tobacco as the local vice.

Two-hundred-year-old Hope Town on Elbow Cay is a lovely day trip that can be arranged through Marsh Harbour's dive operation. Hope Town's red and white horizontally striped lighthouse looks like a Christmas tree ornament.

Early sailors doubtlessly saw it as a real gift. Prior to its construction, there was one wreck a month at Elbow Cay. In 1860 alone, an estimated 112,000 pounds sterling were garnered from wrecks that locals insisted were accidental. Others allege that fires were deliberately set to lure boats onto the reef.

Stop by the Wyannie Malone Historical Museum for a delightful browse through Abaco history. Then enjoy a poolside lunch at Hopetown Harbour Lodge, which surveys the Bahamian blue sea below.

If you're more in the mood for deserted beaches, Great Guana Cay is the place to go. If you don't have a boat, best bet is to take the ferry from Marsh Harbour to Great Guana, then rent a dinghy from the marina and sail around Bakers Point to miles of natural beach and a coral reef only 50 yards offshore. Casserina pines, palms, madeira trees, pigeon plums and poincianas fringe the beach, providing dappled shade.

There are many opportunities for exploring from Marsh Harbour. One option is to hop a freight boat to Nassau. They leave Monday, return Wednesday and make any number of fascinating stops at small cays along the way. It's a great way to see a lot of small islands and really get to know the local residents.

On Abaco Island itself, you can rent a car and (very carefully) drive to several interesting spots. Closest is Seven Mile Beach, a beachcomber's delight. Over 625 species of shells have been found in local waters and many wash ashore here.

Another close treat, about 10 miles north of town, is the Blue Hole just off Great Abaco Beach Highway between Coral Island and Abaco Heights. A ridge surrounds the incredibly blue water. From 90 feet above, the bottom is visible. Orchids, air plants and assorted blue, white, pink and purple blossoms enliven this ideal picnic spot.

The movie <u>Day of the Dolphin</u> was filmed at Abaco Heights. You can see George C. Scott's home in the movie, as well as the tanks and large round pens that housed the dolphins.

There are caves with Indian artifacts around the southernmost community of Hole-in-the Wall, and a bird sanctuary where you might well see the protected native parrot. For all the local spots, you'd be well advised to take a guide. Inquire at the dive shop.

• **Sailing**

Regatta Time, based out of Marsh Harbour, is a major event at the end of June each year.

Conch Inn Resort

• **Diving**

Diving here centers around the reef that Abaco residents insist is the third largest barrier reef in the world. Whatever its ranking, it's long (approximately 150 miles) and beautiful. Most of the dives are shallow to medium. There are no walls but there's plenty of underwater spectacle to satisfy almost any diver.

(1) The Tunnels. The special glow you see at this site is not from the sea. It's from divers holding a wild fish in their arms for the first time. One grouper here is so friendly, divers have held him for 15-minute photography sessions.

The Tunnels is a remarkable dive for reasons other than hugable groupers. It's a honeycomb area of caves, tunnels and caverns that delights both novices and experts. As you wind in and out of caves, the light filters through in spots to create a dappled, forest effect. In others the solid darkness seems eerie. It evokes images of long-forgotten treasure. You half expect someone to jump out brandishing a cutlass.

All kinds of parrot fish crowd this area, so do schools upon schools of blue tangs. In the summer months, the fish get so thick you practically have to push them aside. There's usually a resident green moray around and a barracuda affectionately called Henry.

Sea fans, staghorn coral atop brain coral, feathery anemones, and all the incredible life they attract, make this spot a photographer's dream.

(2) Demira. A 411-foot steel hull sailing freighter that was the last of its kind built in The Bahamas. A hurricane sank it in 1928 in 30 feet of water. The mast is broken, of course, but most of the ship is still intact. It's a good spot for sergeant-majors, chub, grunts and yellowtails.

(3) Cathedral. This dive starts in 10 feet of water and drops to 35. A mammoth room seems lighted so that when you're inside, it's like being in a stained-glass sanctuary. Clouds of silver sides swarm here in summer. A sea garden surrounds the spot. Truly a beautiful dive.

(4) Devil's Blue Hole. Depths range from 150-215 feet and keep going. It's an inland blue hole that consists of fresh water for the first 40 feet below the surface; then there's a mix of salt and fresh water for about the next 20 feet. There are stalactites on the sides, some crab and blind fish, but this is not an area of prolific life. A line has been staked to ensure divers don't exceed 215 feet.

(5) Coral Archway. A coral archway from 20-30 feet leads to a lovely sea garden. Coral heads come to the surface here, so you can weave among them. Usually you'll see a shark of some variety or another on this dive, especially reef sharks. Also numerous are parrot fish, grunts, chubs and southern sennets.

(6) Medusa's Lair. A hole through the reef that leads into a very lively sea garden. Both hard and soft corals abound here, especially finger, plate, leaf, elkhorn and brain. Depth is 20-30 feet.

(7) Tombs. A cave, at 20 feet, has only one entrance and is extremely dark; the kind of place you'd expect to find the Creature from the Black Lagoon.

(8) Carousel. An open coral head, approximately 100 feet across, which you can swim in and around like a carousel gives this site its name. You can't get lost because everything connects to everything else. At 20 feet, this is a good spot to see tropicals, gray snappers, jackknives, yellowtails.

(9) Mini-Drop. On the outside of the reef, this is a sheer drop of 15-40 feet along a coral wall. There's an abundance of gorgonians, sea fans, sea whips and ferns here in all different varieties. Good place to see hawksbill and loggerhead turtles, parrot fish, snappers and an occasional stingray.

(10) Twin Sisters. A macrophotographer's delight. All kinds of tiny things at this well-lighted spot at 20 feet. Look closely for flamingo tongues, banded coral shrimp, arrow crabs, feather duster worms and Christmas tree worms. Corals proliferate here as do reef and tropical fish.

(11) Maxi Cave Bay. Proof that barracuda have a sense of humor. There was an old one that used to hang out on the edge of the cave. Whenever divers emerged from the dark, he'd suddenly poke his face in front of their masks. You could almost see him grin. He's gone now, but there are a host of others that aren't, including other barracuda, an occasional nurse shark, southern sennets, groupers, parrot fish and tiers of elkhorn and brain coral. There are parts of an old wreck, including a big wheel 10-foot across. Maximum depth is 30 feet.

(12) USS Adirondack. This Union battleship sank in 1862. It has two 11-inch bore cannons and 12 of its original 22 smaller cannons. Maximum depth is 27 feet. Good place to see turtles.

(13) Train Wreck. Two complete locomotives went down here and you can still see their wheels, ballast, boilers and engines. This train wreck is the most intact in The Bahamas. Good light, tons of colorful fire coral and sea fans make this a photogenic spot. Just be careful what you touch. Depth is 10 feet.

(14) Grouper Alley. There used to be 12 tame groupers here until someone speared them. Though the remaining groupers have become understandably skittish, this is still an excellent dive. At 40 feet it's an area of caves and caverns. There's an eel here, plus occasional turtles, sharks and a host of tropicals. One cave chute has a lot of banded coral shrimp.

(15) The Towers. Magnificent heads of entwining corals tower up from 60 feet. At 30 feet there's an extensive caving area full of silver sides and yellowfin groupers.

(16) Jolly Tar. A 60-foot ship sunk behind Fowl Cay in 85 feet of water and nearby a Puffin sailboat that sank at about 60 feet. Both are just remains now.

/Johnson

Walker's Cay

Geographically Walker's Cay may be part of the Family Islands, but one glance reveals it's a very distant relative. After all, how many of its kin have been featured on <u>Lifestyles of the Rich and Famous</u>? This is the resort where Richard Nixon and Bebe Rebozo sipped martinis and discussed world-shattering policies as the sun slid into the coral-reefed sea.

Walker's Cay is still very posh. The resort's high wood-beamed ceilings help create the sense of a 1940's men's club where those of similar perspective gathered.

The island is small but offers several notable sights. One is a lovely wood and stone chapel that features a humorous painting of a young novitiate working on a painting of his superior. In the novitiate's version, the superior looks dignified and inspired; the model he's trying to paint, however, is fast asleep.

Visitors are also welcome to stop in at the Aqualife Research Corporation's fish farm. Housed in a specially-designed building over half the size of a football field, the farm is attempting to propagate commercial numbers of marine tropical fish for sale to public and private collectors. Originators are hopeful that success in this delicate and temperamental enterprise could open new economic opportunities throughout the islands.

Sports

Walker's offers a full range of sports in addition to diving: tennis, volleyball, fresh and salt water swimming, shuffleboard, waterskiing, windsurfing, boating, snorkeling and --especially-- fishing.

• Fishing

Host to the world's largest private billfishing tournament, mid-April, Walker's Cay has seen more IGFA records set than any other single resort. As you would expect, this is a prime location for deep sea fishing.

• Diving

The resort course certificate handed out by the Walker's Cay dive operation reads: "Explored the deep, challenged the open waters and survived." Not that survival is an issue. The dive operation here has never lost anyone (except perhaps a few less-dedicated souls who got waylaid at the bar and never made it to the boat). As in the rest of Abaco, the typical diving is shallow reef diving with prolific fish life. The shallowness means excellent light and extended bottom times, ideal for photography as well as sightseeing.

The breakers around keep out the current and push the visibility past 100 feet. Most sites are

/Johnson

coral heads in sandy bottom; many break the surface at low tide. There are caverns throughout. This area is just being charted. It will easily provide 40-50 distinct sites.

(1) White Hole. A great place to challenge tame groupers to "fish tag." They'll even follow you through the coral heads that form a honeycomb of coral caves. Abundant marine life exist in only 35 feet making for an excellent photo opportunity.

(2) North of Tom Brown's. A beautiful shallow dive in 25 feet, and a good spot to become acquainted with area reefs. This thriving coral garden features delicate vase sponges and a wide variety of colorful tropicals.

(3) Old Wreck. Here an encrusted wreck offers excellent macrophotography. Purple featherdusters, bright yellow and blue basket starfish and undulating sea whips populate the wreck and surrounding reef. A pet octopus lives in the sponge-covered anchor winch. Also prolific are gray and queen angels, queen triggers, blue chromis and the yellow and black striped sergeant-majors.

(4) Jeannette's Reef. This magnificent reef was named for one of diving's most popular underwater models who considers this her favorite dive site. It's lush with both hard corals and delicate soft gorgonians, bordered by an eel garden. Great place for night dives.

(5) Charlie's Canyons. According to locals, there are still ancient cannon to be found here. Easy to spot are schools of French grunts, friendly Nassau

grouper and wide-eyed squirrelfish that live among the canyons and crevasses. Depth is 25 feet.

(6) Nick's Reef. Imagine being surrounded by a school of silver minnows so thick you can't see your dive partner. Thousands of fish live inside the reef in a majestic high cathedral. When the sunlight filters through the ceiling fissures, the fish life appear to extend on indefinitely. It's a maze of caves and caverns in only 35 feet with excellent bottom time.

(7) Sue's Reef. Float in silence and wander hidden through a system of ledges and canyons, at an average depth of 25-30 feet. Pugnacious damsels, snapper and grunts form an honor guard around the magnificent elkhorn rosettes.

(8) Queen's Reef. An unusual coral formation rising 50 feet from the bottom creates a natural amphitheater at 60 feet. These majestic coral heads are permanent home to multitudes of colorful fish, including angel, parrot fish, grouper, snapper, grunt and other tropicals.

(9) Queen's II. Here at the outer edges of the Little Bahama Bank you have the chance to come face-to-face with deep-water fish, the big pelagic species such as kingfish, amberjack and mackerel. Even schools of dolphin are occasionally sighted here. It's at a depth of only 35 feet. Bring your camera.

/Bell

(10) Broad Bottom. Just as the name implies, the shallow corals just three feet below the surface billow out onto a huge, broad sand bottom 30 feet below. All down this mini-wall, caverns and tunnels cut through the coral--the perfect spot for lobster. If you've never caught lobster before, ask your guide to show you how.

(11) Travel Agent Reef. A perfect dive for snorkelers and novices. In only 10 feet of water, it's a stunning coral garden teeming with brightly colored tropicals, ideal for natural light photography.

(12) New Sue's. A hobbit-like home coral colony that attracts a varied population of crabs, anemones and gorgonians.

/Bell

Andros, Bahamas

Small Hope Bay

Andros

Andros is the largest of the Bahama islands, but the least populated, developed or even explored. It's a huge scattering of islands and cays interwoven by freshwater creeks and inlets. Much of the land is swamp, while vast areas of pine forests hide countless small lakes and blue holes.

The usual aborted attempt was made to start a plantation economy on Andros in the late 1700's. With the abolition of slavery, blacks from other islands came here in search of farm land. So, too, came Seminole Indians from Florida, though the date of their arrival is disputed.

There are only two dive operations on this island and they're widely separated. Rest assured that you will never see a second boat at your dive site. The reef is huge and only a scattering of sites has really been explored. Frequently the divemasters will just stop the boat, throw out an anchor and go exploring with everyone else. Some of the dive sites discovered this way have been named for the divers who first chanced upon them. If you've always longed to have something named for you, this is the place to go.

Small Hope Bay Lodge, located in central Andros, fulfills the promise of the name "Family"

Island. The oldest dive operation in The Bahamas, Small Hope was founded 27 years ago by the man who still runs it, aided by his wife and children. Guests number no more than 40.

Casual is the word here, laid back and homey the atmosphere. Guests share meals and conversation. Children--who are welcomed and tended to while parents dive--eat dinner together in their own games room. There are "toys" for adults, too, including a hot tub at the beach, sailboats, windsurfers and a hammock.

Small Hope is near the settlement of Fresh Creek. The name comes from a tidal creek that runs miles into the interior before connecting to small freshwater lakes where bonefishing is excellent. Fresh Creek is the main harbour on the island's north coast.

The Androsia Batik Factory is located nearby. You can tour this cottage industry and see the design and production of a fabric that sells in some of Nassau's finest shops.

If beaching is your preference, head the seven miles north to Staniard Creek, considered by many to be one of the finest beaches in The Bahamas.

Some 40 miles north of Fresh Creek, outside of Nicholls Town, lies Andros Beach Hotel & Villas, with its Undersea Adventure dive operation. This spot is more private than Small Hope, less communal. The elegantly landscaped setting features tall palms, flowering shrubs and a beachside freshwater pool. Guests are usually dedicated divers. Those who come here enjoy time spent with no telephones, no television and no distractions except what they choose to create.

Nicholls Town provides a pleasant spot for a leisurely stroll. The settlement's two main roads are called Swamp Street and Blood Alley, obviously not named by a public relations agent. Don't let the names deceive you, however. Nicholls Town is a typically small, vividly painted and definitely peaceful Bahamian community.

A walk around the town will lead you to the pink, white and yellow school with green classroom walls; the lime-green police station with its old British style blue lantern; the pale apricot post office; and houses painted a very distinctive shade of yellow.

If you feel more ambitious, ask a local to show you Evans Blue Hole. The water's no longer blue, however. So many trees surround it, that it's become discolored, but it's still a lovely site.

Small Hope Bay

A few hundred yards from Evans Blue Hole is a shallow limestone cave. It's surrounded by trees with incredibly straight, multiple roots, some as big around as pillars.

Charlie's Blue Hole, some three miles northwest of the airport, is cleaner and bluer than Evan's. It's a lovely spot with small palms and pines ringing it.

Andros is clearly not the island to choose if you want casinos, glamor or glitz. But it's ideal if you want the amenities of modern living combined with quiet seclusion and truly exquisite diving.

• Fishing and Sailing

Marine facilities are limited on Andros. Fishing charters can be arranged in the larger communities. Reef and bone fishing are excellent. Big-game fishing has not been developed except in the north. For small sailboat rentals, try Congo Town.

• Windsurfing

A small number of board rentals are available at Nicholl's Town, Behring Point and Fresh Creek.

• Diving

Andros, Small Hope Bay Sites: The wall diving is particularly exceptional, sloping to 120 feet before the 6,000-foot vertical plunge. Remember that much of the reef here remains un-

explored. Except in a few cultivated sites, you can't feed the fish. They haven't seen enough divers to feel comfortable with the species.

(1) Coral Caverns. If ever there were mermaids, this must have been their home. Pillar corals tower 20 or more feet, intertwining in an incredible array of tunnels and caverns. As you swim through the tunnels, light filters through at different spots. Silver sides flood the holes, at times making it impossible to see past them. The bottom is sand. You can sit and gaze out at huge pillars that look like something from the Acropolis.

The caverns range from 70 to 90 feet. There's a false wall at about 70 feet that drops to 140 feet where the vertical wall begins. But this isn't really a wall dive. The caverns themselves are so beautiful, you'll yearn to spend all of your time exploring them, and want to return.

(2) Turnbull's Gut. A wall dive of intense proportions. Generally this is done as a split dive, with the initial time spent at 120 feet. You'll go over the wall itself at this point and gaze down into the abyss of 6,000-plus feet. The wall here offers black coral, sea fans, huge lettuce coral and a host of fish. Then you swim back into a huge crevasse that emerges some 100 feet later on top of the wall at 70 feet.

Andros, Bahamas

(3) The Catacombs. Pillars tower like giant mushrooms along the edge of the wall at a 90-foot depth. The coral is huge, capped and interweaving with large sand patches.

(4) Coliseum. This starts at 60 feet and slopes to a plane at 80. Big coral pillars rise in succession. There's open channels, abundant coral and lots of groupers.

(5) Blackwell's Bliss. This starts at 60 feet and drops to 90. It's full of tunnels, similar to Cozumel but without the current. Black coral abounds.

(6) The Dungeons. Thirty-foot high pillar coral interconnects to form dungeon like caves. They start at 90 feet and rise to 60. The Dungeons are located on the edge of the wall.

(7) Giant Staircase. The wall here starts at 90 feet, then slopes down at irregular angles so that it looks as if a giant stepped down it to form a staircase. At the bottom of the dive, the wall drops off to 6,000 feet.

(8) The Wall. This is a split dive. The first stop-off is 70 feet. Then you can go down to a ledge at 185 feet. The ledge is 40 feet long and 8 feet wide. There's a wide assortment of fish, corals and sponges.

(9) Cara's Caverns. Here a chimney-like effect is created by a cavern that opens into a tunnel. The tunnel does an S turn and comes out on the wall at about 90 feet. It's packed with fish in spring and summer, especially silver sides.

(10) Great White Sand Patch. This is a quiet dive that offers a real treat. If you settle on the coral that surrounds a large sand patch, you see hundreds of burrowing garden eels emerge from the sandy bottom. These shy, slender creatures, burrow at the slightest disturbance.

(11) Ocean Blue Hole. If you didn't know where this one was, you'd probably never find it. It's like a big crater, maybe 300 feet across, at a depth of 40 to 100 feet and splits a plateau right down the middle. The water is a light turquoise. Black shafts lead inland from the main cavern but should only be explored by well equipped divers with cave certification. There are huge rock "sculptures" throughout the main cavern.

(12) Marian. The Navy flipped this barge and couldn't salvage it. The ship is 100 feet by 40 feet in about 70 feet of water. There's also a large crane that the Navy attempted to use in the salvage operation. A lot of big fish hang out here. The wreck was just sunk this year so don't expect it to be coral encrusted yet.

(13) Barge. This is an LCN landing craft that was sunk in 1963, at about 70 feet. Corals abound as do fish, including tame grouper to feed. A safe wreck and an excellent spot for photographers.

(14) Rosi's Garden. A big flat coral bed at 50 feet, interspersed with sand patches. There are tons of colorful Christmas tree worms and featherduster worms. A great spot for photographs.

(15) Brad's Mountain. A big coral bed that rises from 50 feet up to 15 in an unusually peaked formation. It's tunnelled for exploring the various coral and sponges and fish including groupers, snappers and chubs.

(16) The Islands. Huge coral heads flare out on top at depths ranging from 10 to 30 feet. The effect is that of open caves and tunnels at an unusually shallow depth. It looks like little islands with lagoons. The light makes photography a delight.

(17) Red Shoal. Round giant coral heads range 50 feet across. When you look at this shallow 15-foot area from the surface, it looks like solid coral. But you soon realize you're staring at fish so numerous, they form an almost solid surface.

(18) Lovehill. A white sandy garden with clumps of coral that pierce the surface. This is an unusually square area that resembles a decorated swimming pool. It has lots of small corals, gorgonians, Christmas coral and tropicals.

(19) Trumpet Reef. Named for the schools of trumpetfish that swarm here. There also are yellowtails and grunts in an elkhorn coral garden at about 15 feet.

(20) Sea Turtle Ridge. Usually you see at least one 3 to 4-foot loggerhead turtle at this spot. There's a ridge of solid dense coral ranging from 40 to 50 feet.

• Andros Undersea Adventures Sites

(1) Potomas. This 250-foot cargo ship ran aground before World War II and was subsequently split in half by a hurricane. The bow section is relatively intact and definitely coral-encrusted. It's safe to swim through, but it provides a thrill for those not experienced in wreck diving -- so does the five-foot barracuda that likes to call the hull home, not to mention the nurse sharks that are frequent visitors.

The wreck is surrounded by an underwater forest. The ocean floor is covered with branches of staghorn coral that seem like fallen tree limbs. Gorgonians and coral grow with the deranged beauty of cacti. Silversides and parrot fish and

Small Hope Bay Diving

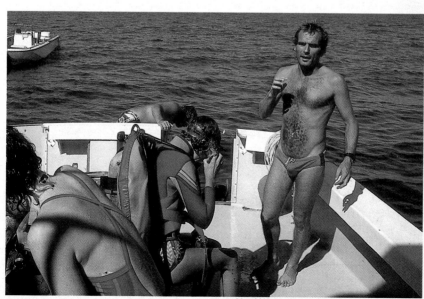

Neal Watson's Undersea Adventures/Bell

Neal Watson's Undersea Adventures/Bell

other colorful creatures flit around like butterflies. This site is shallow enough to be great for snorkelers and paradise for photographers.

(2) Chinaman's Hat. This spot begins at 50 feet, slopes to the wall at 90, drops to 140 and then plummets to 3,000. A mountainous pillar coral looks like an old Chinaman's hat. Deep gullies and ravines form at 90 feet, with room for only one diver at a time. The gullies range 50-60 feet long. Barracuda are usually seen here. One nine-foot Atlantic stingray sometimes appears. When he lifts up off the bottom, it look as if he's pulling up the whole ocean floor.

(3) Lighthouse Reef. At 70 feet, this spot has 6-foot mounds of plate coral, schools of 20 and 30-pound parrot fish, large lobster and numerous octopi. It's a good kickoff point for a wall dive. The ledge drops to 160 feet. You can swim over the top of the wall at 200 feet and look down on a royal purple infinity. Many experienced divers call this the spookiest dive of their experience.

(4) Enchanted Forest. This site gets its name from the many different colors of coral per square foot in this spot, which has a maximum depth of 20 feet. Elkhorn coral grow 7-10 foot across. There are bountiful fish and numerous cleaning stations where fish such as groupers stop to get their gills cleaned by small shrimp they would normally eat.

(5) Queen Angel Reef. This is a large sandy area at 35-75 feet with isolated coral heads branching off into a coral ledge. Queen angelfish are abundant. On one side there's a sandy patch, on the other a solid reef that slopes to 65 feet.

(6) Petrified Forest. At 60 to 90 feet, this is a good spot for seeing large plate coral, sea fans and large grouper feeding on the upwelling current that comes over the wall. Moray eels, a variety of sharks and large turtles are often spotted. An old sailing ship apparently went down here over 200 years ago. Six cannon and a rusted 9-foot anchor, plus pottery and plates, have been found in this spot.

(7) Black Coral Canyon. The canyon starts at 55 feet. There's a strong surge here. Lots of coral including black coral, large brain formations and pillarheads.

(8) Six Palms Ledge. A long ledge with a sandy lower side, ranging from 48 to 72 feet deep. This area is full of holes and crevasses that are home to nurse sharks, groupers, trunkfish, butterfly fish, conch, porkfish, garden eels and both sting and electric rays.

(9) Conch Alley. A series of overhanging ledges and undercuts beginning at 35 feet, this area houses a tremendous variety of conch, parrot fish, grunts, coral and lobsters plus the occasional shark, moray and turtle. Incredible abundance.

/Nivens

(10) Salad Bar. A field of coral so named because there's so much variety, it seems like a tossed salad. A dive at 17 to 20 feet, the coral includes staghorn, elkhorn, plate, brain, three types of fire, sea fans and others.

(11) Caves and Caverns. Sand, eel grass and turtle grass surround this area of caves, arches and ledges. This is an area of limestone caves where the bottom literally fell out, which is how they were formed. Located around 15-20 feet, the area attracts lobster, crab, snapper, grouper, grunts and occasional sharks. (12) Cathedrals Ancient pillar coral towers in formations reminiscent of church spires. Some go as high as 12-15 feet, reaching to the surface. This is a good area for rays, jacks and snappers.

(13) Lobster Bar and Grill. A trench 130 feet long by 40 wide passes through this coral reef at a depth from 15 to 25 feet. Its ledges literally crawl with lobster at night. There's also a lot of parrot fish asleep in their cocoons, spiny lobster, octopi and sharks.

(14) Ali Babbah's Cave. Ali Babbah the Grouper is a friendly, 45-55 pound grouper who lives in this cave. The top starts at 28 feet and drops to 45. You can feed Ali.

(15) Three Sisters. Three massive conglomerations of elkhorn coral that are about 50 feet wide and 150 long look a lot alike. They are a haven for fish, in only 15 feet of water and provide a perfect breeding ground, so there's a lot of baby fish around. There also are brittle stars, lobster and moray eels.

(16) Horseshoe. At 15 to 20 feet, there are unusual stands of elk and staghorn coral making a horseshoe shaped formation.

(17) Grouper Gully. Caves, ledges, holes, caverns and cracks form this area at 48 to 77 feet. There isn't much coral but big beasts live in these holes.

(18) Black Canyon Wall drops to 105 feet before making its vertical plunge. On the wall there are black coral, sea whips, tube sponges and luminescent anemones. A good spot for sharks and rays.

(19) Lighthouse Reef Wall. A panoramic ledge at 100 to 165 feet that looks out over a vista of deep purple infinity before dropping to 3,000 feet.

(20) Mary's Escape. A series of surge channels that start at 60 feet. The channels are 20 feet deep and look like someone ran giant fingernails along the bottom of the ocean. There's a lot of marine life here, including rays and sharks.

Neal Watson's Undersea Adventures/Bell

/Nivens

Bahamas 20 (52)

Mama Rhoda Reef/Nivens

Chub Cay

/Nivens

Chub Cay is paradise for those who want to get away from it all...but not too far. Chub is one of 30 larger cays in the group known as The Berry Islands. None was permanently settled until freed slaves were transported to Great Stirrup's Cay in 1836. Even then these islands were pretty much overlooked for the next 100 years. Finally in the 1930's, a wealthy English woman purchased Big Whale Cay and started the trend of turning these small isles into a private Shangrila.

One of these, the privately owned Chub Cay Club, only recently opened some of its club doors to non-members and features a country club atmosphere amid a Family Island environment. That translates to yachts that cost more than many people's houses, satellite color TV in every room and accommodations that resonate of the good life -- but without the casinos and night clubs or assorted restaurants, shops and landmarks of larger islands like New Providence and Grand Bahama. Incidentally, if you happen to own a 737 or smaller plane, you can land it at the club's large paved air strip.

Chub Cay's beach is a Hollywood version of the species -- wide white sand fringed by palm and pine, bordering water so clear you can see conch shells on the ocean floor.

Berry Islands, Bahamas

This isn't exactly an island you can tour. What you can do is enjoy the club's offerings: a full-service marina, houseboats to rent, a swimming pool, tennis courts and fishing of all types.

• Fishing and Sailing

There are good marina facilities at Chub Cay. Chub Cay also hosts the series finale of The Bahamas Billfish Championship Tournament, in mid-June. Chub has long been a popular fishermen's resort. Big-game and most smaller game fish are found in offshore waters to the southwest and bonefishing is quite good around Chub. This is partly because of the cay's location, which is where the deep "Tongue of the Ocean" meets the shallow Bahama Bank, forming a nutrient-rich pocket that feeds blue and white marlin, sailfish, wahoo, dolphin, yellowfin tuna, grouper, snapper, barracuda, amberjack and a whole host of finned creatures.

• Diving

What's good for the fisherman is, in this case, good for the diver as well. The fishwatching is unsurpassed. So, too, is fish shooting...with a 35-millimeter camera. The Chub Cay Undersea Adventures dive operation specializes in underwater photography. The operation's photo pro/divemasters will also offer individual instruction with advance notice.

Divers who come to Chub Cay tend to be fairly dedicated and usually take at least two dives a day. This area features unusually abundant fish life, as noted previously; a wall that starts at 80 to 90 feet and drops sharply; and shallow reefs near shore that are excellent for snorkeling as well as scuba diving.

(1) Mama Rhoda Reef. It's the ocean's equivalent of a Japanese garden complete with bonsai trees; you have to keep reminding yourself that you're underwater.

The elkhorn and staghorn coral formations here are uniquely scrunched up, as if deliberately sculpted that way. Depth is only 10-20 feet and the water surface seems like a glass ceiling. Wave action scatters the penetrating sun, sending ripples of light across coral and the rolling sand bottom. If you wanted to write "The Zen of Diving," this spot would be a must.

You'll often see spotted eagle rays here and large schools of angelfish, trumpetfish, grunts and tropicals. At low tide much of the coral breaks the surface. Then it becomes like a hedge to meander around.

The shallowness, reflective sandy bottom and clear visibility imbue sea life -- and photographs of it -- with striking, intense color. This site was recently made part of the protected Bahamas National Trust. If you dive it once, odds are you'll dive it again.

(2) Canyons and Caves. This is a line of reef riddled with caves and tunnels, paralleling the shore. The immediate area starts at 20 feet and drops to 50. You'll see thousands of silversides plus angelfish, triggerfish, spadefish, eels, barracuda and the occasional ray, turtle and nurse shark. If you continue swimming, you'll encounter more sand channels then end up on a 45 degree slope that starts at 60 feet and goes to 150 before a vertical drop. Visibility throughout the area is excellent.

(3) Shutterbug Reef. This and the next two sites are part of the Monument Valley area. Shutterbug is a profusion of high profile coral heads at 25 to 45 feet. There's lobster, moray eels and a pair of tamed French angelfish, Pierre and Marie, waiting to greet you. Parts of the movie Splash were filmed here.

(4) Angelfish Reef. In 40-60 feet, this site features another friendly pair of angelfish, Hansel and Gretel. They are definitely not camera shy.

(5) Plane Wreck. A vehicular underwater graveyard with a 4-seater Piper aircraft, an old Ford van and a Toyota truck at 40-60 feet.

(6) Pelagic Reef. One of the deeper Chub Cay dives, this one starts at 60 feet and drops to 120 at the base of the reef. It's a likely place to encounter a shark or two plus large schools of fish and makes for a beautiful two-tank day trip. The dive is usually done with a picnic lunch between tanks. Count on a one hour boat ride and a lot of pelagics.

(7) Flast Point. Huge orange elephant sponges dominate this 60-foot site. So do Nassau groupers. Local dive guides have seen schools of up to an astonishing 300 groupers.

(8) Fish Bowl. This is a wall dive that starts at 60 feet and drops. The reef here runs about a hundred yards long. There's abundant schooling fish and a lot of plate coral.

(9) Overlook Wall. This reef formation is 60 feet on top, then drops another 20 feet and gradually slopes to a pretty substantial drop-off at 150 feet. Keep a close eye on your depth gauge.

Bimini

When referring to Bimini, most people are talking about the island of North Bimini where most of the activity takes place. This island is only 7 miles long and 700 feet wide at its widest point. The majority of the islands' 2500 residents live on the southern two miles of the island and all but a few of the hotels and marinas are less than 1/2 mile from the seaplane ramp.

Never has so small an island received so much notoriety as Bimini. Ernest Hemingway first came here in the early 1930's to fish and write. He later immortalized the island's beautiful setting in his novel Islands in the Stream.

As you stroll through town, the ambience of the island takes over. Most visitors have their shoes off in the first 10 minutes and rarely have them on again until it's time to leave.

The first hotel you come to is Captain Harcourt Brown's Hotel & Marina. Just 50 yards from the seaplane port, Brown's was built in the 1940's for the few fishermen who visited the island. Although it hasn't changed much over the years, it is still a favorite of the "old salts" who return here year after year. For upscale accommodations, the best is probably The Bimini Big Game Fishing Club. Owned and operated by the Bacardi Rum Company, the club offers modern, spacious rooms, tennis courts, a freshwater swimming pool and two fine restaurants on the premises.

For a flavor of old Bimini, many people prefer to stay at The Compleat Angler

Nowdla and Bill with "Brownie"

Bimini from the air/Bell

Hotel. This 15-room hotel and bar was home to Hemingway while he was in Bimini and you can still rent his old room. The downstairs bar and lounge rooms are decorated with hundreds of photographs documenting Bimini's history as the big game fishing capital of the world (one-third of all the world record game fish have been caught off her shores).

Other hotels in the island include: Bimini's Blue Water, Weech's Bimini Dock and the Sea Crest Hotel, all located in the heart of town.

At cocktail time, visitors can find as many different places to go to as there are tropical drinks to sip. A trip to Bimini would not be complete,

Bimini, Bahamas

however, without at least one stop at The End of the World Saloon. A small shack with beach sand as a floor, this spot is popular in the late afternoon after a day of diving or fishing. After dark, however, everyone seems to end up back at the Compleat Angler. The popular native band, The Calypsonians, plays island music most nights to a packed house.

For a change of pace, visit the Fountain of Youth on South Bimini, a mostly agricultural island reachable by ferry from Alice Town. Ponce de Leon scoured the island searching for the Fountain. He found a spot he initially thought might be it. Although history doesn't record Leon's getting any younger, visitors to Bimini often report that the island makes them feel that way.

• Fishing

Bimini offers a wide range of boats and guides, four noteworthy marinas and good accommodations for the angler. Reef species and bonefish are caught year-round. Wahoo are strong in winter, dolphin in early spring and white marlin from New Year's through June. Blue marlin run all year, but mostly in spring and summer.

Many of the world's big game fishing records have been set locally. There are tournaments throughout the year, including the Hemingway Championship Tournament in March; the Championship Tournament (Open) in May; the Blue Marlin (All Billfish) Tournament in June; the Big Game Rodeo in August; and the Small BOAT Tournament in September. Other popular fishing competitions occur here at least once a month.

In keeping with the overall atmosphere of the island, there's also a Native Fishing Tournament in early August that has been variously described as a spoof on the big tournaments and an eight-day drunk. Prizes are awarded for the youngest and oldest anglers, the smallest fish, the least amount of fish and any other non-award anyone can devise.

• Diving

In addition to being spectacular, the diving in Bimini is also unique, with the prolific marine life being its main attraction. Sitting on the eastern fringe of the Gulf Stream, a constant supply of fresh nutrients amplifies the food chain to such an extent that the sheer number of fish here often takes even the most experienced divers by surprise. The constant northern flow of the Gulf Stream, just one mile offshore, also blesses Bimini with some of the clearest waters to be found anywhere in the world. This combination of marine life and clear water makes Bimini a favorite spot for professional photographers and researchers.

The sole dive operation on the island is Bill an Nowdla Keefe's Bimini Undersea Adventures. The operation offers all-inclusive dive packages with a number of hotels on the island. Packages include round-trip airfare from Miami or Ft. Lauderdale, accommodations and diving. Packages with meal plans are also available. Bimini's proximity to the States allows an avid diver to do as many as eight dives over a short three-day stay with Undersea

Hawksbill Reef/Keefe

Mysterious Stones of Atlantis/Keefe

Adventures. Bill and Nowdla run the dives themselves, with the help of Bill's younger brother Chris and personally see to it that each of their guests experience the best that Bimini has to offer. Though relatively young (31 and 24, respectively) Bill and Nowdla have many years of experience in Bahamas diving and Bimini in particular. Their combination of expertise and enthusiasm make for both a friendly and enjoyable dive trip.

Bimini's repertoire of diving includes reefs, wrecks, drift dives and visits to as yet unexplained archaeological sites. Here are but a few of the best:

(1) Moray Alley. Found in 60-70 feet of water, this site hosts large formations of popcorn-like coral heads separated by sand channels.

(2) Hawksbill Reef. Set in 45 feet of water, this site served as the location for many episodes of the TV series The Last Frontier by Canadian cinematographer and naturalist John Stoneman.

(3) Rainbow Reef. This shallow site, 25-30 feet, was chosen as the first Underwater Marine Sanctuary in The Bahamas in September of 1986. Skindiver Magazines's Rick Frehesse lists this as one of the best dives in all The Bahamas.

(4) Tuna Alley and Victory Reef. This area, 12 miles south of Bimini, offers world-class diving by anyone's standards. The barrier-type reef slopes from 40-90 feet, with many caverns and crevices to be explored.

(5) The Sapona. Lying in 15-20 feet of water, the Sapona serves as an artificial reef. Coral and vari-colored sponges abound, as do pufferfish and schooling fish and stingrays.

(6) Turtle Rocks. One brain coral at this site is 18 feet high and estimated to be 6,000 years old.

(7) Big Heads. The name comes from the massive brain coral formations here. One exceeds 18 feet in height and spans 20 feet across.

(8) Pickett Rocks. Good spot for macrophotography.

(9) Kinks. An area of scattered brain corals in 55 feet, there are large cables left here from underwater observatory used by both Cousteau and National Geographic to study the mass migration of the spiny lobster in the early '70's.

(10) Continental Shelf Drift Dive. A Bimini Undersea Adventure specialty, this dive is an interesting and hard to describe treat. Call Bill and Nowdla for more information.

Valentine's Diving/Parrish

Ramora Bay Club/Bell

Harbour Island & Cotton Bay

On Harbour Island, people will stop what they're doing to take you where you're going. For free. What do they want? They want you to come back -- and send your friends. Harbour Islanders say the "only" thing their island has to offer is sea, (pink) sand, sun and smiles. All are in ample supply.

Harbour Island became a popular spot with Loyalists, who brought slaves to work early plantations. Dunmore Town, the island's main settlement, was the original capital of The Bahamas. Throughout most of the 19th century, this island was a booming shipbuilding and agricultural center. When shipbuilding died out following World War II, the population fell from 2,500 people to 743. Tourism has renewed prosperity and population, which doubtless helps account for the relaxed good will of the island's inhabitants.

At sunset the boat taxi from North Eleuthera to Harbour Island crosses pale blue water that reflects a salmon pink sky with an effect much like an impressionist painting. It's a great time and place to first glimpse lovely Dunmore Town.

White picket fences frame pastel houses, many of which were built in the 1700's. You'd never know it since most of the houses are impeccably maintained, making a photographer's paradise. Enriching the picture is a proliferation of colorful flowers: orange and purple bougainvillaea, hibiscus and oleander with hummingbirds darting among them. Night blooming jasmine perfumes the narrow streets. Most houses have names: Strawberry House, Loyalist Cottage, Royal Termite, Lemon Tree. Many of these are vacation homes for US residents. Some island houses can be rented. Contact Geraldine Albury, PO Box 45, Dunmore Town, Harbour Island, (809) 333-2278.

Just past the Government Dock on Bay Street, you come to a huge tree known as The Fig Tree. It's not entirely clear why, as the tree doesn't produce figs. In days of old, craftsmen carefully constructed schooners in the tree's shade. Now all kinds of festivities are held here, including town dances. Local bands are excellent; at least one has toured Europe.

The best way to see Dunmore Town is to wander around. It's too small to really get lost. If you get confused, just ask. Anyone will be happy to steer you straight. There are gift shops, churches, a straw market (beside The Fig Tree), fruit and vegetable stores with locally grown produce, an art gallery and fishing boats and yachts sailing by in the harbour.

Eleuthera, Bahamas

When you work up an appetite, you can always dig into some conch or lobster pizza. If pizzas aren't your thing, there are plenty of other spots to choose from, including one five-star rated restaurant. Ask anybody you see for recommendations. You'll get them aplenty.

This small island fronts the harbor on one side, the ocean on the other. Oceanside are beaches that at low tide expose coral-crushed pink sand. It's a wonderful spot for beach activities, including excellent shelling. The beaches are a short walk or drive from town. Rent bicycles, motor scooters and golf carts to putter around.

There are two dive operations on Harbour Island -- Romora Bay Club and Valentine's Dive Center. Located in Dunmore Town, both cater to families and beginning divers rather than the three dives-a-day crowd. This attitude is partly due to the nature of the diving and partly to the nature of the island. Because non-divers enjoy the general ambience as well as available activities like tennis, fishing, watersports, beachcombing, shopping and just strolling, Harbour Island is an ideal family spot.

Dive spots rival those anywhere, especially in the shallow to medium depths. There are no walls, although there are deep dives to 110 feet. Shallowness allows greater bottom time for exploring the spectacular reefs around the island. It's an ideal area for underwater photographers, experienced divers who enjoy lengthy dives and those just learning the sport. Many families come to Harbour Island with only one certified diver and leave with a whole crew.

• Fishing and Sailing

The southern tip of Eleuthera is a well-known gathering place for the big fish. Bonefishing is very good along the eastern shores and reef fishing is excellent. There are marinas at Harbour Island, Spanish Wells and Rock Sound that offer charter fishing. Small sailboat rentals are available at Harbour Island.

• Golf

Imagine stretches of undulating green grass, blue sparkling ponds, softly rustling trees and a sense of serenity so pervasive you can't help but relax. Where is this edenic spot? On the fairways of The Cotton Bay Beach and Golf Club, that's where.

But don't let this idyllic scene lull you into a false sense of security. This 7,068-yard par 72 championship course, designed by Robert Trent Jones provides a challenge at every hole. The strategically placed water-holes, tight greens and devastating sand traps require every bit of concentration.

Located in Rock Sound along the Atlantic Ocean, the Club provides every amenity: complete pro-shop, bar, lounge, snack-bar, lockers, showers, club rental and electric golf carts. And while golfing connoisseurs will enjoy the challenge presented at each hole, recreational golfers will find this the perfect place to get in a game amid a truly spectacular setting. Free golf clinics are available for those wishing to perfect their putting or driving strokes. For those of us whose divots fly further than our balls, the Club provides private lessons at hourly and half-hourly rates.

• Diving

Most divers here are vacation divers. Most are certified, although the dive operation does offer certification and resort courses. More couples than families come here. Large groups are rare.

Diving resembles that of Harbour Island; some of the sites are the same, though you will rarely see a second boat at any site. The Current Cut dive is world-famous, attracting many experienced divers to both islands, though it's closer to Spanish Wells.

(1) Current Cut. Some people call it diving a jet stream, others riding an underwater roller coaster. Though comparisons vary, there's no dispute on one point: this dive is definitely an adrenalin rush.

Between Eleuthera and the smaller Current Island is a 75-yard channel that links Eleuthera Sound and the open sea. Tide changes cause millions of gallons of seawater to pass through this narrow gap at speeds from 5 to 10 knots. The central depth is 65 feet, with walls on both sides and potholes lining the coral bottom.

The swift current sends divers spinning, flying and tumbling over, under, around and occasionally into coral, crevasse, ravine, hole and ledge.

Divers generally make three passes of 10-12 minutes each. Be sure to wear a wetsuit for protection. Realize before you start that the current is stronger than you; if ever the term "go with the flow" had meaning, this is surely the place to practice it.

(2) The Plateau. Want to go mountain climbing with fish? This is the spot. From depths of 70-90 feet, coral and rock formations rise like mountain foothills to within 35 feet of the surface.

Small openings weave amid the formations. Swimming along the bottom, glance up at the rock walls and you'd swear you were in a canyon. There are even ocean meadows -- large sand patches dotting the hills.

Some of the individual coral heads here are huge. And shaped a lot like giant mushrooms. When a queen angelfish drifts past, you half expect it to say "Off with their heads!"

Rainbow parrot fish, friendly groupers, squirrelfish, snappers, damsels, chromis, triggerfish, black durgeons, creole wrasses, chub and horse-eye jacks abound. Occasionally you'll see a hawksbill turtle or long-snouted trumpet fish. Here, too, are iridescent, pale blue ruffled nudibranchs just waiting for your strobe.

(3) Blow Hole. This unique spot has been featured in film and print. Over the eons, splashing water has carved a hole in the top of a rock. Now when waves smash the shore with sufficient force, the water is forced up through and out the hole. It looks just like a whale spout.

This is an area of rock rather than coral. Huge boulders have fallen into the water. One formation is called Chapel Rock. Its archways are encrusted with sponge and corals. It's a different spot, ideal for macrophotography. The water must be calm to

Cotton Bay Golf

dive this spot, however. Depth ranges from 25 to 45 feet.

(4) Whale Point of The Sea Gardens. Good collection of hard corals at this site, which varies from 12 to 40 feet in depth. Schools of fish are plentiful, especially grunts, snapper, black dur-

Cotton Bay Club

geons, chubs and jacks. This used to be a prime spot to view whales during migrations, but in recent years the whales seem to have chosen other routes.

(5) The White Hole. This is an area of huge white-sand bottoms surrounded by ornate coral formations. Starting in 40 feet of water, it slopes to 110 feet, with an average depth of 50 to 55 feet. The colorful sponge, fascinating formations, clear water and varied coral heads made this a tremendous photography site, especially for silhouettes. Keep an eye on your depth gauge, however. This spot is so mesmerizing, you could accidentally end up at a deeper spot than planned. Lobster, octopus, starfish, turtles, hogfish and large pelagics are sometimes seen here.

(6) The Arch. Miller's Reef parallels the eastern shore of Harbour Island at a depth of 70 to 120 feet. On one side at 110 feet is a plate coral archway that's 80 feet across. Schools of fish swim around the top; a solitary barracuda hangs out beneath. Black coral dots the reef.

(7) The Cave. This spot is also located on Miller's Reef, at a depth of 120 feet. The entrance to a cave leads back about 35 feet. There aren't many fish inside, but the sponge life is especially colorful. A fine sandy bottom makes this dive best for small groups of divers. Spotted eagle rays and sharks are sometimes seen.

(8) Miller's Reef. Three miles of parallel reef. This is a great spot for exploring uncharted territory.

(9) Ocean View. Part of Miller's Reef, this area is similar to the Plateau with ridges, canyons and lots of coral. The water is exceptionally clear. There's a good variety of marine life, especially tropicals. Deepest point is 110 feet.

(10) The Grotto. Here the reef rises from 100 feet to 60. The grotto at 80 feet is a large hollow mound of coral permeated with crevices and caverns. Large schools of fish frequent the area, as do occasional sharks.

(11) Harbour's Mouth Drift Dive. An area of hard limestone bottom with small coral head outcroppings, this is a good spot to view turtles, rays on occasion, schools of snappers and other fish. Some artifacts have collected here due to the 1-2 knot current. This means you might find a 17th century bottle, not Columbus' personalized rum keg. Depth 20-35 feet.

(12) Long Point. A sandy basin with encrusting sponges. Food area for nudibranchs, including the orange-striped racing model and rays. No live coral. Depth 15-40 feet.

Harbour Island/Bell

Harbour Island/Bell

(13) Carrnavon Wreck. A 186-foot Welsh steel freighter that ran upon Devil's Backbone in 1916 and settled in 30 feet of water. All the cargo holds and engines are open so you don't need lights. The superstructure is gone, but the huge anchor, engines, boilers and propellers remain. There's so much algae that many of the fish are too occupied eating, allowing you to get close for pictures.

(14) Cienfuegos. A passenger liner that sank in 1895. Its twisted remains lie near the Train Wreck, in 10-35 feet of water. Most prominent features are a big boiler and the main drive. You can swim through the smokestack.

(15) Train Wreck. The scattered remains of a steam locomotive that sank (with the barge carrying it) in 1865. The only identifiable parts are the wheels, boiler plate and planks from the original wooden barge. There's ample marine life here, including peacock flounders. This is a fish feeding station. At 15 feet, it's good for snorkelers and for photography as well as scuba.

(16) Tunnel Reef. This is a shallow dive most people want to repeat. Coral rises from a white sand bottom at 25 feet to near the surface. You can get inside the coral heads. There are pet fish here, colorful sponges, chubs, lobsters, sea anemones, flamingo tongues, arrow crabs, sea biscuits, milk conches, sea fans and occasional southern stingrays.

(17) Bridgepoint. A collective term for several sites, all in the 40-70 foot range. There are coral outcroppings, then a drop-off that goes down to 110 feet. Spotted eagle rays are sometimes seen here, as is a lecherous loggerhead turtle. This 300-400 pound mammoth likes to goose divers in the rear.

(18) Egg Island Lighthouse Reef. Located due west from Egg Island in 45 feet of water are three large coral heads rising from a sandy bottom, providing a home for an abundant and varied community of sea life. Inhabitants include grouper, angelfish, wrasses, blue chromis and barracuda. The corals and sponges here are colorful and varied.

(19) The Gardens. A large expanse of varying corals rich in sea life lies about a mile from Current Cut in 35 feet of water. All colors of the rainbow are found here. Large schools of grunts and goatfish, parrot fish, trumpetfish, queen angels, groupers and an occasional ray can be viewed and photographed. The invertebrate life is even more diverse and colorful than the fish life.

(20) Split Reef. Just a few hundred yards from the Gardens are two large and one small coral heads lying in 50 feet of water. The largest looks as if it has cracked. There are tunnels running through the two bigger heads and sometimes large

/Nivens

fish such as tiger groupers are found in them. The purple sea fans, brilliant sponges and vivid anemones make it a colorful dive for both observer and photographer. With some luck, you can get a picture of the reef's resident five-foot barracuda.

(21) The Freighter. About five miles off the Current Cut lies the rusting hull of a 250-foot Lebanese vessel which, in 1971, caught fire and was purposely run aground. The wreck sits perfectly upright in 25 feet of water with her superstructure above the surface. As the wreck decays, various parts of the ship's structure and cargo are scattered across the sea floor. The hulk attracts great numbers of fish including parrots, blue tangs, grouper, squirrelfish, French angels and many yellow stingrays. The area is also a macrophotographer's dream, with nudibranchs, various shrimps, arrow crabs and worms.

(22) Roxanne's Castle. This large coral formation located on Southwest Reef lies with its base in 50 feet of water. It rises like a medieval castle to within 15 feet of the surface. Sponges of all types, shapes, sizes and colors are plentiful around the reef. The photography is vivid and varied. There are also many caves and caverns holding diverse forms of invertebrate life.

(23) The Insides. Another excellent site for snorkeling or scuba. Large formations of elkhorn coral rise to within inches of the surface. The water's depth varies from 15 feet on the shallow side to 35 on the open ocean side. Caves, tunnels and many small coral canyons abound. Many of the smaller tropical reef fishes -- sergeant-majors, damselfish, butterfly fish, hamlets and wrasses -- can be seen, as can an occasional turtle.

(24) The Caves. Located near Ridley's Head in 15 to 20 feet of water lies a labyrinth of underwater caves and tunnels. The top of the reef remains just below the surface, making it an idea area for snorkeling. Scuba divers, on the other hand, can enter and explore the many narrow passages and chambers. Yellowtail snapper, blue tangs, parrot fish, wrasse and small jacks abound. Inside the caves you can find squirrelfish, big-eyes and copper sweepers. This location also makes an excellent night dive.

(25) Meek's Patch. Just off Meek's Cay in 8 to 10 feet of water is an interesting collection of small coral heads where all types of marine life thrive. Yellow stingrays, porcupine puffers, grey angelfish, grunts and triggerfish, plus small spotted moray eels, lobster, crab and octopus are seen here. Colorful plume worms and a wide variety of anemones make for great macrophotography. A good spot for snorkelers, too.

Bonefishing, Peace and Plenty/Lloyd

Exuma

Beginning about 35 miles southeast of Nassau, the Exumas are a cluster of 365 small islands and cays bounded by shallow banks and coral heads on the west and Exumas Sound on the east.

Great Exuma is the largest of the islands and George Town the center of its settlements. From George Town you can rent or hire a speedboat or sailboat and spend the day exploring any of the neighboring uninhabited cays. Further north, from Wax Cay to Conch Cut, lie 176 square miles that comprise the Exuma Cays Land and Sea Park. This spectacular area is specifically designated for diving, snorkeling, boating and shelling. Limited fishing is also permitted.

Those who like beaching but not boating can catch the ferry to nearby Stocking Island. The leeward beaches are great for snorkeling and walking.

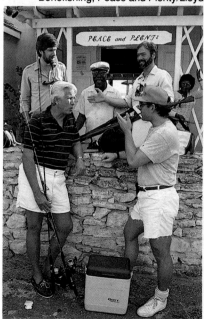

Peace and Plenty/Lloyd

Exuma, Bahamas

Exuma Divers/Lloyd

Sports

• Fishing

Exumas has some of the best bonefishing in the world. Over 50% of the flats are fished by wading. Fishing here is great all year long, and particularly strong in the winter. The bonefish here are <u>big</u>, typically three to seven pounds, and often reaching nine or ten pounds. These tailing fish are the wildest of the wild, providing muscle-bulging, back-straining excitement -- they can literally strip your reel in a second.

To get to these bountiful flats, make arrangements with the Peace and Plenty Hotel, Exumas' main fishing charter. They provide a comprehensive bonefishing package, including accommodation and travel arrangements. Peace and Plenty works in cooperation with renowned fishing guide Roger Martin. With 12 years experience in the Bahamas, he knows the ins and outs of this sport.

Each year, the Peace and Plenty Hotel and Roger Martin host both the two-part George Town Bonefishing Bonanza (late October, early November) and the Bahamas Bonefish Bash (late January). In addition to running the tournaments, they're also putting together a school for fishing guides, which will teach Bahamians the intricacies of the big time fishing business. And, they're exploring opportunities for additional bonefishing facilities in the as yet undeveloped Berre-Terre, at the north end of Exuma.

For more information, contact the Peace and Plenty Hotel (see our Directory) or call Roger Martin in the US at (305) 852-5931.

• Sailing

Sailing regattas include: the wild and wonderful cruising regatta in March; the Family Island Regatta during the final weekend in April every year at George Town; and the Annual New Year's Day Cruise at Staniel Cay. Sail and powerboats can be rented from George Town marinas or at Staniel Cay.

• Diving

Exuma's dive operator is based in George Town. Exuma Divers is a small, personalized operation that benefits from the Bahamian nature and expertise of its owner, Wendle McGregor. Wendle offers package deals with affiliated hotels. He also rents tanks and provides information on boat rentals.

(1) Angelfish Blue Hole. There are so many fish and they swarm in such friendly multitudes, you sometimes have to get someone else to feed them so you have room to maneuver. The Angelfish Blue Hole is 36-40 feet in diameter at a depth that starts at 30 feet and drops to about 90.

(2) Mystery Cave. This is a tunnel type formation usually treated as a cave dive. Jacques Cousteau and company explored this site. Neither they nor anyone else has yet charted an end to it. At 660 feet, the cavern still kept going.

A number of other excellent sites exist, some of which are: Landlocked Blue Hole; Stingray Reef; Lost Camera Reef. Conch Cay Shoals; Flower Garden; West Channel; Jay's Place; Duck Cave; Black Rock and The Post.

UNEXSO

Grand Bahama

Introduction

With the overwhelming bulk of its development occurring in just the last 30 years, Grand Bahama is short on history. It's also short on congestion -- but it's long on casinos, luxury hotels, nightclubs, restaurants, resorts, golf courses and all the amenities many tourists prefer.

Grand Bahama also offers any watersport you can think of, plus excellent diving through UNEXSO, one of the oldest and most extensive dive programs in the Caribbean. UNEXSO operates out of both Freeport and the West End's Jack Tar Hotel, an all-inclusive resort similar to a Club Med.

Editor's Note: During our stay on Grand Bahama, we made the acquaintance of writer/resident Remar Sutton. "Bubba" is co-authoring the book Inside Grand Bahama: An Unauthorized Native Guide. He kindly gave us permission to print the following excerpt. This book (available in Grand Bahama in late 1988) will be invaluable resource for anyone planning a Grand Bahama trip.

History

Spanish explorers sailed into the shallow waters of these northern islands and the name Gran Bajamar (the great shallows) began to appear on 16th century maps. From this designation grew the island's, and the country's, name.

Woe to the mariner who failed to heed the warning in the name, too. The treacherous waters around Grand Bahama have claimed many ships, including numbers laden with treasure taking the "Golden Road" back to Spain, the Gulf Stream route through the Florida Channel. Only a few have been found, an intriguing fact for divers.

Little happened on the island until the Abaco Lumber Company began to harvest the timber that covered the island. In 1946, this company attracted the interest of Wallace Groves, an American who'd lived in The Bahamas for some time. From his involvement grew the idea of developing a new city around a new harbor and the idea of a free port.

In 1956, enactment of the Hawksbill Creek Agreement gave the Grand Bahama Port Authority headed by Groves the right to develop certain properties and to create and manage the city as a free port.

Grand Bahama, Bahamas

Dolphins

Exploring Grand Bahama

Getting around Grand Bahama outside of the Freeport/Lucaya area can be a challenge. If you'd like to explore at your own pace, a rental car is your best bet. They are readily available, but rather expensive. Motor scooters and bicycles are also easily rented and a good choice for exploring in and around Freeport and trekking to the nearer outlying areas.

If you wish to see some of the sights, but do not wish to go it alone, there are various tours available. Just check with the tour office in your hotel. In addition to the around-the-island bus tours, visitors enjoy the many available boat trips. The sunset cruises and glass-bottom boat are favorites.

Freeport and Lucaya

Though we recommend that you explore some of the great beaches away from the city, you can certainly start your exploration in town. First, as you look around, realize that thirty years ago Freeport and Lucaya were pine woods -- period. So the town is a planned community designed to accommodate much future growth.

When exploring Freeport on foot, you may want to start with The International Bazaar. Designed by a Hollywood set designer, the bazaar does have an air of make-believe about it, but it is filled with shops which range from the T-shirt and souvenir variety to those offering imported luxury goods.

If you're interested in island crafts, you'll enjoy browsing in the Straw Market where the vendors are happy to chat as they work on strawcraft, jewelry and woodcarving.

For a taste of everyday commerce, stroll down the mall to Churchill Square. Here amid the hustle and bustle of shopping and banking, you can watch vendors cleaning conch and selling them from the back of their trucks. Or step around behind the Pantry Pride and see if any of the stalls in the Bahama Market have any sapodillas, mangos, island limes or other native fruit for sale.

Editor's Note: Don't miss the great new Port Lucayan Marketplace. This is an outdoor mall, island style, which opened in June 1988. It is a fun collection of over 80 shops, restaurants and bars with great nightly entertainment. It is located on Bell Channel, with it's own marina, connected to the UNEXSO dive center and The Dolphin Experience by the Waterwalk. We'd also recommend you spend time at Lucaya's elegant Garden of the Groves.

Bahamian Villages

Within easy biking distance of Lucaya (and not too far from Freeport, either) are two small communities which can give you an idea of what village life is like outside the boundaries of the Port Authority's development.

Williamstown strings out along the beach west of Lucaya. To get there, bike down Royal Palm Way (you'll need a map for security), take a right on Coral Road, a left on Bahama Reef Boulevard, then a left on Beach Way Drive. This road will bring you to the sea and a sign warning you that you are leaving the bonded area. A right takes you through Williamstown. Note the Traveler's Rest, a good native restaurant. Once through town, the paved track turns to dirt. About six hundred yards down on the left, between the road and the beach, is the Williamstown cemetery, enclosed in a low drywall stone fence. Typical of most island cemeteries, it is located on a dune because it is the only deep topsoil on the island.

Smith's Point, on Taino Beach east of Lucaya, is surrounded on all sides by new development, but keeps its identity with pride, as its entrance sign reveals. To get there follow the signs for The Stoned Crab, but instead of turning there, look for the Smith's Point sign just to the east. Here you can get good Bahamian food at the Outrigger Restaurant (and perhaps play a game of darts in the

UNEXSO Pool Checkout/Bell

bar) or stop at the White Wave Club and chat with the friendly, knowledgeable proprietress about the island's past.

Out to the Beaches

Grand Bahama has many miles of white, deserted beaches just right for a private picnic or an afternoon away from it all. In fact, before development, walking along the beach was the only land route from village to village.

Lucayan National Park is a perfect place to explore the island's ecosystems as well as to see caverns that are part of the world's longest underwater cave (seven miles in the system). Twenty-five miles from downtown, the park is best reached by car, though scooters are a possibility.

Start by walking up the trail from the parking lot to see Ben's Cave and Burial Mound Cave. Both are sinkholes where collapse of the cavern roof has allowed access to the cavern systems. The Bahamas National Trust, which oversees the park, has provided stairways into the caves and explanatory plaques.

Then take the boardwalk over to Gold Rock Beach. The walk (a brisk 10 minutes one way or a leisurely 20) offers a view of all the island's land eco-zones. As you come out of the mangrove swash, Gold Rock Beach stretches out before you inviting a stroll, sunbathe or swim. Gold Rock, an atoll is in the distance.

Barbary Beach is equally lovely, quiet and closer to Freeport and Lucaya. It has the added attraction of The Hermitage, one of the island's oldest buildings. Built as a Baptist Church in 1901 and later the hermitage for a Trappist monk, the building is typical of old island construction. It was recently restored. Barbary Beach is perfect for a picnic; many seem to enjoy snorkeling just off shore. To get there, take the East Sunrise Highway over the Grand Lucayan Water Way and follow the signs to Barbary Beach (essentially a right at the first traffic circle, but look carefully for the signs--they're easy to miss).

Go West!

A trip to Grand Bahama would not be complete without a trip to West End, the village with "a past," and a rakish one at that. Home to gunrunners in the Civil War and rumrunners in the 20's, West End more than any other Grand Bahamian village has the exotic air of what we picture as an island village a la Hemingway and Hollywood.

You can reach West End by rental car or take an organized tour. Harry's American Bar is another favorite stopping off place. And you can see Grand Bahama's most extensive village communities if you turn off the highway and go through Eight Mile Rock.

Recompression Chamber

West End Diving Center/Bell

Sports

• Auto Racing

The Grand Bahama Vintage Grand Prix takes place in Freeport, the first part of January. Freeport also hosts the Annual Supercross Motorcycle Race, the last week of October.

• Dolphin Experience

Imagine being able to swim with dolphins. Even more, imagine becoming their friends. There's some kind of kindred spirit we share with these intelligent mammals that makes us yearn for a closer relationship with them. Now, through a unique program offered by the Underwater Explorers Society you can do just that. Bimini, Cayla, Robala, Stripe and Lucaya are five friendly and fun-loving Atlantic Bottlenose Dolphins waiting to make your acquaintance. Just put on your snorkel equipment and jump into the safe calm waters of the enclosure behind UNEXSO's dive shop. Soon the dolphins will also be released daily into the open waters so that divers can meet them in their natural environment.

Opportunities are also available for assistant trainers and seminars.

• Fishing and Sailing

There are well-equipped marinas at Freeport/Lucaya and West End and charter fishing is readily available. The Bahamas only Yellowfin Tuna Tournament occurs in Freeport in August and various other all-fish and billfish competitions are staged here, usually in the spring and early summer.

Sailing regattas and yacht racing are also based in Freeport. Consult our Directory for The

Bahamas Sports Line, which offers up-to-date information on these events.

• Golf

The Bahamas is now an official golf destination of the PGA tour. As you would expect, they offer a variety of excellent courses. All the courses in The Bahamas are par 72, 18-holes; except for one par 36, 9-hole course in Grand Bahama. There are five challenging 18-hole courses on this island:

(1) and (2). The Bahama Princess Hotel and Golf Club offers two championship courses--the 6,420-yard Emerald and the 6,450-yard Ruby.

(3). The Lucayan Golf and Country Club is Freeport's first golf course, built in 1962. This is championship course that both novice and expert can enjoy.

(4). The Jack Tar Village course is a 6,800-yard, course that favors the strong driver. Ocean views abound.

(5). The Fortune Hill Golf and Country Club course is a scenic, 9-hole, 3,453-yard course.

Numerous amateur and pro tournaments occur at these clubs every month. For information on which events might be happening during your stay, consult our Directory for The Bahamas Sports and Aviation toll-free number.

• Riding

In Freeport, the Pinetree Stables offers guided trail rides and private or semi-private lessons.

• Running

The Annual Princess 10K road run (6.2 miles) in Freeport, takes place in late January. The Ting Road Race (6.5 miles) in early November, is another Freeport run.

• Rugby

The Freeport International Rugby Festival is held at the beginning of April.

• Tennis

There are plenty of guest and non-guest courts at the larger Freeport hotels. In the West End, there are sixteen courts for hotel guests only.

• Watersports

Waterskiing and parasailing are both available at the Holiday Inn in Freeport. The Jack Tar Village in West End can also provide waterskiing and for an alternative parasailing spot, try the Atlantik Beach Hotel.

• Diving

The Underwater Explorers Society (UNEXSO) has developed its expertise for over 22 years and expert it is. On one dive we took, another diver ascended too quickly from 90 feet. A small embolism soon caused him chest pain. Immediately the UNEXSO staff (using their on-call medical experts) diagnosed his problem and skillfully treated him in the BASRA double lock recompression chamber. When the diver emerged six hours later, his only complaint was that he'd missed dinner. Even more important than this example of their effective crisis management, is their everyday emphasis on safety. Each diver, regardless of experience must check-out in their 18-foot diving pool before getting on a boat.

(1) Blairhouse. At first glance this reef seems unmarked. There are no surge channels, no tunnels. As you swim over it, however, you'll see small openings in the star coral. Take a closer look. Like Alice and the rabbit hole, you'll no doubt find yourself checking things out. What you'll discover is a whole series of grottos with

openings about 3 feet wide and 10 feet high, some of which extend for 50-100 feet.

Emerge from the holes and survey a reef alive with two-foot black coral trees and soft corals waving in the gentle current. You might spot sea turtles, perhaps even mating on the surface.

The reef here drops from 60 feet to 85, forming a kind of mini-wall. A small blue hole feeds this stretch. Twice daily it blows out a nutrient-rich mixture of fresh and salt water, which accounts for the prolific fish and plant life that make Blairhouse as enchanted a spot as any Alice found.

(2) Pillar Castle. Marked by a large stand of pillar coral and extensive stands of elkhorn coral, Pillar Castle is a favorite site for photographers. Depth averages 15 feet.

(3) Treasure Reef. Two million dollars in silver and gold was discovered here by skin divers in the 60's, booty from a Spanish galleon that sank in the 1600's. Rumor says divers occasionally find more. Small grottos and schools of grunts, goatfish and other small fish make the site popular even without treasure. Depth 20 feet.

(4) Fish Farm. Parrots and durgeons hang out here. Turn over the rocks on the bottom and find large numbers of spaghetti worms, brittle stars and small urchins, all favorite food for wrasses. Small nurse sharks have learned to hover here in hopes of small tidbits, too. The underwater terrain favors lobsters.

(5) Littlehale's Lair. At 40 feet, Littlehale's is characterized by large, scattered coral heads 15 feet in diameter rising 10 feet off the bottom. Littlehale's is also marked by large colonies of tournazuets hanging onto the soft corals. The southern stingray grazes on the sand flats around this site. Depth ranges from 40 to 60 feet.

(6) Angels Camp. At times colorful angelfish "court" around the large coral formations at 50 feet. There's a colony of red anemones and many basket sponges.

(7) Hydro-Lab. During the late 60's Perry Oceanographics Underwater Habitat was located at this mid-reef site. The lab has since been relocated, but left behind is the mooring slab for the communications hookup. Next door is the old UNEXSO recompression chamber, complete with fixtures. Depth is 50 feet.

(8) Plate Reef. Enormous plates of star coral form a protective armor over long, partially covered canyons. Depth is 80-90 feet.

(9) The Caves. One spot where any big animal in the sea may happen by: spotted eagle rays, turtles and the like. The cave is here, too, an 11-foot surge channel, where the coral has grown over the top to form a cave stretching 50 feet.

(10) Theo's Wreck. One of the newest and most dramatic dive sites is Theo's, a 230-foot steel freighter on its side in 100 feet of water. The prop and rudder perch precariously on the edge of the ledge. Large holes in the ship's hull and deck enable divers to safely swim in and out and guides love to tell all about the ghost legend a true-to-life murder created.

West End Sites

(11) Tarpon Alley. Located off the western tip of Grand Bahama, tarpon and other sites are considered part of the "virgin reefs," so called because of the limited number of divers who venture here. Nearly everyone sees large tarpon, some over eight feet in length and all tame. The coral formations and caves stretch for miles.

(12) The Sugar Wreck. Several miles northwest of Memory Rock lies a large sandy spit running in a southwesterly direction. You are on the "Little Bahama Bank" in about 20 feet of water. The sugar wreck appears as a large dark patch amidst the turquoise water. The three remaining hunks of a steel-hulled barge attract thousands of colorful fish, some very large barracuda and occasional nurse sharks.

(13) Memory Rock (Mount Olympus). Due west of the sugar wreck, there's a narrow reef dropping to 80 feet. Spotted eagle rays, at times 20 at once, swim by here on the way to deeper water. Continuing west, massive coral heads burst forth from the ocean bottom. Horse-eye jacks feed here in the thousands. Mount Olympus itself is a large mountain of plate coral. Black coral trees abound and large, deep water sea fans cover the bottom. Depth 80-100 feet.

(14) Zoo Hole. Ninety minutes from UNEXSO lies a 30-foot hole in the earth. Twice daily cool, nutrient-enriched water flows up from thousands of feet below out through this opening. As a result of the "delivered" food, great numbers of animals live in the cavern. The Zoo Hole is a cavern dive to 110 feet.

UNEXSO also uses Owl Hole and Mermaids Lair for cave diving specialty certification.

Stella Maris Dive Boat/Bell

Long Island

Many divers go to Long Island for precisely the reason otherwise sane people might hesitate -- to swim among the sharks. This is one of the few places in the world where the dive program guarantees you'll see one.

Don't get the wrong idea. You won't see sharks on most dives here and certainly never in the swimming pools. The shark experience is carefully cultivated, as described in the Shark Reef dive listing below. There are other reasons to come to this island, which might well be named Long & Skinny since it's never more than five miles across. The difference between what you'll see on the two coasts, however, is striking.

The island's diving and most of its recreation, centers around Stella Maris Inn in the northeast. Much of Stella Maris sits atop a hilly ridge that surveys both coasts. The Inn also owns beaches on the leeward side of the island where it offers barbecues, parties and various watersports including water and jetskiing, sailing, windsurfing and fishing.

Sports

Just about all sporting activities on Long Island center around the Stella Maris Inn and its various facilities. The marina is small but well-

equipped and offers group fishing trips for deep-sea, bottom or reef angling. The Inn has two daytime tennis courts, bicycle rentals and waterskiing and jetskiing operations. Windsurfing boards are free to guests.

Deep-sea and bonefishing are excellent. You can also rent sailboats, motor boats and houseboats for day or overnight trips. Rental planes are available for private pilots.

The Stella Maris dive operation serves the gamut from novice to highly experienced divers. Its basic certification courses use an 18-foot salt water pool that's one of only two in The Bahamas. Sites include the rarely-seen walls around Conception Island. The Inn also offers dive packages in conjunction with neighboring Rum Cay, so that divers can spend several nights at each facility.

• Diving

(1) Shark Reef. This is a controlled dive and one of the safest you'll ever take. No one has been injured in all the years it's been done. You know that. Still...

Once you arrive at Shark Reef and have carefully (very carefully) checked all your equipment, you roll off the boat and into the water. You regain your equilibrium only to promptly lose it again at the sight of huge sharks swimming beneath you. The sharks are accustomed to this routine, even if you're not; they know the boat means food and they're ready and waiting.

The divers descend to a coral reef and sit. Be sure not to sit on the fire coral that flourishes here. So far it's done a lot more damage than the sharks. Once all the divers are seated, the divemasters toss a pail of dead fish into the adjoining sandy patch. The sharks--usually eight or more--hit the pail a few times until they get the fish out. Then it's a feast. Once dinner's done, the sharks circle around in search of other possible tidbits. The divemasters hold long pointed sticks that they use to lightly prod any shark that gets too close. Of course everyone knows that if a shark really wanted to chomp down, that little stick would be about as effective as a toothpick stopping a tank.

Though it may sound wild, the dive is actually very controlled and calm. This is a fun dive unless the word "shark" sets you quivering in your flippers.

(2) Poseidon Point. You can swim to this site, which is only about 30 yards offshore on the Atlantic side, at average depths of 40 feet. It's a long reef riveted by caves. You can dive through the larger ones. Elkhorn and staghorn coral proliferate, as do large groupers, barracuda and various angelfish. Occasionally you'll see a nurse shark or turtle.

(3) Grouper Valley. Named for the masses of groupers that homestead here. Jewfish are also abundant. This is an excellent fishing as well as diving spot. Depth 40 feet and deeper.

(4) Coral Gardens. It looks like Hollywood must have constructed this site of small caves and towering staghorn coral, but it's a natural formation. One stand of staghorn is 25 feet tall and 50 feet long. The coral starts at a maximum of 40 feet and grows towards the water rather than the surface

(5) Eagle Ray Reef. A good spot for seeing eagle rays, at a depth around 40 feet. This is an area of coral formations and a sandy floor. The visibility and light make this an excellent spot for photography.

(6) North Island Wall. A steep wall that begins at 110-120 feet and goes down. There's a sandy area on top of the wall. On its edge, black coral and huge purple tube sponges flourish. A good spot for seeing billfish.

(7) Barracuda Hole. Horse-eye jacks, hogfish, grunts, snapper, goatfish, grouper and angelfish swim among high stands of coral. It rises from a 40-foot sandy bottom.

(8) Deep Reef. Off Cape Santa Maria, the coral here is huge and pillaring. It starts at a depth of 90 feet and rises over 40-foot high.

(9) Blue Tang Reef. North of Cape Santa Maria, this site, at 35 feet, abounds with tropical fish, including blue tangs and six varieties of shrimp.

(10) Trumpetfish Reef. Named for the fish that populate this reef, as do scorpionfish and pink flamingo tongues. Soft gorgonians are more abundant than are hard corals.

(11) Flamingo Tongue Reef. Flamingo tongues tend to travel in groups here, at a depth of about 30 feet. They generally

/Nivens

Long Island, Bahamas

are found in the purple and yellow sea fans that flutter here.

(12) Grouper Village. The coral here is particularly lovely. There used to be half a dozen tame groupers at this site that you could hand feed. Unfortunately, it's a prime example of the dangers of this pastime, at least for the fish. They have yet to learn to distinguish divers from fishermen.

(13) Harry's Coral Heads. This is like a small canyon that doesn't close. The coral formation is broken in the center, thus letting in a lot of light for photography. There are lots of brain and flower coral, sea fans and sponges. Depth is 35 feet.

(14) The Coral Heads. Individual coral patches that house big schools of blue chromies and other small tropicals are found at 35 feet.

(15) Angelfish Reef. Tall and massive coral heads at 50 feet. Hundreds of other smaller heads surround. Schooling fish and groupers are common. You'll often see barracuda and rays, including the occasional manta.

(16) Barracuda Heads. The reef here is approximately 70 feet long and 40 across at a depth from 45 to 50 feet. A few large coral heads surround the area. There's a large cave on top of the reef and it features lovely formations of black coral.

(17) The West Wall. Starts at 110 feet and plunges. A picturesque wall dive.

(18) Exuma Reef. A 20-mile reef formation that starts at 40 feet and drops off at from 150 to 200 feet. This is a search and find dive, for there are no landmarks. There are, however, turtles, rays and sharks.

(19) Santa Maria Deep Reef. A beautiful, virgin coral reef about three-quarters of a mile in length. The leeward side features a mild drop onto white sand to shore, while the ocean side has dramatic cuts and drop-offs towards the wall and "bottomless" edge.

(20) Conception Island Wall. The wall starts at 55 and runs to 100 feet before plunging into the netherworld. Black coral is plentiful. You'll often see large turtles like loggerhead and hawksbill.

(21) Southhampton Reef. This is an old steamship wreck that's about 100 years old. Parts including the shaft, anchor and chain are scattered for about 200 yards. The depth averages 25 feet.

(22) Ships Grave Yard. This is a series of wrecks, one of which is the British freighter Comberbach, built in 1940 and used for hauling for 45 years. Featherdusters are common here, as are big

Stella Maris

groupers and a large barracuda. The boat has not been stripped. It's sitting upright, just like it was in dry dock. The Wilmar is another ship in the area, a wooden vessel at 42 feet that was sunk in 1981. It's lost much of its shape. Two moray eels live there, as do numerous arrow crabs.

Stella Maris

Stella Maris

New Providence, Bahamas

DIVI Bahamas Beach Resort & Golf Club

New Providence

This island certainly offers what most people associate with Nassau: casinos, luxury hotels, cruise ships, duty-free shopping, excellent international restaurants, historical landmarks and discos galore.

If you prefer something more secluded, New Providence Island can provide that, too. The dive operations and their affiliated hotels on the island's northwestern end seem more like Family Island hideaways, yet they're still within an easy drive of Nassau proper.

Downtown Nassau is a busy shoppers' mecca with a host of places to spend money and not regret it two weeks later. On the western edge of the city is the strip known as Cable Beach. It was named for the first telephone cable connecting The Bahamas and the United States, laid in 1907. Today Cable Beach is another area of large luxury hotels, some of the older ones beautiful examples of colonial architecture, plus a second casino.

Paradise Island is the site of large luxury hotels and a casino; it's connected to Nassau proper by a bridge. Paradise Island and Cable Beach hotels have their own private beaches. Interspersed along these areas and in vast stretches west of Cable Beach are lovely beaches open to anyone.

Those whose day begins after dark will find plenty to entertain them. Casinos with Las Vegas style revues, modern discos, Bahamian nightclubs, movies and restaurants of almost any cuisine are open any night/day of the week.

There is much to see here and several ways to see it. You can walk to most of the central sights. Or hire a horse-drawn carriage. Public buses and jitneys provide a third alternative, organized tours a fourth. Bahamahost taxi drivers have to pass government tests on island history and culture. They can be hired by destination or by the hour.

We'll start our tour at Paradise Island and come inland, make a quick detour east, then head west on Bay Street towards central Nassau and beyond.

Paradise Island was the setting for many of 007's escapades in the movie <u>Thunderball</u>. Its primary attractions are its luxury hotels, yacht harbors and the Casino.

Those who like quieter spots should visit Versailles Gardens and Cloisters on Paradise Island's eastern end. A walkway leads to a small gazebo that overlooks Nassau Harbour. This is a lovely spot to picnic or refresh.

Crossing the Paradise Island Bridge, you come to Potter's Cay, a fish, fruit and vegetable market with more than 50 small stands. The colorful produce, vividly painted fishing boats and the bright clothing worn by many vendors make Potter's Cay photographers' heaven.

As you come off the bridge, head east on East Bay Street a short distance until you come to Fort Montagu. Facing Paradise Island, this is the oldest of Nassau's forts. It was built in 1741 to defend against a Spanish attack.

Slightly east of the fort is Blackbeard's Tower, said to have been used by the notorious brigand in the pirates' heyday of 1703-1714. Originally the practice of looting ships was government-sanc-

NASSAU UNDERSEA ADVENTURES & CORAL HARBOUR DIVERS/Bell

tioned...as long as the target was enemy ships. The Crown licensed what it called "privateers," who made a bountiful living from plunder.

From the Tower, head back west towards Central Nassau. Take Shirley Street to Kemp Road for a visit to the Antiquities Museum. It displays many items brought up from the sea floor.

Take Kemp (which becomes Fowler) back to East Bay Street and head west again. In approximately ten blocks, you'll intersect Deveaux Street, location of the Pirates Museum. It's located in the <u>Bonhomme Richard</u>, a reproduction of an 18th century frigate.

If you're interested in a glassbottom submarine tour of surrounding reefs and shipwrecks, walk across the street to the Mermaid Marina. A boat leaves twice each morning, afternoon and night.

Continuing along East Bay, you'll soon intersect East Street. Take a left to Fort Fincastle. Shaped like a paddle- wheel steamer, the fort was built in 1793. The famous -- or infamous -- Queen's Staircase is 65 steps of stone, 102 feet high leading to the fort. Locals who are eager to show you around these sites report that it took 600 slaves 16 years to construct the staircase. If you're tired and it's a hot day, it might take you that long to climb it.

Next to Ft. Fincastle is the city's white water tower, decked with lights in the shape of a crown. They're lit up many nights. The water tower is 230 feet high. You can walk up or take an elevator to the top for a spectacular, panoramic view of the entire island.

From Ft. Fincastle, take East Hill Street west one block to Parliament Street. Make a right and you'll be at the Royal Victoria, Nassau's first hotel (constructed 1859-1861). During the American Civil War, the hotel's verandas teemed with captains, pilots, Confederate officers, spies and their belles.

Across from the Royal Victoria is Parliament Square, which houses many government buildings. To shop, head back one block to Bay Street. There are plenty of places to leave your money. But don't spend it all before you reach the Straw Market, next to Ministry of Tourism offices. This sprawling, covered market offers every product a person could weave from straw and some things you wouldn't think anyone could. This is a high energy place where you can bargain for prices or just stare in awe at human creativity.

If churches are your thing, walk a few blocks up Market Street and you'll see several, including St. Andrew's Presbyterian (The Kirk), built in 1810.

New Providence, Bahamas

/Bell

Return to your vehicle and Bay Street and head west. A short drive brings you to a delightful cluster of sights. Fort Charlotte protects Nassau's harbor entrance and commands a spectacular view. Flowers, especially hibiscus and bougainvillaea, surround the area.

The nearby Ardastra Gardens should not be missed by bird or animal fanciers. It's a combination park-aviary-zoo. You should also stop across the street at the new Coral World. If your fancy is flora, visit the Botanic Gardens, the fourth in this cluster of delights. Return to West Bay Street and continue west for a drive past lovely tree-sequestered houses and ocean views. This is landscaping and design at its finest. The road is lined with flowering plants.

About a mile beyond Northwest Point is Old Fort Bay, with one of the most hauntingly lovely "ruins" in The Bahamas. Formerly called Charlottville, Old Fort was once site of an ancient sea battery with gun emplacements on the seaward side. Sheltering the house is what is considered to be the biggest tree in the entire Bahamas. It's massive and vine-covered and unbelievably beautiful. Smaller trees cover the walkway to a lovely private beach.

To explore the rest of the island, keep heading west. You'll come to Lyford Cay, a private wealthy community with golf course and marina. You'll pass South Ocean Beach, with a holiday park and golf course. Then continue east through the Pine Barrens, a natural and largely uncharted forest with spectacular tropical orchids. As you emerge from the Pine Barrens, you'll come upon

Adelaide Village, a small, friendly settlement founded by runaway slaves. Stop at one of the local restaurants for a delicious Bahamian lunch. The Bacardi Rum Distillery is a couple of hours by car from here and provides tours. Carmichael Village, a short distance further east, is another former slave settlement.

Sports

Almost all the big hotels as well as some smaller operators offer the popular watersports: water and jet skiing, parasailing, fishing, snorkeling, diving, surfing, sailing in a range of boats, windsurfing and paddle boating. The Nassau area also has two championship golf courses open to the public, over 100 tennis courts, and facilities for squash, bowling and horseback riding.

• Cricket

There are seasonal cricket matches every Saturday and Sunday at Haynes Oval, Nassau, from late April to early November.

• Fishing and Sailing

Charter fishing is available in both Nassau and at nearby Paradise Island and is mostly limited to bluewater angling rather than reef or shallow fishing. Small sailing craft are easily hired at beachfront hotels.

Sailing races and regattas are usually run in March and include races staged by the SORC (Southern Ocean Racing Conference) and the Snipe Winter Championship and Bacardi Cup. Call The Bahamas Sports Line (800-32-SPORT) for the latest information on dates for these events.

• Golf

There are excellent courses in the New Providence area. The DIVI Beach Resort and Country Club course is located in South Ocean (The Bahamas oldest course) and you will find a 6,562-yard course at the Paradise Island Golf Club. Like Grand Bahama, New Providence hosts both amateur and pro tournaments throughout the year.

• Power Boat Racing

Nassau is the host on one side of the ARPA Miami-Nassau-Miami Searace for offshore powerboats (in late summer or early fall).

/Bell

• Soccer

The International Youth Soccer Tournament is held in Nassau, in early July.

• Squash & Racquetball

The Cable Beach Hotel and Casino offers both squash and racquetball. For squash only, try the Nassau Squash and Racquet Club or the Village Club in Nassau.

• Riding

In Cable Beach, the Happy Trails Riding Stables provides trail rides with guides. On Paradise Island, Harbourside Riding Stables offers beach rides and, on occasion, picnics on horseback.

• Running

The Bahamas Discovery Run (13.1 miles) takes place in Nassau in December.

• Tennis

There are extensive court facilities in Nassau and Paradise Island. The Marlboro Bahamas International Tennis Open is held on Paradise Island, in early December.

• Windsurfing

Board rentals and lessons are available at major hotels in Nassau and Paradise Island. Nassau also hosts the Annual Bahamas International Windsurfing Regatta, for both professionals and amateurs, in late January.

• Diving

Three dive operators serve the main Nassau/Paradise Island/Cable Beach hotels and cruise ships: Bahama Divers, Sea & Ski Sports and Sun Divers. All offer resort course diving for those who know nothing more about scuba than that they want to try it, as well as full certification programs and diving for more experienced divers. They focus on the dive sites in the Nassau vicinity. Most spots here are relatively shallow. This, of course, means ample sunlight to enhance the beauty of the prolific coral gardens and the numerous shallow wrecks. This is also a relatively sheltered area, so the diving is usually good even if the weather isn't.

Dedicated divers who come to New Providence usually head for the much less frequented western end. This area has been nicknamed The Underwater Hollywood due to the number of films shot in the locale. That means both spectacular scenery and some pretty interesting wrecks and props that the movie people left behind. But don't get the idea that this is only fluff diving. The wall dives here are as spectacular as you'll find.

Nassau Undersea Adventures, Peter Hughes Dive South Ocean and Dive Dive Dive serve the western end. They're sufficiently spread out that you will rarely encounter another boat at your site. These operators also offer resort and certification courses.

(1) Cove's Rock Trawler. Take this wall dive at night for a really special experience. You'll

/Nivens

/Nivens

/Nivens

drop over the crest of the wall at only 45 feet and descend down a vertical shelf. If you kept going, you'd hit bottom at about 1,000 feet.

Sponges include massive stands of orange elephant ear and purple tubes. You'll see the polyps from the star coral colonies feeding at night. You may spot octopi, parrot fish asleep in cocoons, eels, groupers, lobster, tropicals and any of a host of other creatures.

You sense it before you see it: Eyes gazing at the wall ahead of you will suddenly be drawn up. The bow of this intact wreck hangs over the edge of the wall. On a moonlit night, the resulting eerie silhouette makes you expect to see pirate ghosts stalking the deck. A second look and you're tempted to move for fear the whole thing will at any moment topple over the edge.

This is a new wreck and not yet encrusted but it's certainly well visited by yellowtails, blue tangs, red banded coral shrimp, arrow crabs and a varied assortment of fish.

(2) Never Say Never Again Shipwreck or Tears of Allah. This 100-foot freighter was bought by movie producers from The Bahamas government, which had confiscated the boat from drug smugglers in 1981. The boat stands upright, intact in 40 feet of water. The main part is on a sand patch, the bow in coral. This is a favorite site for wreck diving specialty certification. The boat has

three floors, fake engines reconstructed for the movie, a six-foot green moray and frequently sees great loggerhead turtles. Near by are the remains of the airplane prop designed for the movie Thunderball.

(3) James Bond Reef. In For Your Eyes Only, James Bond and one of his companions were tied and dragged over the coral. There's a reason why this particular spot was chosen for that filming as well as segments of Splash and Wet Gold. It's a spectacularly beautiful 10 acres of abundant coral of almost all descriptions, including sections of giant elkhorn coral that start at 30 feet and tower all the way to the surface. Fish, too, proliferate here, including lobster, crab and numerous tropicals. The timbers of a 17th century Spanish galleon and cannon remains are embedded in the coral.

/Bell

(4) B-25. Off Goulding Cay, this plane crashed in World War II. Pieces are still identifiable including the guns, engine, landing gear and wheels. Lobster and an occasional spotted moray like to take flight in this craft.

(5) Goulding Cay. A terrific site for finding dead shells to collect and keep. It's a sandy area with scattered coral, especially acres of elkhorn. There are also king conches, arrow crabs, coral shrimp, sea fans and the swarms of small fish that mark a fish breeding area. This area was used as a backdrop for Splash and Twenty Thousand Leagues Under the Sea.

/Bell

(6) Porpoise Pen Reef. A pen was constructed here to hold the porpoises used to film the TV series Flipper. It subsequently became the City of Atlantis for Cocoon. All kinds of rays like this spot, as do lobster. It's a macrophotographer's dream with abundant tubeworms, arrow crabs, coral bandit shrimp and shells. The average depth here is 30 feet. The wall begins at 40, however and much of the best scenery -- especially black coral bushes that grow along the wall -- drops to 70 or 80 feet.

(7) Clifton Wall. A tunnel enters the wall here at 40 feet and emerges at 80, where you hover over 6,000 feet of water at the Tongue of the Ocean. On top at 45 feet, it's encrusted with coral and the home of larger groupers and snappers. Looking over the edge into the Tongue, you can see vast amounts of schooling game fish including jacks, dolphinfish and tuna. Frequently, there are also billfish such as marlins and sailfish. To a certain depth, the wall seems almost terraced like rice

/Bell

patty fields. String coral and tube sponges abound, with long strands up to 20 feet. There are crevices, undercuts, ledges and chutes to explore. Visibility is usually excellent.

(8) Tunnel Wall. A dive that begins at 35 feet and could drop to 6,000. It's a honeycomb of tunnels, crevasses and caverns etched in a sheer vertical face.

(9) Thunderball Reef. Used in the movie for which it was named, this sand patch and reef area is an intricate arrangement of sponge, sea fans, basket starfish, coral and fish at 45 feet. Coral heads grow within 10 feet of the surface. There are yellowtails, blue parrot fish, groupers, ghost shrimp and lobsters at night. Sometimes it's hard to see the people for the fish.

(10) Pumpkin Patch. When you first cruise to this spot and look down, you'd swear you were seeing giant pumpkins. In the water, however, you realize you're looking at sponges. A whole mass of sponges: rope, tube, basket, whatever. Some are three feet in diameter. This is a wall dive that overlooks the Tongue of the Ocean. It's the home of many reef and nurse sharks as well as some great barracuda.

(11) The Anchor. A 1,000-pound, 20-foot, 18th century pirate ship's anchor gives this reef its name. There are huge coral heads here and plenty of schooling fish like jacks, pompano and ballyhoo. You have to brush the grunts and snappers away to see the lobsters and crabs hiding inside the coral.

(12) Goulding Cay Wall. This dive goes to 80 feet. It's a truly vertical wall with massive black coral growths and huge fish.

(13) Horse Eye Reef or Pier. An offshore boat pier in 45 feet of water, sponges encrust the pilings. This is a great spot for photographers in search of horse eyed jacks, octopi, needlefish, bluerunners, groupers, angelfish, jewfish and eels.

(14) The Runway. A sand area between the wall and Coral Gardens, this 40-foot dive offers one of your best chances for photographing large sting rays. For unknown reasons, the rays here seem particularly sluggish and difficult to disturb, which makes them ideal models.

(15) The Chute. A sand ramp here drops from 45 feet to 90, where it ends at the wall. Sponges, angelfish, squirrelfish, large grouper and coral predominate.

(16) Lampton's Wall. This site is long on caves, tunnels and passages. It's a great place to explore. Depth ranges from 30 feet to as deep as 115.

(17) Mahoney. This wreck, a 212-foot steel freighter that sank in the 1929 hurricane, is in only 45 feet of water at the deepest, with the main part of the deck at 30 feet. There's lots of growth here, including fire coral, so be careful what you touch. Gorgonians and soft corals surround the wreck. The fish are used to being fed and are quite tame.

(18) Unnamed Wreck. Near the Mahoney, this old freighter is in 45 feet of water. It's only been there a few months, so there isn't much growth but it's intact and very divable.

(19) Trinity Caves. A limestone reef, there are shallow caves here that house many interesting creatures including spiny lobster. Soft corals such as gorgonians and sea fans abound. Sponges cover the cave walls. Look for rays and large fish.

(20) LST Wreck. An excellent shallow dive. This ship was a World War II LST used to haul freight after the war. It's covered with fire coral, sea fans and rope sponges. There's a green moray in the hull that used to be friendly but which has grown skittish from being harassed by too many divers.

(21) Green Cay. A rich area of a flat sandy bottom dotted with large coral heads. Soft and hard coral make this spot particularly colorful, as do the fish that congregate here. Depth is 33-50 feet.

(22) Gambien Wall. At 80 feet there's a stretch of particularly striking reef with prolific fish and coral. At 100 feet there's a vertical drop-off.

(23) Alcora Wreck. At 80 feet, this steel freighter sunk in 1983. It was confiscated by the government from drug runners. The boat was sunk by dive operators and landed upright on the sand bottom. You can swim through its cargo holds. The ports are open and the hull upright.

(24) 20,000 Leagues Under the Sea. Named for the Walt Disney movie, this shallow dive is 30 feet at its deepest point. One of its primary attractions is that you can sometimes see schools of spotted eagle rays. It's a spur and groove reef that stretches for several acres. Tropical and larger game fish abound.

Rum Cay Diving/JC

Rum Cay

The Autobahn on Rum Cay is a little different than its European counterpart. In Europe you can drive 100 -- miles per hour. On Rum Cay you can also drive 100 -- yards; then the island's only paved road ends.

As you might guess, Rum Cay is not the place to go if you crave a vast array of sights, sounds and shops. And don't let the name fool you. This isn't the spot for heavy drinkers, either. Locals say the island was named after an East Indian boat that was wrecked, its cargo of rum washing ashore to line the beaches.

What Rum Cay does offer is tranquil seclusion, a friendly extended family feeling and miles upon miles of relatively shallow (70-100 feet) virgin wall diving. It also features Hot Lips, the famous kissable grouper.

The only settlement on this 30-square-mile island is Port Nelson on the southeastern side. It's a small community that used to be much bigger. Rum Cay was for years one of the largest salt-producing islands in The Bahamas, with an 1852 production of 250,000 bushels. The 1853 hurricane, however, shattered the island and its salt pans. Today only 89 people live in Port Nelson; 25 of them work part-time at nearby Rum Cay Club. Founded in part to help revive the island's economy, Rum Cay is not an exclusive, elite "club" but a casual barefoot get-away.

Twenty nine miles of powdery white beaches extend out from Rum Cay Club. This is premium shelling, picnicking and strolling. It's also one of the few islands in The Bahamas where the reef comes right up to the beach. Carry snorkels and flippers (or scuba gear if you have a sherpa) a short three-quarters of a mile and you are at an excellent snorkel-diving area.

Bordering much of the beach are sea grapes with their edible fruit, papaya and delicate white blossomed shrubs. Melons and mangos are grown locally; take some along for a special treat.

For truly hardy explorers, the Hartford Cave on the island's north side is archaeologically fascinating. There are little-seen Indian drawings. But this is a hard spot to reach. By boat, landing is problematic at best. By foot you have to hack your way through some dense growth. Still, it's a great hike if you want to fantasize about your previous life as Dr. Livingston.

Port Nelson is a much less arduous walk. It's about a quarter-mile from Rum Cay Club to the village. Snowy white egrets dot lawns as you pass. The old cemetery near the end of the Autobahn used to have separate sections for black and white; its tombstones date back over 100 years. The village is a personable, personal place. Stop by Mrs.

Rum Cay, Bahamas

/Bell

/Bell

Bane's Variety Store and Rooming House, Delores' Straw Works or Kay's Bar, which offers hi-fi and dancing. People are laid-back and friendly in this small community and conversations easy to start.

Ruins of the old jail, built from 1800-1850, are very photogenic. It's the basic colonial jail design -- small and square and somehow elegant for its function. A large vine thrives in one of the cells, probably the only thing that ever did.

If you tire of walking, the Club offers free bicycles for its guests and rents sailboats. Fishing is excellent. If you feel lazy, lounge in the hot tub, borrow a book from the Club library or watch movies on the VCR in the video lounge, which has

a good selection of underwater and feature films. Guests have often been here before and even those who haven't soon adapt to the family atmosphere. In other words, they pretty much take over the place.

Sports

Rum Cay is a one-resort island and the Rum Cay Club provides all the sporting activities. This includes small sailboat rentals, bicycles, hiking to Indian caves and windsurfing board rentals.

• Diving

Diving is unusual in that the wall starts as shallow as 60 feet and drops to 200 before its ultimate vertical plunge. Since most sites are on the leeward side of the island, visibility is usually excellent, even in winter. The Club also offers dive packages in conjunction with Stella Maris Inn on nearby Long Island; guests stay several nights at each.

The dive operation echoes the friendly family atmosphere of the Club. Dive gear stays on the boat, so you don't have to build your biceps by lugging heavy equipment.

The dive operation also offers three-hour E-6 film processing in its complete photo lab. You can choose from a full line of Nikonis rental cameras and lenses with Helix and Oceanic strobes.

Rum Cay Club/Bell

Incidentally, dive packages here are a real bargain; they may be the cheapest in The Bahamas.

(1) Snowfields. If ever there were an underwater "winter wonderland," this is surely it. Some 100 yards of glistening white sand stretch over a gently rolling floor to give the impression of snow-covered fields. But unlike normal brown and gray winter landscapes, the scenery here is a riot of color.

Two-feet-tall, vivid orange barrel sponges provide a striking contrast to the white bottom. So do magenta-tipped anemones, red Christmas tree worms, dusty rose featherdusters, purple and yellow sea fans, pale blue ruffled nudibranchs, black coral and a teeming multitude of other life. Look, too, for the colorful coral, clown and cleaning shrimps, as well as the yellow and brown striped arrow crab. This is paradise for photographers, excellent for both macro- and wide-angle shots.

If you're lucky on this dive, you'll see a three-foot-wide stingray lift off from the snowfield. Both southern and yellow stingrays are seen here, as are queen triggerfish, squirrelfish, tangs, yellow fin and nassau groupers, durgeon and enraptured divers.

(2) Westbay Wall. One of the most picturesque wall dives named for the guest who discovered the spot. Brilliant orange sponge, black coral and deep water gorgonians at a depth of 60-100 feet.

(3) Majestic Reef. Hot Lips and a company of 15 pet Nassau groupers reside here. You can kiss Hot Lips if you're so inclined. A word to the wise, however. Hot Lips is fascinated by things that flutter. That includes bikini straps. Hot Lips has disrobed at least one very startled diver. This site also features majestic stands of elkhorn coral and tunnels at 20-30 feet.

(4) Fish Factory. Another spot for pet groupers: Big Mouth and his harem of six. You can hug Big Mouth, who weighs in at 20 pounds. This is a good spot for fish photography. The coral

/RCC

/JC

canyons drop to a sandy bottom in 60 feet and lead out to the wall. Southern stingrays and spotted eagle rays are frequently spotted, as are schools of Bermuda chubs, French grunts and durgeons. Depth is 80-100 feet.

(5) Pinder's Pinnacle. Spectacular pinnacle ascending 35 feet from a sandy bottom at 110 feet. There's an occasional black tip reef shark.

(6) Carousel. Two immense mushroom-shaped coral heads grow on the wall. Long over-hanging ledges and a tunnel maze provide excellent exploration. There's a unique variety of colorful sponges and black coral at only 70-100 feet.

(7) Staghorn Wall. Large stands of staghorn coral balance precariously at the top of the wall at 75-80 feet. One interesting approach to the wall is to follow the opening in the reef near the base of the mooring line. It forms a four-foot arch that leads into a crevice, which in turn enlarges into a sponge-lined canyon. Where it opens on the wall, there's an unusually bright orange, star-shaped sponge. As you go east, two gigantic basket sponges extend over the wall. Depth ranges 70-100 feet.

(8) Blackjack Reef. Scattered coral heads dotting a sandy bottom. Queen conches graze in the eel grass. Good spot for flamingo tongue shells,

gorgonians, sea fans, sponges, sand filefish and yellow jewfish. Depth 10-40 feet.

(9) Menagerie Reef. A horseshoe-shaped reef of staghorn and elkhorn coral, French and Caesar grunts, triggerfish, jewfish, pufferfish, lobster and occasional nurse sharks. Depth 10-25 feet.

(10) Hyperspace. The tunnel that exits on the wall at 120 feet gives the awesome feeling of being in another galaxy. A beautiful carousel on the inside of the reef is 75-90 feet deep. Good place for back-lighted, wide-angle photography.

(11) Cottonfields. At only 5-18 feet off the beach, this is an excellent spot for snorkeling from the beach or dives when you want extended bottom time. Bermuda chubs, parrot fish, angelfish, basket stars, lobster and spotted eagle rays are common.

(12) Sea Gardens. A relaxing dive in shallow water. Sand dollars and lettuce slugs are prolific. Look on the underside of the algae-covered coral heads and ledges for nudibranchs.

(13) Chimney. A spectacular series of large tunnels. One ascends through the reef from 100 to 75 feet. The Chimney is a narrow vertical tunnel, wide enough for diver and camera. The top of a cone-shaped pinnacle comes up to 100 feet.

(14) Dynamite Wall. The tunnel here is large enough to drive a truck through. Stay near the top to prevent going below 100 feet. The tunnel exits

/RCC

on the wall at 140 feet on the bottom. Swimming west along the wall, you find a more restricted tunnel that ascends through a ninety degree chimney in the reef.

(15) Grand Canyon. A prime fish feeding location at 20-50 feet. Look for Radar, a Nassau grouper recognizable by two damaged rays in his dorsal fin; Klinger, a queen trigger who thinks he's a grouper; and Lady Di, a queen angel who can be hand fed. Be sure to allow time to explore the reef life and tunnels at 40-50 feet.

(16) Cathedrals. The top of the wall starts at 55 feet. An amphitheater of coral with a sandy bottom heads into a series of large tunnels and canyons which exit on the wall. Some tunnels go below 120 feet.

/RCC

(17) HMS Conqueror. This ship sank in 1861. Look for scattered wreckage including the mast, cannon, coral-encrusted cannon balls, anchors and small trinkets and bullets. Do not take any relics; they are property of the Bahamian government.

(18) Lighthouse. A new site excellent for night diving. The depth is 50 to 60 feet.

/JC

San Salvador, Bahamas

/Zamrok

San Salvador

Lying just a two and a half hour's plane flight from Fort Lauderdale Florida is an unspoiled diver's paradise called San Salvador (not to be confused with San Salvador, the capital of El Salvador). Part of The Bahamas archipelago, this small 12-mile long island lies some 385 miles southeast of Fort Lauderdale in the Atlantic. San Salvador features some of the world's best diving and it's presented in comfort and style through the island's dive resort, The Riding Rock Inn.

Although it's hotly debated whether or not San Salvador was the first bit of land discovered by Columbus, most experts agree that was indeed his first sighting of the New World.

For such a small island, there are a surprising amount of places to visit, many of them within walking or hiking distance.

Cockburn Town (that's pronounced Cohburn, forget the "ck") is the island's largest settlement. At one time, large boulders used to roll about the ocean floor just off the town point, giving rise to the town's original name, "Riding Rocks Settlement."

You'll need to plan for a full to half day to visit some of the island's other sites, some of which include: The Columbus Monument, at Long Bay, the location of two historical markers com-memorating Columbus' discovery. One, a bronze monument, sits in 20 feet of water, marking the exact spot where the great explorer dropped anchor on October 12, 1492. The other, a white cross on the beach, is the most photographed "site" on the island. This site is also the spot where the Olympic torch was lit on its way to Games of 1968 in Mexico.

Head further south to the Dripping Rock at Sandy Point. Many caverns burrow into the ridges along the coast and these are perhaps the loveliest.

This is only a partial sightseeing list. Ask the front desk for a copy of the handy island tour booklet that maps, in detail, the specific location and time required to reach each destination. Make sure to pack a bathing suit with you to take advantage of the many fine beaches you'll discover along the way.

• Diving

What makes this dive destination so superb? Well, for starters, the water is crystal-clear and there is no current to fight. The visibility is a consistent 100-150 feet. Over 50 excellent dive sites await exploration and even the most experienced diver will find something uniquely captivating. In this veritable underwater cosmos, graceful mantas and rays flit about, magnificently colored corals and sponges paint the crevices, overhangs

Guanahani Dive Ltd./Zamrok

and towering walls, and everywhere schools of fish are commuting to their next destination.

A partial list of the sites includes:

(1) Wreck of the <u>Frascate</u>. A 261-foot freighter located on a shallow reef north of the Inn. Among its attractions are two large boilers now decorated with purple and blue sea fans and clusters of brain, star and pillar corals. But the main feature of the dive is Kermit, the friendly 6-foot long moray eel who dwells there and who appreciates a regular feeding.

(2) The Witches Cauldron. On a sand slope in 70-feet of water, this site is imaginatively named for its huge barrel sponge. One of the biggest in the Caribbean, it measures 8 feet high and 6 feet in diameter. Long, slender finger sponges and large tube sponges also decorate the adjoining wall, as well as pastel colored brain and star corals.

(3) The Hump. A good spot for night diving, only two minutes from the marina, the dive offers a proliferation of marine life. Small red shrimp come out in droves at night and sometimes the orange ball anenome even puts in an appearance.

(4) This wall in French Bay has been described as the "wall to end all walls." An almost constant current supplies the area with nutrients for the vibrant growth of corals in the area. The main attraction here are two large, well lit caves, which

are entered from a large crevice cutting through the wall. Schools of hammerheads, eagle and manta rays frequent the first cave. The second cave, a little distance away, is entered through an arch at 110 feet. It slowly winds its way up through the wall and come out at a sand hole in 60 feet of water.

(5) Cable Crossing. Two submerged communication cables mark the border lines for this dive. In 50 feet of water, the coral heads are home to all kinds of tiny critters and make the site especially popular with macro photographers.

(6) Telephone Pole. Perhaps one of the most breathtaking dives in San Salvador, the drop-off

Riding Rock Inn/Zamrok

Riding Rock Inn/Zamrok

begins in 40 feet of water and slants down to a large lighted cave.

(7) Snapshot Reef. Appropriately named, this site (maximum depth of 20 feet) is home to the very friendly and not at all camera-shy Fred the Grouper.

(8) Devil's Claw. Although ominous in name, this site offers a spectacular abundance of marine life not always found in the shallower reefs.

(9) Hole in the Wall. With fish in abundance, the Hole features two deep, huge crevices slicing through the wall from 50 to 120 feet. Monstrous lobster and king crab hang out here.

(10) Basket Cave. A new, unexplored area just off Grotto Beach, the wall begins at a shallow 35 feet and then plunges away. The wall is covered with a tremendous variety of sponge life, predominately large basket sponges which reach lengths of up to 6 feet long.

(11) Movie Caves. It was near this site that Christopher Columbus first anchored when he set off in 1492. In 20 feet of water, there's a bronze monument commemorating this auspicious occasion. The site itself is full of coral and caves and arches where bottom oriented fish such as fairy basslets, black bar soldier fish, nurse sharks and squirrel fish hide out.

(12) Doolittle's Grottos. This spot is popular for its variety of coral cave and grottos.

Among the other fantastic dives are: Sandy Point Cave, the Rookery; French Bay's End; Elkhorn Garden; Vicky's Reef; Split Reef; Sand Castles and Shark Alley.

Crab, Riding Rock Inn/Tozer

Columbus Memorial/Zamrok

Cat Island

Life here remains out of the mainstream, with thatched-roof friendly Bahamian settlements and various historic spots. On both islands you can rent bicycles, mopeds, automobiles and boats to explore.

Cat Island's rolling, densely forested terrain with high cliffs (by Bahamian standards) overlooking empty white beaches has earned it many visitors' title as most beautiful of all Bahamian isles. At 206 feet, Comer Hill is the highest natural point in The Bahamas.

Sports

Cat Island used to offer diving through Hawk's Nest Club. However, at the time of this writing, the club was closed. Hawks Nest features an eight-slip marina, tennis, windsurfing, deep-sea fishing and sailing as well as diving and snorkeling. Cat Island shows promise as a new area for marlin and yellowfin tuna. Cat Island hosts the Cat Island Sailing Regatta at New Bight in July. You might check with The Bahamas Sports and Aviation department to see if the club has reopened. So few have dived here that most of the fish, coral and fauna have been literally untouched for hundreds of years.

Crooked Island

Describing what's now Crooked Island in his journal, Columbus noted: "There came from the land the scent of flowers or trees, so delicious and sweet that it was the most delightful thing in the world." Native herbs and citrus blossoms still perfume the air, giving Crooked its nickname, "The Fragrant Isle."

Crooked Island offers guest houses and a few small facilities. It's a quiet spot with 12 miles of spectacular beaches where you won't see another soul.

Sports

Boating and bonefishing are offered in addition to diving. Most dive sites, including miles of unexplored reefs and walls, are within a 5-10 minute boat ride of the club.

Green Turtle

Easily reached by ferry from Treasure Cay, 25 miles north of Marsh Harbour, Green Turtle Cay is a peacefully secluded island that delights almost anyone.

Sports

Diving on Green Turtle is from Brendal's Dive Shop at White Sound. Most divers are as laid-back as just about everyone else on this island, averaging only two-three dives a week. Many are new divers taking their resort course on a shallow ocean reef where they can actually stand. It certainly makes understanding the dive operator's instructions a lot easier when you can stand up and keep your head above water.

Spanish Wells

Sports

Four miles long and two wide, Spanish Wells is another good strolling spot. There's plenty to entertain vacationers: tennis, waterskiing, Friday night dances, touring the fishing industry, soaking up sun, reading, diving and special excursions available through the island's only dive operation, Spanish Wells Dive Center. The Dive Center shares dive sites the Ramora Bay Club and Valentine's out of Harbour Island.

Treasure Cay

Sports

Treasure Cay hosts one of The Bahamas Billfish Championship Tournaments in mid-May. Other competitions occur throughout the spring and early summer.

The Treasure Cay Golf Club offers a 6,972-yard, 72-par, championship course.

Bahamas

Abaco, Bahamas - Accommodations

ABACO TOWNS BY-THE-SEA 809-367-2227   48 Units: $130-162 BDPRT
   809-367-2221 803-671-5659 Box 486 Marsh Harbour, Abaco, Bahamas. See: Dive Abaco, Ltd..

CONCH INN RESORT & MARINA 809-376-2800   9 Units: $75-130 BDFKOPRS
   809-367-2233 Box 434 Marsh Harbour, Abaco, Bahamas. Located on the harbour. Private patios overlook marina. Dock-side bar and grill. Waterskiing, snorkeling, diving, boating, aqua bikes, jet skiing available. Hobie cats. Freshwater pool. Organized tours of island by taxi, scooter, cycle and car. Five star restaurant serves local and seafood specialties. Marina offers showers, boating supplies, radio communication and telephone service. Good jumping-off spot for exploring neighboring islands. See: Dive Abaco, Ltd..

GREAT ABACO BEACH HOTEL 809-367-2158   25 Units: $95-195 BDFKOPRSTW
   Box 419 Marsh Harbour, Abaco, Bahamas. All accommodations have balconies overlooking private beach. Five luxury, two bedroom villas and 20 airconditioned rooms, all with private phones. Freshwater pool. Tennis courts. Two bars. Deep-sea and bonefishing trips, scuba diving, snorkeling, car and bicycle rentals arranged. Also sailing sojourns on chartered sloops and schooners or motor boats to explore deserted cays or nearby settlements like Hopetown and Man O' War Cay. Restaurant. See: Dive Abaco, Ltd..

GREEN TURTLE CLUB MARINA 800-327-0787   30 Units: $135-159 BDFKOPRSTW
   809-367-2572 305-833-9580 Box 270 Green Turtle Cay, Abaco, Bahamas. See: Brendals Dive Shop Ltd..

LOFTY FIG VILLAS 809-367-2681   6 Units: $70-70 DFKOPRW
   Box 437 Marsh Harbour, Abaco, Bahamas. See: Dive Abaco, Ltd..

TREASURE CAY BEACH HOTEL & VILLAS 800-327-1584   164 Units: $155-255 BDFGKOPRSTW
   800-432-8257 305-525-7711 2301 S. Federal Highway Ft. Lauderdale FL 33316.

WALKER'S CAY HOTEL & MARINA 800-327-3714   66 Units: $155-700 BDFOPRT
   800-432-2092 305-522-1469 700 S.W. 34th St. Ft. Lauderdale FL 33315. Great, secluded beaches in isolated lagoons. Comfortable rooms and villas and a 75-slip marina with commissary, sundries shop and lounge. Their restaurant serves island-gourmet cuisine. With the finest fishing anywhere, they host the world's largest private billfishing tournament. Full service dive shop on premise. The underwater terrain is fantastic and easily accessible. Private airstrip, two swimming pools and tennis facilities available. See: Walker's Cay Divers.

Abaco, Bahamas - Sports

BRENDALS DIVE SHOP LTD. 809-367-2572   15 Divers: $42-42 BD
   800-468-9876 Green Turtle Cay Abaco, Bahamas. See: Green Turtle Club Marina.

DIVE ABACO, LTD. 800-468-9876   18 Divers: $50-50 DO
   809-367-2787 809-367-2014 Box 555 Marsh Harbour, Abaco, Bahamas. Operation features "The Geriatric Boat," a 30-foot island hopper specially designed for diving; it takes all the work out. No transom. Ladder is on 45 degree angle with wide steps. Two shoulder-high holders for slipping in and out of tank packs. Most dives at beautiful shallow sites, affording expanded bottom time. Excellent for scuba and snorkeling. Resort courses offered plus full certification through and including divemaster. Pkgs. through Aero Coach. See: Great Abaco Beach Hotel.

ISLAND MARINE DIVE SHOP 809-367-2822   6 Divers: $50-50 DO
   Box G Hope Town, Abaco, Bahamas.

WALKER'S CAY DIVERS 800-327-3714   50 Divers: $50-50 D
   800-432-2092 305-522-1469 700 S.W. 34 St. Ft. Lauderdale FL 33315. Full service, PADI dive facility at Walker's Cay Hotel & Marina. Camera and diving equipment rentals, E-6 processing, courses from resort and open water through assistant instructor certification offered. We also have special night dives and packages which include round trip air fare from Ft. Lauderdale, breakfast and dinner (daily), a deluxe double occupancy room, boat dives and more. Call our toll free number for price and reservations. See: Walker's Cay Hotel & Marina.

Andros, Bahamas - Accommodations

ANDROS BEACH HOTEL & VILLAS 800-327-8150   15 Units: $75-115 BDFKOPRW
   305-763-2188 809-329-2582 Box 21766 Ft. Lauderdale FL 33335. The large, airconditioned rooms open onto their own patios that overlook the sea and the freshwater pool. Tall palms provide shade or step a few feet away and enjoy the sun. Graceful landscaping and decor creates a sense of elegance, but the pace here is relaxed and casual. All rooms have two double beds. Their secluded Holiday Villas are small homes each with a kitchen, living room and two bedrooms. Windsurfing available for guests. See: Neal Watson's Undersea Adventures.

SMALL HOPE BAY LODGE 800-223-6961   20 Units: $198-260 BDFORSW
   305-463-9130 809-368-2014 Box 21667 Ft. Lauderdale FL 33335. Laid-back, family owned and operated. Twenty hand-built cabins nestled in pine grove at edge of the sea. Beachfront hot tub, complimentary bikes, windsurfing Sunfish. Excellent diving and snorkeling on 140-mile long barrier reef. Free scuba lessons. Great meals, good conversation. Adults and children welcome. 3 nights-345$, 5 nights-530$, 7 nights-690$ all inclusive PPDO rates. See: Small Hope Bay Lodge Diving.

Andros, Bahamas - Sports

NEAL WATSON'S UNDERSEA ADVENTURES 800-327-8150   28 Divers: $50-50 BD
305-763-2188 Box 21766 Ft. Lauderdale FL 33335. Virgin barrier reef stretches for 140 miles. No other dive boats are around. Shipwrecks, blue holes, wall drop-offs, coral gardens. We have excellent equipment and an easy-to-board deep-V boat. Camera rentals and E6 processing available. Three dives daily and night dives on request. See: Andros Beach Hotel & Villas.

SMALL HOPE BAY LODGE DIVING 800-223-6961   44 Divers: $35-35 BDFOS
305-463-9130 809-368-2014 Box 21667 Ft. Lauderdale FL 33335. World's third largest barrier reef is our front yard. All sites within 10-20 minute ride on flat top boats with large boarding ladders. Three times a week we do mystery dives, where we just throw out the anchor and explore a new place. We name dive sites for guests who help discover them. Dive price includes all equipment except wet suit. Call for special packages. Free resort course for anyone staying at the lodge, Bahamas oldest resort at 27 years. See: Small Hope Bay Lodge.

Berry Islands, Bahamas - Accommodations

CHUB CAY CLUB 305-445-7830   15 Units: $75-75 BDFPRT
809-325-1490 Box 661067 Miami Springs FL 33266. A "total" fishing resort that's quiet, friendly and relaxed. A private club, recently opened to non-members. These are the only accommodations on the island of Chub Cay. They have a comprehensive marina and the best fishing and scuba diving in the Bahamas. Other amenities include a swimming pool, two beaches, tennis courts, airport with Bahamian customs. All airconditioned rooms have satellite TV. They also have a restaurant, commissary and gift shop See: Neal Watson's Undersea Adventures.

Berry Islands, Bahamas - Sports

NEAL WATSON'S UNDERSEA ADVENTURES 800-327-8150   34 Divers: $50-50 D
305-763-2188 305-763-6843FX Box 21766 Ft. Lauderdale FL 33335. One of Neal Watson's full service dive operations, serving the Chub Cay Club. Diversified and exciting diving is just five and ten minutes from the marina. Eagle rays are everywhere. They are geared to serious divers and underwater photographers. Video and slide shows and E-6 processing available. Photography technique and equipment, full certification and resort courses are also available. Full rentals, trips and packages. See: Chub Cay Club.

Bimini, Bahamas - Accommodations

BIG GAME FISHING CLUB & HOTEL 800-327-4149   49 Units: $98-134 BDFOPRT
809-347-2391 305-444-7480 Box 699 Alice Town, Bimini, Bahamas. See: Bill & Nowdlas' Bimini Undersea Advent..
BIMINIS BLUE WATER LTD. 809-347-2166   12 Units: $95-302 BDFOPR
809-347-2291 Box 627 Alice Town, Bimini, Bahamas.
BROWN HOTEL 809-347-2227   24 Units: $40-50 BDFR
Box 601 Alice Town, Bimini, Bahamas. See: Bill & Nowdlas' Bimini Undersea Advent..
COMPLEAT ANGLER 809-347-2122   12 Units: $52-69 BDFOR
Box 601 Bimini, Bahamas. See: Bill & Nowdlas' Bimini Undersea Advent..

Bimini, Bahamas - Sports

BILL & NOWDLAS' BIMINI UNDERSEA ADVENT. 800-327-8150   50 Divers: $50-50 DFW
305-763-2188 809-347-2089 Box 21766 Ft. Lauderdale FL 33335. Dive Moray Alley, the wreck of the "Sapona," the Atlantis Road. Drift along the "edge of the world" suspended in crystal-blue gulf stream waters. We have 20 sets of first rate equipment, 200 tanks, and four divemasters. No minimum number on package deals -- our boats go out even if there's only one diver. See: Browns, Compleat Ang. & Big Game.

Eleuthera, Bahamas - Accommodations

COTTON BAY CLUB 800-223-1588   77 Units: $300-350 BDFGOPRSTW
212-661-4540 809-334-6101 Box 28, Rock Sound Eleuthera, Bahamas. Cotton Bay Club offers the discerning traveler secluded luxury on one of the most beautiful of the Bahamas family islands. Seventy-seven comfortably furnished, airconditioned rooms and cottages are nestled amid stately palms bordered by a 2-mile crescent-shaped beach. Enjoy Continental and Bahamian cuisine and lively entertainment nightly. Golfers can test themselves on their Robert Trent Jones 18-hole championship golf course. Rates include meals. See: Golf and dive operations.

ROMORA BAY CLUB 800-327-8286   30 Units: $115-165 BDFKORSTW
305-760-4535 809-333-2325 Box 7026 Boca Raton FL 33431. A former citrus plantation, this is an intimate tropical resort with lush gardens and a beautifully landscaped setting. Open air hot tub. Gourmet restaurant. Waterfront bar. Club offers a full range of water sports: all types of fishing, windsurfing, sailing and waterskiing, with instruction in all areas. Dive shop on premises. Tennis courts. Bicycles available for touring Dunmore Town. Fronts both harbour and beach, only 550 yards apart. See: Romora Bay Dive Shop.

SPANISH WELLS BEACH RESORT 800-262-0621   21 Units: $90-122 BDFKORT
800-451-8891 305-341-9173 Box 31 Spanish Wells, Bahamas. See: Spanish Wells Dive Center.

VALENTINE'S YACHT CLUB & INN 305-491-1010   21 Units: $90-100 BDFOPRSTW
809-333-2142 809-333-2080 Box 1 Eleuthera, Bahamas. Homelike atmosphere with resort conveniences. Water sports include sailing, scuba diving, all types of fishing, windsurfing and skiing. Lodge has own marina and yacht club. All rooms have airconditioning, ceiling fans, patios. Large fresh water pool. Lodge will take guests to neighboring uninhabited islands for special fresh catch picnic or own private parties. Excellent restaurant and bar. The Reach Up provides open-air bar and dancing. Hot tub. See: Valentine's Dive Center.

Eleuthera, Bahamas - Sports
COTTON BAY CLUB GOLF 800-223-1588
212-661-4540 809-334-6101 Box 28, Rock Sound Eleuthera, Bahamas. Robert Trent Jones, 18-hole championship golf course. Par 72, 7068-yards. No greens fees in the summer for guests of the Cotton Bay Club. Special golf packages available in the winter. See: Cotton Bay Club.
COTTON BAY CLUB DIVING 800-223-1588   12 Divers: $50-50 DO
212-661-4540 809-334-6101 Box 28, Rock Sound Eleuthera, Bahamas. See: Cotton Bay Club.
ROMORA BAY DIVE SHOP 800-327-8286   20 Divers: $50-50 D
305-760-4535 809-332-2325 Box 7026 Boca Raton FL 33431. A small operation offering individualized personal service. Caters to the photographer and those seeking small dive groups. Maximum number of divers per boat is 10. Offers resort and introductory scuba courses through specialty certification. Full photography rentals. Polaroid slide film works great; it's better than waiting to see if the strobes worked. Full rental for scuba and camera equipment. Located at Romora Bay Club. Close dive sites. See: Romora Bay Club.
SPANISH WELLS DIVE CENTER 800-262-0621   24 Divers: $45-45 D
800-451-8891 305-341-9173 Box 31 Spanish Wells, Eleuthera, Bahamas. See: Spanish Wells Beach Resort.
VALENTINE'S DIVE CENTER 800-662-2255X832   30 Divers: $50-50 DFOPRSTW
502-897-6481 809-333-2309 3928 Shelbyville Rd. Louisville KY 40207. They offer free resort courses in the pool each morning, full certification, open-water completions, specialty certifications and free photo coaching. Dive boats and rental equipment are modern and well maintained. Underwater photo equipment rentals are available and a video can be made of your dive. Morning and afternoon trips daily, night dives and full day trips to the famous Current Cut. Special dive packages rates available including hotel & air. See: Valentine's Yacht Club & Inn.

Exuma, Bahamas - Accommodations
OUT ISLAND INN VILLAGE 800-327-0787   88 Units: $110-183 BDFRTW
809-336-2171 809-336-2173 George Town Box 49 Exuma, Bahamas.
PEACE AND PLENTY 800-327-5118   33 Units: $94-98 BDFOPRSTW
305-791-5118 809-336-2551 Box 55 Georgetown, Exuma, Bahamas. Charming, quaint resort. They welcome great expectations. Airconditioned rooms with private balconies. Two cocktail lounges and indoor-outdoor dining. Sit back in informal luxury or enjoy sailing, snorkeling or bonefishing. Exuma Divers just across the street. Their Beach Club, with windward and leeward beaches, is across the harbour by courtesy boat, with food and bar service. Calypso music and dancing under a star-filled sky, twice weekly. See: Exuma Divers.

Exuma, Bahamas - Sports
EXUMA DIVERS 800-327-0787   30 Divers: $48-48 DFO
809-336-2710 Box 110 Georgetown, Exuma, Bahamas. "Let experience be your guide" is their logo. After 14 years on Exuma, they know the best reefs. As well as guided boat dives, they offer resort courses, complete certification, openwater check out, night dives and a special Blue Hole and Mystery Cave dive. Two dive masters. Fishing and snorkeling trips and other special charters available. Complete diving equipment and u/w camera rentals and air fills. Aluminum tanks to 3000 psi and 24-hour E-6 processing. See: Peace and Plenty.

Grand Bahama, Bahamas - Accommodations
ATLANTIC BEACH HOTEL 800-622-6770   175 Units: $115-160 BGRSTW
305-592-5757 305-592-3715FX 1150 N.W. 72 Ave, Suite 375 Miami FL 33126.
BAHAMAS PRINCESS RESORT & CASINO 800-223-1818   965 Units: $110-125 DFGOPRSTW
809-352-9661 212-715-7000 Box F 2623 Freeport, Grand Bahamas, Bahamas.
CASTAWAYS RESORT 800-327-0787   130 Units: $58-88 RT
809-352-6682 Box F 2629 Freeport, Grand Bahamas, Bahamas.
HOLIDAY INN BEACH RESORT 800-465-4329   505 Units: $96-132 BPR
809-373-1333 800-HOLIDAY Box F 2496 Freeport, Grand Bahama, Bahamas.
JACK TAR VILLAGE 305-641-0209   424 Units: $175-175 BDGRS
809-346-6211 305-848-4699FX West End Grand Bahama, Bahamas. See: West End Diving Center.
LUCAYAN BEACH RESORT & CASINO 800-327-0787   247 Units: $120-175 BGRSTW
TX:37225 809-373-7777 1610 S.E. 10th Terrace Fort Lauderdale FL 33316.
XANADU BEACH & MARINA RESORT 809-352-6782   185 Units: $105-160 BFPR
809-352-5799FX Box 111400 Miami FL 33143.

Grand Bahama, Bahamas - Sports

UNDERWATER EXPLORERS SOCIETY (UNEXSO) 800-992-3483   70 Divers: $50-58 D

305-761-7679 809-373-1244 1628 S.E. 10th Terrace, Room 203 Ft. Lauderdale FL 33316. They have a spec'l approach to diving that stresses safety and professionalism The fully equipped shop means they keep your equipment in order and you out diving. They have a special 18-foot checkout pool to help you get ready for the open water. Most of the dive sites are only 10-15 min. from the dock. The variety of diving experiences they offer ranges from shallow, 15- foot reefs to the ridge of the ledge that drops into a 2,000-foot abyss.

WEST END DIVING CENTER 800-992-3483   18 Divers: $39-58 D

305-761-7679 809-346-6211 Box F2433 Freeport, Grand Bahama, Bahamas. They offer extraordinary diving, as good as any in the Caribbean. Dive the nutrient-rich Gulf Stream as far north as legendary Memory Rock. Though they are located in the West End, you will find that they make a great day trip out of Grand Bahama. The West End has a true Family Island feel and this experience should not be missed. Though this is a new facility, the operation is backed by 24 years of experience diving Grand Bahama. See: Jack Tar Village.

Long Island, Bahamas - Accommodations

STELLA MARIS INN 800-426-0466   50 Units: $86-180 BDFKOPRSTW

305-467-0466 809-336-2106 701 S.W. 48th Street Ft. Lauderdale FL 33315. This plantation-style, club-hotel has everything, for up to 120 guests, plus its own international airport, shopping, marina & yacht club. Food is superb. Activities are plentiful. Many are free of charge. Entertainment is pleasant "Out-Island-Low-Key." Prices are moderate. They offer a variety of packages for divers, couples, honeymooners, fishermen & sun worshippers. Packages can include all air transportation, serv. charges, taxes, meal plan & activities. See: Stella Maris Inn Diving.

Long Island, Bahamas - Sports

STELLA MARIS INN DIVING 800-426-0466   66 Divers: $50-50 BDFOPRSTW

305-467-0466 809-336-2106 701 S.W. 48th Street Ft. Lauderdale FL 33315. This tropical island resort provides high adventure as well as relaxed quality diving off three islands. Dive programs cater to the shallow-depth photographer just as much as to the wall and wreck diver. Dive trips go out on a superb fleet of boats from 28' to 72' feet! Day, night and overnight cruises are available (including a special Wreck Cruise). Make sure you dive Conception Island Wall, and the world-famous Shark Reef. See: Stella Maris Inn.

New Providence, Bahamas - Accommodations

BRITANNIA TOWERS 800-321-3000   700 Units: $150-300 BDFGOPRSTW

809-327-3000 EXT:6270FAX Box N4777 Paradise Island, New Providence, Bahamas.

BRITISH COLONIAL HOTEL 809-322-3301   325 Units: $114-210 BDFOPRST

809-322-2286FX Box N7148 Nassau, Bahamas. See: Sun Divers.

CABLE BEACH HOTEL & CASINO 800-822-4200   693 Units: $160-220 BDFGOPRSTW

809-327-6000 809-327-6987FX N4914 Nassau, New Providence, Bahamas.

CASURINAS OF CABLE BEACH 800-327-0787   91 Units: $85-170 BKPR

809-327-8152/4 809-327-7921/22 Box N-4016 Nassau, New Providence, Bahamas.

DIVI BAHAMAS RESORT & GOLF CLUB 800-367-3484 120 Units: $160-200 BDFGORSTW

607-277-3484 809-326-4391 54 Gunderman Rd. Ithaca NY 14850. A golf resort located on the southwest shore of Nassau. Golf course is USGA rated and hosts international pro-am tourneys. Many consider it the best course in the region. The hotel and course overlooks the clubhouse Papagayo. The hotel has a private spectacular 1500-foot beach with its own bar also a gameroom, pool, and TV lounge. The transportation to town is convenient. Rent bikes, scooters, and cars. Dress code. New oceanfront rooms available. See: Peter Hughes Dive South Ocean.

EMERALD BEACH HOTEL 800-222-7466   162 Units: $75-95 BDGOPRTW

809-327-8001 800-237-0041 Box N-7108, Cable Beach Nassau, New Providence, Bahamas.

HOLIDAY INN 800-465-4329   535 Units: $125-185 BDGOPRTW

809-326-2101 809-326-2206FX Box SS6214 Cauarina Drive Paradise Island, New Providence, Bahamas.

NASSAU BEACH HOTEL 809-327-7711   411 Units: $145-215 BDGOPRSTW

800-223-5672 809-327-7615FX Box N7756, Cable Beach Nassau, New Providence, Bahamas.

ORANGE HILL BEACH INN 809-327-7157   20 Units: $68-75 BDFKORSW

800-327-0787 Box N 8583 Nassau, Bahamas. See: Nassau Undersea Adventures.

PARADISE PARADISE 800-321-3000   100 Units: $125-185 BORSTW

809-326-3000 305-891-2909FX Box N-6259 Paradise Island, New Providence, Bahamas.

PARADISE TOWERS 800-321-3000   503 Units: $150-300 BDFGOPRSTW

809-326-3000 809-327-2000 N4777 Paradise Island, New Providence, Bahamas.

ROYAL BAHAMIAN HOTEL & VILLAS 800-822-4200   170 Units: $145-1250 BGR

809-327-6400 809-327-6535FX Box N-7528 Nassau, New Providence, Bahamas.

SHERATON GRAND HOTEL 800-325-3535   360 Units: $150-275 BDFGOPRSTW

809-326-2011 809-326-3193FX Box SS 6307 Nassau, Bahamas. See: Sea & Ski Ocean Sports.

SMUGGLERS REST RESORT 800-328-8029   4 Units: $85-85 B

809-326-1143 Box N 8050 Nassau, Bahamas. See: Dive Dive Dive Ltd..

WYNDHAM AMBASSADOR BEACH HOTEL 800-822-4200   376 Units: $121-160 BDGOPRSTW

809-327-8231 809-327-6727FX Box N3026, Cable Beach Nassau, New Providence, Bahamas. See: Bahama Divers.

New Providence, Bahamas - Sports

BAHAMA DIVERS 809-326-5644   90 Divers: $50-50 BD
    809-322-8431 Box 5004 Nassau, Bahamas.

DIVE DIVE DIVE LTD. 800-328-8029EX246   36 Divers: $50-50 DO
    809-326-1143 Box N 8050 Nassau, Bahamas. Maximum bottom time. You arrive quickly at spectacular dive sites aboard
    the fast, roomy dive boat equipped with long-range radios, oxygen, trauma kit and manned by an expert crew. They usual-
    ly anchor in 35-40 foot waters, where the wall begins before it drops to 6,000 feet. You can have guided tours or dive with
    a buddy. Full certification with personable, expert instructors. Snorkeling trips too. This is not a cattle car operation. Full
    gear rental. See: Smugglers Rest Resort.

NASSAU UNDERSEA ADVENTURES 800-468-9876   50 Divers: $50-80 DF
    809-327-7862 809-326-4528FX Box CB 11697 Nassau, Bahamas. Internationally known for underwater filming in several
    "Bond" movies and "Splash," including shark stunts. Stuart Cove, the owner, gives all of his divers special care that makes
    for memorable diving experiences. Free transportation to shop in Lyford Cay. Five minute boat rides to the island's best
    dive sites. Quality u/w camera rentals. E6 processing. Easily boarded boats. Scuba Pro gear. Introductory to advanced
    and specialty certifications. See: Orange Hill Beach Inn.

PETER HUGHES DIVE SOUTH OCEAN 800-367-3484 20 Divers: $45-45 BDFGOPRSTW
    607-277-3484 54 Gunderman RD. Ithaca NY 14850. Qualified guides visit James Bond movie wrecks and underwater
    sets from Cocoon, Splash, Wet Gold and Twenty-Thousand Leagues Under the Sea, as well as reefs, walls, caverns and
    tunnels. The 1/2 day, introductory scuba experience, complete with pool session and reef dive, is a model of safety. Daily
    trips and hotel transportation available. Instructors on boats at all times. All sites within half an hour. Complete equipment
    and u/w camera rentals. See: DIVI Bahamas Resort & Golf Club.

SEA & SKI OCEAN SPORTS 809-326-3370   20 Divers: $50-50 DOSW
    809-326-3371 809-326-2011EX668 Box N 9141 Nassau, Bahamas. See: Sheraton Grand Hotel.

SUN DIVERS 809-325-8927   115 Divers: $50-50 DO
    809-322-3301 Box N10728 Nassau, Bahamas. See: British Colonial Hotel.

Rum Cay, Bahamas - Accommodations

RUM CAY CLUB 800-334-6869   16 Units: $100-150 BDFRSTW
    305-467-8355 809-332-2103 Box 22396 Ft. Lauderdale FL 33335. Rum Cay's only resort. A luxurious, casual, barefoot
    get-away. They offer spacious guest rooms with private porch, a two-room cottage overlooking the ocean, and three
    economy rooms with a one minute walk to the beach. The Aquarium Bar sits above the ocean. The restaurant offers ex-
    cellent Bahamian and American food. They also have a hottub by the beach, free bicycles,ve- hicles and sailboats ren-
    tals, and a video lounge with extensive film library. See: Rum Cay Club Diving.

Rum Cay, Bahamas - Sports

RUM CAY CLUB DIVING 800-334-6869   32 Divers: $32-32 BDFSTW
    305-467-8355 809-332-2103 Box 22396 Ft. Lauderdale FL 33335. They have two 34-foot flat-top Trimarans and most
    sites are within 10 minutes of the dock. No lugging gear around; it stays on board. Fully equipped dive shop repair cen-
    ter, and photo lab with three hour E6 processing. They rent a full line of Nikonos cameras and lenses with Helix and
    Oceanic strobes. Though prices suggest a cattle car operation, they offer small, personalized service. They don't pack
    you like sardines and throw you off the boat. See: Rum Cay Club.

San Salvador, Bahamas - Accommodations

RIDING ROCK INN 800-272-1492   24 Units: $80-80 BDFPRT
    305-761-1492 701 S.W. 48th St. Ft. Lauderdale FL 33315. The Riding Rock Inn features 24 hotel rooms, restaurant and
    lounge, a fresh- water swimming pool, tennis court and marina. The main building houses the restaurant which special-
    izes in American and Bahamian cuisine, the Driftwood Lounge known for its Island Concoctions, and a large veranda that
    overlooks the ocean. The hotel rooms are all airconditioned with private bath and patio with a view of the ocean or pool.
    See: Guanahani Dive Ltd..

San Salvador, Bahamas - Sports

GUANAHANI DIVE LTD. 800-272-1492   50 Divers: $45-45 DF
    305-761-1492 701 S.W. 48 St. Ft. Lauderdale FL 33315. Guanahani Dive Ltd., located at Riding Rock Inn Marina, fea-
    tures three boat dives daily. The diving here is known for its spectacular walls and abundant fish life. The dive shop (dock-
    side) has a full line of rental equipment. Instruction available - resort courses/full certification/ specialties. Underwater
    Photo Center has E-6 processing, conference center, camera rentals and photo courses. See: Riding Rock Inn.

Bahamas, General Listings - Information

AERO COACH AVIATION & AERO INTL. TOURS 800-327-0010/AIR
    800-468-9876/TOUR 305-359-3080FX P.O. Box 21604 Ft. Lauderdale FL 33335. A diving and sports-oriented airline.
    More than 70 scheduled flights daily from South Florida to 9 Island locations in The Bahamas, including Grand Bahama,
    Bimini, the Abacos, Eleuthera and Exuma. We are an offical sponsor of many of the island regattas. Sports vacation value
    packages are available and our knowledgeable, experienced agents are ready and willing to answer your questions. WE
    KNOW THE BAHAMAS! Call toll-free for air, hotel & sports pkgs.

BAHAMAS SPORTS AND AVIATION 800-32S-PORT
    305-442-4860 255 Alhambra Circle, Suite 415 Coral Gables FL 33134. Open Monday through Friday 9am-5pm EDT.

/Jones

/Roessler

Travel & Sports Guide

Bonaire

Useful Facts

• <u>Airline Connections</u>   ALM Antillean Airlines flies nonstop out of Miami on Saturday and Sunday. They have daily direct or connecting flights from both New York and Miami. Otherwise you fly into Curacao on one of the following: American (daily out of Kennedy with a stop in Aruba) or Eastern (daily out of Miami with a stop in Aruba). ALM makes the short hop from Curacao to Bonaire several times a day, but reservations are strongly recommended. You must reconfirm your outbound reservations 72 hours in advance. Airport departure tax for international flights is NAf18.00/US$10; for local flights it is NAf10.00/US$5.80 (per person over 2 years of age).

• <u>Banking</u>   The exchange rate at time of publication was NAf1 = $.56 US and is likely to remain so since the florin floats with the US dollar. The florin, which is usually referred to as the "guilder," is written NAf. It is divided into 100 cents and issued in various denominations. American Express, MasterCard and Visa are honored at most accommodations, but expect to pay cash at restaurants and shops. Most restaurants, shops and hotels quote prices in the local currency but will happily take US currency (and give change in guilders). Hotels expect you to pay in dollars if you are from the United States. Exchange currency at banks or the airport for the best rates. Banks are open from 8:30am to noon and 2pm to 4pm, Monday through Friday.

• <u>Courtesy & Dress</u>   Casual dress is definitely the way to go both day and night on Bonaire. As much as we personally favor cavorting in scanty beachwear at any time, it is considered a bit much while shopping or dining in town. Simple, easily cared-for cotton slacks, shorts and dresses will fulfill every need on this island.

• <u>Customs & Immigration</u>   When entering Bonaire, all you need to show is proof of US citizenship (a passport is always best, but a birth certificate or a voter's registration card will do), plus return or onward tickets. US residents who are non-citizens must show their alien registration card. Citizens of countries other than the US need to present a passport. You may bring back to the US $400 worth of articles duty-free, including 200 cigarettes and 1 quart of liquor per person. For duty rates on additional purchases and information on special duty-free items and prohibited items, consult either Bonaire customs or write for <u>Know Before You Go -- Customs Hints for Returning Residents</u> or <u>US Customs Pocket Hints</u>. These and other specialized customs publications are available from US Customs, P.O. Box 7404, Washington, DC 20044 or call (202) 566- 8195.

• <u>Driving</u>   On the right, as in the US. All speed limits are posted in kilometers. If you're planning to tour the island extensively, a jeep is recommended, due to long stretches of rough, unpaved road. The main roads are pretty good. Car rentals are available at the airport, major hotels and in town. Scooters, microbuses and pickups are also available. Foreign and international licenses are accepted.

• <u>Electricity</u>   127 volts AC, 50 cycles, which is different from the US system. This is likely to fry some appliances if they are used for long periods of time (you might get away with a short burst on a hair dryer). Check with your hotel about procuring a transformer or locating special facilities for any of your chargeable electronics. Some of the photo shops are set up to charge underwater strobes.

• <u>Events & Holidays</u>   New Year's Day; Carnival Monday, with dancing and parades (Feb.); Good Friday; Easter Monday; Coronation Day (April 30th and you're invited to the Lieutenant Governor's house for a drink, by the way); Labor Day (May 1); Ascension Day; St. John's Day, with folk dancing in

Klein
Bonaire

Miles
0   30   65
0   12   24
Kilometers

Roads

Unpaved Roads

/Bell

various villages (June 24); St. Peter's Day, with song and dance in Rincon (June 28); Bonaire Day (Sept. 6); Annual Sailing Regatta (mid-Oct.); Annual Nautical Races (Nov.); Christmas (Dec. 25 & 26).

• Events, Nikonos Shootout This is a week long underwater photography contest for amateurs, featuring three categories of competition – wide angle, macro and standard lens. Each day contestants are supplied with a free roll of film, donated by Kodak, and then have 8 hours to shoot the film with a Nikonos. Prizes have included trips to Fiji.

• Languages While the official language of the island is Dutch, Papiamento is the language of everyday life. It's a mixture of the Portuguese and the African tongues, with Spanish, Dutch and English sprinkled throughout. This is a young language, perhaps 150 years old and isn't difficult for Americans to learn. "Con ta bai?" (How are you?); "Mi ta bon!" (I'm fine!). Many Bonaireans are multi-lingual and English is spoken just about everywhere. You'll hear Spanish as well.

• Medical A recompression chamber, recently donated by the Royal Dutch Marines, is located at the island's hospital and is fully operational. A typical 4-5 hour treatment costs $1,800 - $2,000. Payment is by credit card or cash.

• Off-Season Dates & Rates In effect from April 15 through Dec. 20. Dates at each hotel vary slightly. You can save 10%-30% by booking for the off-season.

• Taxes & Tipping Accommodations are subject to a 5% government tax and most hotels add a 10% service charge. No tipping is required, unless some extra or unusual service is given. Most restaurants add a 10% service charge to your bill.

• Taxi Fares From airport to Kralendijk, US$5; to Rincon US$15. No meters; determine fare before embarking on a ride. Sample taxi fares are posted at the airport.

• Telephone From the US, direct dial using 011-599-7 plus the four-digit Bonaire number. For example, 011-599-7-8322 connects you to the Tourist Bureau. In Bonaire, just dial the last four-digits. Most lodgings do not have phones in the rooms. Calling a hotel direct is cheaper and quicker than telex, (about $10 US). Most hotels in Bonaire will send telex messages to the US for guests. Some offer FAX machines.

• Time Atlantic Standard Time (Eastern Standard Time + 1 hour). Bonaire does not switch to Daylight Savings Time in the summer.

• Weather Bonaire is in the far south of the Caribbean and does not experience the cold fronts that can shut you out of watersports in

Bonaire

the more northern areas during the winter months. Year round diving is almost guaranteed and the fall diving is exceptional. The only time you really need to be careful is in October and November, when trade winds have been known to shift for one or two days and put the major dive sites on the windward side of the island. Otherwise, sunshine and calm waters are the norm just about any day of the year. Average air temperature is 82 degrees, average water temperature 80 degrees. Trade winds average 16 mph from the southeast but it may be breezier in the winter. Humidity is moderate; rainfall is only about 22 inches per year.

History

The island of Bonaire was "discovered" by Europeans in 1499, during a voyage by Amerigo

Vespucci. No doubt this arrival came as an unpleasant surprise to the Arawak Indians who had been living there for centuries. While their culture disappeared rather quickly, the name Bonaire evokes their memory, since it is a derivation of the Arawak word "bo-nah" or "low country."

Spain made attempts to colonize Bonaire in the 1500's, but it was the Dutch who eventually took control in 1634. At the same time they also occupied the other Netherlands Antilles, consisting of Aruba, Curacao and the Dutch Windward Islands of Sint. Maarten, St. Eustatius (Statia) and Saba.

The Dutch West India Company developed salt mines and agriculture on Bonaire, using slave labor from Africa. When slavery was abolished in 1863, the economy quickly fell apart. It is only since the 1950's (Bonaire's first hotel opened in 1951) that a new economic vitality has returned to the island, in the form of tourism, a modern salt-

producing industry and an oil-distribution terminal that adheres to stringent environmental legislation. You won't find any high rise hotels, however, such as those on Aruba and Curacao.

The 10,000 people currently living on this arid, 112-square-mile coral reef, a scant 50 miles north of Venezuela, are of Dutch, African and Indian descent. Aruba is now an affiliated but independent political entity. Attachment to the mother country of Holland is still strong.

Ecology

Bonaireans are very ecology-minded. Not only is the entire island surrounded by the Bonaire Marine Park (see our diving section), but there is a substantial wildlife preserve at Washington National Park and two smaller bird sanctuaries at the Solar Salt Works and Goto Meer. There are, in fact, over 150 species of birds, including flamingos, as well as iguanas and other native land creatures.

The Bonairean environment is interesting in other ways as well. This is the driest island in the Caribbean and the topography of the interior is often compared to the American Southwest.

Exploring

Bonaire is one island where a rental car is almost a must, because the really interesting sights are not the easily reachable man-made edifices but the more remote masterpieces of nature. There are taxis at the airport and here and there on the island, but no public buses. Taking a tour with one of the tour operators is another alternative.

All hotel and dive operations provide or arrange regular boat tours off island, either to the nearby reefs or to the small, uninhabited island of Klein Bonaire, which is close by and a good place for a leisurely day picnic (as well as great snorkeling and diving). At day's end, a relaxing sunset cruise from 4:30 to 6:30 can be arranged through local resorts such as the Flamingo Beach Resort and the Bonaire Beach Hotel.

One very pleasant way to familiarize yourself with Bonaire is to attend one of the highly enjoyable slide and video shows presented at several of the major hotels.

Exploring Kralendijk

Start your tour at Kralendijk ("Coral Dike"), the island's capital. It's a small town of only 1,500 or so people, a few blocks long with an occasional street pointing inland. On the main thoroughfare, variously called J. A. Abraham Boulevard, Kaya Grandi and Breedestraat, depending on where you are, you'll find most of the shops, lined up in rows of colorful one- or two-story buildings, as well as the Tourist Bureau.

Stop by the Tourist Bureau for a free copy of Bonaire Holiday and a chat with Bonaire's illustrious tour guide, "Cai Cai" Cecilia. He'll probably suggest a walk along Kralendijk's waterfront, where Fort Oranje (a fortlette, actually) and some very handsome historical buildings surround the small plaza called Wilhelminaplein. Nearby is the Fish Market, a brightly painted Greek "temple" in miniature. After your walking tour of Kralendijk, stop for refreshment at the beautiful open-air cafe of the Hotel Rochaline, which overlooks the waterfront near the fish market.

Now you're ready to take on the rest of the island. Put your snorkel or dive gear, camera, binoculars, picnic basket and water (remember, this is arid country) in the car and pick a route.

• Exploring to the north

Kaya Grandi turns into General Debrotweg as it leaves Kralendijk. Just outside of town, the road enters the countryside, called kunuku in Papiamento (the local dialect), following a curving, westerly track along the coast.

Along the main coast road is the transmitter of Radio Nederland Wereldomroep (Dutch World Radio) on the right and the Thousand Steps dive site (now a boat dive) on the left. A bit north, at Karpata, is an intersecting road to Bonaire's oldest village, Rincon, which can be approached later on from the west. At this point the coast road becomes one-way.

The western terminus of the coast road leads to the fence of Bonaire Petroleum's oil terminal and the southern end of Goto Meer, a beautiful lagoon that serves as a popular hangout for flamingos. The road splits here, just a short ways up from the guarded gate, with a right turn taking you to Washington/ Slagbaai National Park and Mount Brandaris, which is the island's highest point at 784 feet. A left turn leads west of Goto Meer to both Nukove, a great snorkeling spot and Playa Frans, a small but active fishing village. These two sites are a side trip you may wish to reserve for an early afternoon.

Washington/ Slagbaai National Park is a huge game preserve (about 22 square miles). It is open

1,000 Steps/Bell

seven days a week from 8am to 5pm, except for major holidays. Entrance to the park is through the towns of Rincon or Onima. There is no way to

/Bell

Bonaire

connect from Playa Frans. We strongly recommend this experience. Entrance tickets are purchased at the gatehouse. Remember to bring food and water. Parts of this tour can duplicate the mid-day desert. There are no concession stands inside the park boundaries. By the way, camping is not permitted in the park.

Visitors to the park can select the 15-mile route or the 21-mile scenic tour. The roads are well marked by yellow and green arrows, but can be rough in spots, as befits a true wilderness area.

Drive past the gatehouse to a salt flat called Salina Mathijs, an area populated by flamingos during the "rainy" season (October-January). A few kilometers farther, there's a side road to the right that leads to Playa Chikito, a nice beach with a strong surf and some simple shade huts. It's a good place to sunbathe and perhaps bodysurf a little, but swimming far from shore is very dangerous. Skeptics should note the memorial plaque displayed nearby.

For serious birdwatchers, a good spot is Poos di Mangel, where a fantastic array of birds gather for happy hour in the late afternoon. This watering place is on a side road to the left as you're rounding the northern tip of the island on the way to Boca Bartol. After getting back on the main road and passing Boca Bartol (the favorite hideaway of a famous Hollywood actor of the past), you're heading south again, with Mount Brandaris in front of you. At Playa Funchi there's excellent snorkeling, as well as a small army of hungry little lizards that will swarm to greet you if you throw pieces of bread on the ground near the stone bench. Nearby, a road branches off to Bronswinkel Well, where hundreds of birds and giant cacti thrive (cactus makes an excellent soup if cooked properly).

Between Playa Funchi and Boca Slagbaai is a cliff road where some shamelessly overweight iguanas occasionally sun themselves. But the chance of getting a good look at them decreases markedly after the first human visitors of the day have rolled by. Boca Slagbaai, the first port on the island and an area once used to pen and slaughter livestock, is now an inviting place to picnic, swim, snorkel and take a nap. Just across the road is Salinja Slagbaai, a salt bed where flamingos often congregate. From this point the road leads back to the gatehouse, but pause along the way for a different view of Goto Meer and its flamingos before leaving the park.

On exiting, go through the village of Rincon and stop at the Amstel Bar for a taste of the local favorite, Amstel beer, brewed with desalinated sea water. After exhaustive testing, we heartily recommend this product. Another possible stop after leaving the park is to take the road to the north coast and Boca Onima, a rocky little inlet where the few remaining Indians on Bonaire are believed to have launched their boats and escaped slavery.

Just a short distance from the pounding surf is the road to the Onima Indian inscriptions. Here, on the ceilings of small shallow sea-carved caves, are pre-colonial symbols and designs dating back 500 years or more. Also look for a second group of caverns and inscriptions that lie behind the green arrow sign pointing to the main group of caves. As you leave the area, look for the twisted trunk of the Brazia tree, the probable source of the original red dye used for the inscriptions.

· Exploring to the south

The south of the island varies considerably from the north in both topography and history. After passing the Punt Vierkant Lighthouse and the Trans World Radio antennae, you'll see some ruins of slave huts from the 1850's, located near the Salt Pier of the Antilles International Salt Company. A 30 foot obelisk stands close by, in the spot where it once guided the salt ships to their moorings. Farther south, on the right and just before you pass an old white plantation house, is Pink Beach, probably the nicest stretch of sand on Bonaire. Two more obelisks and a row of restored slave huts border the beach.

Just across the road begins the lagoon of Pekelmeer, the breeding ground for thousands of flamingos. To protect the birds from disturbance, their sanctuary is off limits to visitors; but if you park and walk quietly along the side of the road, you're almost sure to see some.

At the southernmost tip of the island stands the Willemstoren Lighthouse (Bonaire's oldest existing lighthouse, built in 1837), surrounded by views just begging to be photographed. That huge freighter double-parked on the beach is the Telisa Del Mar, a Honduran ship that ran aground a few years ago.

At day's end, from either Pekelmeer or Willemstoren, you can watch the flamingos trotting elegantly on the water as their long pink and black wings lift them aloft for the nightly sojourn to Venezuela. Rounding the island, the road heads north again toward Lac Bay and then Sorobon Beach, a remote and quiet resort, that offers its own "clothes optional" beach (non-guests pay an entrance fee). There's also a nice bar and restaurant nearby. At the end of the tour, take a short-cut back to your hotel through an inland road intersecting at Sorobon Beach.

• **Exploring off Island**

You may want to take the quick 25-minute hop by air to Curacao, especially if you originally flew directly to Bonaire on ALM; your ticket entitles you to a free round-trip to Curacao as part of the deal.

Food

Eating out in Bonaire can be expensive, although a careful search will turn up several restaurants serving less expensive bar snacks or selected main menu items at reasonable cost. Be sure to try some conch, either fried or as a stew. Iguana soup isn't bad, either, although you might want to try it before you go off to see the island's wildlife.

Most grocery items on Bonaire are expensive because nothing is produced locally. Fruits and vegetables, for example, are shipped in from South America. Drinking water comes from a modern desalinization plant and is very safe and very tasty.

Nightlife

This is not exactly the hot spot of the Caribbean; however, there are some above-water fun spots in Bonaire. The historic Zeezicht Bar & Restaurant, the E Wowo and Dynamite discos have late-night dancing. The Flamingo Beach Resort and Bonaire Beach Hotel have casinos as well as their own entertainment and Habitat has a good bar (check out the "Western night").

Shopping

There are some low-duty shops on Breedestraat, which is a continuation of JA Abraham Boulevard. These specialize primarily in luxuries, but you will also find nearby stores stocking local arts and crafts such as shellwork, coral jewelry and fabric. Store hours are Monday through Saturday, 8am to noon and 2pm to 6pm and for a few hours on Sundays and holidays if cruise ships are in port.

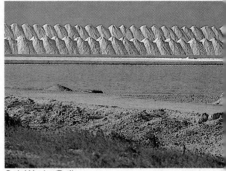

Salt Works/Bell

Obelisk/Bell

Sports

Sports on Bonaire are very water-oriented. There are a few tennis courts and some horseback riding if you ask around, but no golf.

The real sports action is on or under the sea. The water here gives you a dependable visibility of 150 to 200 feet. You can get to many interesting places without a boat. The water's warm and the currents are gentle. There are many experienced instructors and these local pros are will-

Bonaire

ing to lend their considerable expertise. All in all, these are ideal surroundings in which to learn or polish your skills on or under the water.

• Fishing

The deep-sea fishing industry is just getting started. The locals claim that bonefishing is great and you will find white and blue marlin, tuna, dolphinfish, sailfish, kingfish, wahoo, barracuda and snapper. Charters on small boats (up to about 25-feet) can be arranged through the hotels. Complete half-day or full-day packages with food and tackle are available. Spearfishing is prohibited.

The Third Annual Bonaire International Fishing Tournament is March 24, 25 and 26, 1989. Hosted by the Bonaire Nautical Association this tournament attracts participants from South America, Brazil, Venezuela, Aruba, Curacao, Bonaire and the US. This is an open tournament -- any kind of fish can win by weight. The $100.00 entry fee includes a T-shirt and lunch each day on the boat. Individual participants can sign up by contacting the Tourist Bureau. The Grand Prize is valued at $300.00.

• Hiking

The best place to experience nature on Bonaire (other than underwater) is in the 13,500 acres of the Washington/Slagbaai National Park which is supervised by a Dutch environmental group, STINAPA. They've done an exceptional job of protecting the Park's natural wonders: coves, beaches, birdlife and trails. There's a footpath you can follow up to Mt. Brandaris, the Park's highest point and you'll be amazed at the variety of birds

/Dean

(135 different species) including the green and yellow parrots that always fly in pairs. One of the Park's most dramatic spots, Boca Cocolishi, is a bay on the windward side where waves sweep in some 300 yards through a high coral cutout.

• Sailing

The annual Bonaire Sailing Regatta in mid-October attracts serious ocean-racing yachts. This event started about 20 years ago, when local sailors made bets on who could circle the island in the best time. The Regatta has grown into a world class event with races for various classes including seagoing yachts, catamarans, Sunfishes, windsurfers and local fishing boats. The races are subject to international standards and rules. Festivities include Sailor's party, Caribbean Pepperpot festival, volleyball and tennis tournaments, fashion show, beauty contest and an Awards Ceremony. The challenging course circles Bonaire and Klein Bonaire, fighting the South Caribbean trade winds and the rugged North coast. Smaller vessels compete in Kralendijk Bay. Nowadays, while the yachts circle Bonaire, the yachties encircle the town's streets and most of the hotels. Kind of a mini America's Cup, you might say. This is five days of great fun, but room reservations are hard to get without booking well in advance.

The Third Annual Nautical Races are scheduled for November 3, 4, and 5, 1988. This event features speed racing on a marked course limited to small boats 14 to 19 feet. Daily races are in Kralendijk Bay.

• Windsurfing

Bonaire, known as one of the best dive destinations in the world, is now also becoming a windsurfing destination. Windsurfing (including equipment rentals and lessons) is available on the leeward side of the island; because the island is shaped like a boomerang, windsurfers on this side are always protected by land. There is an offshore wind of 20-25 knots, the water is a little choppy with waves of 2 to 3 feet common. On the other side of the island, at Lac Bay, there are flat seas with a strong constant onshore wind. There are organized weekly trips to Lac Bay; check with your hotel.

• Diving

A very enlightened approach to combining reef conservation with liberal recreational use has resulted in the development of the Bonaire Marine Park. Here, practically the entire coastline from

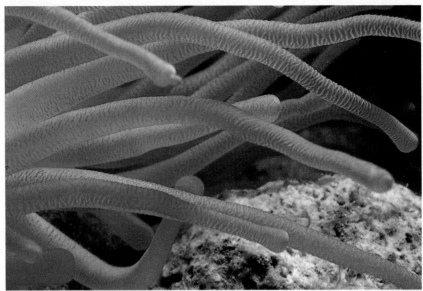

/BBA

/BBA

/Bell

the high water tidemark to a depth of 60 meters (220 feet) is subject to research, mapping, surveys and basic common-sense regulations. The establishment of the Marine Park not only serves to enhance the diver's experience but ensures that this spectacular environment will remain unspoiled for future generations of visitors and islanders. It is for this reason that such imprudent practices as anchoring on the reef, littering, stepping on coral heads, taking coral souvenirs and spearfishing are

Bonaire

not permitted. Just one dive in the Bonaire Marine Park will turn you into an ardent supporter of this underwater Garden of Eden.

Bonaire is the peak of an underwater mountain. It is surrounded by miles of colorful living reefs that are close to shore, with excellent visibility. Dive sites are incredibly diverse. Just steps from many beaches and hotel docks, you can descend 60 to 100 feet or more. Shallow reefs with sloping walls are also easily accessible from the shore or by a short boat ride. Many major hotels and dive operators offer unlimited air at the beach. Divers may even enjoy night dives right off hotel shores or docks.

You won't have to endure "cattleboat dives" either. The dive operators keep the number of divers on any one dive to a reasonable number, either by prearranging schedules among themselves or by deferring to the boat that is first to approach a dive site mooring. You won't see squabbling on the high seas off Bonaire. Some operators post daily dive site schedules so that divers can choose and plan where they want to go.

Bonaire offers great opportunities for underwater photography. The reefs present a rainbow of colors, with many different and spectacular coral formations, including elkhorn and staghorn. Sponges and fish are abundant in all varieties and colors. Divers frequently see eels, barracuda, tarpon, trunkfish, filefish, trumpetfish, angelfish, parrot fish, yellowtails and cleaner shrimp. Christmas tree worms, prevalent at several locations, are particularly colorful. A great delight for many divers on Bonaire is spotting their first sea horse.

At many locations in Bonaire, you will find green and moray eels. Feeding the eels is somewhat akin to feeding the bears at Yellowstone Park. If you know what you're doing and you fed the right bear, no problem. Otherwise, you may be mistaken for a large jar of honey. Eels have poor eyesight and bad table manners. Some of the eels have extensive rap sheets. For the most part the guides suggest that you don't feed the eels. If you want to go ahead anyway, limit your activities to the Sampler dive site.

Bonaire's sloping reefs with wall dives at various depths also contribute to the island's popularity with underwater photographers. There are also great photographic opportunities at shallower depths with, of course, longer bottom time.

Favorite spots for photography include Calabas Reef and the Town Pier.

Bonaire is a favorite dive destination for many diving clubs and groups from around the country -- some visit Bonaire several times each year. A favorite activity is to have your group videotaped with each diver getting a copy of the tape to take home.

Many of the hotels have dive operations on their premises. They also offer evening get-togethers and programs for guests to meet new friends and perhaps a new dive buddy. Evidence of Bonaire's popularity is the great number of repeat divers who return after their first trip.

• Eastern Dive Sites

In general, the windward (east) side of the island features an extensive shelf with small brain coral, sargasso weed and a drop-off that starts about 40 feet out, goes to a 100-foot coral shelf and then drops to the center of the earth. This side also contains a number of older wreck fragments, including cannon and anchors. Unfortunately, you can expect 8-foot seas most of the year. The wind may shift for a day or so in October or November, allowing you to explore the area with an experienced dive guide.

Anytime of the year you may want to try Lac Bay at the center of the dam. Southeast of Lac Bay, the current is strong and entry difficult. North of Lac Bay you will find cliffs. A knowledgeable local suggested that we enter by jumping off the cliff and exit by waiting for the wave surge to carry us back up to the top of the cliff, where we could simply hop out. We'll just take his word for it. In any event, all of the diving on the east side (outside of Lac Bay) requires a strong, experienced diver and a local guide.

• Western Dive Sites

By agreement with Mr. Eric Newton, Director of the Bonaire Marine Park (STINAPA), the dive site names and numbers used below are identical to the listings in the Bonaire Marine Park Guide. We recommend this excellent guide which can be obtained from the dive shops on the island or directly from STINAPA.

Bonaire's famous snorkeling trail was wiped out four years ago by unusual weather conditions. The trail will be reset as soon as the reef has recovered sufficiently. In the interim, Eric suggested Nukove, Playa Funchi, Playa Benge (which is a little rougher) and Klein Bonaire for snorkeling. Eric also counseled against diving

/BBA

around the water plant since the massive intake pipe for the plant is just off the shore.

(3) Pink Beach, aptly named, is a boat dive or shore dive. There is a mooring offshore that marks the start of the dive. Fish life is abundant and the reef is quite striking once you're out 400 feet or so from shore. A large barracuda is seen here on occasion.

(4) Salt Pier and Salt City are in the Antilles International Salt Company's loading pier vicinity. Salt Pier is a very interesting dive beneath the huge loading pier, its massive wooden support pilings offering cover to many small fish. This site is also a favorite with snorkelers.

The Salt City dive site is located about 1,500 feet south of the large buoy that sits on the south side of the Salt Pier. A nice feature of this area is a group of underwater coral islands at the 60 foot level. Fish life is superb and is often seen in large schools. Scad, palometa, groupers and snappers are common.

(6) Angel City, which is the most popular and shallowest dive in the double reef area and, as of September 12, 1984 home to the 1,000-ton freighter Hilma Hooker, Bonaire's most notorious (seized in a drug bust) and spectacular shipwreck (100 feet at the sand). Some of the world's friendliest fish reside at (7) Lake Bowker. The Crotch Gorge and Snake Valley sites are also part of this complex. Although (8) Punt Vierkant is located at the northern end of the Alice in Wonderland complex, it is generally regarded as a separate site.

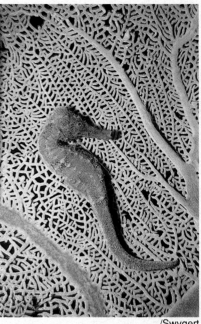

/Swygert

(9) Windsock Steep takes its name from its proximity to the airport. This site is a good snorkeling spot and a popular hangout for barracuda.

(10) Bonaire's most frequently dived site, Calabas Reef features an abundance of sea life and scenery. Giant brian coral and cavernous star corals may be found on the reef slope, as well as many types of sponges. Just north of the Calabas Restaurant pier you'll find the wreck of an aluminum boat at 60 feet covered with Christmas tree worms and fire coral.

Closer to the pier itself is the best snorkeling spot of Calabas Reef. Here you'll see long-spined sea urchins, schools of French and smallmouth grunt and on the pier itself, encrusted stinging coral and orange tube coral. Calabas Reef is also a rewarding dive at night.

(11) The Town Pier Dive is a fun dive located beneath Bonaire's town pier. At depths of less than 30 feet, this site offers extended bottom time. There are a number of eels hiding in old tires under the pier and schools of small fish. The area is especially colorful because of the Christmas tree worms that cover the pilings of the pier.

Bonaire

/Bell

• Klein Bonaire

The island of Klein Bonaire is only a mile off-shore from Kralendijk and its many sites are dived regularly by the operators from the main island. There are quite a few sites chartered and each one has something unique about it. With rare exception, all dives sites at Klein Bonaire are considered boat dives.

(15) Hands Off, a site opened for studying reef damage caused by divers, is similar to nearby (16) Forest. Seas here can turn rough; snorkeling is also good when the seas are calm.

(17) Southwest Corner, a popular site, is rich and colorful with plenty of fish and coral. Left of the mooring, at about 75 feet, is an interesting old anchor.

(18) Twixt and (19) Valerie's Hill are near each other and similar. Black coral and sponges are plentiful and keep an eye out for crinoids. Nearby (20) Mi Duchi is accessible from a small beach, with fairly good snorkeling.

(21) Carl's Hill is an unusually interesting site, requiring multiple dives to see it all. The vertical wall to the east of your boat's mooring features pillar coral, multi-colored cavernous star coral and butterprint brain coral, with a variety of sponges and invertebrates adding to the collage of color. On the shallow terrace up from the wall are gorgonians, fire corals and brain corals. Beautifully formed elkhorn coral will be found closer to shore.

The mooring area is good for snorkeling. In addition to the elkhorn coral, upright plates of leafy stinging coral are found in the shallows. Shoreward, cave-like coral formations are home to porcupine fish.

There is no vertical wall to the west of the mooring, but the dive has its compensations. Swimming west through the stony and soft corals and sponge growths, you'll pass a huge green-purple finger sponge. Just past it is one of the largest purple tube sponges discovered in this area, possessing in excess of 70 tubes!

For a rich coral landscape, try (22) Ebo's Special/Jerry's Jam, a popular spot with two names and many attractions. This area is best known for elkhorn coral. Hubert "Ebo" Domacasse was the first official dive guide on Bonaire and Jerry Greenberg was an underwater photographer.

If you're looking for some real underwater characters, make a dive at (25) Sampler. Presently, this is the only dive on Bonaire where fish-feeding is still encouraged. Since there are a great many eels at this site, it is recommended that you do NOT bring fish into the water as snacks. The smell of a good fish dinner often excites a moray beyond his attention to good manners.

Just off the only sizable beach of Klein Bonaire is (26) No Name. This area is one of the few sites at Klein Bonaire where divers can see mullet. These fish travel the sand shallows foraging about the bottom. Many types of coral are found at all levels, but in deeper water (80 feet) are beautiful roof shingle formations. Black coral is also present.

If you'd like to see black coral in abundance, (27) Ebo's Reef is the place. Remember that collecting black coral is strictly prohibited.

• Back to Bonaire

(28) Something Special is a boat dive that lies offshore of Bonaire between the Marina and the Bonaire Beach Hotel. Its main attraction is a community of garden eels, living on the sand terrace

at a depth of about 60 feet. Care should be taken, however, not to swim north toward the mouth of the Marina, where there is boat traffic.

(29) Front Porch is the name of the site in front of Bonaire Scuba Center. Here lies the <u>Cavilere State Tugboat</u> in 70 feet of water.

(30) La Machaca is an easy dive with several attractions. A small wreck at 35 feet is a nesting site for sergeant-majors. The reef slope begins here and at its lower edge (120 feet), garden eels are found in the sand terrace. On the lower slope are attractive roof shingle formations of sheet and scroll coral.

The site (32) Small Wall is just what its name suggests: a small wall starting 40 feet and going down to 65 feet. Gorgonians are most abundant on the wall, along with colorful sponges. At the lower edge is a small cave sheltering banded coral shrimp. Royal gamma are numerous near the wall.

(33) Petries Pillar is a shore dive named for the pillar coral that grows atop the reef face. Fish life include barracuda and both tiger and yellowmouth groupers. By the way, never dive near the sea intake of the plant!

A shore dive for those who don't mind the steps, a boat dive for those who do, (35) Thousand Steps attracts a wide range of fish: parrot fish, sergeant-majors, wrasses, groupers and so on. Inspect the hollow bases of coral heads and you may find a shovel-nosed lobster. (Are there really a thousand steps? Only if you count each one 15 times.)

(36) Ol'Blue is a shore dive just north of the Thousand Steps that has some interesting coral cover, but just north of here is (37) Rappel, one of the better dives on the island. Today, divers go by boat or swim from Karpata.

Steep buttresses and tame fish are the appeal of (39) Karpata. This site may be dived from shore or a boat.

A very good snorkeling dive, (40) Nukove is located off a little road just before Playa Funchi. There you'll find a small but very nice sand beach and concrete pier. Enter the dive by swimming through a channel cut in the elkhorn coral.

Another out-of-the-way place for snorkeling and shore diving is (41) Boca Slagbaai, but the center of the bay is pretty barren. If you see old cannon at the right side of the bay at about 15 feet, don't be fooled. They are fakes, planted there for a movie called <u>Shark Treasure</u>. The cannon in shallow water at the southernmost corner of the

Bachelor's Beach Apartments

Black Durgon

Bonaire Beach Hotel & Casino

bay are real, however, coming from a small fort above, on the cliff.

(42) Playa Funchi is a very popular snorkeling area for visitors to Washington Park. Best snorkeling is to the north. Look for a variety of coral, large ocean triggerfish and southern stingrays.

Bonaire

Bonaire Sunset Inn & Villas

Buddy's Dive Resort

Cap't Don's Habitat

Carib Inn

DIVI Flamingo Beach Resort

Hotel Rochaline

Sand Dollar   Sorobon

Accommodations

BACHELOR'S BEACH APARTMENTS 407-276-2795   3 Units: $85-145 BDKO
011-599-78073 934 Eve Street Delray Beach FL 33483. Three luxury apartments (2 two-bedrooms, and one studio) with full kitchens and bath. Very private. On the water with great views and a pier. Very good diving off the pier. Inquire about special pricing for the low season.

BLACK DURGON INN 800-526-2370   6 Units BDFKW
201-566-8866 011-599-78846FX Box 775 Morgan NJ 08879. Bonaire's smallest waterfront dive resort. Diving with Bonaire Scuba Center from their private pier. Complete dive services & facilities. Dive the beautiful Small Wall right in front of the Inn. Rooms are large and airy. Cooking facilities. Dine on the patio or relax on the Beach overlooking the water. Bonaire Scuba Center annex on the property. Call for special dive packages. We have 15 years experience diving Bonaire. See: Bonaire Scuba Center.

BONAIRE BEACH BUNGALOWS 717-586-9230   8 Units: $83-90 BDK
011-599-78581 Box 264 Waverly PA 18471. A small, waterfront bungalow complex. All units with two bedrooms, living room, kitchen, bath and large covered patio. Laundry available. Fully furnished with sheets, towels, cooking and eating facilities. Dive right off the private pier. Carib Inn provides dive services.

BONAIRE BEACH HOTEL & CASINO 800-526-2370   145 Units: $110-170 BDOPRSTW
800-223-9815 201-566-8866 c/o Bonaire Tours, Box 775 Morgan NJ 08879. Eleven newly refurnished low-rise buildings on 12 acres of outstanding waterfront property. In addition to all the watersports, the hotel offers lighted tennis courts with tennis pro, mini-golf, horseback riding, a casino and weekly activities program, a 600-foot white sand beach, the Beach Bar and Restaurant, and the Bonaire Scuba Center dive shop. See: Bonaire Scuba Center.

BONAIRE SUNSET INN AND SUNSET VILLAS 305-793-8016   19 Units: $45-210 BDFKW
011-599-78300 011-599-78865FX Box 115 Bonaire, N. A. Seven properties located throughout the leeward side of Bonaire on the water or in town. All units, ranging from studios to villas, have telephones, TV, full kitchen and laundry. Kitchen stocked at your request. Rental car and dive services, tours, watersports, fishing and air reservations arranged. Sunset Inn is located on the water next to Dive Inn. No service charges. Special rates for stays of one month or more. See: Dive Inn.

BUDDY'S DIVE RESORT 212-662-4858   20 Units: $55-85 BDKPRSW
011-599-78647 TX:1900 Box 231 Bonaire, N. A. The economic alternative in the Caribbean. Attractive, spacious, completely furnished bungalows with private kitchen, bath and patio. Across from Playa Lechi and Bonaire Beach Hotel. Personal service with special group rates. Get PADI certified for only $250 in 5 days. 24-hour access to tanks. They now have a location on the water next to Sand Dollar and Habitat. See: Buddy's Dive Resort.

CAPTAIN DON'S HABITAT & HAMLET 800-223-5581   43 Units: $48-175 BDKRW
800-327-6709 212-535-9530 Box 88 Bonaire, N. A. New luxury oceanfront villas with three doubles, airy two-bedroom cottages with living rooms and single and double economy rooms. Kitchen facilities and seaside verandas in many units. Economy rooms are for the budget minded. Don Stewart's 26 years of resort and diving experience have created an intimate diving related community with an air of congenial informality. Their Bonaire Cowboy Night is on Thurs., slide show on Fri. Personalized dive guide service. See: Captain Don's Habitat.

CARIB INN 011-599-78819   10 Units: $49-115 BDK
Box 68 Bonaire, N. A. This small resort has been designed specifically for divers. Ten rooms, six with kitchens. Catering to a quieter type of client. Small intimate dive groups on the boats. No service charge. Maid service provided. Private pier and fully equipped dive shop on the premises. A 10-minute walk from town, very personalized diving. See: Carib Inn.

Bonaire

DIVI FLAMINGO BEACH RSRT/CASINO 800-367-3484   150 Units: $90-200 BDKOPRTW
607-277-3484 011-599-78285 54 Gunderman Rd. Ithaca NY 14850. Waterfront hotel. A short walk into town. Private white-sand bathing beach. Freshwater pool, jacuzzi, two open-air dining rooms. Casino, watersports. Doubles and new studio apartments. Home of the world's first barefoot casino. Dive Bonaire, Peter Hughes Flagship operation, is on the property. Music and dancing every week. Extensive underwater photo shop with a variety of other stores & services. A full-service, 5-Star PADI facility. See: Peter Hughes Dive Bonaire.

HOTEL ROCHALINE 011-599-78286   25 Units: $43-43 R
TX: 1187 Box 27 Bonaire, N. A. This small hotel is on the downtown waterfront and is noted for its fine restaurant. Good service and attractive prices. Entertainment on the weekends.

SAND DOLLAR BEACH CLUB 609-298-2298   38 Units: $125-225 BDKRW
011-599-78738 c/o Travel Barn, 50 Georgetown Rd. Bordentown NJ 08505. New property still under expansion. Each unit facing the sea with full kitchen, spacious balcony. Very deluxe. Beach diving, late-night snack bar and entertainment. Full dive shop, 2 restaurants, marina, additional units planned over the next 3 years. Underwater photo pro on the property. See: Sand Dollar Dive and Photo.

SOROBON BEACH NATURIST RESORT 800-828-9356   25 Units: $120-120 BDKORSW
TX: 1200 011-599-78080 Box 14 Bonaire, N. A. A family-oriented and quiet resort with a clothing-optional private beach. Located on a peninsula between the Caribbean Sea and Lac Bay, cooled by the tradewinds. All the chalets (equipped with kitchen) overlook the water. Inside the barrier reef is beautiful snorkeling over a square mile of coral. The shallow part of the bay in combination with the steady wind makes it ideal for sailing and windsurfing. Diving is with Dive Inn.

Information
BONAIRE TOURIST OFFICE 212-242-7707
011-599-78322 275 7th Avenue, 19th Floor New York NY 10001.

Sports
BONAIRE SCUBA CENTER 800-526-2370   80 Divers: $45-45 DO
201-566-8866 011-599-78978 Box 755 Morgan NJ 08879. At Bonaire Beach Hotel and Black Durgon Inn. Spacious flat-top dive boats with easy water entry and exit. Special dive by truck combines diving with a tour of the island. Packages include unlimited air, tank, BP, wts, and guided boat trips. Operated by Eddy Statia & Al Catalfumo. Snorkeling available. Step off pier onto Front Porch reef. Fully equipped dive shop, boutique and training facility. Complete your open-water certification with us. See: Bonaire Hotel & Casino/ Black Durgon Inn.

BUDDY'S DIVE RESORT 212-662-4858   12 Divers: $24-24 D
011-599-78647 TX: 1200 Box 231 Bonaire, N. A. Full dive shop, dive equipment rental, T-shirts. 24-hour access to tanks every day. Six-day unlimited diving includes tank, BP, wts, night dives and 6 guided reef trips. Boat limited to 12 divers. PADI certification in 5 days for $250. Personal guided trips by instructor. See: Buddy's Dive Resort.

CAPTAIN DON'S HABITAT 800-345-0322   Divers: $35-35 D
802-492-5607 Box 88 Bonaire, N. A. A PADI 5-star facility for all levels of divers. The open-air, full-service dive shop includes the classroom, a photo lab, equipment rooms and sea front patios. Their slogan is "Diving Freedom," and divers can take their tanks and dive anywhere any time of day or night, most often along "the Pike," a half mile of protected reef right in front of Habitat. The qualified staff is always there to assist and advise. Personalized dive guiding and slide show. See: Captain Don's Habitat & Hamlet.

CARIB INN 011-599-78819   20 Divers: $38-38 D
Box 68 Bonaire, N. A. Bruce Bowker's full service dive facility. Small personalized dive operation. No more than 12 divers per boat. Fast boats get you to all the dive sites. No service charge. An ideal hassle-free dive experience. Over 15 years experience. Tank rental is for entire day. NAUI & PADI instruction all levels. See: Carib Inn.

DIVE INN 011-599-78761   16 Divers: $8-25 DOSW
TX: 1900 011-599-78513FX Helmut Road, #27 Bonaire, N. A. Located next to the Bonaire Sunset Inn, 100 yards north of Flamingo Beach. The owner is the trained recompression operator for the hospital. German, Dutch and English spoken. Unlimited shore diving. Inexpensive packages. Resort courses. PADI open-water certification courses $215 (4-person minimum). BBQ on Klein Bonaire, snorkel trips, boat and night diving, Sunfish, windsurfing, waterskiing and fishing trips ($125 everything included) available daily. See: Bonaire Sunset Inn and Sunset Villas.

PETER HUGHES DIVE BONAIRE 800-367-3484   185 Divers: $50-50 D
607-277-3484 011-599-78285 54 Gunderman Rd. Ithaca NY 14850. Two dive shops located on the grounds of the Flamingo Beach Hotel & Casino. Top-of-the-line Scuba Pro and Sherwood equipment, custom-designed dive boats with special tank racks. Complete underwater photography operation available. Offering personalized service with 2 dive shops and 10 boats. Dive groups can schedule their own boat. Individuals have a variety of dive sites to choose from. A great place to meet divers from all parts of the world. See: DIVI Flamingo Beach Rsrt/Casino.

SAND DOLLAR DIVE AND PHOTO 609-298-2298   52 Divers: $25-25 D
011-599-78738 c/o Travel Barn, 50 Georgetown Rd. Bordentown NJ 08505. The dive facilities here match the high quality of the accommodations. E-6 processing and full dive packages available. See: Sand Dollar Beach Club.

Key: The accommodations price range is based on the high season rate per night, double occupancy. The Liveaboard price range is per berth, high season. The dive price range is based on the cost of a two tank dive. Letter codes: Beach (or on the water), Diving, Fishing, Golf, Other watersports, Pool, Restaurant & Bar, Sailing, Tennis, Windsurfing.

Cayman Islands

/Bell

Travel & Sports Guide

/Johnston

/Bell

Cayman Islands

Useful Facts

• Airline Connections   Cayman Airways, to Grand Cayman twice daily from Miami (3 times on Fridays and Sundays) and 5 times weekly from Houston. Flights from Grand Cayman to Jamaica 3 times a week. Services to Cayman Brac and Little Cayman twice daily, except Tuesday. Air Jamaica Ltd. has 3 flights weekly from Grand Cayman to Kingston and Montego Bay. Northwest Airlines and Eastern have direct flights daily from Miami to Grand Cayman and one flight from Memphis. All airlines require you to reconfirm your flight reservations 72 hours in advance of departure. The airport departure tax is US$7.50 = CI$6.00.

• Banking   Currency conversion: CI$1 = US$1.20. The exchange rate is fixed by an International Monetary Fund agreement; restaurants and shops will convert at a higher rate to cover bank charges, so it's best to use the banks. The official currency is the CI dollar, but the US dollar is in wide circulation. Both are accepted by hotels, stores, sports operators and restaurants. Change is usually given in CI dollars. Many bars, restaurants and shops do not accept credit cards. Hotel rates are usually quoted in US dollars, but restaurant menus are often in CI dollars, making the food seem cheaper than it actually is to the inattentive diner. Banking hours are Monday-Thursday, 9am-2:30pm; Friday, 9am-1pm and 2:30-4:30pm

• Courtesy & Dress   The Caymanians are somewhat conservative regarding skimpy beachwear in shops and public buildings. Casual but proper is the key.

• Driving   On the left or as some might say, on the "wrong" side of the road. If you fail to remember this, the Cayman Islands provide adequate reminders -- like trucks coming at you head on, for instance. Yellow lines on the road indicate no parking. Most traffic signs are of the European "common sense" variety. Stop behind stationary buses (the doors open into the center of the road).

• Electricity   US standards.

• Events and Holidays   New Year's Day; Ash Wednesday; Good Friday; Easter Monday (with a sailing regatta at Seven Mile Beach); Botabano Carnival Week (April); Brachanal, on Cayman Brac. It's a carnival with a Mardi Gras flavor (April 26); Discovery Day, celebrating Columbus' discovery of the Caymans (third Monday in May); Million Dollar Fishing Tournament (June); Queen's Birthday (June); Constitution Day, with regatta (July); Pirates Week (Oct.); Remembrance Day (Nov.); Christmas and Boxing Day.

• Languages   English.

• Medical   There is a 12-bed government hospital on Cayman Brac and a fully staffed hospital in George Town on Grand Cayman.

• Off-Season Dates & Rates   From May to December, rates drop 10 to 30 %.

• Taxes & Tipping   A tourist tax of 6% will be added to your hotel bill. Many restaurants add a 10%-15% service charge.

• Taxi Fares   Fares are regulated by the government according to distance.

• Telephone   The islands have a modern automatic telephone system. Locally, just dial the last 5-digits in our Directory.

• Time   Eastern Standard Time. No Daylight Savings Time.

• Weather   The Cayman Islands enjoy some of the best weather patterns in the Caribbean and are outside the "Hurricane Belt." Winter temperatures range from 70 to 80 degrees and summer temperatures run from 80 to 90 degrees. The climate is even and balmy. There is really no bad time to travel here. In fact, travelers actually benefit during the "off-season." The slightly warmer temperatures are easily offset by the substantially lower accommodation rates. Breezes from the northeast cool the hottest days. The rainy season is May through October.

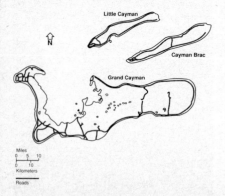

Little Cayman

Cayman Brac

Grand Cayman

Miles
0   5   10

0   10
Kilometers

Roads

Cayman Islands

/Roessler

History

Lying on a stretch of four-star beach on any one of the three Cayman Islands, it's difficult to think of yourself as a mountaineer. But there you sit, on the flat tips of a gigantic range of undersea mountains called the Sierra Maestra Range. A short distance offshore, the coral island on which you rest drops-off dramatically, plunging to depths a mile or more. Just a few miles south of the Caymans lies the deepest part of the Caribbean, the Cayman Trench, 12,576 feet deep.

Standing on the deck of his ship, Christopher Columbus probably held somewhat less dramatic thoughts about the three small and flat islands he chanced upon during his last voyage. These solitary land masses in the West Caribbean ocean, probably uninhabited at that time, offered little to record in a ship's log, other than the abundance of green sea turtles; hence the islands were called Las Tortugas. The present day name (based on the Caribe Indian word for crocodile) came from the Wolfenbuttel map of 1530.

Spain ceded the islands to Great Britain in 1670. More than 200 years after their discovery, the first permanent settlers (debtors, deserters and shipwrecked sailors) arrived on the island. Later visitors to the islands were not quite so distinguished. After 1713 the islands fell into the hands of pirates. The notorious but no doubt fun-loving pirates Sir Henry Morgan, Edward Teach (known as Blackbeard to his more intimate acquaintances) and Neal Walker, to name but a few of the merry band, all walked the beaches of one or more of these islands, fighting, drinking, scheming and, if the locals are correct, stashing their loot. It was here in the Caymans that Blackbeard wounded Israel Hinds, who was later immortalized in Robert Louis Stevenson's <u>Treasure Island</u>. Grand Cayman's low profile makes it practically invisible against the horizon--a good hideaway.

More settlers arrived in the 1730's, mostly Scottish fishermen and since that time the Caymans have absorbed an interesting mixture of English, Scot, Irish, Welsh and West Indian. In 1788, on a dark November night, a convoy of 10 Jamaican merchant ships were sailing past Grand Cayman when the lead ship <u>Cordelia</u> struck a reef on the East End. Unfortunately, her signal to warn off the other ships was mistaken for the order to come up close, and one by one the remaining nine ships plowed into the reef. Their crews were saved by the heroic efforts of the islanders and not a life was lost.

Until 1962, the Caymans were under British rule as a dependency of Jamaica. When Jamaica became independent, the Caymans chose to remain under British rule. In 1972, the Caymans

Cayman Islands

received their present constitution. The islands are a loyal British Crown Colony, a democracy of elected representatives with a governor general appointed by the Queen.

With a large interracial population and strong ties to England, harmony and stability reign in the Caymans. The fact that there is no property or income tax probably helps, too. The islands have one of the highest per capita incomes in the Caribbean.

The Caymans first received attention as a tourist destination in the 1950's when the Saturday Evening Post ran an article labelling the Caymans, "The Islands Time Forgot." That's over now. In less than 20 years Grand Cayman has become the largest offshore banking center in the western hemisphere. With over 500 banks, it's on a par with Switzerland or Liechtenstein. Strict secrecy laws permit depositors to remain incognito. The Caymans are considered one of the finest tax havens in the world. And the islands have directed just as much attention to tourism as they have to banking.

Within the last ten years, prosperity and growth have come to Grand Cayman, which now has the highest standard of living in the Caribbean. Hotels, condominiums, numerous restaurants, an increasing variety of nightlife and a fleet of fishing and dive boats make it a busy place. Yet the East End District still retains the appeal of the days when fewer people knew of its attractions. Buildings are limited to treetop height, which for the palm, is about four stories.

Cayman Brac/Bell

During the last week of October, the Cayman Islands commemorates their buccaneering history with the outrageous Pirates Week. More than just a celebration, this is a national festival. Local residents and visitors come together in a mutual celebration. Everyone gets into the spirit and dons a costume. You'll find patch-eyed Blackbeards and lusty wenches everywhere: in banks, at stores or just frolicking on the beach.

The week begins when the Queen Anne's Revenge, an authentic pirate ship replica, attacks George Town's Hog Sty Bay. Amid the ensuing panic and booming cannons, the Chief Pirate and crew saunter ashore and "capture" Grand Cayman and its governor. Once in possession, a colorful parade, complete with floats and island beauties, makes its way through town, and music from steel drum bands fills the air. The week's activities include beauty, song and underwater photo contests, athletic competitions, underwater treasure hunts, sailing regattas and fishing tournaments. The week of revelry climaxes with a gala costume ball and there's rum punch aplenty to quench your thirst between activities. If you plan to visit during this time of year, make advance reservations, as it's immensely popular.

For a more subdued vacation look to Little Cayman. For as Grand Cayman has embraced progress and technology, so Little Cayman has avoided it. Situated about 80 miles northeast of Grand Cayman, this little island of only 10 square miles offers a respite from the more hectic Caribbean ports-of-call. There are fewer than 50 permanent residents, no rental cars, no airconditioning, no paved roads, no massive accommodations and only one public phone to call your broker. In a word, this is where you go for serious sportfishing and unhurried, uncrowded, but nonetheless superlative, diving experiences.

Cayman Brac offers more in the way of amenities than Little Cayman, but it's still very laid-back compared to Grand Cayman. As the word spreads that Cayman Brac offers a rural pace, clear water, friendly people and most creature comforts, it's bound to get busier.

Ecology

Turtles and iguanas, once numerous, are now practically extinct in the wild. The cream-colored land crabs and the hare-like agoutis have also become rare. But there are still more than 100 species of birds to observe on the islands throughout the year.

Ironically, it is Cayman's flatness and lack of lush vegetation and tropical streams above the shoreline that promotes some of the world's most breathtaking scenery below it. Unlike the waters surrounding mountainous, soil-rich islands, these waters are not full of the silt run-off which clogs coral polyps and inhibits their growth. Due to the limestone topography and the nutrients provided by the mangrove swamps, Cayman waters have spectacular and abundant marine life and exceptional visibility (up to 200 feet).

Cayman Brac, sister island to Little Cayman and about the same size, is regarded by many visitors as the prettiest of the Cayman Islands. The array of tropical vegetation is impressive, as is the wildlife in the air and under the sea. Certainly Cayman Brac has the most noticeable topography of the three islands, with a limestone bluff running along the island to an easterly elevation of 140 feet. Hence the name "Brac," the Gaelic word for cliff. These eastern cliffs are riddled with caves and the inevitable stories of pirates' treasure secreted within. But who knows? It's worth a look.

Among Grand Cayman's more outstanding geographical features are truly beautiful beaches and the spectacular coral formations which surround most of the island. You're probably a bit weary from hearing each Caribbean island tout it's "spectacular beaches," but the Caymans and Grand Cayman especially, have a legitimate right to boast.

Th best beaches on Grand Cayman include: Seven Mile Beach; East End, at Colliers, by the Tortuga Club; Cayman Kai, on the North Side; Rum Point & Water Cay, also on the North Side; and Sand Cay on the South Sound; Pease Bay past Bodden Town.

Exploring Grand Cayman

Grand Cayman is, if you haven't already guessed, the largest of the three islands, lying 480 miles due south of Miami. It measures 22 miles long by 8 miles wide. Roughly 21,700 people live on Grand Cayman and they enjoy their reputation as a friendly folk.

There's a lot to see here, both above and below the waterline. Grand Cayman attracts more divers than any other single island in the world. And if you don't feel like getting wet, Grand Cayman of-

Elizabethan Square/Bell

fers the only commercial submarine rides in the world. The small two passenger subs of RSL (Research Submersibles Ltd.) dive to 800 feet, well beyond the safe limit for scuba diving. The

Rugby/Bell

Cayman Islands

Atlantis submarine only dives to 150 feet, but seats 28 passengers, so it is a great way for non-divers to experience the undersea world.

Topside, Grand Cayman can be toured easily in one day's time by taxi, bus or limousine. Or take charge yourself and rent a bicycle (for short tours), motorcycle or automobile. Motorcyclists must wear a helmet and cannot drive on the beaches. Cars are easy to rent and a US driver's license will suffice.

Tour services on the island aren't limited to bus rides, either. You can take shopping tours if that's your idea of a big day out or you can book a very pleasant circle-the-island lunch and snorkeling tour, which should be called "snunch" but isn't.

Taking a ride with a local cab driver can also be fun. No doubt you'll be entertained with plenty of local folklore about various geographic and historical sites and the more fanciful the historian, the better for you. Taxis on Grand Cayman do not run by meter, but on a rate set by the government according to distance. Although Caymanian cabbies are an honest lot, it's a good idea to ask the rate before you leave on a taxi tour.

George Town (pop. 5,000), the islands' capital, can be explored in a few hours. George Town is the hub for shopping and business. Although shopping is not a primary attraction of the Caymans, George Town's free port shops offer imported merchandise and native crafts. More importantly, it provides good access to the watersports operators. It lies in Hog Sty Bay, which has been developed into the island's main

/Bell

harbor and it's shoreline is composed of ironshore, not sand.

On the seafront are a number of old buildings including Elmslie Memorial Church, a restoration of a 19th century church and the remains of Fort George, built in the 17th and 18th centuries to protect the island from attacks by pirates.

To see the rest of the island, proceed south from George Town into South Sound, a pretty residential area, containing some of the most beautiful and exclusive homes on the island, with good examples of traditional Caymanian architecture. A bit further along you'll see the Rugby Club's field as well as some private tennis and squash courts, on the north side of the road. The South Sound, sheltered by its barrier reef, contains a wreck at the western entrance.

Soon South Sound merges with the Bodden Town Road in an area called Prospect. An active settlement once flourished here and a fort built in 1780 stood nearby. All that's left is a monument to the past, since the entire town of Prospect was destroyed in a hurricane in 1846. On the east side of Prospect Point is the little Prospect Beach, with another wreck on its sheltering reef.

Near Savannah, at Spott's Bay, is Bat Cave Beach, aptly named after a cave where bats still live. You can explore the cave, but you'll have to do it on hands and knees: it's got a low ceiling. A bit north are the Matilda Ponds, the nesting place of rare birds. Watch for big land crabs crossing the road.

Further along the Bodden Town Road you'll pass an old cemetery on the shore side. While locals may be tempted to call these "pirate graves" within hearing of a wide-eared tourist, evidence suggests they are the burial site of some early pioneers.

Soon you'll come to Pedro's Castle (formerly St. James Castle). It is often billed as the oldest structure on the island (built in the 1700's) and a former pirate haunt, but it actually lay in ruins from 1877 until 1970, when it was restored after a fashion. It's now a popular local bar and restaurant and has a great view.

Just a little further east is Bodden Town, named for one of the first two settlers of the island, a deserter from Cromwell's army. A small, quaint settlement on the southside of the island, the former capital of the Cayman Islands shelters in Bodden Bay. Once the island's largest settlement, Bodden Town suffered from frequent pirate raids and is still partially surrounded by ruins of a defensive wall erected to deter pirates. Look for the Pirate's Caves, an underground tunnel system that may have served as a hiding place for those charming thugs who roamed the Caymans in the 17th and 18th century. Note also the Guard House, some old cannons and the slave Walls. You might inquire about the local history here. Bodden is one of the island's most common surnames.

A few miles further east is the village of Breakers, which has a restaurant worth stopping for. It's called the Lighthouse Club, for obvious reasons and you can sample some of the local dishes and drinks.

Past Half Moon Bay, heading toward the East End district, you'll pass the spewing "Blow Holes," sprays of water shooting like geysers through the limestone rocks, so loud conversation is often impossible. Rounding the eastern end of the island, you'll spot a portion of an anchor embedded in the ocean floor. This is reported to be an old relic of the legendary "Wreck of the Ten Sails," but local historians merely grin if you ask them to prove it. Farther northeast is Borling Bluff lighthouse. Beyond this is Gun Bay, with a picturesque church, belfry and churchyard.

As you pass Collier's Village and the Tortuga Club, you'll see the remains of an old liberty ship, visible from the road. This is the Ridgefield, which struck the reef in 1943 or 1962, depending on whom you ask.

At Old Man Bay on the North Side, you can either head back down south through the savannah country or continue westward to Rum Point, a popular spot blessed with a lovely beach and stand of pine trees. Nearby Water Cay is also worth a visit. A trip from George Town to Rum Point, done at a relaxed pace, will take about 3 hours. On the return trip, take the north-south road at Old Man Bay, which offers a look at some interesting terrain and, if you're lucky, a glimpse of the local parrots.

North of George Town, on Seven Mile Beach you'll find dive boats, parasailing, glass-bottom boat trips, sail boat rentals and other watersports. Swimming is among the Caribbean's finest.

North of Seven Mile Beach in the West Bay District are two other attractions if you'd like to play full-fledged tourist. One is the Cayman Turtle Farm, where over 4,000 hatchlings a year are released to the open sea to replenish the wild turtle population. It is the only establishment of its

/Bell

kind in the world, with thousands of turtles ranging in weight from six ounces to 600 pounds. The turtles were originally hatched from imported eggs, but, since 1973, the farm's turtles have laid eggs in captivity. The farm also exports turtle meat, leather, tortoise shell and cosmetics.

East of the Turtle Farm is the village of Hell, named many years ago for the blackened limestone spires found in the area. The idea here is to mail your friends a postcard from the Hell post office and then have some refreshment at The Club Inferno. Now you can say you've been there and back.

At the northwest end of the North Sound is the fishing village of Botabano. This is a starting point for boat trips to the Northern Barrier Reef. It's also a fine place to buy fresh lobster.

Exploring Cayman Brac

A local taxi guide, hired at Gerrard Smith International Airport (a relatively new addition

Cayman Islands

/Bell

which accommodates 727 jet flights directly from Florida) can take you on a nice tour of the island. The 1,700 inhabitants (locally known as "brackers") live almost exclusively on the sheltered north coast and Spot Bay is the island's largest village. Most Brackers are descendants of Scots and Englishmen. With only two small beach front hotels, tourism activity is limited. This is a quiet place.

The island's most dramatic feature is the bluff -- a gradual incline of coral and limestone rock, starting at sea level on the west end of the island and going up to 140 feet, then dropping straight down to the sea at the East End. If you follow the south coast road, at the northeast end you'll find a number of caves with stalactites. The caverns honeycombing the limestone bluff are reputed to contain treasure left by long ago pirates and in some of them you can still find three foot long iguanas, which are now almost extinct. The northeast point has a light house (165 feet) standing on the edge of the island's steep-sided promontory and it commands a great view.

Explore the barrier reef of living coral surrounding the island by snorkeling. The reef starts a few dozen yards from shore and stretches for miles, with sea fans, sea anemones, sponges, caves and archways, just to name some of the delights you'll find here. The island's best beaches, Tiara Beach and Brac Reef Beach, are found near West End.

/Bell

Cayman Islands

At some point, stop at the Cayman Brac Museum on the main road at Stake Bay. It houses a fascinating collection of local tools and artifacts all donated by the islanders.

Exploring Little Cayman

Little Cayman is the smallest island of the three. It's only 10 square miles in size and has less than 50 full time residents. There's no air-conditioning, the roads are unpaved and the runway is a grass strip. Little Cayman has changed little since Columbus discovered it and much of it is still covered by mangrove swamps. The island's primary visitors are sport fishers and scuba divers (Little Cayman has some of the best bonefishing in the world). The pink sand beaches and the variety of tropical birds are the island's main above-water attractions. The south coast is one unspoiled beach after another, protected by an almost continuous line of reefs. South Town is the island's main settlement.

A lighthouse stands at the rocky western end of the island. Nearby is Bloody Bay, where scuba divers prospect for old wrecks.

Check out Owen Island, a tiny uninhabited paradise off the southwestern coast. It's a perfect place for a picnic.

FOOD

There is no really "native" Caymanian cuisine, but the islands offer a variety of adaptations, from traditional West Indian food to Italian, Chinese and yes, even Burger King. Local taste treats include conch (say KONK, please), seafood and curries. You can get turtle dishes (soups, stews, steaks) without guilt, since the turtles are raised at the Turtle Farm and not hunted in the wild. You might want to try codfish and ackee, a local favorite breakfast dish. Ackee fruit is poisonous until it ripens and bursts open. When cooked it tastes somewhat like scrambled eggs. You can find the local fruits (mango, papaya, sweetsop and soursop) made into delicious pies, cakes and puddings. Most, but not all, restaurants accept credit cards so check before dining.

Since most food staples in the Caymans are imported from the US or other islands, they tend to be expensive. Restaurant bills often run to $30.00 per person. While it would no doubt be great fun to sample a different Caymanian gourmet restaurant every afternoon and evening (you could: Grand Cayman has over 70 restaurants),

/Bell

/Dean

Cayman Islands

you may want to give your wheezing budget a break by considering the alternatives: less expensive eateries and cooking for yourself. The big fast food chains have also taken up residence. But you should try the small local establishments that offer more interesting, inexpensive meals.

Another way to keep overall expenses down is to rent or share a condominium or apartment that has its own cooking facilities. There are supermarkets in George Town and West Bay, as well as smaller grocery stores in those locations and in Prospect. Food shopping on Cayman Brac is quite limited and practically non-existent on Little Cayman.

Water in the Cayman Islands comes either from a desalinization plant or from small cisterns that use trapped rainwater and is safe to drink unless otherwise noted. Water on all the islands is scarce, however, so keep the showers short.

Nightlife

Entertainment on Grand Cayman ranges from nightclub acts and dancing to concerts, live theatre and movies. Consult the local paper for the up-to-date list.

At the moment there is stiff competition for the top rating between the Treasure Island's Islander Night Club and the Holiday Inn. Traditionalists maintain that the atmosphere and the island-flavored music at the Holiday Inn is the

/Bell

only place to wile away the balmy night-time hours. On the other hand, The Islander Night Club's combination of live entertainment and tunes spun by the local D.J. have been drawing some serious night-owls.

At Ports of Call, it's open-air dancing. The Sons of the Beach at Long John Silvers offers 60's music. For a flaming limbo act, try the Wreck of the Ten Sails. If movies are more your pace, go to The Cinema on West Bay Road. Live performances are offered at The Cayman National Theater.

Shopping

While Grand Cayman offers a wide assortment of duty-free items from around the world, the specialties of the Cayman Islands are black coral, shell and semi-precious stone jewelry, straw weavings and turtle products. In general, it's a good idea to know the approximate prices in US stores for some of the non-specialty, duty-free goods being offered, such as perfume, china and the like. You may find that only the sale items are a real bargain.

For local crafts, try the Viking Gallery, Harbour Drive on the waterfront. (tel.9-4090) It has two floors of handicrafts, hand-painted skirts and tops, native bolt material and local paintings.

Sports

Sports buffs will find an incredible variety of activities, both in the water and out. Landlubbers can choose from aerobics, darts, golf, running, squash and tennis, while water enthusiasts will find diving, fishing, parasailing, sailing, waterskiing and windsurfing.

• Aerobic/Weight Training

If you just can't leave those gym shoes at home, the Cayman Nautilus Fitness Centre has excellent health club facilities. Choose from Nautilus and free weights, aerobic classes, dance classes, Lifecycles and whirlpools. Visitors are welcome and daily, weekly and monthly rates are available. Located near the airport on Crewe Rd. (809-949-5132).

• Cricket

The cricket season gets under way in March. Matches are held on the Agricultural grounds on Smith Rd. Check the local paper for exact time and location.

• Darts

Its easy to find a friendly game of darts in Grand Cayman. Many pubs host games and

Cayman Islands

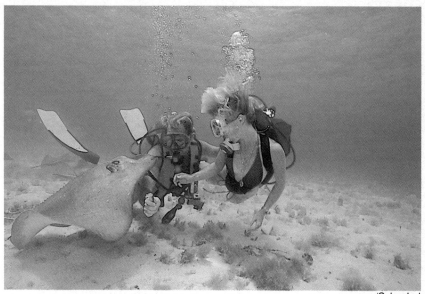

/Schnabel

League games are held Wednesday evenings. Check the local newspaper for location and time.

• Fishing

Sport fishing may not be the most popular sport in the Caymans (first place goes to scuba diving), but it sure is running a close second. June is the time for the highly competitive Million Dollar Month Tournament. Anglers from all over the world compete for the grand prize: one million dollars (US), to the sportsman who breaks the All Tackle Atlantic Blue Marlin record of 1,282 lbs. The winner receives additional prizes including a luxury condo in Cayman, a new Sportsfisherman, a new Porsche and a lifetime pass on Cayman Airways. And if that's not enough, additional prizes include $100,000 (US) for the Cayman record Blue Marlin and $100,000 for the White Marlin record in five different categories. Other prizes are awarded as well and cash-winning fish will be mounted free of charge. For entry forms and information contact the Million Dollar Office in the West Wind Building, George Town.

Fishing is great all year round, a license may be required. April through August is the best for marlin. In the Spring, wahoo, mahi mahi and blue and yellowfin tuna are caught in abundance. You will also find grouper, snapper and bonefish.

You can also get a guide to take you progging for langouste (a large crayfish) in a glass-bottom boat. This crayfish is caught with a pronged stick and then boiled in seawater.

At Little Cayman you can fish the Pygmy Tarpon found in the huge pond near South Hole Sound. And you might check out the bonefish that gather at the shoreline of the Sound. The billfishing is reputed to be quite good. Check with one of the Little Cayman lodges listed in the Directory.

• Golf

On the west side of Grand Cayman stretch the emerald greens of The Britannia. Designed by Jack Nicklaus, the 3-in-1 course offers a 9-hole regulation course and an 18-hole executive layout. There's also a special 18-hole game made possible with the unique Cayman Ball, also designed by Nicklaus, which reacts like a conventional ball, but travels half the distance. This challenging course is complete with blind tee shots and pot bunkers.

• Parasailing

A big hit off of Seven Mile Beach, this sport combines parachuting and waterskiing...kind of. Instead of skiing behind the tow rope, the boat lifts

Cayman Islands

you above the white water in a colorful parachute.

• Rugby
Experienced players are invited to drop in on practices held each Tuesday night on the field on South Sound road. Rugby is a Fall sport and you will find the best games on Saturday afternoon.

• Running
Cayman clubs host a variety of Fun Runs and Cross Country Runs. Check the local paper for the current events.

• Sailing
Easter Monday is the date for the annual Sailing Regatta on Seven Mile Beach. The following resorts have slips, freshwater, ice, and other supplies for larger sailing vessels: The Kaibo (809-947-9064), Governor's Harbour (809-947-4204) and Lime Tree Bay (809-947-4045). Many enterprises and hotels offer boat rentals and/or charters. Novices will appreciate the practically untippable Sunfish, while more seasoned sailors will enjoy Lasers, 470's, Hobie and Prindle catamarans. Many of the operators located along Seven Mile Beach offer sailing instruction as well. Charter Boat Headquarters (809-947-4340) specializes in rentals and charters.

• Squash
The Racquet Club off Elgin Ave. near the police station has courts open to the public. Courts are available most afternoons and evening. Rentals are available and reservations are necessary, (809-949-2054).

• Tennis
For three weekends in March players take up their rackets for the Cayman Tennis Open. Visitors are welcome to participate. In November, the Cayman Islands Tennis Club on South Sound Road hosts the Cayman Island Open Tennis Tournament. This exciting event draws men and women from the US and Caribbean countries to challenge locals and each other in doubles and mixed doubles. The club has four excellent courts, with pros available for individual and group lessons. More than 30 courts are scattered about Grand Cayman, with quite a few located along Seven Mile Beach.

• Waterskiing
Cayman's calm waters make it the ideal waterskiing resort. Waterski boats and equipment are readily available for rent and your hotel can put you in touch with the various operators.

• Windsurfing
Windsurfing rentals can be arranged through most hotels.

• Diving
Diving in the Cayman islands is rated in the top four best sites in the world. Among the prolific marine life that thrives in these nutrient rich waters, gorgonians and sponges flourish here in unusual number, variety and size. For example, there are many sea fans surpassing four feet in diameter and enormous barrel sponges, including one of the world's largest, measuring in at over five feet in diameter. The waters are warm, and unless you're going to be doing some intricate diving around fire corals and hydroids, you won't need a wetsuit. Be aware that the Caymans have a code of ethics for divers to follow.

• Grand Cayman Diving
Grand Cayman has more identified dives sites than any other dive destination we are aware of. The diving here is divided into the four points of the compass.

• The west side dives:
The west side (which includes Seven Mile Beach) has the following sites:

Big Tunnels. Scores of archways, tunnels and overhangs form an underwater museum. The most notable is an enormous coral archway, measuring 30-40 feet in diameter, which exits on the edge of famous Cayman Wall. Black gorgonian fans frame the outside of the archway and barracuda and horse-eyed jacks are frequent visitors.

Oro Verde. Purposely sunk in 1980, this wreck dive is perfect for novices and experts alike. In 50 feet of water, she lies fully intact in a rich spur and groove formation of coral and reefs. Fishy passengers include vivid queen parrot fish and yellow butterfly fish.

Other dives sites on the west side include: Spanish Anchor, Trinity Caves, Sand Chute, Eagle Bay Rock Orange Canyon, Big Dipper, Burger King Reef and Killer Puffer Reef. Most of the dive operators are located in this area.

• The north side dives:
Tarpon Alley. This large coral ravine some 80 feet below the surface is where the tarpon hang out. Swimming in packs of 40 to 50, they cruise the narrow coral ravine, while southern stingrays take off and land on the sandy flats.

Spanish Bay Reef. Located directly off the Spanish Cove Resort, this site is known for its gorgeous mini-wall with prolific macro marine life

Cayman Islands

/Bell

and rays. As always under the Caymans, you can hear the gentle static of parrot fish munching on the coral. Also excellent night dives.

• The east side dives:

The Maze. This site gets its name from the labyrinthine network of narrow and deep intertwining corals canyons that wend about like an undersea Grand Canyon. It's visited by turtles, groupers and sharks and decorated with black coral and myriad sponges.

Other east dives include: Scuba Bowl '85, Shark Alley, Grouper Grotto and Ramunda Wreck.

• The south side dives:

Cebert's Chute. This sand chute curves through a coral cave and empties out onto a magnificent wall overhang.

River of Sand. Glistening white sand slopes from a depth starting at 45 feet and down to 100 feet where it spills out over the edge of the South East Wall. This curious site is said to represent an underwater glacier.

Tunnel of Love, Three Sisters, Iron Shore Gardens, The Lodge Anchor, Palis Wall, Elkhorn Gardens and Spot's Wall are other south side dive sites.

The south and east side sites are readily accessible by Cayman Kai and the Cayman Diving Lodge.

/Bell

Cayman Islands

DIVI Tiara Beach Resort in Cayman Brac

• Cayman Brac Dive Sites

There are only two operators in Cayman Brac: Brac Aquatics and Peter Hughes Dive Tiara Beach. Here are some of the sites they dive in Cayman Brac and Little Cayman.

The following are north side wall sites:

Aiport Wall. This wall starts at 65 feet with a gentle slope to 100 feet then you find a 90 degree drop off.

West Chute. This sand chute runs along one wall with vertical reefs growing perpendicular to the wall. The coral heads start about 45 feet. There is a mini wall in the sand chute.

Middle Chute. Like west chute, coral heads have formed on the wall at 60 to 65 feet. The chute at its base is 80 feet.

Cemetery Wall. Here are two parallel sand chutes that start at 50 feet then drop off the wall at 110 feet. Between chutes is a large ridge that stays at 70 feet to the edge of the wall. Look for lots of sponges on the ridge and face of the wall.

• North side shallow diving:

End of the Island Reef. 25 to 50 feet sloping mini wall. Gorgonians, large formations of mountainous star coral. Pillar coral about 10 feet high. Tame french angel fish await your arrival. Barracuda wait for the angle fish.

Expect visibility of 100 feet or so on shallow dives. Outside of the walls the visibility goes up to 150 feet on a good day.

• South side wall diving:

The Hobbitt. Big barrel sponges you can sit in at 100 feet. Strong current.

Anchor Site. One of the favorite sites on the Brac and old large anchor (15 feet or so) stuck in the coral at 100 feet.

Bat Caves. 80 feet to the coral bottom. This is a continuous reef without any sand. Lots of soft coral and sponges. Caves are found through out the wall at 60 feet, exiting outside the wall at 80 feet.

In addition there are a number of shallow south side shallow reefs: Tarpon Reef, Lighthouse, Sergeant Major Reef, Butterfly Reef, Elkhorn Forest, Blowers Reef, Public Beach, Coconut Grove and Prime Fredrick.

• Little Cayman Diving

Little Cayman Dive Sites are accessed by the Cayman Brac operators, the Little Cayman operators and the liveaboards. The two main areas are Bloody Bay and Jackson's.

Bloody Bay Wall. Named for the many shipwrecks and battles that occurred here, the Philippe Cousteau named this site one of the three best in the world. Located off the north shore and peaking at just 18 feet below the water's surface, this wall drops a breathtaking 600 feet. Among the world's truly unique sites, it features a rare form of platinum yellow pipe sponge, as well as blue cup sponges, pink vase sponges and black coral trees.

Three Fathom Wall. This spot is perfect for diving as well as snorkeling. Featured in this coral garden at the end of Bloody Bay are tunnels and crevices filled with purple sea fans, feathery seawhips and technicolor fish.

Jackson dive sites include: Paul's Anchor, Nancy's Cup of Tea, Meddows, Jacksons Reef and Bus Stop.

Key: The accommodations price range is based on the nigh season rate per night, double occupancy. The Liveaboard price range is per berth, high season. The dive price range is based on the cost of a two tank dive. Letter codes: Beach (or on the water), Diving, Fishing, Golf, Other watersports, Pool, Restaurant & Bar, Sailing, Tennis, Windsurfing.

Cayman Islands

Cayman Islands - Information
CAYMAN ISLANDS DEPARTMENT OF TOURISM 212-682-5582
  809-949-7999 420 Lexington Ave., Suite 2312 New York NY 10170.
CAYMAN ISLANDS DEPARTMENT OF TOURISM 305-444-6551
  809-949-7999 250 Catalonia Ave. Coral Gables FL 33134.
RESERVATIONS, CAYMAN ISLANDS 800-327-8777
  305-448-3634. All of the accommodations shown in this directory and dozens of condo units not listed here may be booked through this central reservation service.

Cayman Brac, Cayman Islands - Accommodations
BRAC REEF BEACH RESORT 800-327-3835   40 Units: $90-100 W
  800-233-8880 809-948-7323 Box 72279 Tampa FL 33602. See: Brac Aquatics Ltd..
CORAL ISLE LODGE 809-948-7213   8 Units: $30-40 BR
  West End P.O. Cayman Brac, Cayman Islands.
DIVI TIARA BEACH RESORT 800-367-3484   58 Units: $120-180 BDOPRSTW
  607-277-3484 809-948-7313 54 Gunderman Rd. Ithaca NY 14850. Friendly, friendly, friendly. That's the word for the world renowned DIVI resorts. A partial listing of our amenities includes the Turtle Pier Bar ,new underwater photography facility, a long beautiful beach, a freshwater pool, jacuzzi, lighted tennis courts, paddle boats, windsurfing and organized beach volleyball. We offer full meal plans, slide show of the island, car and scooter rentals, shopping, fishing trips, and diving with Peter Hughes. See: Peter Hughes Dive Tiara.

Cayman Brac, Cayman Islands - Liveaboards
LITTLE CAYMAN DIVER 809-948-7429   8 Berths: $150-175 BDR
  Box 84 Cayman Brac, Cayman Islands.

Cayman Brac, Cayman Islands - Sports
BRAC AQUATICS LTD. 809-948-7429   42 Divers: $45-45 DW
  809-948-7331 Box 89, West End Cayman Brac, Cayman Islands. See: Brac Reef Beach Resort.
PETER HUGHES DIVE TIARA 800-367-3484   56 Divers: $50-50 BDOPRTW
  607-277-3484 809-948-7313 54 Gunderman Rd. Ithaca NY 14850. Part of Peter Hughes Diving, an organization based on professionalism, safety and quality. They handle all your gear from arrival to departure including setup and storage. With the fastest dive boats in the Cayman Islands, their two weekly trips to Little Cayman are right quick. Plan for two dives in the morning with your afternoons free. They provide beach diving and transporta- tion for shore dives. Complete dive shop and underwater photography operation. See: DIVI Tiara Beach Resort.

Grand Cayman, Cayman Islands - Accommodations
AMBASSADORS INN 809-949-7577   18 Units: $59-59 R
  TX:4432 Box 1789 Grand Cayman, Cayman Islands.
BEACH CLUB RESORT 809-949-2023   41 Units: $138-215
  Box 903 Grand Cayman, Cayman Islands.
CAYMAN DIVING LODGE 800-262-7686   15 Units: $90-90 BDR
  809-947-7555 404-424-7500 331 Washington Marrietta GA 30060. See: Cayman Diving Lodge.
CAYMAN ISLANDER 800-922-7555   67 Units: $89-89 R
  800-423-7555 95528 5821 Hollywood Blvd, Suite 203 Hollywood FL 33021. See: Bob Soto's Diving, Ltd..
CAYMAN KAI RESORTS 800-223-5427   26 Units: $120-120 BDORTW
  305-554-9350 809-947-9555 3201 SW 94th Avenue Miami FL 33165. See: Cayman Kai Resorts.
COCONUT HARBOUR 809-949-7025   35 Units: $75-165 BDFOPW
  809-949-4054 809-949-7468 Box 2086, South Church Street George Town, Grand Cayman, Cayman Isl. See: Don Foster's Dive Grand Cayman.
GRAND CAYMAN HOLIDAY INN 800-421-9999   213 Units: $148-238 BDFGOPRSTW
  809-947-4444 901-767-1230 5100 Poplar Street Suite 2219 Memphis TN 38137. See: Bob Soto's Diving, Ltd..
GRAND PAVILION 809-947-4666   57 Units: $175-395 PRT
  809-947-4666 EXT-302-FX Box 69 Grand Cayman, Cayman Islands. See: Don Foster's Dive Grand Cayman.
HYATT REGENCY BRITANNIA 800-228-9000   235 Units: $200-750 BDFGOPRSTW
  809-949-1234 809-949-8528FX Box 1698 Grand Cayman, Cayman Islands. See: Nick's Aqua Sports, Ltd..
PLANTATION VILLAGE BEACH RESORT 809-949-4199   70 Units: $165-290 BDFOPSTW
  809-949-6230 TX:4412 Box 1590 Grand Cayman, Cayman Islands.
SCUBA SAFARI DIVE LODGE & GUEST HOMES 809-949-3742   2 Units: $86-100 DK
  TX:72339 Box 2029 Grand Cayman, Cayman Islands. See: Scuba Safari.
SPANISH COVE 800-231-4610   63 Units: $60-95 BDPR
  809-94-93765 800-232-1034 Box 637 Grand Cayman, Cayman Islands. See: Spanish Cove.
SUNSET HOUSE 800-854-4767   42 Units: $75-110 BDFOPRSW
  809-949-7111 TX:4367 Box 479 Grand Cayman, Cayman Islands. See: Sunset Divers.
TORTUGA CLUB 800-327-8223   14 Units: $100-125 BDR
  800-432-8894 809-947-7551 241 East Commercial Blvd. Fort Lauderdale FL 33334.
TREASURE ISLAND RESORT 800-874-0027   290 Units: $145-380 BR
  809-949-7955 Box 1817 Georgetown, Grand Cayman, Cayman Islands. See: Treasure Island Divers.

Cayman Islands

Grand Cayman, Cayman Islands - Liveaboards
CAYMAN AGGRESSOR 800-348-2628   BDR
    95551 504-384-0817FX Drawer K Morgan City LA 70381.

Grand Cayman, Cayman Islands - Sports
ATLANTIS SUBMARINE 809-949-7700   28 Divers: $48-56
    809-949-7827 TX:4450 Box 1043 Grand Cayman, Cayman Islands.
BOB SOTO'S DIVING, LTD. 800-262-7686   125 Divers: $25-45 DO
    809-949-2022 809-949-8731FX Box 1801 Grand Cayman, Cayman Islands. See: See Hotel listings.
CAYMAN DIVING LODGE 800-262-7686   28 Divers: $45-45 D
    809-947-7555 Box 11, East End Grand Cayman, Cayman Islands. See: Cayman Diving Lodge.
CAYMAN DIVING SCHOOL 809-949-4729   Divers: $26-26 D
    Box 1308 Grand Cayman, Cayman Islands.
CAYMAN KAI RESORTS 800-223-5427   44 Divers: $43-43 DFOTW
    305-554-9350 809-947-9055 Box 1112 Grand Cayman, Cayman Islands. See: Cayman Kai Resorts.
CROSBY'S WATER SPORTS 809-947-4049   100 Divers: $25-25 BDOR
    809-949-3372 Box 714 Grand Cayman, Cayman Islands.
DIVER'S WORLD 809-949-8128   Divers D
    809-949-8128FX Box 917 Grand Cayman, Cayman Islands.
DON FOSTER'S DIVE GRAND CAYMAN 809-949-7025   110 Divers: $45-45 DFOW
    809-949-5679 809-949-8651FX Box 151 Grand Cayman, Cayman Islands. See: See Hotel listings.
EDEN ROCK DIVING CENTER 809-949-7243   Divers: $11-11 BD
    Box 1907 Grand Cayman, Cayman Islands.
FISHEYE PHOTOGRAPHY 809-947-4209   15 Divers: $45-45 D
    809-947-4209FX TELEX:4336 Box 2123 Grand Cayman, Cayman Islands.
NICK'S AQUA SPORTS, LTD. 800-228-9000   48 Divers: $45-45 BDOR
    809-949-1234 312-876-9116FX 10 S Riverside Plaza, Suite 2 Chicago IL 60606. See: Hyatt Regency Britannia.
PETER MILBURN, DIVE CAYMAN 809-947-4341   22 Divers: $40-75 D
    809-947-2189 TX:4432 Box 596 Grand Cayman, Cayman Islands.
QUABBIN DIVERS 809-949-5597   90 Divers: $45-45 D
    TX:4210 Box 157 George Town, Grand Cayman, Cayman Isl.
RESEARCH SUBMERSIBLES LTD 809-949-8296
    809-949-7421FX Box 1719 Grand Cayman, Cayman Islands.
RIVERS SPORT DIVERS, LTD. 809-949-1181   Divers: $40-40 D
    Box 442 West Bay Grand Cayman, Cayman Islands.
SCUBA CAYMAN 809-949-3873   33 Divers: $40-40 D
    Box 746 Grand Cayman, Cayman Islands.
SCUBA SAFARI 809-949-3742   6 Divers: $50-50 D
    TX:72339 Box 2029 Grand Cayman, Cayman Islands. See: Scuba Safari Dive Lodge & Guest Homes.
SEA SPORTS 800-949-3965   16 Divers: $50-50 D
    809-949-3965 Box 431, West Bay Grand Cayman, Cayman Islands.
SPANISH COVE 800-231-4610   40 Divers: $38-38 D
    809-949-3765 Box 637 Grand Cayman, Cayman Islands. See: Spanish Cove.
SUNSET DIVERS 800-949-7111   40 Divers: $40-40 BD
    809-949-7111 TX:4363 CP Box 479 Grand Cayman, Cayman Islands.
SURFSIDE / RUM POINT 800   50 Divers: $40-40 DOW
    809-949-7330 809-947-9098 Box 891 George Town, Grand Cayman, Cayman Islands.
SURFSIDE WATERSPORTS, LTD. 800-468-1708   80 Divers: $40-40 DOW
    809-947-4224 Box 891 George Town, Grand Cayman, Cayman Islands.
TORTUGA CLUB 800-327-8223   15 Divers: $35-35 DFOPSTW
    800-432-8894 809-947-7551 Box 496, George Town Grand Cayman, Cayman Islands. See: Tortuga Club.
TREASURE ISLAND DIVERS 800-874-0027   75 Divers: $35-35 D
    809-949-7777 Box 1817 Georgetown, Grand Cayman, Cayman Islands. See: Treasure Island Resort.

Little Cayman, Cayman Islands - Accommodations
PIRATES POINT RESORT LTD. 809-948-4210   6 Units: $145-145 BDFRW
    Little Cayman, Cayman Islands.
SAM MCCOY'S DIVING LODGE 203-438-5663   7 Units: $170-200 BDR
    809-948-8326 c/o Road Least Trav., 14 Rochambeau Ave. Richfield CT 06877. See: Sam McCoy's Diving Lodge.
SOUTHERN CROSS CLUB 317-636-9501   10 Units: $220-220 BDFKOPRSW
    809-948-3255 1005 E. Towen #1 Merchant Plaza Indianapolis IN 46204. See: Southern Cross Club.

Little Cayman, Cayman Islands - Sports
SAM MCCOY'S DIVING LODGE 203-438-5663   24 Divers: $30-30 D
    809-948-8326 c/o Road Least Trav., 14 Rochambeau Ave. Ridgefield CT 06877. See: Sam McCoy's Diving Lodge.
SOUTHERN CROSS CLUB 317-636-9501   120 Divers: $50-50 DFOPRSTW
    809-948-3255 1005 E. Towen #1 Merchant Plaza Indianapolis IN 46204. See: Southern Cross Club.

/Dietmar Reimer

Travel & Sports Guide

/Jones

Curacao

Useful Facts

• Airline Connections   ALM (Antillean Airlines) offers daily nonstop flights from New York and Miami with two flights per week from Puerto Rico. ALM is the sole provider of inter-island flights between Aruba, Bonaire, Curacao and Sint Maarten. ALM also offers various flights from points in the Caribbean and South America on a regular basis. Eastern flies daily from Miami. American Airlines also flies daily from New York. BWIA flies direct from Trinidad/Tobago three times per week; Aeropostal arrives daily from Venezuela. KLM offers regular flights from South America and Europe. Air Jamaica flies from Kingston three time per week. Avianca has three weekly trips out of Columbia. Once a week you can fly to Surinam on Surinam Air. Viasa flies to Caracas three times per week. Dominicana flies out of the Dominican Republic three times per week. The airport departure tax is NAf 10 = US $5.75.

• Banking   The unit of currency is the Netherlands Antilles florin, or "guilder" as it is often referred to. Written as NAf, the guilder is divided into 100 cents and issued in many denominations up to 500 guilders. Banks offer the best exchange rate. The NAf is tied to the US dollar and remains constant at NAf 1.74 = US $1.00. US currency is readily accepted on Curacao. Major credit cards, such as American Express, MasterCard and Visa, are honored at all major hotels, and most shops and restaurants. Most banks are open from 8:30am to noon, and 1:30pm to 4:30pm, Monday through Friday.

Curacao

↑
N

Miles
0   10   20

0   10   20

• Courtesy & Dress   Curacao is warm and arid; light cotton clothing seems to work best. Nights are cool however, so a light sweater is handy. Some casinos require jackets. Formal business dealings may require dressier clothing. As in most of the Caribbean, the island residents regard bathing suits as beach wear only, not quite proper for shopping and dining out.

• Customs & Immigrations   Visitors arrive at Curacao International Airport. Proof of citizenship, a completed immigration card and a return or onward ticket are required for entry into the country. The best proof of citizenship is always your passport, but a birth certificate or voter's registration card will suffice. The baggage claim area is close to the Immigration counters, and taxis are readily available when you're ready to head for your accommodations.

• Driving   Foreign and international licenses are accepted. Cars drive on the right on roads that are generally in good condition.

• Electricity   110-130 volts, 50 cycles. This is not quite the same as the US; and some appliances may overheat if used for extended periods of time. Check with your hotel about the use and charging of delicate electronic equipment.

• Events & Holidays   New Year's Day; Chinese New Year (January); Carnival (weekend before Lent); Harvest Festival (March); Passover, Good Friday, Easter, Queen's Birthday (April); Labor Day (May 1); Ascension Day, Whit Sunday, Curacao Flag Day (July); Rosh Hashonah, Yon Kippur (September); St. Nicholas Day, Kingdom Day and Antillian Flag Day, Christmas, Boxing Day (December).

• Events, Carnival   Carnival is an interesting event, and the time for big, joyous celebrations in Curacao. The various festivities of the event actually take place over the course of the month leading up to Ash Wednesday, the beginning of Lent. There is a Carnival Parade for children prior to the Carnival Parade (Gran Marcha). The main parade is a huge, colorful affair complete with costumes, floats and music bands winding through the streets of Willemstad. The Sunday of the Parade and the following day (Carnival Monday) are official holidays on the island.

/Dean

• Languages   Dutch and the local Papiamento are the native tongues, but English and Spanish are spoken widely.

• Medical   These are among the best in the Caribbean. There are two major, well-equipped hospitals, and the general standard of health on the island is high. There is a Drager recompression chamber at St. Elizabeth's Hospital, run by Dr. Edwin Valeriano and three qualified technicians, at least one of whom is on 24-hour call. Hospital phone is 24900, doctor's phone is 82603.

• Off-Season Dates & Rates   From April 15 through December 15. Dates may vary slightly at each hotel.

• Taxes & Tipping   Hotel charges include a 5% government tax and a 10% service charge.

• Taxi Fares   Taxis are not metered, but drivers carry rate cards. Determine your fare beforehand. Most cabs are identified by roof signs and the TX or BUS suffix on license plates. Typical fare from the airport to a hotel in or near Willemstad is US $10.00. All fares generally increase 25% after 11 pm. Taxis may be hired for tours.

• Telephone   From the US dial direct using the number in our directory. For a local call, only dial the last 6 numbers.

• Time   Atlantic Standard (Eastern Standard + 1 hour) year round.

• Weather   A pleasant year round climate, with average temperature of 80 degrees and an annual rainfall of 22 inches. Rainiest months are November and December; humidity is then typically 76%.

History

Curacao is an island of many distinctions, one of which is not having been discovered by Christopher Columbus. History awards that accomplishment to one of his lieutenants, the Spaniard Alonso de Ojeda, who sighted the 38-

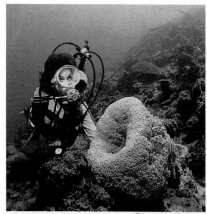

/Dietmar Reimer

Curacao

mile-long island in 1499 with an assist from Amerigo Vespucci. As was the case with the sister islands of Aruba and Bonaire, the peaceful Arawaks had beaten the Europeans to the island by at least a few centuries. These native peoples were quickly displaced under the relentless Spanish conquest. White settlers arrived in the early 1500's.

The Dutch made a grab for Curacao in 1634 and were successful in wresting it from the Spaniards. They soon renamed the principal town of Santa Ana, calling it Willemstad, and turned it into the main port for The Netherlands West India Company's commercial enterprises in that region of the world.

In 1642, Peter Stuyvesant took over the governorship, which we might assume groomed him within a short time for the important post of governor of New Amsterdam, later to be known as New York City. From the mid-1600's until the early 1800's, the English and French struggled with the Dutch over the proprietorship of Curacao.

Dutch control of Curacao was firmly established by the Treaty of Paris in 1815. By this time, a slave economy was established on the island, and in addition to shipping and slave trading there were attempts to build up a plantation system. The arid climate, however, was not conducive to that effort.

When King Willem of the Netherlands abolished slavery in 1863, the economy of Curacao quickly deteriorated and remained in that state for about 50 years. Then, in 1915, the Royal Dutch Shell oil refinery and the Panama Canal brought Curacao to life again.

Contemporary Curacao is still a busy place, with a multi-national population of over 160,000 people. While the oil and dry dock revenues have fallen off in recent years, and new US tax regulations in 1984 adversely affected the island's banking industry, Curacao's beauty, architecture, weather, superb port, cosmopolitan atmosphere and reputation for friendliness have all helped to attract new revenues from tourism.

Ecology

Like many Caribbean nations, the Netherlands Antilles has become increasingly concerned with the delicate ecology of their islands, much to the benefit of both residents and visitors alike.

A 4,000-acre wilderness preserve, called Christoffel National Park, has been established in

the western part of the island. This area, easily accessible by car, helps to preserve indigenous flora and fauna, including orchids, rare palms, the evergreen wayaca and such wildlife as iguanas, rabbits, donkeys, wild goats, many species of birds and the small Curacao deer. Mt. Christoffel dominates the park, and is the highest point in the Leeward Dutch Antilles at about 1,230 feet.

Life under the sea is also given sanctuary in Curacao since the establishment in 1983 of the Curacao Underwater Park, which extends 12.5 miles from the Seaquarium at Bapor Kibra to East Point. While strictly protected, the beautiful reefs and shipwrecks within this park are made accessible to divers. An underwater snorkel trail has been provided, along with concrete moorings that prevent anchor damage to reefs from dive boats.

A spectacular new facility, the Curacao Seaquarium, allows the non-diver to appreciate the exquisite variety, and delicate balance, of undersea life in this part of the world. In fact, the Seaquarium boasts the world's largest collection of Caribbean fish and invertebrates, with over 400 types on display.

All in all, Curacao has made significant strides in protecting and managing one of its greatest resources: its natural beauty.

Exploring
• Willemstad

If one had to name a Caribbean city that excels in architectural artistry, Willemstad would be a prime candidate. Easily toured on foot, certain quarters of this city, such as Punda, offer the visitor a chance to step back in time to view the streets and houses of 17th century Holland. The oldest surviving building within the city dates from 1708 (once a social club, it is presently occupied by the merchants Penha & Sons), while some of the still-standing walls of Curacao's many forts harken back to the years of the Dutch conquest of the island. A stroll around Willemstad is educational and, best of all, free!

A good place to begin your pedestrian tour is at the Curacao Plaza Hotel, which sits right at the intersection of the St. Anna Bay (a canal, really) and the Caribbean Sea. The actual foundations of the hotel are part of the old Waterfort, dating from 1634. As you look at the sea wall, you'll notice the remains of the massive iron chains that were once stretched from this fort to the Riffort across the canal, effectively barring invaders from the harbor's entrance.

Around the corner, one of the newly restored Waterfront Arches at the Curacao Plaza houses a tourist information office. You might also want to take in the view of the Caribbean from the back of the Plaza. Nearby is a statue commemorating Manuel Piar, a hero of Curacao who distinguished himself as a general under Simon Bolivar, the renowned revolutionary who eventually liberated South America from the Spaniards.

Across the Plaza Piar sits Fort Amsterdam, which now serves as the Governor's Palace and the Central Government House. Also within the fort is the Fort Church, dating from the mid 1700's, and yes, that is a real cannonball resting in its southwest wall.

As you face north, look for what is certainly our favorite attraction on Curacao, the Queen Emma Pontoon Bridge. This unique movable bridge was built in 1888 by Leonard B. Smith, the American consul. A native of Maine, he had previously brought both ice and electricity to Curacao, and then proceeded to make himself a tidy sum off the tolls collected from this bridge enterprise. Although in modern times it supports only the city's foot traffic on its aging back (you're looking at the third version, a 1939 model), the bridge still swings open faithfully perhaps 20 or 30 times a day to allow the passage of vessels from around the world. And how do you cross St. Anna Bay when the pontoon bridge is letting a ship through? Easy. Willemstad provides you with a free ferry ride. These attractive little boats are called "havendienst."

Across the bridge you'll end up in the Otrobanda district (literally, "the other side"), around the Brionplein, or town square. The statue of Pedro Luis Brion is nearby, and is dedicated to the memory of this native son who inspired the island's defenders to repel the British a number of times in the early 1800's. In 1814 he served as an admiral under Simon Bolivar, fighting for the liberation of both Venezuela and Colombia.

West of the square is St. Anna's Church, and a few miles past that (a long walk), on Van Leeuwenhoekstraat, sits an old plantation house. This is the Curacao Museum, which houses a very interesting assortment of antiques, paintings and art objects, as well as artifacts representing the island's former inhabitants, the Caiquetio Indians.

/Dean

Its gardens contain an attractive display of the island's flora.

Cross over the pontoon bridge again to the Punda side and walk along the waterfront on Handelskade. Here you pass some of Willemstad's most handsome buildings, quaint structures with mustard walls and roofs made of red tile carried over as ship ballast many, many years ago.

If you cross over the Wilhelmina drawbridge, you'll be in Scharloo, the old Jewish quarter settled by wealthy merchants during colonial times. This part of town contains plenty of Old World architecture, ranging in period from the early 1700's to Victorian times. The census office is particularly well-restored and worth a look. A hill called Mt. Arrarat serves as a backdrop to this neighborhood, and a lovely white statue of the Madonna sits atop it.

Nearby an American flag is flying. This is what the Curacaoans call Roosevelt House, a gift of gratitude from the Netherlands to the United States for help rendered during World War II. The building is now the site of the US Consulate. Further along St. Anna Bay, where it opens into the huge harbor of Schottegat, sits Fort Nassau, a 19th century structure. The fort has a restaurant inside and offers a fine view of Willemstad. The consulate and fort are a bit too far for a casual stroll, so plan on taking a taxi ride or a rental car if you're going up that way.

Returning once more to the Wilhelmina drawbridge, turn left on Columbusstraat and you'll reach the Mikve Israel Emanuel Synagogue, one of the oldest (1634) synagogue buildings in the Western Hemisphere. The entrance is on Hanchi di Snoa. Of particular interest is the sand floor, a Sephardic (from Sephardim,

Curacao

a Jewish sect that fled the Spanish Inquisition) tradition which memorializes the desert pilgrimage of the Israelites during their escape from Egypt. Be sure to visit the courtyard museum next door.

Walking down Pietermaai toward the waterfront, there's a very fine example of colonial architecture, the Department of Finance building. Walking back to the pontoon bridge along Breedestraat brings you to the 272-year-old Penha building, at the foot of the bridge, and also to the end of your tour. It's time to find a cool drink and rest your feet!

• Exploring the Island

Curacao's beautiful countryside, called "kunuku" in the Papiamento language, is quite a contrast to the bustle of business and industry that characterizes much of Willemstad. Here, an occasional windmill, along with charming old Dutch plantation houses from colonial times, combine with cactus and the ubiquitous, wind-bent divi-divi tree to create a memorable landscape.

Touring the western side of Curacao will put you in touch with the island's beaches, wildlife and old plantation homes or "landhuizen."

Going back to Daniel and proceeding west leads to Boca San Pedro, a very picturesque stretch of coastline. Continuing on this road, you'll come to the lovingly restored Landhuis Ascension, used by the Royal Dutch navy as a social center. Open house there is every first Sunday of the month.

At Landhuis Savonet is the entrance to the St. Christoffelberg National Park, a 4,000-acre wildlife preserve. The roads through the park are in good condition and well-marked, making driving or hiking a pleasant experience. You can take a footpath to the top of Mt. Christoffel (1,239 feet) or drive along a 35-mile network of roads that lead to some impressive lookouts. The park is open daily from 8am to 3pm, but no one may enter after 2pm, since it takes a little over 3 hours to complete the road tour. Guided tours are available at 9 and 10:30am and at noon. By the way, there are no facilities in the park itself, so bring a snack with you. You can, however, buy beer and soda at the park entrance. Also, be prepared to pack your trash out.

At Boca Tabla, it's worth a stop to look at (and listen to) a cave created by the wild surf on the north coast. Just walk down the gorge, near where you park, and before you step into the ocean, turn

left. This is Thunder Cave, quite a nice spot. Further along, at Playa Kalki, just before North Point, is a pleasant and quiet beach with good snorkeling offshore.

The road swings south toward Knip and some nice beach coves, such as Knip Bay (nice beach, free, popular with the locals), Jeremi Bay and Boca Santa Cruz. Many of the little villages along the way, such as Soto, Pannekoek and Willibrordus, all have old plantation homes, most of which are private, however. At Soto you can look down over Boca Santa Marta. This area was the last refuge of the Indian inhabitants of the island. A stop at Landhuis Jan Kock, on the road to St. Willibrordus, offers a good view, refreshments and music (most weekends).

The fishing village of St. Michiel, with an old fort and a beach, is on this same road. You may also want to take a dip at nearby Blauw Bay, where snacks and other facilities for bathers are available.

Touring the eastern side of Curacao puts you in a somewhat different environment. There's more development and industry here, as well as a long tradition of agriculture. Your first stop out of town on Penstraat should be Curacao's new Seaquarium complex, an impressive cluster of six-sided buildings housing more than 60 pools and tanks and an outstanding collection of Caribbean marine life. The Seaquarium sits on the stranding site of the Orange Nassau, which broke up here in 1906. The Bapor Kibra (Broken Ship) bar is a favorite spot for sunset watchers.

On the east side of the bay stands Fort Beekenburg and its imposing battle tower; to the west is Jan Thiel, a residential area with a private beach. Locals must pay an entrance fee but you can go in for free.

Just before you reach Caracas Bay, there's a side road going east to Spanish Water, a well-developed harbor for yachts and a good place for sailing enthusiasts to rent a boat.

Heading back, take the road to Santa Rosa (a bit more northerly than the road you came on), and swing toward the northern coast and St. Joris Bay. The entire area is agricultural in nature, with five old plantation homes in close proximity.

Although your island tour ends when you drive the 9 miles or so back to Willemstad, keep in mind that Curacao is a richly textured place, and there's always something new to discover if you take the time to explore.

Curacao

Food

Now here's an island you can sink your teeth into, figuratively speaking. Curacao offers travelers a wide variety of cuisine, including Dutch, Caribbean, Indonesian, Latin American, Chinese, French and Italian fare.

Among the items you're likely to see are sopito, a fish soup flavored with coconut; funchi, the Caribbean's version of the tortilla; and keshi yena, which is Edam cheese stuffed with meat, shrimp or chicken, and then baked. Other tasty menu items include zult, which is pickled pigs ears and soppi juana, otherwise known as iguana soup. Conch is prepared in many different ways, such as a stew called carco stoba. Naturally, there's rijsttafel, the traditional and spicy Indonesian "rice table" feast of many courses. For the homesick eater, there are various meat and fish dishes quite familiar to Americans as well as the typical fast-food restaurants one sees back home.

Drinking water on Curacao is obtained from desalinization and is quite pure. Of course you could sample some Curacao, the orange liqueur for which the island is famous. The distillery that manufactures this drink offers tours.

Nightlife

Willemstad is as busy at night as it is during the day. The city's buildings are often illuminated, and the four nearby casinos play on until the early hours of the morning. There are also places to dance, piano bars, some local theatrical productions and, near the airport, a famous bordello. Dining out can be rather entertaining in itself, with many of the restaurants operating out of century-old buildings.

Shopping

You want shopping? They've got plenty of it, mostly concentrated in Willemstad's two major districts, Punda and Otrobanda. The variety of goods is bewildering and international in scope. One could spend an entire day just wandering from store to store, many of which are located on spotless, airy plazas closed off to vehicular traffic. The best place for South American and Caribbean handicrafts is on Columbusstraat. Shopping hours in town are from 8am to noon, and 2pm to 6pm, Monday through Saturday. US dollars are accepted everywhere, and you'll get change in US currency. The credit cards honored by each store

/Serberie

are usually posted in the windows or at the cashier's station.

/Bell

Curacao

/Dietmar Reimer

/Dietmar Reimer

/Serberie

/Dean

/Dean

/Bell

/Serberie

Curacao

Sports

Curacao boasts three sports stadiums, and a wide variety of sporting events are always going on, including soccer and baseball.

For joggers, there's the Rif Recreation Area, laid out on the south shore, just west of downtown Willemstad. The entire complex, still under development, extends for 2 kilometers. It starts at the Curacao Caribbean property and goes west up to the Mundo Nobo water plant. In addition to a jogging track, there's a beach, too.

Most hotels provide equipment for watersports, but some places are better equipped than others. Between them all you should be able to find windsurfers, Sunfish, pedalboats, jetskis, snorkeling equipment and fishing tackle.

• Fishing

Private boat charters for sightseeing (about US $50 per hour for a party of four or more) or deep-sea fishing for marlin, sailfish, tuna, dolphin and wahoo (about $300/half-day, $500/full-day, party of four) are readily available. Short tours on glass-bottom boats can be taken for as little as $6 a person.

• Golf, Tennis and Squash

Island visitors are welcome at the Curacao Golf and Squash Club which is situated near the main office of the oil refinery in Emmastad. The 9-hole golf course (played two ways for an 18-hole total) is a bit of a challenge given the stiff trade winds and the sand greens. It's a par 70, and the total distance is 6,156 yards for men and 5,342 for women. Caddies are available, and rentals include clubs and pull carts. Under tall trees you will find a club house with a bar and snack facilities. There are also two squash courts available every day of the week between 8:00 and 4:30. Arrangements can be made by calling the Dutch golf pro, Jan Cramar, a day in advance, at 62664.

There are tennis courts at most hotels, as well as at the Curacao Sports Center, where you're more likely to pick up a game with a local.

• Riding

Horseback riding can be arranged in the countryside.

• Sailing

For the nautical types who come to visit Curacao by yacht, the Curacao Yacht Club, located at Spanish Water, offers various facilities and services including mooring, gasoline and a bar and restaurant. Each year the Club organizes a fishing tournament, the Blue Water, which takes place in April. For information call 673038 or write to Box 870 in Willemstad.

• Sunfish Senior Olympics

Well into the summer season (generally in August), the Inter-American Sunfish Senior Olympics takes place on beautiful Spanish Water which is a protected bay joined by a small channel to the sea. The entrance fee for this fun event includes the use of Sunfishes, round-trip transportation between the airport and hotel, an opening party, barbecue, folklore show and an awards dinner to wrap up.

• Windsurfing

The best place for windsurfing in Curacao is in the Marie Pompoen Area. This area starts at the Seaquarium and runs towards the capital of Willemstad. The winds average 12-18 knots at the hotel and blow in the direction of left to right as you face the water.

Just 50 yards off the beach, the ocean gets extremely deep (1,500 feet) and is considered an intermediate to advanced area. What you find outside are waves of generally 3-5 feet that never crest or break like waves in a shallow area. This makes for spectacular open ocean sailing conditions only 50 yards away from where you launch. With the wide selection of equipment at the Highland Center, the proper board and rig can be found for every level of ability.

The Annual Open Windsurfing Competition takes place at the beginning of the summer in June. Sponsored by KLM and ALM airlines, the event happens along the south coast of the island. Noteworthy among the previous participants in the Competition are Olympic gold medal winner Stephen van der Berg (the Netherlands), silver medalist Scott Steele (US) and bronze medalist Bruce Kendal (New Zealand).

The Competition consists of an Olympic triangle course, a long distance course, jibe slalom, speed slalom and course racing. Invitations are typically extended to a dozen or so world class teams to encourage their participation although the event is an open one. Spectators come from all over including the US, Canada, the Netherlands, Belgium, France, Venezuela and the Caribbean.

• Diving

Diving in Curacao is a relatively recent development and you will find areas around the island that are in their original state. The coral is not broken off or chipped, the heads are healthy and the fan coral has all its fans.

There are three main areas to dive when you visit Curacao: The Underwater Park, the leeward side of the island outside of the Underwater Park and Klein Curacao. The Underwater Park is well managed and the diving is exquisite. You will find more shallow wall-diving here than anywhere else in the Caribbean. In the park, the east point is untouched, since there is no beach access and the dive operations do not go there on a regular basis.

For all of Curacao, the current runs about 1 to 2 knots from the southwest.

If Curacao diving is in its infancy, then Klein Curacao diving is embryonic. The dive operators are just starting to make regular trips to this island. If you want to do some real underwater exploring, try a day trip to Klein Curacao.

• The Underwater Park

The Guide to the Curacao Underwater Park is your best source of information on the park. It may be obtained directly from the Netherlands Antilles National Parks Foundation by writing to: STINAPA c/o CARMABI, Box 2090, Curacao, Netherlands Antilles.

All of the park sites have mooring buoys. Buoys numbered 1, 2 and 4 can be dived from shore. The director of the park recommends that snorkelers try the wide and quite varied shallow terrace of PBH (1); the coral garden at Bapor Kibra (2) (when the sea is calm); the ledge under the mooring buoy at Boka di Sorsaka (3); the soft coral formations between Piedra di Sombre (5) and Kabes Baranka (6); Towboat (8), a wreck dive for snorkelers; and Piedra Pretu (15) with its dense coral cover.

The park dive site numbering system for the descriptions below coincides with the numbers on the mooring buoys. There are another ten or twenty unmarked dive sites within the park. You should also note that the best diving in the park tends to be shallower than at the best diving sites around the rest of the island.

(1) PBH features a variety of species on a shallow terrace, which is slightly wider than average and very good for snorkeling. The mooring is close to Princess Beach Hotel. Porgies and groups of squid are often seen on the terrace as well as a variety of colorful fish.

(2) Bapor Kibra (Papiamento for "broken ship") is named after a shallow, partly exposed

/Dean

wreck. The main attraction of this site is the lush, exceptionally pretty, shallow-water coral garden.

Attractive for shallow dives and snorkeling, (3) Boda di Sorsaka features a very colorful deeply undercut ledge at 17 feet. Near the mooring, the ledge -- covered with orange tube coral and purplish pink algae -- separates two shallow terrace plateaus. A 10-minute swim to your left, facing the sea, will bring you to a vertical wall that reaches from the drop-off down to 67 feet. It is covered with purple, green and brownish pink cavernous star coral.

The terrace at (4) Jan Thiel is relatively wide. The reef is most beautiful at depths of 50 to 60 feet. Near the mooring is a very pretty, lush coral garden with a stretch of yellow pencil and head corals, and lots of gorgonians.

(5) Piedra di Sombre features both a spectacular wall and a lush shallow reef community. With many sponges and corals, including oc-

casional flat plates of sheet coral and tube sponges, the scenery is superb.

Near the entrance of Caracasbaai is (6) Kabes Baranka, best translated from Papiamento as "Tip of the Cliff." Coral in the drop-off zone is lush and varied, as are the many gorgonians and sponges, especially the large orange sponge and the do-not-touch-me sponge.

(7) Lost Anchor is just inside the geological wonder of Caracasbaai, a bay formed by a catastrophic onshore landslide in which 375 million tons of limestone rock disappeared into the deep sea. This site features an old heavy chain that runs from the terrace at 10 feet straight down the reef slope as far as the eye can see (those who have followed the chain down 283 feet report no end in sight).

(8) Towboat is named after the "really cute" tugboat that lies in protected waters just 17 feet deep. This well-known site is so shallow that even snorkelers can enjoy it. The 25-foot long boat has a fully intact hull, which is covered with brain corals in various colors. The wreck offers excellent opportunities for both wide-angle and close-up photography.

The shallow terrace at (9) Kabaya stretches offshore for almost 670 feet, which is exceptional for the normally narrow fringing reef. Take a westerly course from the mooring to the drop-off (only a short swim). Here you find a vertical wall that stretches from 33 to 100 feet. The wall itself is covered with black corals, black wire coral and encrusting sponges. The wall is intersected by two gullies that create dramatic light effects in the mooring at a low sun angle.

With fish in abundance, (10) Punt'i Piku offers both shallow walls and terraces. Just a 5-minute swim to the right of the mooring (facing the sea) is an interesting steep wall, stretching from 33 to 60 feet down. Left of the mooring is a rich coral community with big coral colonies down to about 50 or 60 feet.

There are always numerous fish at (11) New Port, just east of the entrance to Fuikbaai. In the mooring area, the terrace is dominated by head corals and gorgonians.

The shallow terrace at (12) Punt'i Sanchi is 500 feet wide, but choppy seas can be expected. Depending on the current, you can go right (facing the sea) where the reef slope is quite unusual, or go left of the mooring where a steep wall begins in front of the point, from the drop-off down to 50

feet. Gorgonians and cavernous star coral are abundant on the wall, whereas on the slope below giant brain coral, mountainous star coral, flower coral and leaf coral are more common.

The mooring at (13) Barank'i Karanito lies right next to a 33-foot-wide field of club finger coral. A 10-minute swim to the right of the mooring will bring you to a short wall that stretches from the drop-off down to 67 feet, with a ledge at 50 feet. The coral reefs to the right of the wall take on an undulating appearance, and the terrace between the mooring and the wall is especially lush.

The sea is usually choppy at (14) Guliaw, but the diving is rewarding if you don't mind a rough boat ride. Coral cover is high on the upper slope and the terrace, which is divided in two by a step at 27 feet. Staghorn coral occurs down to 50 feet, an unusual depth for this species.

(15) Piedra Pretu features both a spectacular vertical wall and a very lush shallow terrace community, slightly protected by the tip of the island. The mooring lies just right of the wall, near the edge of an extensive field of staghorn coral.

• Other Curacao Dive Sites

In addition to the sites in the Underwater Park, there are a dozen other noteworthy diving spots around the island.

At the (17) Mushroom Forest, offshore from Sanu Pretu (Papiamento for black sand), the coral formations 50 feet under resemble (surprise) huge mushrooms.

(18) Sponge Forest, in 45 to 80 feet of water, supports a wide variety of sponges.

(19) Franklin Special--ask your divemaster about this site.

(20) Lost Anchor is an anchor from an old frigate in 50 feet of water.

(21) The Valley is a double reef system extending to 80-foot depths, forming an underwater valley.

Swimming out from the shore (a long swim) at (22) Knip Bay, you will find a shallow (40-feet-deep) reef.

(23) Black Coral Beach (Boca Hulu in Papiamento) has, as you might expect, black coral offshore between 60 and 150 feet down. This is a beach dive.

(24) The "Gorgonians" shore dive puts you in a field of gorgonians at 40 feet.

Swimming out from (25) Playa Jermi beach you will encounter abundant star coral as well as a forest of garden eels. The local divemasters do not recommend eel feeding.

At (26) San Juan Bay the shoreline reef is 60 feet deep.

(27) Club Beach at Vaersen Bay is a private beach for the police department, so you will need permission to dive here. The dive starts with a long swim from shore to an area with lots of sunken cars in 30 to 40 feet of water.

(28) Blauw Bay is a wall dive that starts at a depth of 20 feet and goes to 150 feet. It can be dived from boat or shore and is considered one of Curacao's premier dive sites.

The medium-sized freighter (29) Superior Producer rests in 100 feet of water just off Holiday Beach. When this ship went down, the owners made some vain attempts to salvage the vessel itself, but the cargo generated far more interest among free-lance operators. The salvage divers' mad scramble met with mixed success: due to the depth of the wreck many would-be booty hunters ended in the hospital for recompression. Now that things have calmed down, it makes for a very interesting deep dive.

· **Diving Klein Curacao**

Though there are only a couple of named sites on Klein Curacao, don't let that mislead you -- there is a whole lot of diving here. The island is a 2-1/2 mile oval with a lighthouse, pier and some fishermen's huts. It lies 16 miles due east of Curacao. The boat ride from the Seaquarium is about 50 minutes, so most trips are arranged for two dives, with lunch in between. You won't find any shade on the island so come prepared -- also come prepared for 150-foot visibility.

(30) The Long Wall parallels half of the island, from the eastern to the southern extremes. The wall is 50 yards offshore and starts in 30 feet of water. At the south point the wall drops to 120 feet at the base.

(31) North Point begins in 20 feet of water, 100 yards from shore, drops off to 80 feet, and then resumes a gradual slope.

Avila Beach Hotel

Coral Cliff Resort & Beach Club

Curacao Caribbean Hotel & Casino

Curacao

Curacao Plaza Hotel & Casino

Holiday Beach Hotel & Casino

Hotel Holland

Las Palmas Hotel & Vacation Village

Princess Beach Hotel & Casino

Trupial Inn

Key: The accommodations price range is based on the high season rate per night, double occupancy. The Liveaboard price range is per berth, high season. The dive price range is based on the cost of a two tank dive. Letter codes: Beach (or on the water), Diving, Fishing, Golf, Other watersports, Pool, Restaurant & Bar, Sailing, Tennis, Windsurfing.

Accommodations

AVILA BEACH HOTEL 800-223-9868
45 Units: $60-98 BDRW
212-397-1560 011-599-9614377 Box 791, Willemstad Curacao, N. A. This historic governor's mansion "Pen of Belle Alliance" is furnished in old- Dutch-style with 45 airconditioned rooms and lovely tropical terraces. Try their open-air dining under rustling palm trees, or the Schooner Bar overlooking the Caribbean, for afternoon tea and cocktails. They have a private cove for year round swimming and barbecues. This is one of the very special places in Curacao. Relaxed elegance at its best.

CORAL CLIFF RESORT & BEACH CLUB 800-782-5247
35 Units: $70-130 BDFORSTW
011-599-9641610 TELEX:1008 Box 3782, Santa Martha Bay Curacao, N. A. Situated on a bluff overlooking the Santa Maria Bay. They're little enough to care. You'll be surrounded with panoramic vistas of sea & sand, breathtaking sunsets and the carefree tropical atmosphere found only in beautiful Curacao. Every room faces the ocean and has a private veranda. For action, there's fishing, sailing, tennis, shuffleboard, swimming, snorkeling and much more. Located just 35 minutes from Willemstad, Coral Cliff has it all!! See: Coral Cliff Diving.

CURACAO CARIBBEAN HTL & CASINO 800-223-9815
200 Units: $90-300 BDFOPRSTW
212-840-6636 800-444-1010 JF Kennedy Blvd. Box 2133 Willemstad, Curacao, N. A. Modern resort living combined with our island's colorful past. Guest rooms and suites with private balconies. Located just five minutes from town. The fort's ancient battlements rim the garden's star-shaped pool and beach. They offer watersports, scuba diving, and motor boating. You will also find a fishing pier, tennis courts, sauna baths, shopping, and a casino. Elegant and informal dining. Lounge and club with dancing and entertainment. See: Seascape.

CURACAO PLAZA HOTEL & CASINO 800-223-1588
240 Units: $90-135 DOR
212-661-4540 011-599-9612500 Box 229, Willemstad Curacao, N. A. Located in downtown Willemstad at the harbor entrance. Every room offers a magnificent panoramic view of the city or sea. The property is being totally refurnished to the standards of the most discriminating traveler. They have three exciting settings for dining and entertainment, all overlook the harbor entrance, pontoon bridge or pool terrace. For the night owl, the casino is open until 4am, international entertainment in the bar and Sabines nightclub. See: Dive Curacao & Underwater Curacao.

HOLIDAY BEACH HOTEL AND CASINO 800-223-9815
200 Units: $95-105 BDRTW
212-840-6636 011-599-9625400 25 West 39th Street New York NY 10018. Each room has its own balcony with a spectacular view of the ocean, just right for breakfast in the Curacao morning air. Casino action, beach barbecue parties and a host of other activities allow you a wide choice of things to see and do. Within walking distance of the famous Queen Emma Pontoon Bridge and fabulous Willemstad shops, the Holiday Beach serves as your center of activity throughout your stay. See: Underwater Curacao.

HOTEL HOLLAND 011-599-988014
30 Units: $69-69 R
011-599-981120 TX: 1405 FD Rooseveltweg 524 Curacao, N. A. Feel at home when away from home with the Vrolijk family. Hans Vrolijk is a qualified commercial diver. They offer fresh and clean, airconditioned guest rooms. The decor is dramatically Dutch. They're very close to the Curacao International Airport, and Curacao's sunshine, fabulous fishing, fine beaches, great restaurants, fashionable shops and dazzling casinos. There's a fine popular restaurant and cocktail lounge to meet and mingle with locals.

LAS PALMAS HOTEL AND VACATION VIL. 800-622-7836
200 Units: $160-165 BOPRTW
203-849-1470 011-599-9625200 Piscadera Bay, Box 2179 Curacao, N. A. A first class resort: beautiful beach, watersports, an olympic-size pool, kiddie pool, lighted tennis courts, aerobics, excellent cuisine, coffee shop, casino and nightly entertainment. They have beautiful rooms in the main building of carefully located villas (great for groups of 4-6). Shopping facilities, "mini market" and drug store on premises. They offer family packages. Make sure you visit the watersports center. See: Las Palmas Reef Divers & Watersports.

LIONS DIVE HOTEL & MARINA 800-451-9376
72 Units: $110-110 BDOPRSW
212-840-6636 011-599-9611644 25 West 39th St. New York NY 10018. Located on Curacao's largest white sand beach, this resort has been developed to be the ultimate dive resort. All the units are airconditioned with a view of the sea, queen beds, color tv, phone and private balcony or terrace. Guests have direct access to the Curacao Seaquarium complex which includes Masterdive - a professional retail diveshop. Very reasonable 6-day dive packages are available. Complete watersports available. E-6 and 24 print processing. See: Underwater Curacao.

PARK HOTEL 011-599-9623112
80 Units: $33-33 R
011-599-9625240 Frederikstraat #84, Willemstad Curacao, N. A.

PRINCESS BEACH HOTEL & CASINO 800-782-5247
205 Units: $90-130 BDFGOPRSTW
212-840-6636 011-599-9614944 Dr. M.L. King Blvd #8, Willemstad, Curacao, N. A. Near town, on the beach, and right next to Curacao Underwater Park and Seaquarium, lots of dive packages. Rooms are modern with a relaxed atmosphere. They have a coffee shop, weekly barbecues and daily happy hours. Special costume parties, dancing, and casino. Pool, tennis, nearby golf course. Watersports including diving, sailing, windsurfing, snorkeling, deep-sea or bottom fishing. Family packages and convention facilities available. See: Dive Curacao & Underwater Curacao.

TRUPIAL INN HOTEL 011-599-978200
74 Units: $44-60 PRT
TX: 1410 Groot Davelaar Weg 5 Curacao, N. A. Curacao's great new highlight, newly refurbished with phone, cable color TV and air con. in every room. Just 10 minutes from the heart of the shopping district, with the best of the city, yet retaining the tropical tranquility that only residents enjoy. The beautiful facilities include a pool with a bar, tennis courts and one of the island's finest restaurants. Weekend dancing and folkloric shows under the stars. Sauna and massage center. Solar hot water.

Curacao

Location of the new Lions Dive Hotel & Marina/Dean

Information

CURACAO TOURIST BOARD 800-332-8266
212-751-8266 011-599-977339 400 Madison Ave., Suite 311 New York NY 10017.

Sports

CORAL CLIFF DIVING 800-782-5247   15 Divers: $50-50 D
011-599-9641610 TELEX:1008 Box 3782 Curacao, N.A. This facility dives Curacao's fabulous South coast. They offer a complete dive accommodation package: 12 boat dives (PADI) divemaster, unlimited beach diving, breakfast & dinner meal plan and an ocean view room. When you are ready for your perfect Caribbean dive vacation, call them for their current packages. The diving is very good and the environment is extraordinary. See: Coral Cliff Resort & Beach Club.

DIVE CURACAO & WATERSPORTS 800-223-9815   10 Divers: $50-50 D
212-840-6636 011-599-9614944 Dr. Martin Luther King Blvd. Curacao, N. A. We offer a full service dive operation (including PADI cert.) run by divers for divers. Located at the Princess Beach Hotel and Casino, just at the north edge of the Curacao Underwater Park, offering wreck, cave, wall reef and night dives. With the Princess Beach, some very affordable 3 to 7-day packages are offered combining great diving with accommodations at the resort. See: Princess Beach Hotel & Casino.

LAS PALMAS REEF DIVERS & WATERSPORTS 800-622-7836   Divers BDO
203-849-1470 011-599-9625200 Box 2179 Curacao. Located at a private beach 500 yards from the mall lobby of the Las Palmas Hotel & Vacation Village. For the diver there are shore and boat dives incl. wreck and night diving, underwater photo, equipment rental and service, PADI certifications including open-water, advanced & divemaster. If you're not into diving try: windsurfing, deep sea fishing, volleyball, waterpolo, or tanning floats. Bar & Restaurant right on beach. Special packages available. See: Las Palmas Hotel and Vacation Vil..

MASTER DIVE SHOP 011-599-9611772
Box 3582, Santa Martha Curacao, N. A. This is a well-equipped dive shop located at the Seaquarium. All of the diving for this shop is done through Underwater Curacao.

MISTRAL CENTER 011-599-9614944
c/o Princess Beach Hotel, ML King Bvd #8 Curacao. This is the new Mistral center set up at the Princess Beach Hotel. Some of the best windsurfing in Curacao is located right at their door steep. This is also the location of the annual windsurfing championships. With a complete supply of rental boards for the experienced and lessons for the beginner, this operation should be contacted if you plan to windsurf in Curacao.

SEASCAPE 800-422-0866   40 Divers: $50-55 DOSW
212-697-7746 011-599-9625000 Curacao Caribbean Hotel, Box 2133 Curacao. This operation offers wreck, reef, wall and night diving. There are dive and accommodation packages throughout the year including special low season discounts. Chris Richards, with 12 years of dive experience in Curacao, heads the operation. This operation has all new boats and dive equipment. In addition to diving, they offer a complete range of watersports and activities such as sunset cruises and beach BBQ's. See: Curacao Caribbean Htl & Casino.

UNDERWATER CURACAO 800-782-5247   48 Divers: $55-55 BDORSW
011-599-9616666 011-599-9616670 c/o Curacao Seaquarium Curacao, N. A. Their shop is fully equipped and ready to provide all your equipment needs. Because they are located at the Curacao Seaquarium, they have short quick rides to all of the dive sites in the Marine Park. In addition, they offer regular trips to Klein Curaco. All divemasters are top-flight professionals. They are able to provide you with a complete package of diving and lodging. When you are ready for extraordinary diving, give them a call. See: Lions Dive Hotel & Marina.

French West Indies

St. Barts

/Kelly

Travel & Sports Guide

/Kelly /Chez Guy

Useful Facts

• Guadeloupe Airline Connections   A i r France flies direct from Miami and San Juan; from other US cities American Airlines flies via San Juan. Air Canada flies from Toronto and Montreal. Inter-island airlines include: LIAT, Air Guadeloupe, Air France, American Eagle, Air St. Barthelemy and Caribes Air Tourisme.

• Martinique Airline Connections   T h e r e are direct flights from Miami and San Juan on Air France. For other US cities, American has connections via San Juan. Inter-island airlines include: Air France, Air Martinique, LIAT, and American Eagle.

• St. Barthelemy Airline Connections   Most flights route through Sint Maarten, St. Thomas and Guadeloupe; weekend flights from San Juan. Winair and Air St. Barthelemy have ten-minute connections from Dutch Sint Maarten. (A pleasant and relaxing alternative is the high-speed catamaran sailing craft which leave from Dutch Sint Maarten, making the passage in about 1 1/2 hours). Air Guadeloupe flies from Esperance Airport on French St. Martin and from Guadaloupe. Virgin Air and Air Guadeloupe fly from St. Thomas.

• St. Martin Airline Connections   You arrive at the Dutch Juliana Airport via American from New York, Boston, Los Angeles and Dallas/Fort Worth. ALM flies from New York; Pan Am from New York and Miami, and Eastern from Miami. Other US cities are served via San Juan. Inter-island connections can be made by Eastern, ALM, Air Guadeloupe, LIAT, Winair and Air France, BWIA and Air St. Barthelemy. In addition to scheduled service, several charter flights are available.

• Banking   The French franc is coin of the realm in the French West Indies. 6.2FF = US $1.00, subject to fluctuation. Traveler's checks and some major credit cards are accepted. US dollars are widely accepted, although banks give the best exchange rate. Banking hours vary from island to island. Most banks observe the French custom of taking a long, relaxed midday break. Banks

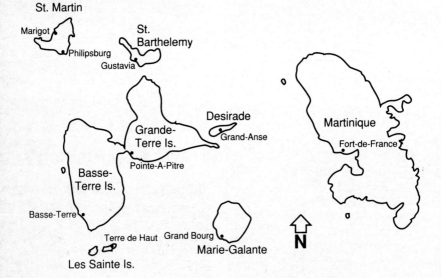

St. Martin

Marigot

Philipsburg

St. Barthelemy

Gustavia

Desirade

Grand-Anse

Grande-Terre Is.

Martinique

Fort-de-France

Pointe-A-Pitre

Basse-Terre Is.

Basse-Terre

Terre de Haut   Grand Bourg

Marie-Galante

N

Les Sainte Is.

Miles
0 4 8
0 4 8
Kilometers

• Cities

French West Indies

Guadeloupe/Kelly

are open Monday through Friday, from 7:30am to noon and 2:30pm to 4pm on Martinique; from 8am to noon and 2pm to 4pm on Guadeloupe. Banking hours are 8am to noon and 2pm to 3:30pm on St. Barts, 9am to noon and 2pm to 3pm on St. Martin, Monday through Friday.

• Courtesy & Dress   Casual dress in town; swimsuits and bikinis are appropriate for ocean-side only, although hotel beaches are topless. Bring a coverup and hat to prevent sunburn. For evenings informal chic is appropriate. Men might wish to wear jackets in fine restaurants, but ties are not required.

• Customs & Immigrations   For stays of up to 3 months, US and Canadian citizens need either a passport (current or expired within the past 5 years) or proof of citizenship such as a birth certificate or voter's registration card plus a photo ID. An onward or return ticket is also required. No arrival or departure taxes are collected on commercial flights except on St. Martin and St. Barthelemy. Items for personal use, such as tobacco, cameras and film, are admitted without formalities or tax, provided they are not in excessive quantity. For other items, French regulations apply.

• Driving   Like the US, the French West Indies are known for good roads, though some mountain routes are challenging. Secondary

roads in remote areas may be steep, winding and rough. Car rental agencies operate at airports, major hotels and in the major towns. Advanced reservations are recommended, especially in high season.

• Electricity   American-made appliances will require French converters, plugs and transformers.

• Events & Holidays   New Year's; Carnival (Feb.); Ash Wednesday; Mid-Lent (March); Easter Monday; Labour Day (May 1); Slavery Abolition Day (May 1); Ascension Thursday; Pentecost Monday; Bastille Day (July 14); Schoelcher Day (July 21); Assumption Day (Aug. 15); All Saints Day (Nov. 1); Christmas Day. On Martinique, Cultural Festival (July); Festival of the Sea (Sept.); Pro-Am Imperial St. James Golf Tournament (Nov.); Semi-Marathon (Dec.); Bi-Annual International Guitar Festival (alternate years, Jazz Festival) (Dec.); On Guadeloupe, Tour de la Guadeloupe bicycle race (Aug.); Cook's Festival (Aug.); St. Cecilia's Day (Nov. 22); On St. Barts, Patron Saint Day (Aug.24); La Route du Rose regatta (Dec.). On St. Martin, Food Festival Day (May); Concordia Day (Nov. 11). Carnival in Martinique and Guadeloupe is the liveliest of holidays with big parades and other events which come to a climax between Samedi Gras (the Saturday before Ash Wednesday) and Mercredi des

French West Indies 3 (147)

French West Indies

/Cavezzale

Cendres (Ash Wednesday) and culminate with the burning of the "Vaval."

• Languages   Predominantly French, with a Creole dialect. You'll find some English-speaking waiters and resort employees, but bring your French phrase book and give it a try. You are sure to make new French friends in the process. More English is spoken in St. Martin and St. Barthelemy.

• Medical   Martinique and Guadeloupe each have modern hospitals and numerous clinics, as well as recompression chambers. St. Martin has two hospitals (one in Sint Maarten, on the Dutch side); St. Barts has one clinic, in Gustavia.

• Off-Season Dates & Rates   From mid-April to mid-December rates are lowest.

• Taxes & Tipping   A service charge of 10-15% is included on the tab at most restaurants and in most hotels. In resort areas there is up to one dollar per person per day local tax.

• Taxi Fares   Rates vary from island to island. Check official fixed rates at the airport or your hotel to estimate charges. You may want to double-check the price with the taxi driver before departing. Night fares are 40% higher on Martinique and Guadeloupe, 25 - 50% higher on St. Martin, and 50% higher on St. Barts.

• Telephone.   From the US to Martinique dial direct using 011-596 + the local number for station-to-station; for person-to-person, 01-596. From the US to Guadeloupe, St. Martin and St. Barthelemy dial 590 instead of 596. Phoning abroad from hotels with direct dial phones is easy. Otherwise overseas calls must go through the hotel operator or be made at the front desk. Ask about service charges in advance. The use of "Telecarte"

(phone card) makes local and international calls easier and less expensive. Telecartes are sold at all post offices and other outlets marked "Telecartes en Vente Ici" ("Telecartes are sold here") and are used in phone booths marked "Telecom." Telex area code for Martinique is 300. For the other islands it's 340.

• Time   Atlantic Standard (Eastern Standard + 1 hour). Daylight Savings is not observed. The French tell time in 24-hour increments, e.g. 1pm is 13 hours.

• Weather   Coastal temperatures vary from 72 to 86 degrees. Inland temperatures in mountainous regions are 66 to 81 degrees. Average water temperature is 70 degrees. Constant trade winds from the east-northeast, known as "les alizes," temper the climate.

Editor's Note:

As a sports destination, the French West Indies is just now being discovered by Americans. If your interest tends to the land-based sports, you will find many sports, such as cycling, with a strong French heritage. Anyone interested in watersports will find miles of protected reefs, crystal clear waters and bountiful marine life surrounding all of the French islands. The windsurfing is exceptional, and the diving has been rated by Cousteau as one of the 10 best areas in the world.

It's easy to start diving in the French West Indies. First-time divers start with a free "resort course" in their hotel swimming pool. Interested students can sign up for a supervised dive on a shallow reef the next day under the watchful eye of a qualified guide.

Experienced divers with their own equipment will find that dive clubs on St. Barts and St. Martin are using American, as well as French tanks, so compatibility with American-made regulators and BC's is no problem. Several dive clubs on Guadeloupe and Martinique use only Spirotechnique (French) equipment, which requires an adaptor when used with certain American brands of regulators and BC's. You may wish to bring your own adaptor for diving on these two islands or call ahead to check on equipment compatibility. Don't forget to bring your "C" card.

Guadeloupe

History

Guadeloupe's history parallels that of its sister island, Martinique. Arawak Indians arrived from Venezuela about 2,000 years ago, Carib Indians conquered the island in approximately 1000 AD and Columbus arrived in 1493. He named the island for Santa Maria de Guadelupe de Estremadura in gratitude for protection from severe weather during the voyage. The Carib name was "Karukera" or Island of Beautiful Waters.

French settlers arriving in 1635, drove the Carib Indians to other islands, built sugar plantations and refineries and brought in slaves, often from the coast of Guinea. Britain struggled with France for control of the island for the next two centuries until France's claim was finally ratified by the Treaty of Paris in 1815. Slavery was abolished in 1848 and indentured laborers from the East Indies were brought in to work the plantations. Today 330,000 people live on the island's 530 square miles.

Guadeloupe owes its individuality to this rare combination of diverse cultures -- French, African and East Indian.

Ecology

Guadeloupe is an archipelago made up of several islands. The largest are Grande-Terre and Basse-Terre, which together form the butterfly-shaped land mass known as Guadeloupe. Except for Guadeloupe's administrative capital (Basse-Terre), the island's major cities and resorts are located on the eastern wing, Grande-Terre. This area has gently rolling hills and natural attractions such as the rugged Pointe des Chateaux. The western wing, Basse-Terre, is noted for its 74,100-acre Parc Naturel, a protected national park covered with dense forests, mountains, dramatic waterfalls and the Soufriere Volcano. Another protected area, this one underwater, is the Parc Naturel surrounding Pigeon Island off Basse-Terre's western coast.

Exploring

Allow several days to fully explore this lush, tropical paradise. Begin your tour with some morning sightseeing in Pointe-a-Pitre, the largest city on Guadeloupe. Shops are closed from 1pm until about 3pm, so plan your shopping accordingly. For local color visit the open air market near the harbor and the main cluster of shops and boutiques on the Rue Nozieres. Stop into the Office du Tourisme, (corner of Rue Delgres and Schoelcher, tel: 011-590-82-0930) for information about sightseeing and to pick up a good map, and a free copy of the Guadeloupe Bonjour guide.

The rest of the island can be explored by bus, taxi or rental car. The island's new buses, usually Mercedes, are comfortable and inexpensive. They cover a very extensive network and can take you to most villages on either Grande-Terre or Basse-Terre. Taxis are expensive, as the roads are long and winding. Rental cars are your best bet, but be sure to reserve one in advance, especially during high season. Details on organized island excursions offered by local tour operators can be had from the tourist Office and from hotel desks.

/Kelly

French West Indies

Grande-Terre

From Point-a-Pitre, set off on the Riviera road along the southern coast of Grande-Terre. In Bas du Fort, visit the Fort Fleur d'Epee with its wooden drawbridge entrance and continue east, past the resort town of Gosier and several busy fishing villages. Stop to photograph the colorful boats with nets spread out to dry in the sun and don't forget to plan an afternoon plunge at one of the white sand beaches between Sainte Anne and Saint Francois.

After St. Francois, continue east to the popular Plage de Tarare (clothing optional) and enjoy the view from Pointe des Chateaux where wild surf pounds against black castle-shaped rocks. Don't miss Le Moule, a 17th century village with an impressive Arawak Indian Museum (Musee Edgan Clerc) and the Grands Fonds area, distinguished by its hills (mornes) and deep valleys (fonds).

Guadeloupe/Kelly

Along the inland road through Abymes you will pass vast mangrove swamps, and the fishing villages of Port-Louis and Anse Bertrand. Continue north to Pointe de la Grande Vigie for a spectacular view of offshore islands. Return via Le Moule continue south to Saint Francois or complete the loop to Pointe-a-Pitre.

Basse-Terre

Basse-Terre alone deserves several days' touring time. Bring your map and guidebook and drive out of Pointe-a-Pitre across the bridge over the Riviere Salee. Turn south until you reach the Route de la Traversee, leading inland through the Parc Naturel to the Caribbean Coast.

At Malendure Beach enjoy the view of Pigeon Island. Excursion boats ferry passengers back and forth all day for snorkeling and picnicking recreation.

Cousteau has described the reefs off Pigeon as among the world's ten best dive spots. Several dive clubs right on the beach rent equipment and offer guided dives for all experience levels.

Within the 74,100 acres of Guadeloupe's Natural Park you'll find hundreds of natural attractions, including spectacular waterfalls, hot springs, the dormant Mt. Soufriere volcano and miles upon miles of forested hiking trails. Man-made sights include Parc Zoologique, La Griveliere Coffee Plantation, Fort St. Charles, the Arawak rock engravings at the Parc Archeologique des Roches Gravees and several small and charming villages. A guide to the complete tour of this park is available at the Office du Tourisme in Pointe-a-Pitre. For natural beauty and dramatic vistas, it is an unforgettable experience. Bring your camera and plan a leisurely tour with plenty of time to stop and savor the quiet spirit of this untouched landscape.

Another itinerary covers the north of Basse-Terre, including some of the finest beaches of Guadeloupe at Clugny and Deshaies.

Return via the road de la Traversee through the Parc Naturel.

Off-Island Exploring

Guadeloupe is the jumping-off place for the smaller islands of La Desirade, Marie-Galante and Iles des Saintes (Les Saintes Islands). They can be reached either by air or by boat or ferry and are most popular as day-trip destinations, although all have overnight accommodations as well. Be sure

French West Indies

to make reservations. hilly, pretty les Saintes is emerging as a hide-away destination on a miniature scale, yet complete with small hotels, restaurants, water sports, an even a historical fort, a museum and a botanical garden. Marie-Galante, an undiscovered, rural, friendly island with fine beaches and a few rum distilleries, is best suited for visitors who seek a different, soothing experience. Visiting these islands is like taking a step back in time, since many of the island residents still make their living from the sea. There are very few cars on these islands, many lovely white sand beaches, and ox-driven carts can be seen transporting sugarcane.

/Kelly

Food

Much in the French tradition, eating in Guadeloupe is a celebration, so much so that the island's most colorful and major annual event is none other than the Festival of Women Cooks (Fetes des Cuisinieres). Like the terrain and culture, the cuisine offers rich contrasts: from sophisticated French classics to haute Creole cuisine to authentic family-style Creole specialties. From elegant dining rooms to simple family porches to charming beachside lunch spots, the choice of restaurants is such that visitors are known to actually plan their sightseeing around their meals. Local favorites include crabes farcis, or stuffed land crabs; accras, a fritter stuffed with salt codfish; sea urchins; freshly caught seafood including crayfish, lobster and conch; and gratin of cristophine, a local squash. Also, try "soupe de pecheur" (fisherman's soup), and "blaff," a French West Indies bouillabaisse. Local dark rum, aged for 5 to 25 years, is served as an after-dinner drink.

Nightlife

Many hotels offer dinner-dancing and entertainment by folkloric groups. Check with your hotel desk or visit the Centre des Arts et de la Culture in Pointe-a-Pitre to find out what cultural events are happening during your visit. There is usually a large selection of performances, from a Haitian ballet to jazz or mime from Paris. The island also has several nightspots, including discos and two casinos, one in Saint Francois and the other in Gosier (no slot machines). Casino hours are 9pm to 3am. A nominal entrance fee is charged at both casinos. Gambling age is 21 (proof of identity, with photo, is required) and the drinking age is 18.

Shopping

The main shopping streets in Pointe-a-Pitre are Rue Schoelcher, Rue de Nozieres and Rue Frebault. You'll find a good selection of high quality French perfumes, fashions, leather goods and other luxury items at French prices.

A 20% discount is available on perfumes and luxury items if you pay with traveler's checks or credit cards in specialized stores. Outside Pointe-a-Pitre there are two new shopping malls at Bas du Fort, with restaurants, supermarkets, department stores and entertainment.

Local products and handicrafts are available at many shops, and also at the waterfront open-air market. Take home local gold jewelry, gourmet foods from France, exotic spices, coffee beans and dark or light rum, wood carvings, and recordings of local Creole bands. Also worth a look are some antique shops and art galleries.

Sports

Guadeloupe offers varied land and water sports. Spectator sports include soccer, horse racing, cycle racing and cockfighting.

Watersports, however, are the real attraction for Guadeloupe vacationers. An archipelago made up of several nearby islands, Guadeloupe lends itself exceptionally well to sailing excusions for one or several days. Glass-bottom boats conduct snorkeling trips to the underwater Natural Park at Pigeon Island off the western shore of, Basse-Terre. Saint Francois reef and the Ilet du Gosier are other popular snorkeling sites. Beaches surround the entire island, most being sheltered and excellent for swimming. Public beaches have few facilities, and hotel beaches charge for changing

/Rosenberg

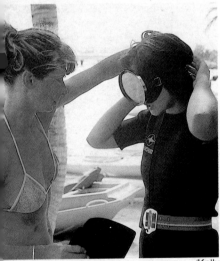

/Kelly

rooms and towels. The most popular of the nudist beaches is at Pointe Tarrare.

• Bicycling

Guadeloupe is a wonderful place to cycle as reflected by the many touring and rental operations on the island. You can also experience the "Tour de la Guadeloupe," a 10-day international race held every August. This event has helped make cycling a major sport here. In Pointe-a-Pitre, Velo-Vert has tours (with maps and bikes

supplied) that cover 270 miles; contact Christian Rolle at Motobecane for information (011-590-831-574). For rentals in Gosier, you can try Cyclo-Tours (011-590-841-134); in St. Francois there are Le Flamboyant (011-590-844-551), Rent-a-Bike at Meridien (011-590-845-100) and Loca BR (011-590-844-780). Also, for information on cycling tours from the US to Guadeloupe, contact Country Cycling Tours, 140 W. 83rd Street, New York, NY 10024 (212-874-5151).

• Fishing

Deep-sea fishing for barracuda and kingfish happens from January to May. December through March is the time for tuna, dolphin, and bonito. Check out the Port de Plaisance Marina in Bas du Fort for the deep-sea fishing boats (011-590-827-494). As an alternative, inquire at the Fishing Club Antilles in Bouillante (011-590-867-377) and Guadeloupe Chartaire in Pointe-a-Pitre (011-590-823-447).

• Flying

Les Ailes Guadeloupeennes at Raizet Airport (011-590-821-899) has two Cessnas and four Cherokees (2- and 4-seat). Foreign private pilots must go through the Civil Aeronautics Board at Raizet for a license. Also, Hamak Hotel's Sagatour in St. Francois has a twin-engine 5-seat Partenavia and a pilot-instructor (011-590-885-999).

• Golf

At St. Francois, one of Guadeloupe's most dynamic and popular resort areas, is the Golf de St. Francois, designed by Robert Trent Jones. The course is about 22 miles east of the airport and Pointe-a-Pitre. The 6,755-yard, par 71, 18-hole course offers a multitude of challenges including water traps, sizeable bunkers and trade winds. There are lockers, a club house with pro shop, and a bar and restaurant all along with equipment and cart rentals (011-590-884-187).

• Hiking

The Parc Naturel de la Guadeloupe in Basse-Terre offers some of the most terrific hiking in the Caribbean. Trails are well-marked and lead through tropical rain forests to waterfalls and mountain pools suitable for swimming. The Organisation des Guides de Montagne in the Maison Forestiere at Matouba arranges guided excursions for one to twelve persons. Contact M. Berry (011-590-814-575).

La Soufriere is a volcano featuring a challenging ascent rising to 4,813 feet. The hike up re-

/FWITB

quires about two hours, and be sure you have sturdy footwear and rainproof clothing. The volcano's slopes are rocky and quite steep with a minimum of plant growth due to the sulphurous fumes and heavy rainfall (about 400 inches a year). From the parking area on the Savane a Mulets, follow the Chemin des Dames to the Fente du Nord at which point the Piste Verte continues up to the summit area. Some sections of the trails are difficult, and visibility may be reduced by mist, but there are excellent views on clear days.

If you like waterfalls, the Chutes du Carbet, which emerge from the east side of the volcano as boiling hot springs, plunge down dramatically in three separate areas. From the parking area, it's a half-hour walk down to the first falls, Troisieme Chute du Carbet. From there, climb 15 minutes to the 360-foot high Seconde Chute du Carbet. An hour and a half beyond is the Premiere Chute du Carbet, the highest of the three (375 feet).

A few small hotels and inns arc scattered on the outskirts of the Parc Naturel.

• Horseback Riding and Racing

Le Criolo, Alain Brossard's riding school in St. Felix, has about 30 horses and 10 ponies and offers lessons, tours and picnic excursions (011-590-843-890). Also try Le Relais du Moulin in Chateaubrun, just outside Ste. Anne (011-590-882-396). Horse races are scheduled periodically at Bellecourt, Baie-Mahault and the St. Jacques Hippodrome at Anse Bertrand.

• Sailing

A major yachting center, Guadeloupe has three very good marinas. Largest and best-known is the Bas du Fort Port de Plaisance. Near the southeastern tip of Grande-Terre is the Marina de la Grande Saline in the elegant St. Francois resort area. The small Marina de Riviere-Sens, at Gourbeyre, is the best mooring for tours to La Soufriere volcano. Additionally, there are a number of small, well-protected anchorages with jetties, notably at Deshaies on Basse-Terre, in Les Saintes and in Marie-Galante. There are several sailing schools and yacht rental agencies, some of which allow one-way boat rentals between Guadeloupe, Martinique and St. Martin at no extra charge.

• Tennis

A total of about 30 courts, many lighted for night play, are located on the grounds of Guadeloupe's larger hotels. Additional facilities, lessons, and short-term memberships are available to hotel guests at a half-dozen tennis clubs located in various towns and resorts off the island. Contact the Guadeloupe Tourist Office for details (011-590-820-930).

French West Indies

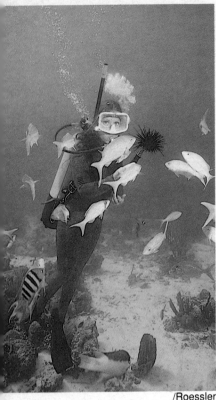

/Roessler

• Windsurfing

Windsurfing is very popular on Guadeloupe, and the beachfront hotels offer rentals and lessons. The "Ronde du Rhum" and "Funboard World Cup" were international events held here in 1987 and are scheduled again for 1989.

• Diving

It's difficult to say how many dive operations there are on Guadeloupe. The number depends on your definition of "dive operation." Approximately 15 hotels offer scuba (plongee) among their varied watersport activities. What this usually means is that one of the island's CMAS (French Federation Certified) dive instructors has a contract with the hotel to give free pool "scuba initiation" classes. Interested participants are invited to sign up for an open-water dive, usually on a shallow reef at Pigeon Island or in the lagoon at the Meridien Hotel on Grande-Terre.

A quick 5-minute boat ride from Malendure Beach is the renowned Underwater Cousteau

Reserve at Pigeon Island, which Jacques himself has called "one of the 10 best places to dive in the world." Dive operators enforce their own preservation policy to discourage divers from taking anything from the area. Spearfishing with tanks is prohibited.

There are two diving clubs with boats on the beach at Malendure, across from Pigeon Island. One is Chez Guy, a club catering to islanders and tourists alike, with at least one English-speaking instructor. The other is Nautilus Club, which is, by their own description, private and non-commercial. Most of the hotel instructors use Chez Guy and Nautilus boats when diving at Pigeon Island. A few now have their own boats. A couple of glass-bottom boats provide diversions for non-divers who accompany non-divers to Malendure.

Pigeon Island is actually two tiny islands with 4 or 5 anchorages, each with its own set of attractions: giant boulders, hot springs, walls and an abundance of colorful marine life. There are sites along the Guadeloupe coast north and south of the Cousteau Reserve, but few divers go further astray along Basse-Terre's west coast. The windward coast is considered too rough for diving. Les Heures Saines is a fully-equipped operation in Deshaies at the former Club Med site.

The Ilet a Fajou, which lies in the Grand Cul de Sac Marin is a special spot north of Baie Mahault. It is seldom visited, yet well worth a look for its virgin corals, including elkhorn, rarely seen elsewhere on the island. Alain Verdonck at the Creole Beach Hotel offers 2-dive day trips to Fajou.

There are several inhabited islands around Guadeloupe with good diving, including 2 sites on Marie-Galante (via boat from Pointe-a-Pitre) and at least one site on Petite-Terre. The fully equipped Centre Nautique on Les Saintes organizes dives to 4 or 5 excellent sites (15-minute flight from Guadeloupe).

Guadeloupe is blessed with warm waters and great visibility all year round. The reefs are generally safe and relatively shallow, yet it's best to dive with a guide to be sure of finding the best sites.

/Kelly

Martinique

History

The Arawak Indians, a peaceful and quite advanced cultural group from Venezuela, arrived in Martinique over 2,000 years ago. They were conquered by the fierce Carib Indians 1,000 years later, who remained warlike enough to intimidate Columbus when he sighted the island in 1493, preventing him from coming ashore until a return trip in 1502.

French settlers were the first Europeans to establish a foothold on the island in 1635, although the King of France didn't officially annex it until 1674. France and Britain fought over possession of Martinique until 1815 when it was restored to France. Diamond Rock, a 600-foot pinnacle off the southern coast, is an enduring reminder of the struggle between France and England. In 1804, British soldiers, using it as a sloop of war, held out against French forces for eighteen months. British ships passing the rock still salute it as the HMS Diamond Rock.

In 1848, due to the efforts of Victor Schoelcher, slavery was abolished on the island and in-

St. Pierre/Kelly

dentured laborers were brought from India and China to work the plantations.

Food, language and customs on Martinique all reflect the island's varied cultural heritage. The original French settlers, slaves from Africa, and Asian laborers have all made their unique contributions to the Creole cuisine, the local patois and the many traditional festivals and celebrations.

The 320,000 inhabitants of the 425-square-mile island participate in a local economy based on agriculture (mainly sugarcane and bananas), tourism and rum. Martinique is a Department and Region of France; residents vote in French elections and enjoy a standard of living comparable to French citizens, with free public schools and good medical facilities.

Ecology

When Columbus landed on Martinique, he described it as "the best, most fertile, most delightful and most charming land in the world." The same unspoiled tropical forests, beaches and hills can still be seen today within the boundaries of the Parc Naturel Regional, 232 square miles of lush vegetation and protected animal life, covering more than half the island's total area. The park areas include the volcanic region around Mont Pelee, several botanical gardens, an arboretum, the Montravail forest near Ste. Luce and the Caravelle peninsula on the Atlantic Coast. Underwater areas surrounding Martinique, which exhibit the same unspoiled beauty, are also carefully protected under government regulation.

Exploring

A complete tour of Martinique can take several days; but there is room here to mention

/Kelly

only some of the highlights. Pick up complete sightseeing information, a detailed map, and a free copy of the Choubouloute, Bienvenue en Martinique or Une Histoire d'Amour Entre Ciel et Mer brochures at the Office of Tourisme in Fort-de-France (on the waterfront, Blvd. Alfassa, 011-596-637-960). Exploring on your own is made easy by an excellent road network combining highways and small, winding roads which reward adventurous visitors with some splendid panoramas.

Martinique is the "Isle of Flowers" and the Martiniquais' fondness for nature is most apparent in th island's many flower plantations, nurseries, and lovingly-tended private gardens which are open to the public.

Begin at Fort-de-France, an attractive small city built on steep hills around the harbor. Start your walking tour from La Savane, the city's central park, planted with trees and flowers from all over the island. At the south end of the square, 17th century Fort St. Louis guards the harbor's entrance. Across form the park on the Rue de la Liberte, the three-story Musee Departemental houses exhibits from all periods of Martinique's history. Further north on the same street is the Schoelcher Library, named for the man instrumental in abolishing slavery in the French West Indies. This Rococo building was first dis-

played at the Paris exposition in 1889. It was then dismantled, shipped piece by piece to Martinique and reassembled. The Schoelcher Library also houses temporary exhibits, as do the city's various ar galleries and other museums.

After your tour of Fort-de-France several modes of transportation are available--taxi, bus, ferry or rental car. Before heading off in a taxi, check standard rates with your hotel. "Taxis collectifs," minibuses and station wagons marked "TC," are a reliable means of transportation and are less crowded than the larger local buses. The main terminal is at Pointe Simon on the waterfront. Ferry rides are a pleasant alternative for visits to Point du Bout, Anse Mitan or Anse-a-l'Ane. Renting a car offers greater flexibility and easiest access to Martinique's beaches and out-of-the-way scenic attractions. Information n organized tours offered by local tour operators is available at the Tourist Office and at the front desk.

Twenty miles south of Fort-de-France is Trois-Ilets, birthplace of the Empress Josephine, wife of Napoleon I. Visit La Pagerie, a small museum filled with mementos from Josephine's life, and the new Maison de la Canne (Sugarcane Museum). Also, take a stroll through Parc Botanique, one of the botanical gardens.

Further west is Pointe du Bout, the main resort area of the island. Follow the coast road through Anse-a-l'Ane, known for its Musee d'Art en Coquillage ("seashell art") and the fishing village of Anses d'Arlets. Heading east, you arrive at Le Diamant with its striking view of Diamond Rock and beyond, a string of white sand beaches. You may wish to stop for a hike on one of the trails through the Foret de Montravail before continuing on to the villages of Marin and Ste. Anne, and finally to Les Salines Beach at the southernmost tip of the island.

To the north on the Atlantic side is the 1,654-foot peak of Mount Vauclin, the highest point in southern Martinique. Drive to the top for a panoramic view, then north through the port of Francois and west through vast plains of sugarcane to Fort-de-France.

To travel the northern loop, drive out of Fort-de-France through Schoelcher and the fishing village of Bellefontaine. Carbet, further north, was Columbus' port-of-call in 1502 and the site of the first French settlement in 1635. Paul Gauguin lived here for a time before going to Tahiti. There is a Centre d'Art Musee Paul Gauguin in Carbet which displays letters and reproductions of paintings by the artist.

St. Pierre, a few miles north, was once known as the "Paris of the Antilles" and was then the former capital city of Martinique. On May 8, 1902, the eruption of Mont Pelee wiped out the city, killing all but one of its 30,000 inhabitants (a convict, incarcerated underground). The Musee Volcanologique displays photos and relics from the original town, along with a collection of clocks stopped at exactly 8:02am when the cloud of scorching gas enveloped the city. St. Pierre never regained its original splendor.

Turn inland to Morne Rouge, a town at the foot of Mont Pelee. From here you can drive the narrow, winding and often rutted road toward the summit. At 2,500 feet the road ends and a four-or five-hour strenuous hike, with the aid of an experienced guide, will take you through a rain forest complete with ancient trees, giant ferns, tropical vines and a profusion of flowers.

Cut inland to the Atlantic coast and drive north to Grand Riviere, a fishing village built along the wind-lashed coast. Retrace your route to the main road and continue south through fields of pineapple, cocoa, sugar, banana and coffee to the Presqu'ile de la Caravelle peninsula, part of the

St. Pierre/Kelly

/Kelly

French West Indies

Parc Naturel. Here are beautiful, calm beaches for swimming and sunning. Visit the lighthouse and the ruins of the Chateau Dubuc before heading inland toward Fort-de-France.

Off-Island Exploring

Short boat excursions around the small offshore "islets," such as Ilet Ramier, Ilet la Perle and Diamond Rock are fun day-trips.

Food

Martinique is renowned for the excellence and variety of its restaurants, housed in chic city establishments, rustic dining rooms or romantic beachside settings. Two types of cuisine, both of them outstanding, predominate: traditional French and island Creole. Fresh seafood is ubiquitous and can be prepared any way you like. The leisurely midday meal is an important one on Martinique. Don't expect fast service, so allow plenty of time for a relaxing lunch. The same goes for dinner.

Rum begins the meal and may be ordered in a variety of ways; a "petit punch," straight, with ice and sugar syrup with a squirt of lime juice or in a "planteur" punch with fruit juice. A "decollage" is straight rum and often starts the day. And everyone knows the familiar daiquiri and pina colada.

Nightlife

Most of the action after dark centers around dinner-dancing and entertainment at the resort hotels. Learn to dance the famous "beguine" or see it performed at various hotels by Les Grands Ballets de la Martinique. There are several local nightspots in Fort-de-France featuring piano bars and native bands, with a zouk or jazz beat, in addition to the discos in the larger hotels. Check on current events in the latest issue of Bienvenue en Martinique or Choubouloute. Both La Bateliere and Meridien Hotels have casinos for blackjack and roulette (craps also at La Bateliere). No slot machines. Gambling age is 21 (a photo ID is required), drinking age is 18. An admission fee is charged at both casinos.

Shopping

In Fort-de-France, shop the boutiques for fashions and import items and the open-air markets for fresh produce, spices and local handicrafts. The Centre des Metiers d'Art sells high quality local basket work, pottery and other handmade wares. Bolts of madras are sold everywhere. Rums can be purchased from sixteen different Martinique distilleries. Bring your camera, but courtesy dictates that you ask permission before photographing the local residents. many stores offer a 20% discount on luxury items paid for by travelers' checks or certain credit cards.

Sports

It is for its watersports that Martinique is best known. Regattas covering various distances or even circling the island are held regularly. The island is surrounded by white sand beaches in the south, dark grey in the north. As it is in the rest of the Caribbean, swimming on the Atlantic Coast can be dangerous except at the Vauclin and Presqu'ile de la Caravelle Nature Preserve. Always inquire about safety in advance with the islanders.

Public beaches have few facilities and resort hotels charge non-guests for facilities and towels. The best snorkeling is off the south coast near Sainte-Anne, off the Anse Mitan and Anses d'-Arlets. Offshore snorkeling from glass-bottom boats can be arranged from La Bateliere Hotel and Pointe du Bout hotels. Many hotels offer lessons and rentals for windsurfing and waterskiing. Spectator sports include horse racing, bicycle racing, soccer, cockfighting and snake versus mongoose matches.

• Bicycling

In cooperation with local bicycle organizations, the Parc Naturel Regional de la Martinique has designed biking itineraries "off the beaten track." Call 011-596-644-259 for information. Bicycles are available for rent from Vespa (011-596-716-003), Funny (011-596-633-305) and Ts Autos (011-596-634-282) in Fort-de-France.

• Fishing

The most popular catches in Martinique are tuna, barracuda, dolphin, kingfish and bonito. Most hotels can make arrangements for deep-sea fishing. Bathy's Club at the Meridien, for example, offers daily fishing trips on its 37-foot Egg Harbor. Up to four persons can fish at one time, and the boat accommodates six.

For surfcasting, try Cap Macre, Cap Ferre and Cap Chevalier in the southeast.

• Flying

Antilles Aero Services (011-596-516-688) and Air Foyal (011-596- 512-904), both at Lamen-

/FWITB

tin Airport, rent two- and four-seater Cessnas and Cherokees, with or without a pilot. To fly on your own, you must first get the French license from the CAB at Lamentin. This is done by presenting your license. Helicopter tours of the island are marketed through Helicaraibes at 40, rue Ernest-Deproge, Fort-de-France (011-596-733-003).

• Golf

The Golf de l'Imperatrice Josephine is at Trois Islets, a five-minute, one-mile drive from the leading resort area of Pointe du Bout and 18 miles from the island's capital of Fort-de-France. Designed by Robert Trent Jones, the course is tough but beautiful. It's 18 holes, 6,640 yards and a par 71. You'll find carts and clubs for rent and an attractive restaurant called Le Country (011-596-683-281).

This course hosts an increasing number of annual tournaments including the Imperial St. James, held every third week of November. Golf is a major attraction for cruise passengers calling at Fort-de-France.

• Hiking

Inexpensive guided excursions in which tourists can participate are organized year round by the Parc Naturel Regional de la Martinique, Caserne Bouille, Fort-de-France (011-596-731-930). Serious hiking tours include a two-hour climb with a guide up Mont Pelee through thick foliage and overgrown trails. The top is often wrapped in clouds. Less difficult, but still requiring skill, is the trek through a dense coastal rainforest between Grand Riviere and Le Precheur. Fairly easy are the hikes along the Gorges de la Falaise.

/Roessler

French West Indies 15 (159)

French West Indies

Guadeloupe/Kelly

Guadeloupe/Kelly

Guadeloupe/Kelly

Martinique/Jacobs

St. Barts/Jones

St. Barts/Jacobs

Guadeloupe/Kelly

French West Indies

Martinique/Cavezzale

• Tennis

Martinique offers a plethora of tennis courts in addition to the 20 courts located on hotels' premises. These private clubs welcome hotel guests as temporary members when courts are available. In addition, there are three courts, all lighted for night play, at the Empress Josephine Golf Course in Trois-Ilets, a five-minute drive from Pointe du Bout.

• Diving

Martinique is a good destination for divers who also enjoy above-water activities. It has plenty of shallow dives as well as more challenging diving, including walls, breakers, caves and wrecks for more experienced "plongeurs."

The water is warm and visibility is about 100 feet most of the year. No spearfishing is allowed with scuba gear.

Underwater, Martinique is primarily known for four separate areas: in the south, Diamond Rock and Anses d'Arlets; in the north, Cap Enrage and the Baie de St. Pierre.

Diamond Rock is the most challenging site and is located off the southern tip of the island. Anses d'Arlets is famous for its easy diving, cliff walls, colorful corals and plentiful plant life.

Cap Enrage, which translates as "angry point" features giant scrapes out of cliff wall forming underwater caves, 10 feet deep and 60 feet long. The caves are home to thousands of soldier fish, triggerfish, longlure frogfish and lobster. Pure white sand, colorful coral and the sheer cliff walls make this site (actually three separate sites) dramatic and exciting. Depths range from 10 to 90 feet.

The island's best known dive area is off St. Pierre. In 1902, Mont Pelee's abrupt eruption sank all but two of the ships in the harbor at the time; only they were able to set sail in time to escape danger. Today the rest lie on the bottom for divers to explore. Within the harbor there are at least 12

• Horseback Riding

Martinique offers a number of equestrian itineraries, some along scenic beach routes, others through tropical hillside greenery. Excursions and/or riding lessons are available from the following: Ranch de Galochat near Anse d'Arlets (011-596-686-397); Black Horse Ranch near La Pagerie in Trois-Islets (011-596-660-004); and La Cavale near Diamant on the road to the Novotel (011-596-762-294).

• Sailing

Martinique is a major gateway to St. Vincent and the Grenadines and is a paradise for sailing, whether done close to shore on Sunfishes and the like, or on yachts that can be chartered bareboat or crewed, for a sunset cruise, by the day, week or month. The beautiful Bay of Fort-de-France and the pretty Anse Mitan provide anchorages favored by seasoned yachtsmen. The new, well-protected marina at the southern end of town of Marin is attracting notice. Boat rental agencies are plentiful and the long-established Pointe du Bout Marina is a particularly good source for day-long sailing excursions on large catamarans and schooners. Typically, they'll head for St. Pierre on the north and Diamond Rock in the south and might stop for snorkeling, swimming and a beach picnic lunch. One-way yacht rentals between Martinique, Guadeloupe and St. Martin are also available at additional cost. For trips on typical Martinique fishing yawls or glass-bottom boats, inquire at the Tourist Office or hotel front desk.

separate wreck sites to visit. Some are too deep for casual diving, but most can be dived. They include an Italian yacht, a 50-meter sailing ship, several cargo ships, barges and a tug. The <u>Dalia</u>, sunk in 1930, can be reached by a short swim from the town pier.

Another excellent dive site is Ilet La Perle, at the end of the coast road north of Precheur. There's sometimes rough water here and a strong current between the beach and a large, surface-breaking rock. Stay close to the rock to avoid the current. Look for barjack, moray eels, lobster, small grouper, large yellowtail, snapper and chub.

Other sites include: Abymes, Baboudy, Pointe La Mare, Riviere Claire, Fond Boucher, Case-Pilote, Cap Vetiver, Caille Vetiver and Anse Dufour.

• Windsurfing

Besides beachfront hotels, many of which offer windsurfing lessons, there are countless windsurfing haves. Competitions often take place in the Bay of Fort-de-France. Among the best spots is Cap Michel, near Cap Chevalier in the south, but there are no rental facilities.

St. Barthelemy

History

Columbus, who discovered the island in 1493, named St. Barthelemy (St. Barts) after his brother, Bartolomeo. The French made an attempt at settlement in 1648 but were driven off by the fierce Carib Indians. Settlers from Brittany and Normandy tried again in 1673 and successfully established

Corossol/Kelly

/Jacobs

a farming community on the island. French buccaneers used St. Barts as a home-port for launching raids against Spanish galleons and British merchant ships.

St. Barts was briefly held by the British in the mid-18th century and, in 1784, was sold to Sweden in exchange for duty-free trading rights with Gothenburg. The Swedish renamed the harbor Gustavia. In 1878 the French repurchased St. Barts for 320,000 gold francs. Today most of the 4,000 inhabitants are fair-haired, fair-skinned descendants of the original Norman, Breton and Swedish inhabitants. St. Barts' men are renowned for their seafaring skills. Farming is still an important island industry, as is the tourist trade.

St. Barts is part of the Guadeloupe archipelago. Residents are French citizens and participate in French elections.

Ecology

St. Barts is an 8-square-mile speck of island plopped in the Caribbean 15 miles southeast of St. Martin. Its 14 gleaming white beaches and small green mountains contrast harmoniously with savanna-type stretches divided up in tiny plots. The island has become a vacation hideaway favored by celebrities who are attracted by its tranquil beauty, privacy and elegantly casual European feel, and who are eager to get away from their fast-paced lives at home.

Exploring

Gustavia, the capital, is a delightful town whose harbor is one of the most photographed in the Caribbean. Drop in at the Office de Tourisme, located in the Mairie de St. Bart (City Hall, rue August-Nyman, 011-590-276-008) to pick up a map or a free copy of <u>Shhhh. St. Barts</u> guide or <u>St.</u>

Barth Magazine. To take in the town's ambience and to best see its buildings, of which the most impressive date back to the Swedes and early French settlers, explore Gustavia on foot and browse the shops along its narrow streets. Snack on crispy palmiers at the patisserie near the post office and sip capuccino at a bistro.

To tour the rest of the island you'll probably want to rent a car. Having your own transportation allows you the freedom to lounge on the beaches and take pictures to your heart's content. Motorbike and scooter rentals are also plentiful. For information on sightseeing tours by minibus or taxi, contact the Tourist Office or hotel desk.

From Gustavia, head northwest to the villages of Corosal and Colombier where some of St. Barts' historic traditions are still in evidence today. Some men wear long-sleeved white shirts tucked into dark pants and a few women still wear long-sleeved dresses and shoulder-length sunbonnets or quichenottes dating back to 17th century Normandy. The women make and sell reed handicrafts, baskets, hats and other woven specialties.

Farther north, below the Pointe a Colombier, is the bay where David Rockefeller built his Caribbean vacation home. It's a half-hour walk to this beach, reputedly the most beautiful on the island. Returning toward the south, drive to the beach at Baie des Flamands and enjoy the privacy and seclusion of yet another St. Barts' beach, but watch out for unexpectedly strong currents here. Complete the loop by veering off along the northern coast to the Baie de St. Jean. Visit the shops and enjoy the many watersport activities available here.

East of St. Jean is Lorient; stop for fresh-baked bread at the small bakery. For panoramic views, turn inland toward the mountainous area of Vitet, the island's highest point. From Lorient you can also follow the shoreline road east to Marigot and Grand Cul de Sac, then south to Grand Fond. The houses here, with their red and green roofs and low stone fences are distinctly reminiscent of Normandy. In fact the entire island has a European flavor, quite unique in this part of the world.

For more beautiful stretches of sandy beach, head for the Grande Saline or Anse du Gouverneur. Getting there via primitive mountain roads is rough but well worth the bumps.

Off-Island Exploring

There are full-day charter sails from Gustavia to Ile Fourchue, an uninhabited island northwest of St. Barts. Enjoy a day of swimming, snorkeling, cocktails and picnicking. Many of the other nearby islands -- Les Petites Saintes, Gros Ilet, La Baleine -- can be visited through the Marine Service or Yacht Charter Agency in Gustavia.

St. Jean Bay/Kelly

Sailing to St. Barts/Kelly

/Cavezzale

Food

Dining has become a stellar attraction on St. Barts. Season after season, young chefs who have trained in France's greatest restaurants choose to work on St. Barts. There are nearly 60 restaurants on the island, serving primarily French and Creole specialties. Prices are high, but so is the quality. Service is generally slow; relax and enjoy the experience. There's plenty of locally-caught fish, excellent French wines and freshly baked breads. Prices at the local grocery are also expensive, as most food is imported.

Nightlife

If you've come to St. Barts for its romance, beauty and excellent diving, you won't miss the absence of casinos and neon signs. In Gustavia you may linger over a late dinner and watch the twinkling lights in the harbor. Then end the evening with a stroll on the beach. There's also a local beer and wine bar at Le Select where you can play dominoes with visiting yachties. There is live jazz in Gustavia in season. Autour du Rocher and La Licorne, both in Larient, are two dancing possibilities.

Shopping

St. Barts, once had a reputation as a smuggler's port, and is still reputed to have some good bargains on imports, mostly on French luxury items in duty-free shops. Local buys include woven straw-work, summer fashions made from island-designed fabrics, island-made, natural beauty lotions, paintings, drawings and lithogrpahs by resident artists. It's also fun to buy reed work from the women who make it in Corossol and Colombier.

Sports
• Fishing

Deep-sea fishing expeditions can be arranged through Yacht Charter Agency and La Marine Service. Popular catches include tuna, bonito, dorado, marlin and barracuda.

• Sailing

Besides Gustavia's harbor (13 to 16 feet deep) which can accommodate about 40 yachts, there are fine anchorings ar Publie, Corossol and Colomier. A colorful event on the yachting calendar for 1988 is the Route du Rose, a regatta of tall ships which leaves St. Tropez (France) in early November and is expected to reach Gustavia by December 4. From December 5 to 10, a Salon du Rose will be celebrated throughout St. Barts, climaxed by a race of the tall ships (about 12 of them) on December 11.

For anything connected to yachting, Loulou's Marine in Gustavia (011-590-276-274) is a good place. The staff speaks English, and the bulletin board is a treasure trove of local yachting infor-

French West Indies

mation. Other good sources of information are La Marine Service (011-590-277-034) and Yacht Charter Agency (011-590-276-238). These companies offer half-day sails, sunset cruises and full-day sails for the uninhabited Ile Fourchue and a stop at the Bay of Colombier.

• Tennis

There are only six hotel tennis courts, but you'll find courts at Le Flamboyant Tennis Club (011-590-276-982), the Youth Association of Lorient and the Sports Center of Colombier (011-590-276-107).

• Windsurfing

St. Barts is ideal for windsurfing. Regattas frequently take place around the island. There are two major windsurfing locations, St. Jean and Grand Cul de Sac. Off the beach at St. Jean, the winds blow from right to left with a reef area 100 yards offshore that provides good wavesailing for the more advanced. The Cul de Sac may be one the finest locations in the Caribbean for beginners learning the basics. The bay is protected on three sides by a white sandy beach. The opening on the outside area is lined by a shallow reef that protects the inside from open ocean swells. The water is waist deep. The winds run at 10-16 knots.

Wind Wave Power operates out of the St. Barths Beach Hotel and the Grand Cul de Sac Beach Hotel. In addition, rentals and lessons are also available from Atlantis, Grand Cul de Sac and St. Bart Wind School in St. Jean near the Tom Beach Hotel.

• Diving

There are several diving options on St. Barts and lots or virgin unerwater territory. Dive With Dan, a PADI certification facility, at the Emeraude Plage Hotel (011-590-276-478) and Club La Bulle (011-590-276-893), both on St. Jean beach, are good places to check out, as is La Marine Service (011-590-277-034) in Gustavia. The PADI Diving Center there is operated by Guy Blateau, a licensed divemaster with both PADI and French certification. There is also a branch at the Guanahani Hotel (011-590-276-660), at Grand Cul de Sac.

A 5-mile-wide shallow reef encircles St. Barts, with a maximum depth of 60 feet, allowing long underwater times. One of the more dramatic spots is La Baleine, where you can swim to the top of an underwater sea mount and enjoy spectacular views in all directions. At other sites there are caves, tunnels, breakers, walls and lots of fish.

Most sites are easy to reach and many can be dived at various depths. Only on the windward reefs is diving usually limited to experienced divers and hardy swimmers. Currents can be strong here and the longer boat rides through choppy water are not for the queasy sailor.

Just around the corner from Gustavia Harbor are four sites they call Les Petités Saintes, named after nearby islands. Expect to see turtles, rays, nurse sharks and large parrotfish. If you're lucky, pompano or dolphins will come out to play with you among the colorful sponges and corals.

Further offshore near Gros Ilet are three sites. The most distinct features at these spots are large rock formations forming a 40 foot wall. Large barracuda are often spotted here, as well as thousands of smaller damsels and other schooling reef fish. Grouper, snapper, moray and lobster frequent these waters. There's no current and the visibility is usually good.

La Baleine is the above mentioned towering sea mount - a great vantage point with a 360-degree view. A long rock-lined underwater boulevard with a sandy surface sprawls in front of the mount. Don't be surprised (or alarmed) to see large barracuda here, good-sized lobster and nurse sharks. Two intact wrecks are a 10-minute swim away. Most of the attractions at these sites are at depths of 50 to 60 feet.

Pain de Sucre, Sugar Loaf, is considered the best dive on St. Barts. Located in open-water at the edge of the island's encircling reef, this spot drops off from 20 feet and 60 feet to...who knows? There's a large cave plus a number of smaller ones housing lobster and grouper, and a tunnel where large barracuda like to hang out. This is a great spot for photos because of the abundance of colorful corals and sponges. Part of the site is shallow, 20 feet, and marked by a dramatic elkhorn forest.

Les Deux Baleines, The Two Whales, is 20 minutes from Gustavia. There's sometimes a current here because of the site's open-water position. There are a number of caves housing moray eels and lobster, and stingrays and nurse sharks in the area. Maximum depth is 60 feet.

Farther north, in the general vicinity of Pointe a Colombier, the waters of the Atlantic and the Caribbean meet in a dramatic setting with two 60-foot walls and many small caves. Rays, eels and barracuda frequent the area. Many large sponges and colorful corals are found here. In addition to the above sites, there are innumerable leeward dive sites and a number of sheltered coves along the windward coast which have yet to be discovered.

St. Martin

History

St. Martin is a study in contrasts, the major one being the juxtaposition of two different nationalities on the 37-square-mile island. The French side has a population of 18,000, and the smaller but more heavily populated Dutch side (Sint Maarten) has 20,000 residents.

The island was first visited and named by Columbus in 1493. The Dutch claimed Sint Maarten in 1631, and French settlers also arrived in the 1630's. Rather than fight about their relative territorial claims to the island, the two countries worked out an amicable arrangement and have co-existed peaceably since 1648. It is not known how the actual border was drawn but one legend describes a walking contest in which the Frenchman walked a little faster, thereby winning a larger share of the island. Today the border is marked only by an obelisk and by greeting signs that say "Welcome" in French and Dutch.

/Kelly

St. Martin, part of the French Department and Region of Guadeloupe, is governed by a sub-prefect appointed in France. Residents vote in French elections. Visiting St. Martin is like being in France...except for the palm trees, creole food and calypso music. Most everyone speaks English, but it is always fun to brush up on your French or pack your phrase book for reference. The French language and customs serve to make St. Martin an even more exotic Caribbean destination.

Duty-free shopping, sun-soaked relaxation and excellent cuisine, make tourism the number-one industry on both sides of the island.

Ecology

Aside from several tourist-oriented centers, most of the island remains a tropical paradise. The green rolling hills have a quiet, pastoral beauty. Many of the beaches that adorn the island's coast still offer solitude and seclusion.

/Kelly

/Kelly

Exploring

From the US you'll arrive at the Sint Maarten airport on the Dutch side. Take a taxi to your hotel on the French side. Rental cars cannot be picked up at the airport. Arrangements can be made to have one delivered to your hotel or pick it up at a rental office in town. The whole island is within reach with a few gallons of gas. A complete island tour can take as little as a few hours, or as long as you wish. Professional sightseeing companies offer various guided tours. Inquire at your hotel desk.

For a comprehensive background on the island, get a copy of the free Discover St. Martin/St. Maarten guide at your hotel. If you plan to do a self-guided tour, pick up a copy of What to Do in St. Martin before setting off on your adventure. Bring your bathing suits, towels and suntan lotion and be prepared to beach-hop along the way.

Taxis are expensive; if you prefer to be driven around, agree to the fare, route and waiting times before pulling away from the curb. Buses run from 6am to midnight on a coastal route around the island. The fare from Marigot to Philipsburg is US$.85.

The capital, Marigot, resembles a small French town, transported and reassembled in a tropical setting. Continental restaurants, boutiques and houses with wrought iron balconies -- even sidewalk cafes line the narrow streets. Along the quay, islanders sell produce and fresh seafood.

Drive out to the resort town of Grand Case and savor fine dining and an enchanting view across the horseshoe-shaped cove. The living is easy here and the pace relaxed, quite slow by American standards. It's no place to be in a hurry. Traveling east out of Grand Case, you'll pass through Orleans, or French Quarter, the oldest French town on the island. There are no monuments or museums but many of the original homes have been maintained or restored by private owners. Plan to stretch the short drive back south by visiting St. Martin's east coast beaches, including the "clothing optional" Orient Bay and Baie de l'Embouchure (also good for surfing).

A fun attraction is the "Live Eagles Show," presented on a hilltop on Pointe Pirouette Road, where eagles and falcons perform 7 days a week, accompanied by a spoken commentary.

Off-Island Exploring

Several motorboats and ferries leave Marigot each day for the 15-minute crossing to Anguilla and the 55-minute ride to St. Barts. Other vessels transport passengers from Philipsburg to Anguilla or the four neighboring islands to the south. Also, you can island-hop via airplane in ten to twenty minute jumps. For casual jaunts, arrange with a passing fisherman for a ride to and from one of the many tiny offshore islands.

Food

Gourmet dining gives this island much of its tourist appeal. There are about twenty restaurants in Marigot, an equal number in Grand Case and even more scattered along the shoreline and inland. As you'd expect, there's outstanding French cuisine on the island, plus spicy Creole variations. Prices are generally "tres cher," for both restaurant and supermarket food, since most ingredients must be imported.

Nightlife

There's something for everyone in St. Martin, depending on how you like to spend your evenings. Enjoy a leisurely dinner followed by a quiet stroll along the beach or dance until the wee hours at the Privilege Disco at Anse Marcel or at Night Fever near Colombier. A few of the larger hotels offer live entertainment. Casinos are a short ride away on the Dutch side.

Shopping

There's plenty of good shopping in Marigot, all of it duty-free. If you plan to do any serious shopping, check the prices of the items you want at home, first, for com-

/Kelly

parison. There are many boutiques and import stores near the marina at Port La Royale and near the town's main harborfront square. Look for bargains on perfumes, cosmetics, fashion accessories, sportswear, lingerie, porcelain and French crystal. For local crafts, fresh fruits, shells and spices, make a morning trip to the open market near the harbor. A few resident artists also open their studios to visitors.

Sports

St. Martin's 36 beaches, tucked away in picturesque bays and coves (called anses) provide the setting for a variety of watersports. The water is exceptionally clear, making for great swimming, snorkeling and scuba diving. Many of the hotels have complete watersport centers offering lessons and equipment rentals for windsurfing and waterskiing. Yacht and deep-sea fishing charters can be scheduled in Marigot and Grand Case. The resort hotels also offer just about every above-water sport.

• Fishing

Fishing boats can be chartered for an hour, half day, full day or week. Dolphin, kingfish, and barracuda can be fished from December to April, and tuna all ytear. The new, 35-foot Sushi is based in Marigot's Port La Royale Marina and can reach St. Barts in 20 minutes and Anguilla in 10. Details in Anguilla (809-497-2846).

• Horseback Riding

Caid & Isa, a new horseback riding facility at St. Martin's Anse Marcel, is operated by longtime professional, Brigitte Duzant. It's located just next to the resort hotel, L'Habitation. Eight paso fino horses are stabled here, and you can take them over the hills of Anse Marcel to the private beach of Petites Cayes (011-590-873-333).

/Cavezzale

French West Indies

• Sailing

St. Martin is a perfect departure point for short cruises. Sailing excursions from both Marigot and Philipsburg to such offshore islands as Anguilla, Saba, Statia, St. Barts and St. Kitts, often include snorkeling and picnics, and can be arranged through most hotel desks or through Dynasty, a new yacht charter company (011-590-878-521) at Marigot's Port La Royale Marina. It is also possible to charter a boat in St. Martin and leave it in Marinique or Guadeloupe at no extra cost. Recommended moorings on the French side of St. Martin include: Baie Rouge, Nettle Bay, Marigot Bay, Friar's Bay, Happy Bay, Grand Case Bay and Anse Marcel.

One of the newest and best-equipped marinas on the island is Port Lonvilliers which has docking space for 105 boats from 29 to 73 feet in length and has all the yachting amenities (011-590-873-194 or 011-590-873-333). The Port La Royale Marina at Marigot Bay also has all kinds of services, shops and restaurants.

• Tennis

Besides hotel courts Le Privilege, a sports complex overlooking L'Habitation at Anse Marcel, has sic lighted courts and two squash courts.

• Windsurfing

Almost every beachfront hotel has facilities for windsurfing and Sunfish sailing. Windsurfing lessons are also available.

• Diving

For serious divers who also enjoy a variety of above-water activities and for first-time divers as well, St. Martin is an ideal (as well as idyllic) destination. There's as much, or more going on below the surface as above. Visibility averages 120 feet and on calm days up to 200 feet. Temperatures are warm all year round, ranging from 72 to 82 degrees, and only from December through April are wet suits advisable. The reefs are shallow (30-80 feet) and the fish and plant life abundant and unspoiled.

All the diving on the island is done from boats, as most sites are some distance offshore. It's always a good idea to dive with a qualified guide from one of the shops, as the sites are difficult to locate without help. Groups are generally quite small.

All St. Martin hotels will arrange for dive excursions upon request. Most of them work with Maho Watersports at Mullet Bay on the Dutch side of the island, a long-established dive operation that caters to all experience levels.

There's no wall diving here, but there are plenty of other dramatic reef structures to explore: caves, spectacular breakers, deep channels, ravines and the wreck of a small tug boat which was sunk intentionally as a dive attraction.

The fish life along the north shore is particularly dramatic. In addition to large schools of familiar reef fish, you'll find large rays, snappers, groupers, barracuda, nurse sharks, moray eels and even dolphins. Barracuda and nurse sharks are common in these waters; they're as fascinated by the divers as you will be with them.

Although there is no government-enforced reef protection policy, spearfishing and the collection of live specimens are strongly discouraged and are not allowed on guided trips.

There are a total of 15 regularly-visited dive sites around the island, 5 of these along the northern coast. For descriptions of the Dutch side sites, refer to St. Maarten in the Netherlands Antilles section of the Travel & Sports Guide.

Eagle Ray Rock, is just outside of Grand Case beach with depths from 20 to 21 feet. The reef covers about 2 acres in the middle of a sheltered bay, where a group of about 30 quite tame moray eels live. Also, two beautiful eagle rays with wing spans of 6 feet and overall lengths of 8 feet or more can be seen here. The rays are curious creatures who occasionally will gently caress divers with one of their wings as they swim past -- definitely a memorable experience!

Creole Rock is a site quite near Grand Case. The water is nearly always calm here, extremely clear, with no currents. This is a shallow reef at 10 to 25 feet with colorful hard and soft coral formations and schools of small tropical fish.

Located between Tintamarre Island (a.k.a Flat Island) and the mainland of St. Martin is Spanish Rock, a spot which offers a complex rock formation with many channels and ravines. It's another shallow 10 to 30-foot dive, but conditions can sometimes be rough here. Expect to see lots of fish and crustaceans, including angels, nurse sharks and lobster.

Further offshore, near Tintamarre Island, a small tugboat has been sunk to create a dive site. Fully intact, about 40 feet long, it is lying on its keel on a sandy bottom with some interesting plant life attached to the hull.

French West Indies

Bois Joli Hotel, Guadeloupe

Le Coucou des Bois, Guadeloupe

Novotel Fleur d'Epee, Guadeloupe

Relais Du Moulin, Guadeloupe

Calalou Hotel, Martinique
Manoir De Beauregard, Martinique

Diamant-Les-Bains, Martinique
Novotel Diamant, Martinique

French West Indies

Emeraude Plage, St. Barts

St. Barths Beach Hotel, St. Barts

West Indies Management Co., St. Barts

Club Le Grand Beach Resort, St. Martin

Le Belle Grand Case, St. Martin
Le Royale Louisiana, St. Martin

Laguna Beach Hotel, St. Martin
Ecotel, GUADELOUPE

Key: The accommodations price range is based on the high season rate per night, double occupancy. The dive price range is based on the cost of a two tank dive. Letter codes: Beach (or on the water), Diving, Fishing, Golf, Other watersports, Pool, Restaurant & Bar, Sailing, Tennis, Windsurfing.

French West Indies - Information

FRENCH WEST INDIES TOURIST BOARD 212-757-1125
212-247-6468 FX 610 5th Avenue New York NY 10020. Or contact your nearest French Government Tourist Board. There are offices in San Francisco, Los Angeles, Chicago, Dallas, Montreal and Toronto.

Guadeloupe, French West Indies - Accommodations

ARAWAK HOTEL 800-223-6510   160 Units: $145-180 BDFOPRSTW
011-590-842424 011-590-902187 BP 396, 97162 Pointe-a-Pitre, Guadeloupe, F.W.I. See: Aqua-Fari & International Club.

AUBERGE DE LA DISTILLERIE 800-223-9815   15 Units: $100-120 PR
212-840-6636 011-590-942591 Route de Versailles, Tabanon 97170 Petit Bourg, Guadeloupe, F.W.I.

AUBERGE DE LA PLONGEE - CHEZ GUY 011-590-988172   20 Units: $51-56 BDFKSW
011-590-988584 TX:919436GL B.P. 4 97132 Bouillante, Guadeloupe, F.W.I. At "Chez Guy", you will find a beautiful remodeled hillside villa overlooking the sea. With 20 beds in nice bedrooms, 3 bathrooms and kitchen facilities, the Auberge offers a calm, relaxing alternative to expensive and impersonal vacation living. There are also several independant airconditioned bungalows. A 7-night stay starts at $360 inc. 2-single tank dives per day, one night dive. Free stay for every ten participants. Breakfast. Free Airport transport. See: Chez Guy.

BOIS JOLI HOTEL 800-223-9815   21 Units: $124-198 BDFOPRSW
011-590-995038 011-590-902187 FX 97137 Terre De Haut, Les Saintes Guadeloupe, F.W.I. Located three kilometers from the village of Bourg in natural settings and facing the sea. They offer a unique view of the "Pain de Sucre." Two beaches to choose from, one of which is naturist. This place is preferred by those who fully enjoy the pleasure of the sea. Here, you will find very good cuisine and a place to relax. Prices include breakfast and dinner.

ECOTEL-GUADELOUPE 800-528-1234   44 Units: $116-116 DOPRTW
011-590-842020 011-590-902187 FX 97190 Gosier Guadeloupe, F.W.I. Located in a garden with luxurian vegetation 5 km. from Pointe-a-Pitre, and very close to Gosier and the beach. Free transportation to and from the beach. Spacious rooms with bathtub, telephone, TV, individual airconditioning. Complimentary breakfast upon request in room. Lunch by the pool at "Pap Pap" Snack bar. Dinner at the "Galion" offer specialties of the island or American food. Clear field for "petanque," ping pong, all watersports at nearby beaches

GOLF MARINE CLUB 800-223-1510   74 Units: $156-214 R
011-590-886060 011-590-842626 FX Box 26 La Marina 97118 St. Francois - Guadeloupe, F.W.I.

HOTEL MERIDIEN ST. FRANCOIS 800-543-4300   271 Units: $130-325 BDFGOPRSTW
011-590-884071 FX 011-590-885100 Box 37 97118 St. Francois, Guadeloupe, F.W.I. See: Meridien Diving.

L'ESPERANCE 011-590-988663   12 Units: $36-36 DR
011-590-987017 Box 1, 97132 Pigeon Guadeloupe, F.W.I. See: Les Heures Saines.

L'ILET DE LA PLAGE 011-590-842073   15 Units: $95-95 BDFKOSW
TX:919174GL Residence Touristique, 97190 Le Gosier, Guadeloupe, F.W.I.

LA CREOLE BEACH HOTEL 011-590-842626   156 Units: $123-158 BGRW
011-590-902187 FX Box 19, 97190 Gosier, Guadeloupe, F.W.I.

LE COUCOU DES BOIS 800-223-9815   10 Units: $71-71 R
212-840-6636 011-590-954225 Montebello, Petit-Bourg, 97170 Guadeloupe, F. W. I. Lea is waiting to welcome you with a big, generous heart that characterizes "Le Coucou des Bois." This small tropical paradise is nestled between the sea & mountains, on the edge of the Natural Park w/ hiking trails and easy access to magnificent beaches of fine sand. You will discover the forest and a new sport "Petanque." Lea will treat you to the delights of the traditional Guadeloupean cuisine, particularly her speciality "ouassous" known island-wide

NOVOTEL FLEUR D'EPEE 800-221-4542   180 Units: $186-186 BDFORSTW
011-590-908149 EXT:396FAX Bas du Fort, 97190 Gosier, Guadeloupe, F.W.I. Situated on a white-sand beach we are surrounded by a lush tropical garden. We offer beautiful airconditioned guest rooms with a tremendous view of the Soufriere volcano. There are plenty of watersports complimentary for guests. Meeting facilities are available along with fine dining and live entertainment.

PLM AZUR MARISSOL 800-223-9862   200 Units: $120-212 BDFGKOPRSTW
212-757-6500 011-590-908444 Bas-du-Fort, 97170 Gosier Guadeloupe, F.W.I.

RELAIS BLEUS DE LA SOUFRIERE 011-590-800127   24 Units: $73-91 R
011-590-902187 TX:919522 97120 Saint-Claude, Guadeloupe, F.W.I.

RELAIS DU MOULIN 800-223-9815   40 Units: $160-160 BDPRT
212-840-6636 011-590-882396 Chateaubrun, 97180 Sainte Anne, Guadeloupe, F.W.I. In the middle of the countryside, around a sugar-mill, 10 minutes from the beach and 30 kilometers from the airport, between Ste. Anne and St. Francois, Relais du Moulin has 2 bungalows and 20 duplexes, with swimming pool, restau- rant & bar offering French and Creole cuisine. Everyone has airconditionning, shower, living room, refrigerator, and a terrace. Bungalows have a bathtub and microwave. Sports on the premises include tennis, archery & horseback riding.

SALAKO HOTEL 800-223-1510   120 Units: $96-96 BDOPRSTW
212-477-1600 011-590-842222 Box 8, 97190 Gosier Guadeloupe, F.W.I. See: Aqua-Fari & International Club.

TOUBANA 800-223-9815   57 Units: $80-190 BFRTW
212-840-6636 011-590-882578 Box 63, 97180 Ste. Anne, Guadeloupe, F.W.I.

French West Indies

Guadeloupe, French West Indies - Sports

AQUA-FARI & INTERNATIONAL CLUB 011-590-842626   30 Divers: $60-60 BDR

011-590-902187FX TX:919836 Creole Beach Hotel, Pointe de la Verdure 97190, Le Gosier, Guadeloupe, F.W.I. Dive the Cousteau Reserve and the Fajou reef with English speaking CMAS, NAUI and PADI instructors. This unique operation is a joint venture between Alain Verdonck (French) and John Lehew (American), with dive centers in several major hotels and on the beach at Pigeon. Fully equipped with new French and American gear. Special group rates and dive packages available. See: Creole Beach, Hotel Arawak, Salako.

CHEZ GUY 011-590-988172   50 Divers: $40-40 BD

011-590-820296FX Pigeon, 97125 Bouillante, Guadeloupe, F.W.I. Conveniently located on the Malendure beach at Pigeon, just a five minute boat ride to the underwater Cousteau Park and other West Coast dive sites. If you have a rental car, going directly to Chez Guy can cost less per dive than going through the hotel instructors. In fact, many of them use Guy's boats. Several scheduled dives a day. Group rates and packages available. Their newly refurbished 45' sailboat is available with skipper and hostess on request. See: Auberge de la Plongee - Chez Guy.

LES HEURES SAINES 011-590-988663   25 Divers: $70-70 DR

011-590-987017 011-590-902187FX Box 1, 97132 Pigeon, Guadeloupe, F.W.I.

MERIDIEN DIVING 011-590-885100   14 Divers: $50-50 BD

011-590-884071FX TX:919733 Box 37, St. Francois, 97118 Guadeloupe, F.W.I. See: Hotel Meridien St. Francois.

Martinique, French West Indies - Accommodations

CALALOU HOTEL 800-223-9815   36 Units: $161-161 BGORSTW

212-840-6636 011-596-683178 Anse-A-L'Ane, 97229 Trois Ilets, Martinique, F.W.I. At Calalou hotel, you will find comfortable rooms with airconditioning and a restaurant reknown for its French and Creole specialties. There is a beautiful carousel nearby for children (or adults!) right on the white-sand beach which lets you enjoy swimming, waterskiing, sailing or watersports. They offer special rates for horseback riding. The hotel is located in a magnificent park, rich with greenery and flowers. Don't miss it !

DIAMANT-LES-BAINS 800-223-9815   24 Units: $65-72 BDFOPRSW

212-840-6636 011-596-764014 97223 Le Diamant Martinique, F.W.I. A small cozy family style hotel, right off the sea, facing the Diamant Rock. It offers single rooms and bungalows. You will enjoy a boat trip which will give you a chance to admire the famous Diamond Rock from close-up. Each room has airconditioning, telephone, television and a lounge. Pool on the premises. Situated right above the beach, you will enjoy Martinique in a very special way.

IMPERATRICE HOTEL 800-223-9815   24 Units: $49-68 R

212-840-6636 011-596-630682 2 rue de la Liberte Fort-de-France,97200 Martinique, F.W.I. Facing "Park de la Savane", this hotel has 24 airconditionned rooms with direct telephone line, bathtub & TV. Restaurant & bar offers French and Creole cooking. It is the center of activities of several clubs in Fort-de-France and is only 15 minutes from the beach. 10% reduction for a 7-day stay. Her brother is opening Imperatrice Village on the beach of Anse Mitan in Jan. of '89. Will have 59 units moderately priced from $60 to $70.

LA BATELIERE 800-221-1831   200 Units: $138-204 BDOPRSTW

011-596-614949 FX:011-596-616229 97233 Schoelcher, Martinique, F.W.I. See: Tropicasub Diving Center.

LA DUNETTE HOTEL SAINTE ANNE 011-596-767390   18 Units: $53-102 BFRW

011-596-767431 011-596-606668FX 97227 Sainte Anne, Martinique, F.W.I. At this (2-star luxury) hotel, you practically have your feet in the water. La Dunette means "Avant du Bateau" (front of a boat). The restaurant special- izes in seafood and French cuisine. Piano bar every Friday evening. They offer airconditioning, television and a living room. Possibility of all watersports on the beach. We also organize outings on Hobie Cats, horse- back riding, fishing, windsurfing. Visit Martinique with them.

LE BAKOUA 800-221-4512   140 Units: $200-278 BDFGOPRSTW

011-596-660202 011-596-762287FX Point du Bout, 97229 Trois Ilets, Martinique, F.W.I. See: Bathy's Club.

LEYRITZ PLANTATION 800-223-9815   54 Units: $98-150 KPRT

212-840-6636 011-596-785392 97218 Basse Pointe, Martinique, F.W.I.

MANOIR DE BEAUREGARD 800-223-6510   27 Units: $126-126 FRS

011-596-767340 011-596-736693FX Chemin des Savines, 97227 Sainte Anne, Martinique, F.W.I. You will remember things past in elegant 18th century surroundings. On the road to the Salines, one of the island's loveliest beaches, Manoir de Beauregard is the ideal spot for rest and relaxation. We offer rooms furnished with island antiques, airconditioning, telephone, access to a telex machine, a swimming pool and a very good restaurant. Special rates for groups.

MERIDIEN HOTEL 011-596-660000   303 Units: $175-200 BDFOPRSTW

TX:912641 011-596-660074FX 97229 Trois Ilets Martinique, F.W.I. See: Bathy's Club.

NOVOTEL DIAMANT 800-221-4542   174 Units: $198-508 BDFGOPRSTW

011-596-764242 011-596-762287FX Pointe de la Chery, 97223 Le Diamant, Martinique, F.W.I. Located on the quieter southern coast, this is a complete three-star resort in a lush tropical setting on Point Diamant. There are four beaches, one pool, two tennis courts. Watersports include sailing, windsurfing, pedal boats, fishing and the Sub Diamond Rock Dive Club on premises. All rooms are airconditioned, with phone, radio and terrace. Live entertainment and disco. Shops and hairdresser also on premises. Dive packages available.

PLM AZUR CARAYOU 800-223-9862   200 Units: $120-168 BDFOPRSTW

212-757-6500 011-596-660404 Pointe du Bout, 97229 Trois Ilets, Martinique, F.W.I.

Martinique, French West Indies - Sports

BATHY'S CLUB 011-596-660000   30 Divers: $60-60 D
  TX:912641 011-596-660074FX c/o Hotel Meridien, La Pointe du Bout, 97229 Trois Ilets, Martinique, F.W.I.
CARIB SCUBA CLUB 011-596-780227   20 Divers: $50-50 D
  011-596-660074FX 97221 Carbet, Martinique, F.W.I. See: Grain d'Or.
HELICARAIBES 011-596-733003
  40, rue Ernest-Deproge Fort-de-France, Martinique, F.W.I. Helicopter tours of the island are marketed through Helicaraibes. A one-hour charter tour of Martinique by helicopter from Lamentin Airport costs approximately 685 $ (3765 F). Sightseeing excursions by plane are available through a number of companies, including Air Martinique (Tel. 510990), located at Lamentin Airport.
SUB-DIAMOND-ROCK 011-596-764242   22 Divers: $66-66 D
  TX:912392 011-596-762287FX Novotel Diamant, Point de la Chery 97223 Diamant Martinique, F.W.I. See: Novotel Diamant.
TROPICASUB DIVING CENTER 011-596-614949   30 Divers: $46-46 BD
  011-596-627172 011-596-616229FX c/o Hotel La Bateliere 97233 Schoelcher, Martinique, F.W.I.

St. Barthelemy, French West Indies - Accommodations

EL SERENO BEACH HOTEL 011-590-276480   20 Units: $250-270 BPRTW
  TX:919039 011-590-277547FX Box 19 97133 St. Barthelemy, F.W.I.
EL YPADO HOTEL 800-932-3222
  401-849-8012 011-590-276018 97133 Gustavia St. Barthelemy, F.W.I.
EMERAUDE PLAGE 011-590-276478   30 Units: $143-268 BDFKOSW
  TELEX:919-167 Box 41 91733 St. Barthelemy, F.W.I. Directly on the beautiful bay of St Jean, this casual hotel, set in a tropical garden, offers a choice of 30 spacious accommodations & personalized service. Each bungalow is fitted with a ceiling fan, features airconditioning, direct-dial phones and has a fully equipped kitchenette opening onto a large terrace. Within walking distance are 2 shopping centers and about a dozen restaurants. PADI diving at the hotel & a variety of watersports on the beach.
FILAO BEACH 800-932-3222   30 Units: $300-375 BOPRSW
  401-849-8012 011-590-276224 Box 167 97133 St Barthelemy, F.W.I.
GRAND CUL DE SAC BEACH HOTEL 800-223-6510   52 Units: $120-193 BDFKOPRSTW
  011-590-276273 011-590-902187FX Box 81 91733 St. Barthelemy, F.W.I.
MANAPANY COTTAGES 800-932-3222   24 Units: $290-550 BDKPRTW
  011-590-276655 011-590-277528FX Box 114 97113 St. Barthelemy, F.W.I.
ST. BARTHS BEACH HOTEL 800-223-6510   36 Units: $192-192 BPRTW
  011-590-276070 011-590-902187FX Box 81, 97133 Grand Cul de Sac, St. Barthelemy, F.W.I. Situated on a narrow peninsula at the Northeast end of St. Barts, next to Grand Cul de Sac Beach Hotel. All rooms have an ocean view, balcony, air-conditioning, shower, refrigerator and telephone. Beautiful white-sand beach where windsurfing school is available. Saltwater pool and tennis court on property. Just three miles from the airport. Preferential rates for three, five or seven-day stays.
TOM BEACH HOTEL 800-932-3222   12 Units: $120-160 BDFKORSW
  011-590-277096 011-590-276043 Box 94, 97133 St. Jean St. Barthelemy, F.W.I. See: Marine Service Scuba Diving Club.
TROPICAL HOTEL 800-223-6510   20 Units: $180-180 DFOPSTW
  212-832-2277 011-590-276487 Box 147 97133 St. Barthelemy, F.W.I.
VILLAGE ST. JEAN HOTEL 800-932-3222   25 Units: $110-200 KR
  401-849-8012 011-590-276139 Box 23 91733 St. Barthelemy, F.W.I.
WEST INDIES MANAGEMENT CO. 800-932-3222   313 Units: $110-800 BDFKOPRSTW
  401-849-8012 401-847-6290FX Box 1461 Newport RI 02840. West Indies Management Company (WIMCO) is the exclusive US representative for STBARTH Real Estate on St. Barths and French and Dutch St. Martin/Maarten and rents over 300 villas. If you're thinking of renting a private villa, call 800-932-3222 and speak to an informed agent who has seen all of the select villas. WIMCO also handles the hotels on St. Barths and St. Martin/Maarten and arranges car, plane and yacht charters. Vendome Guide available. Pls Call.

St. Barthelemy, French West Indies - Sports

MARINE SERVICE SCUBA DIVING CLUB 011-590-277034   Divers: $70-70 BDO
  Quai du Yacht Club, 97133 Gustavia St. Barthelemy, F.W.I.
WIND WAVE POWER 800-635-1155
  215-348-9813 c\o Windsurfing Vacations, Box 1097 Doylestown PA 18901. Equipment: the full range of Tiga production boards and custom boards with Gaastra and Neil Pryde rigs. Private and group lessons available. See: Grand Cul de Sac Beach Hotel.

French West Indies

St. Martin, French West Indies - Accommodations

CLUB LE GRAND BEACH RESORT 800-221-1831   177 Units: $250-375 BDFKOPRSTW

800-221-1832 011-590-875792 Box 99, 97150 Marigot, St. Martin, F.W.I. At this resort, you can be right next to Marigot's restaurants, shops and waterfront and still enjoy the quiet serenity of the private grounds and white sand beach. All units, ranging from studios to three-bedrooms, have airconditioning, kitchenettes, telephone and color TV. Enjoy the island's largest freshwater pool or take advantage of thier complimentary sailing, snorkeling and windsurfing equipment. Prices include everything in the Hotel.

CLUB ORIENT 800-828-9356   61 Units: $120-325 BKORT

TX:919953 011-590-873385 7630 N.W. 63rd St Miami FL 33166.

CORALITA BEACH HOTEL 800-223-5695   40 Units: $135-135 BFKOPRTW

212-725-5880 011-590-873181 Box 175, 97150 Baie Lucas, St. Martin, F.W.I. On the sunny north coast of St. Martin, in the French West Indies, is a small and intimate hotel with great class, much in the spirit of the island itself. For here, at the charming Beach Hotel, overlooking the Caribbean, each guest receives the personal attention & service for which Coralita has become known. Every room is on the beach where all watersports and activities are available nearby. Swimming pool & tennis court on location. UW fishing.

GRAND CASE BEACH CLUB 800-223-1588   75 Units: $175-290 BDFKOPRSTW

011-590-875187 EXT:25FAX Box 339, 97150 Grand Case, St. Martin, F.W.I. See: Under The Waves.

L'HABITATION DE LONVILLIERS 800-847-4249   253 Units: $190-390 BDFKOPRSTW

212-757-0225 212-586-5970 c/o Mondotels, 200 West 57th St. New York NY 10019. See: L'Habitation de Lonvilliers Diving.

LA BELLE CREOLE A CONRAD INTERNATION HTL 800-445-8667   156 Units: $225-490 BORSTW

212-980-6680 011-590-875866 301 Park Ave. Suite 1851 New York NY 10022.

LA BELLE GRAND CASE 011-590-878346   8 Units: $75-150 BDFKOSTW

97150 Grand Case St. Martin, F.W.I. The newest luxury Inn in St Martin, La Belle Grand Case offers year round cooling breezes, panoramic views of Anguilla and sits on one of the island's loveliest beaches amidst green sea grapes and picturesque West Indian houses. All apartments are ocean front, with airconditioning, livingroom & balcony. This is where artists paint & fishermen still head out to sea. Try snorkeling windsurfing, day-sailing, fishing and horseback riding. Island tours arranged.

LAGUNA BEACH HOTEL 800-223-6510   64 Units: $180-290 BDGKOPRTW

011-590-878997 212-759-5968FX Baie Nettle 97150 Saint Martin, F.W.I. This 3-Star Hotel is perfectly situated approximately one mile from Marigot between the sea and Simpson Bay. Each of the 64 airconditioned rooms features a water-view balcony, telephone, radio, TV with American channels and video. Watersports on the property include windsurfing, waterskiing & pedal boats. They offer beautiful nestled beaches and a wonderful lagoon, warm waters, soft sand, freshwater swimming pool, three tennis courts & golf at Mullet Bay.

LE GALION BEACH HOTEL 800-223-6510   62 Units: $130-175 BDFKORSTW

212-832-2277 011-590-873177 Box 1, 97150 Marigot St. Martin, F.W.I.

LE PIRATE HOTEL 800-666-5756   100 Units: $115-175 BDFKOPSW

011-590-877837 011-590-919669 97150 Marigot St. Martin, F.W.I.

LE ROYALE LOUISIANA 800-221-4542   75 Units: $95-147 GRT

011-590-878651 Av. du General de Gaulle, Marigot 97150 St. Martin, F.W.I. The Royale Louisiana with its enchanting and exotic charm is located in the heart of the busy capital of the French part of the island and right near the beaches, golf course, tennis courts and watersports. Le Royale Louisiana offers you "Comfort a la Francaise" with rooms and suites around a patio and is fully equipped with airconditioning, color television and VCR, direct line, office type desk, snack bar, telex, car rental, excursion desk.

St. Martin, French West Indies - Sports

L'HABITATION DE LONVILLIERS DIVING 800-847-4249

212-757-0225 011-590-873333 c/o Mondotels, 200 West 57th St. New York NY 10019. See: L'Habitation de Lonvilliers.

UNDER THE WAVES 011-590-875187   Divers FOSW

TX:919089 011-590-902187FX Grand Case Beach Club 97150 Grand Case, St. Martin, F.W.I. See: Grand Case Beach Club.

Hotel photographs courtesy: French West Indies Tourist Board (FWITB). Credit: D. Thim, C Aries, J. Petrocik, C. Graffin, M. Clement, R. Ockelmann, S. Goldsmith, L. Greifer, P. Kaplan, Martinique Tour Off., J. Rosenberg, Guadeloupe T. Off., Rel du Moulin, V. Brunt, M. Garanger.

In some cases, the descriptions included in this guide were provided to Travel & Sports by the hotel.

/Johnston

El Morro/Jones

/Jones

Travel & Sports Guide

Useful Facts

• Airline Connections   The busiest in the Caribbean, San Juan's international airport serves as connecting hub for 50 percent of air traffic in the region. There are dozens of direct flights to Puerto Rico from major US cities via American Airlines, Delta, Eastern, TWA and American Trans Air. From San Juan, make connections for inter-island flights to most other parts of the Caribbean. From either the international or municipal airports in San Juan, there are daily flights to other towns within Puerto Rico including Humacao, Ponce, Mayaguez, Aguadilla, Culebra and Vieques.

• Banking   Puerto Rico is a commonwealth of the United States and uses the US Dollar. Principal banks include the Banco de Ponce, Banco Popular, Chase Manhattan, City Bank, Royal Bank of Canada, Scotia Bank, though most major US banks have branches on the island. Banking hours are 9:00am to 2:30pm. Credit cards and traveler's checks are widely accepted.

• Courtesy & Dress   Puerto Ricans are gentle and friendly people; the island feels more like Latin America than the States. Swim wear is fine for the beach and leisure wear for the resorts, but elsewhere a little dressing up is in order. Nighttime in San Juan is somewhat formal -- fancy dresses for the ladies, jackets for men.

• Customs & Immigrations   There are no customs regulations or restrictions for US citizens. However, be prepared to have all of your bags X-rayed when returning home;

Puerto Rico

they are inspecting for agricultural products but will allow you to hand carry film.

• Driving   All the same rules as any part of the United States, except that the signposting is in Spanish, the distance markers in kilometers and the gas sold in litros (slightly larger than quarts).

• Electricity   US standards.

• Events & Holidays   All traditional US holidays, plus: Epiphany or Three Kings Day, a day for gift-giving (Jan. 6); Birthday of Eugenio De Hostos, Puerto Rican patriot and writer (Jan. 11); San Sebastian Street Fiesta in San Juan, featuring processions, dancing and paso fino horses on display in the old city (Jan. 18-20); Abolition Day (March 22); Jose de Diego's Birthday (April 17); St. John the Baptist Day, marked by feasting and dancing, particularly at the beach (June 23-24); Luiz Munoz Rivera's Birthday (July 17); Commonwealth Constitution Day (July 25); Dr. Jose Celso Barbosa's Birthday (July 27); and Puerto Rico Discovery Day (Nov. 19).

• Languages   Spanish is the principal language of the island. However, most everyone understands English and most speak at least some. You will, however, feel most comfortable if you too understand and speak some Spanish.

• Medical   Among the finest in the Caribbean. There are physicians and hospitals in all major cities and stateside insurance policies are honored here. Puerto Rico has two recompression chambers, both used by the US Navy, at the University of Puerto Rico at Mayaguez and at Roosevelt Rose. There's even a specialty dive-medicine staff at Mayaguez to serve Navy divers.

• Off-Season Dates & Rates   Rates drop 25 to 50% from April 15 to December 15 at many of the resorts who depend on international tourists. At certain more rural locations, the bulk of business is from Puerto Ricans who vacation during the summer months; hence off-season at those accommodations is during the winter months. Holidays (Christmas, Easter, Thanksgiving and long weekends) are very, very busy since many of the Puerto Ricans who have emigrated to the States travel to visit relatives at these times.

• Taxes & Tipping   There is a 6.6% sales and hotel tax; this and other taxes will be added to your bill. A 15% tip is customary for

/Hobby

restaurants and nightclubs; check to see whether the tip has already been added to the bill.

• Taxi Fares Taxis are metered throughout the island, by law and are readily available at tourist locations. All cabs have special lights and license plates. Traveling from the international airport to downtown San Juan costs about $8; you may be surcharged for baggage.

• Telephone Puerto Rico has modern, reliable telephone service. A local call costs only 10 cents. Information is 123. For directory assistance in other parts of Puerto Rico, dial 129 first; for overseas information dial 128. The direct long distance dialing code is 137; for person-to-person, collect and calling card calls dial 130. To call elsewhere in the 809 area code, dial 137 plus the seven-digit number. At the center of the phone book are blue pages in English; this section is reproduced and is available at most hotels and the airport.

• Time Atlantic Standard (Eastern Standard + 1 hour). The island doesn't observe Daylight Savings Time, so during that part of the year the time is the same as Eastern Standard.

• Weather Puerto Rico enjoys year round summery temperatures, averaging in the mid-80's November to May. In the mountains, it's about 10 degrees cooler in the summer and 20 degrees cooler in the winter. Most days have brief showers, but rarely is there a sunless day. The north coast gets twice as much rain as the south coast. The dry season is December to March.

Introduction

"Transculturation" might not get you any points in Scrabble, but Puerto Ricans know what it means: paella and Big Macs, salsa and Madonna, sugar cane fields and petrochemical plants, 15th century convents and 21st century hotels. Many islanders today say they have two parents - - a Spanish mother and an American father.

Both heritages are apparent. You can explore Old World towns, 400-year-old forts and convents and Gothic cathedrals or lose yourself amid modern floor shows, championship golf courses, designer stores, art galleries and symphonies -- all on the same day. The medieval is often adjacent to more modern conveniences such as excellent telephones, utilities and roads. The only stumbling block for most tourists is the language, but this is more an inconvenience than an obstacle. Most Puerto Ricans understand English, though some are shy about butchering it in conversation with those whom they call "Continentals." This reluctance is easily overcome; just mutilate a little

Puerto Rico

Spanish and most people will quickly venture their undoubtedly more proficient English.

There's yet a third heritage that gives this island so distinct a flavor. Unlike elsewhere in the Caribbean, some Indians survived here as did their name for the island, "Borinquen," which is still used. The Indian bond with the land still inspires Puerto Rican culture; everywhere you go, well-tended gardens flourish, even beside the most weathered shack.

It's easy to understand why the Indians viewed this land as sacred. Rain forest, desert, beach, mountain, cave, ocean, river -- Puerto Rico offers astonishing variety.

Ecology

Puerto Rico is the easternmost and smallest of the Greater Antilles islands. Mountains cover 60% of this 110 by 35 mile island; the central range bisects the island as it climbs to its highest altitude of 4,389 feet at Cerro la Punta.

Numerous rivers flow down from the mountains to distinct coastal plains. The northern (Atlantic) coast is wet and green. On the southern (Caribbean) coast prickly pear cactus, yucca and mesquite grow in an "Arizona" landscape. Towards the northwest, an unusual topography of haystack hills, caves and sinkholes mark the terrain. In the southwest, mangroves have created a unique canal system.

The highlight of Puerto Rico's endless natural beauty may well be the cloud-cloaked El Yunque Peak in the Caribbean National Forest. This 28,000 acres is all that remains of the vast rain forest that once covered much of the island (indeed, much of the entire northern Caribbean). A moist hike or horseback ride takes you past 240 species of trees, some thousands of years old, 50 species of ferns, 20 varieties of wild orchids and a riotous multitude of flowers.

Another unique ecological environment can be found on Mona Island, 50 miles off the west coast of Puerto Rico. Like the Galapagos Islands, this virgin, largely unexplored island has species both indigenous and rare. Mona is a protected island, under the management of the National Park Service and the Puerto Rican Natural Resources Department. Accessible only by a sometimes difficult, long boat ride, the island is available for sport diving to those who make special advance arrangements and are willing to rough it.

History

When Columbus dropped anchor at Borinquen (Puerto Rico's earlier name), he was greeted with offerings of gold nuggets. The Taino Indians soon regretted their naive generosity, however, as waves of fortune-hunting Spaniards descended on their peaceful island.

Thanks in part to the enthusiasm of ambitious Ponce de Leon, a lieutenant of Columbus', Puerto Rico ("rich port") quickly became Spain's most important military outpost in the Caribbean. Concerned about potential threats from European enemies, Spain began constructing massive defenses around San Juan.

Spanish might was required to quell repeated rebellions by desperate Indians and to keep watch over the slaves imported to work the growing sugar and tobacco plantations, although fewer Africans were brought here than to most Caribbean islands. The Spanish settlers brought no women on their ships. To populate the country, the Spanish took Indian women. This historic intermingling has resulted in a contemporary Puerto Rico without racial problems.

When Puerto Rico's meager gold supply was exhausted, islanders struggled to develop an agricultural economy. Cattle, sugar cane, tobacco and coffee were the main investments. However, a series of repressive regimes failed to make the island either profitable or docile. Finally the Spanish granted Puerto Rico semi-autonomy. Islanders celebrated when they elected their first free government, but a few months later the American Army invaded. In the treaty ending the Spanish-American War of 1898, Puerto Rico was ceded to the United States.

Puerto Rico remains a US territory; its residents became US citizens in 1917 and in 1952 the island assumed the status of a semi-autonomous commonwealth voluntarily associated with the US. The debate continues as to whether Puerto Rico should seek independence, become the 51st state or continue with the status quo. Since World War II Puerto Rico has developed a strong industrial base and today is a leading exporter of electronic equipment and pharmaceutics.

Exploring

We'll start our tour with San Juan, where glamorous one-year-old high-rises overlook 400-year-old churches. The population is just under one million or a third of the entire island. Part of this city, one of the oldest in the Western Hemisphere, is a chic glamour strip of hotels and casinos resembling the Miami oceanfront. But if you like history, Spain or just graceful buildings, you'll love Old San Juan. It's a 465-year-old neighborhood that was originally conceived as a military stronghold, but its seven square blocks have evolved into a charming residential and commercial district. When the United Nations designated world-class historic sites such as the Taj Mahal, it also named six monuments in Old San Juan.

Begin your tour at the Tourism Company at 301 San Juan Street or at nearby La Casita Tourist Information Center near Pier One.

Art lovers will want to visit the Fine Arts Museum at the corner of Fortaleza and Cristo or the San Juan Museum of Art and History at Norzagaray and Mac Arthur, which exhibits Puerto Rican art and hosts concerts and festivals. Opera buffs should stop at the Pablo Casals Museum at 101 San Sebastian Plaza de San Jose.

El Morro -- the word itself sounds powerful and this six-level fortress certainly was. Rising 140 feet above the sea, its 18-foot-thick walls proved a formidable defense. It fell only once, in 1538, to a land assault by the Earl of Cumberland's forces. They were driven out, however, by dysentery. The fort is a maze of tunnels, dungeons, barracks, outposts and ramps.

Begun in 1540, The San Juan Cathedral is an authentic and rare New World example of medieval architecture. Look for its elegant circular staircase and four vaulted Gothic ceilings. The body of Ponce de Leon has lain in a marble tomb here since 1913, close to the mummy of a Roman martyr, San Pio, interred in 1862.

San Jose Church, the second oldest in the Western Hemisphere, is noted for its spectacular vaulted ceilings and its magnificent 16th century crucifix.

Casa Blanca was built as a reward for Governor Ponce de Leon, who died in Florida before he could move in. His family, however, stayed in residence for over 250 years. Following restoration, Casa Blanca is now a museum of 16th and 17th century family life.

Another way to see many of Old San Juan's sights is to cruise or tour the harbor by ferry or tour boat.

/Hobby

/Hobby

Puerto Rico

As Puerto Rico's population and industrialization grew, the city spread from its origins in Old San Juan. Several delightful attractions in and around San Juan, listed below, are easily reached by bus, taxi or car.

Rio Piedras was a separate municipality from its founding in 1714 until united with San Juan in 1951. It is home to a lovely botanical garden located at the Agricultural Experimental Station.

Those willing to confront the metro traffic, can return to the coast along Ponce de Leon Avenue and will eventually reach the Fine Arts Center. It's the largest, best-equipped facility in the Caribbean, hosting internationally and locally renowned performers, concerts, plays and operas.

The fastest-growing city of Puerto Rico, Bayamon offers a historic zone that includes a plaza, church and mall.

The route between Bayamon and Catano passes the grounds of the Barrilito Rum Plant, site of a 200-year old family house and a 150-year old windmill.

Exploring "en la isla" is an opportunity to explore rain forests, mountains and varied beaches. This term, meaning "out on the island," refers to anywhere beyond the San Juan metropolitan area.

There are so many places to go and so many ways to get there that your choice of route will depend on your own scenic preferences. You can stay on coastal roads to circle the entire island or take interior routes through the rain forest and mountains.

If you head east out of San Juan towards Luquillo Beach, there's a turnoff a few miles outside that will take you to El Yunque and the 28,000-acre Caribbean National Forest, the only tropical rain forest in the US National Forest system. Among the crags, waterfalls, ferns and wild flowers are many marked trails to enjoy on foot or rental horse.

If you return to or stay on the coastal highway, you'll soon reach Luquillo Beach, which offers a full range of recreational opportunities. The road continues into Fajardo, once a sleepy fishing village on the tip of a miniature peninsula, it is now a major sailing and boating center.

Many visitors head for Vieques, some 6 miles east of Fajardo. Snorkeling is excellent, especially at Blue Beach. The island also offers phosphorescent Mosquito Bay.

Halfway between Puerto Rico and St. Thomas lies an archipelago consisting of a main island, Culebra, and over 20 smaller islets and an outstanding coral reef. Travelers to Culebra are charmed by its calm atmosphere, beautiful white-sand beaches, clear waters and incredible reef.

With a population of 300,000, Ponce is Puerto Rico's second-largest city. The beautiful downtown Plaza is a worthwhile stop, with lovely fountains, a cathedral and local bench-sitting citizens. The outrageous red-and-black, century-old wooden firehouse, Parque de Bombas, is a landmark and still used.

From Ponce, follow coastal Highway 2 west past attractive beaches and an unusual dry cactus forest. At Route 304, turn seaward to La Parguera, a small and friendly fishing village. Plan to stay past sunset on a moonless night at nearby Phosphorescent Bay where a special variety of luminescent plankton, "dinoflagellates," glow like blue fire in the dark. As you stir your hand through the water, you'll leave sparkling swirls.

Perhaps the most scenic of routes is the appropriately-named Panoramic Route, connecting Yabucoa in the southeast with Mayaguez on the west coast by way of the Cordillera Central, the mountain backbone of Puerto Rico.

Sooner or later, you'll get to the port city of Mayaguez. Its elegant plaza has a stone walk and

Golf at Palmas del Mar

benches, bronze figures and a statue of Christopher Columbus on a globe pedestal.

Rincon to the north, is nestled between La Cadena Mountains and a series of beaches facing the Atlantic to the north and the Caribbean to the south. The half-dozen reef-lined Atlantic beaches have become a winter mecca for skilled surfers since the World Surfing Championship was held here nearly twenty years ago.

The Aguadilla area beyond is best known to visitors as the center for mundillo lace-making and for picturesque, coconut-palm-shaded beaches, which extend along northwestern Puerto Rico from Crash Boat around Borinquen Point to Jobos and Isabela. Some 50 miles west of Mayaguez is rugged Mona Island, where sea birds share their colonies with yard-long iguanas.

Food

As you might expect in any cosmopolitan city, you can get nearly every type of international cuisine in San Juan. In the city, expect to pay top dollar for dining, especially if your taste runs towards fashionable decor and formal service. If you're a bit more adventurous or on a budget, opportunities for delicious, cheap and moderately priced meals exist, even in the city. Puerto Rico still has a significant agriculture industry, which means you can eat fresh, local food at a reasonable price.

Rum is the national drink. Much is still made on the island and is quite cheap, usually cheaper than the cocktail mixer. Some of the more famous Puerto Rican brands include Bacardi (formerly of Cuba), Don Q and Barrilito. There are several tasty Puerto Rican-brewed beers as well. For those who prefer non-alcoholic beverages order fresh fruit punch made from any combination of locally grown tropical fruits.

Try a couple of genuine Puerto Rican meals as part of your island explorations. If you're en la isla, you can get a feast of rice, beans, vegetables, plantains, chicken or seafood, prepared Puerto Rican-style, for well under $5.00. In San Juan, the Puerto Rico Tourism Company hosts a LeLoLai cultural festival nightly at various hotels. Included is an evening's folkloric entertainment and a buffet of native delights. In addition to Puerto Rican cuisine, there are also many Spanish and Cuban restaurants.

A Puerto Rican favorite are pasteles, which look like small rectangular packages. Actually, they're ripe plantains stuffed with beef or pork and wrapped in banana leaves tied with string. Another staple is tostones, a side dish of green plantains. Along with arroz con ganduras (yellow stewed rice with pigeon peas) and lechon asado (whole roasted piglet), you have a meal. For desert, consider tembleque (coconut pudding), flan (light caramel custard) or sopa borracha (cake

Puerto Rico

Klugel/Jones

with a heavy dose of rum). Complete the meal with strong, Puerto Rican coffee.

Nightlife

The nightlife of Puerto Rico is unequalled anywhere else in the Caribbean. There are international-caliber casinos at the Carib Inn, Caribe Hilton, Condado Beach, La Concha, Condado Plaza, Dupont Plaza, El San Juan, Quality Royale, The Palace and Ramada Hotels. Out on the island, you can gamble at the Hyatt Regency, Cerromar Beach and Humacao. Men are required to wear jackets at most casinos, but don't worry if forget to pack yours, as free courtesy jackets are available to all who need them.

San Juan is the cultural and entertainment capital of the Caribbean. This is partly because Puerto Ricans are festive night people, partly because of enterprising Cuban refugees and partly because of transculturation with the United States. In sum, there's a lot of night activity and cultural diversity in the theatre, dance, opera, concerts, nightclubs and galleries.

Also worth experiencing is an evening of La Plena, Puerto Rico's traditional music, featuring instruments which are handmade on the island -- the guicharo, cuatro (a small guitar), guitars, bongos, maracas, the timbal, panderos (large tambourines) and congas. Ballad themes vary, but typically tell stories about important happenings in the neighborhood or send messages of love.

Every town celebrates fiestas patronales, a six-to-ten day party honoring their patron saint. Enjoy dancing in the streets, music and fiestas.

The free, readily available, monthly guide for tourists, Que Pasa, provides details on patron-saint festivities, nightclubs, music and dance, folkloric festivals, theater, film and other special events during your visit. You can also check the newspapers; the Sa Juan Star is the English newspaper.

Shopping

Puerto Rico is the world's leading rum producer and many visitors buy a few bottles. Take note that there can be a duty bringing alcohol stateside. Another bargain is cigars -- grown, shaped, filled and rolled on the island.

Foremost among Puerto Rico's traditional crafts is the carving of santos, small wooden figures of saints or religious scenes. Mundillo, intricate handmade bobbin lace originally produced in Spain, is fashioned by artisans into doilies, bands, collars, tablecloths and other dainty items. There are two traditional styles: entredos with two straight borders and puntilla with one straight border and one scalloped border.

Another popular craft is masks, such as the coconut vejigantes used in Loiza saint festivities

Puerto Rico 8 (184)

/Jones

or papier mache masks popular at Ponce Carnival. Fine hammocks are still made in Puerto Rico. Musicians seeking cuatros or full-sized guitars should go straight to the artisans at Ciales or Ceiba. On weekends, there's an artisans' market with dozens of stalls at El Centro Convention Center.

Looking for designer clothes, luggage, shoes and homesick for a mall? Take your credit card for an elegant stroll along Ashford and Magdalena Avenues in Condado, whose 200-plus stores constitute the largest shopping center in the Caribbean.

Sports

Long a tourist mecca for those seeking its city glamour and nightlife, Puerto Rico also warrants attention as a sports playground.

The most popular spectator sports in Puerto Rico are baseball, basketball, horse racing and cock-fighting. Professional baseball is in season October through January; cock-fighting runs November through August.

Sports enthusiasts will also find horseback riding along the palm-lined beaches, tennis and year round championship golf courses. But real adventure lies in Puerto Rico's watersports, including scuba diving, snorkeling, sailing, windsurfing, surfing, deep-sea fishing, lake fishing, boating and ocean swimming. You can get a paddle boat, water skis or almost any aquatic toy.

• Camping

Hundreds of beaches rim Puerto Rico and its offshore sister islands, ranging from the busy stretches alongside metropolitan hotels to deserted beauties next to rural pasture land. In Puerto Rico, all beach front property is legally accessible to the public; however, there are many public beaches with easy access and services for the visitor. For details and information about camping, call the Department of Recreation and Sports at 722-1551.

• Fishing & Sailing

In Puerto Rico, you can charter a sail or motor boat, privately or shared, with or without crew, for a half-day, day or week from a variety of vendors across the island, from downtown to Palmas del Mar to La Parguera.

Out in deep water, abundant white and blue marlin, bonito, albacore, Allison tuna, bonefish, tarpon, jack, king, dolphinfish, sailfish, grouper and wahoo are targets for the hook. Deep-sea fishing enthusiasts can participate in many tournaments in Puerto Rico; thirty world records have been broken here. Professional guides are available for hire.

Inland, numerous lakes in the hills and mountains have been stocked with catfish, large-mouth

/Jones

bass, peacock bass, tilapia and sunfish. Anglers with their own equipment can get details about fishing holes from the Department of Natural Resources (722-5938).

• Hiking

For hikers, there are Commonwealth Forest Reserves, scattered around the island. These range from bird-filled mangrove forests along the coast to dense sierra palm forests in the mountains. Most unusual are the reserves in karst country, extending from Manati to Aguadilla. For information, contact the Department of Natural Resources Forest Service (724-3724).

• Surfing

The Puerto Rican surf has challenged tube-shooters and curl-riders since the World Championships were hosted at Rincon in 1968. In and around San Juan, summer sees surfers head to La Concha and Aviones in Pinones; in winter they ride Pine Grove in Isla Verde, Stop Eight and Condado Beach Lagoon. Arecibo and La Pared in Luquillo keep surfers happy on the north coast year round while they head to Los Tubos next to Tortuguero Lagoon in Vega Baja only in the winter. Up in the northwest corner, Aguadilla and Jobos, near Isabela, are the year round spots; Rincon and Punta Higuero lure winter wave-catchers. Surfers also ride Ensenada Honda in Culebra.

• Diving

Several factors make diving here delightful. Freshwater run-offs attract teeming multitudes of fish, including large pelagics not normally seen so close to shore. Also, since so few divers have explored these waters, coral thrives in astonishing abundance.

Another asset is the dive operators. The Puerto Rico Water Sports Federation, an alliance of Puerto Rican-owned watersport businesses, is dedicated to rendering services to local and international tourists. Member businesses have regular hours and services. They must be fully insured and meet all legal requirements of doing business in Puerto Rico. Membership is not automatic and depends on an interview and site inspection in addition to meeting established criteria. Federation members are committed to the goal of providing reliable, professional, safe, quality watersport activities for tourists. Puerto Rico's waters are regulated by the US Coast Guard.

Volcanic Puerto Rico is encircled by a fringing reef that follows the shoreline and extends into bays and inlets. Because frequent rains and fresh water rivers flow from her mountains to the sea, Puerto Rican coastal waters are prone to be a little murkier than the rest of the Caribbean. There are a few places where visibility exceeds 100 feet, but even the more normal range of 70 feet is still a good three times what you're lucky to get in California or much of the States. Plus, the run-off attracts fish -- and mammoth "mermaids."

Mermaids? That's what sailors reported when they first saw manatees. Though at one time common in the Caribbean, we know of no other island that can now claim their presence. Another Puerto Rican treat is the Spring migration of the humpback whales.

San Juan and the island's Northern Coast have several good learn-to-dive locations. Experienced certified divers will want to head for the dive sites along the northwest, south and northeastern shores. Much of the reef and underwater world of Puerto Rico and her sister islets is relatively unexplored. It doesn't take much persuasion to convince most dive operators to take you out where no man or woman has dived before. Customized trips, for small and large groups, can be arranged with advance notice. It's their business to serve US divers and they love to dive.

• North Coast Dive Sites

San Juan. In the shadows of the glamorous, high-rise Caribe Hilton, the casino-to-coral time is a matter of minutes, for right here you can do two interesting shore dives. The Inside Reef, so named because it is completely enclosed by a barrier, hosts over 50 varieties of tropical fish you can feed by hand. This dive is shallow and protected. The Outer Reef has caves, caverns, the occasional lobster and great photography opportunities on clear days. Caribe Aquatic Adventures, a full service dive shop, is on the premises of the Hilton.

Fajardo. Snorkelers here can enjoy shallow waters near the beach; divers will want to take boats to deeper areas and to the offshore islands of Icacos, Palominos and Palminitos. Mangroves and coconut palms tuft these offshore islands, surrounded by gin-clear water. Below, brilliant tropical fish swim around soft sea fans and castles of coral structures, in 12 to 30 feet of water. You can arrange for a trip via Fajardo, including land transportation from San Juan, with Mundo Submarino, Caribe Aquatic Adventures or Caribbean School of Aquatics. From Fajardo, there are also various boats departing for Vieques and Culebra.

• East Coast Dive Sites

Palmas Del Mar. Here, where the coastline overlooks cloud-capped El Yunque Rain Forest, look for whales as they make their annual migration taking them between Puerto Rico and the US Virgin Islands. On a slightly different tack, you

can also take a monkey-watching cruise to Cayo Santiago (Monkey Island) where scientists from all over the world travel to study the 800 macaques (or rhesus) monkeys inhabiting the island. Brought from Africa in the 1930's, the family and social habits of these monkeys have been closely observed since then. The entire island is a laboratory and visitors are not permitted on land. But you can anchor in 6 feet of water and watch the monkeys from a boat (the snorkeling here is good as well).

Basslet Reef is a marvelous mile-long dive spot only five minutes from the harbor. Ranging from 35 to 60 feet deep, the reef features an abundance of marine life, several overhangs, caves and tunnels.

Only 15 minutes off the coast from Palmas is The Drift, where you can cruise along with many species of tropical fish among stands of large sponges.

"The Reserve" is for experienced divers, running between 65-90 feet. With excellent visibility

Puerto Rico

(75-150 feet), it is a great place to photograph the myriad blue chromis, butterflys and morays that frequent this site. The angels here are big (as large as hubcaps) and lucky divers will encounter playful porpoises and even a curious whale.

Another site is <u>Vieques Island</u>. Waters are very clear in this area of reefs and grass beds with many dives in less than 50 feet. Impressive stands of elkhorn coral break the surface in many places. Grouper, angelfish, moray and lobster -- make appearances and large numbers of barracuda frequent the area. Mature conches are surprisingly abundant as are giant barrel sponges. Do not be surprised by a curious porpoise in a shallow reef. Popular sites here include Green Beach, Dog's Paw and Caballo Blanco and there is a lot of virgin diving territory to explore. The Palmas del Mar is serviced by Coral Head Divers, located at the Palmas del Mar Resort.

<u>Culebra</u>. The archipelago of Culebra is a sleepy divers' paradise awaiting discovery just a half-hour plane ride from San Juan. There are affordable tourist accommodations and services, including Caribbean Marine Services and others.

Along the northern west coast of Culebra is Impact Area, which abounds with schools of small reef fish and live corals. Fan corals, 4 to 5 feet across and huge gorgonians thrive here. Schools of blue chromis hover over larger brain corals and star corals. This is one healthy coral reefs. Top of the reef is 40 or 50 feet down, with another 20-to-30 foot drop to the sandy bottom. This is an excellent reef for photography, with rarely any current.

Off Culebra's west coast are three tiny islands. Here, large boulders are strewn atop one another, creating multiple hiding spots for schools of fish. At times these schools are so large you cannot see through them. The Arch, north of the northernmost cay, is a huge rock formation through which you swim into a large central hole. Corals have grown under the archway and photography is a must. Maximum depth is 50 feet.

The waters around the southern cay are also strewn with boulders. Rock Wall on one side starts at a depth of 15 feet and drops to 50 feet. Along this wall are schools of grunts, angelfish and jacks. There are so many fish of so many varieties you don't know where to look first. There is a current here. At Amber Jack Hole to the south, the large boulders cover the sandy bottom. This is a cleaning station where thousands of schooling fish live. Also expect schools of amberjacks, french angels,

grunts, squirrelfish and rays. Some tricky current at times. Bring your camera.

• South Coast Dive Sites

<u>Ponce</u>. Puerto Rico's south coast is popular with local divers, largely because of the Great Trench of the South (El Gran Beril del Sur), which runs from the Virgin Islands, passing along the southern edge of Vieques and the continental shelf, to just off Cabo Rojo on Puerto Rico's west coast. It's home to a delightful variety of marine creatures and offers plenty of drop-offs between 50 and 80 feet in depth, ideal for sport diving.

Caja de Muertos (Coffin Island), Cayo Cardona, Cayo Ratones and Cayo Caribe form a horseshoe-shaped barrier reef from Ponce to Tallaboa to the west. Only 15 to 35 minutes from Ponce, the reefs are 15 to 40 feet off the islands and teem with life.

Formerly a fisherman's colony, Coffin Island is now a park administered by the Department of Natural Resources. You can dive from the shore to depths of 15 to 40 feet. Since this is a preserve, there's no spearfishing; in fact, many fish have been tamed. A marked, snorkelers' nature trail is currently under development. Camping is permitted on the island. Marine Sports & Dive Shop, based in Ponce, offers regular dive excursions here. San Juan-based Mundo Submarino often brings divers here as well. The Coffin Island ferry runs on the weekend from the Ponce pier.

<u>Bahia de Guanica</u>. On the southwest tip of the island, take a 100-foot dive off the continental shelf, over the 1,200-foot drop-off below. There are trenches and crevices with all kinds of marine life and some big fish. Visibility here is usually 100 feet, occasionally up to 200 feet. The drop-off is about 4 miles from the bay. There are also shallow coral dives in the area. Mundo Submarino leads boat excursions here.

• West Coast Dive Sites

<u>La Parguera</u>. Roads allow good access to the southwest corner of the island, where there is plenty of unexplored diving for the adventurer. This beautiful area, 2 1/2 hours from San Juan or 1 hour from Ponce, also offers unique underwater ecosystems at Phosphorescent Bay and in the mangrove canals. There are several dive operators including Parguera Divers, in La Parguera.

A 25-minute boat ride brings you to the wall, which starts at 45 feet, slopes to 90 and then drops-off thousands of feet. The visibility is usually about 100 feet. Shelf Edge is an area at 130 feet

/Johnston

Puerto Rico

Caribe Aquatic Adventures

Coral Head Divers

Marine Sports

Parguera Divers

where unusual canals run perpendicular to shore. Big fish are often seen between the high coral walls here. Nearby is Las Vosas, a shallower dive with coral head patches on holes with a sandy bottom. Pinnacles, 15 minutes from shore, is a popular spot for rays and moray eels. Here the coral is unusually arranged in formations like successive Christmas trees at a depth of about 60 feet, with visibility typically 60 to 75 feet.

The area also has many interesting shallow dives. Vertical patches of coral on a sandy bottom mark Majimo Reed, only 6 minutes from shore in 20 to 60 feet of water. Close by is Gato (Cat) Reef, starting in 10 feet and sloping to 50 to 65 feet. Gato is a popular night dive.

The scientific research area of Enrique Reef gives the night diver an opportunity to immerse him- or herself in 30 to 50 feet of phosphorescence and is a mere 5 minutes from shore.

Mona Island. Definitely for the adventuresome, a 5-6 hour boat ride from the west coast, takes you to the wildlife reserves of Mona Island and its mini-twin Monito. They are prime dive spots for those willing to spend a few days rough-

ing it. Many virgin, living reefs with abundant marine life are found at depths averaging 80 feet. You will also see seals playing by the rocky cliffs. This trip is available only through Marine Sports & Dive Shop and Parguera Divers.

• North Coast Dive Sites

Isabela. A spectacular beach dive off Bajuras Playa. Swim just 40 feet to the first of a series of underwater caves and swim-throughs stretching hundreds of yards along the beach. Schools of blue tang, sergeants, spotted drums, angels and rays and invertebrates such as lobster, crab and shrimp inhabit the caves. Dive the Isabela and Aguadilla areas with La Cueva Submarina in Isabela.

Aguadilla. The area around Aguadilla, particularly the Crash Boat site, has long been popular with local divers, especially when the wind blows from the NE and other sites are too rough to dive. It's a beach dive, just 30 feet from the old Naval dock. Swim among the old pilings down a gradual slope to a reef teeming with fish and covered with coral.

Accommodations

CARIBE HILTON INTERNATIONAL 809-721-0303   667 Units: $189-285 BDFOPRSTW
TLX: 2733 Box 1872 San Juan PR 00903. The Caribe Hilton International is a self-contained world of exciting activities and entertainment, set amid 17 lush tropical acres. San Juan's Premier Resort is ideally situated between Old and New San Juan and located on the area's only private beach. See: Caribe Aquatic Adventures.

CARIBE PLAYA 809-839-6339
Highway #3, Kilometer 152.5 Patillas PR 00723.

CLUB SEABOURNS, INC. 809-742-3169
Box 357 Culebra PR 00645. See: Caribbean Marine Services.

CONDADO PLAZA HOTEL & CASINO 800-468-8588   565 Units: $130-195 BDOPRSTW
809-721-1000 999 Ashford Avenue, Santruce Condado PR 00907. See: Coral Head Divers.

EL SAN JUAN HOTEL & CASINO 800-468-2818   392 Units: $280-335 B
809-791-1000 Box 2872 San Juan PR 00902. See: Coral Head Divers.

FAMILY GUEST HOUSE 809-863-1193   15 Units: $25-56
Carretera Croabas 987 HC-00867 Box 21399 Fajardo PR 00648. See: Scuba Shop.

FLAMINCO RESORT & FISHING CLUB 809-742-3144   F
Box 241 Culebra PR 00641. See: Caribbean Marine Services.

HOLIDAY INN OF PONCE 800-465-4329   120 Units: $92-125 R
Ponce PR 00731. See: Marine Sports & Dive Shop.

LA CONCHA HOTEL 800-468-2822   233 Units: $135-245 BDRTW
809-721-6090 Ashford Avenue Box 4195, Condado San Juan PR 00905. See: Caribbean School of Aquatics, Inc..

MELIA HOTEL 800-221-6509   77 Units: $50-65 R
Box 1431 Ponce PR 00731. See: Marine Sports & Dive Shop.

PALMAS DEL MAR 800-221-4874   205 Units: $130-390 BDFGORSTW
809-852-6000 TLX:3450830 Box 2020 Humacao PR 00661. A unique residential resort on 2,750 acres of lush tropical beauty by the sea, 40-min. from downtown San Juan. There are restaurants galore, and activities include: Scuba, snorkeling, deep-sea fishing, sailing, waterskiing, windsurfing, and other watersports; golf, tennis, horseback riding, cycling, jogging, a wellness center, a casino and more. The Scuba package includes 7 days and 6 nights for $1150 to $1400 depending on the time of year. See: Coral Head Divers.

PARADOR GUAJATACA 809-895-3070   38 Units: $52-60 BR
Box H Quebradillas PR 00742. See: La Cueva Submarina.

PARADOR VILLA PARGUERA 800-223-6530   50 Units: $37-55 BDOPRSW
809-899-3975 Route 304, La Parguera Lajas PR 00667. See: Parguera Divers.

POSADA PORLAMAR 809-899-4015   16 Units: $25-55
Box 405, La Parguera Lajas PR 00667. See: Parguera Divers.

TRAVELODGE OF PUERTO RICO 809-728-1300   91 Units: $115-130 BR
Box 6007, Loiza Station Isla Verde Avenue, Santurce PR 00913.

Information

PUERTO RICO TOURISM COMPANY 800-223-6530
212-541-6630 809-721-2400 1290 Avenue of the Americas New York NY 10104. IN FLORIDA CALL: 305-381-8915, IN CALIFORNIA CALL: 213-874-5991

Sports

BENITEZ FISHING CHARTERS 809-703-0292   F
809-724-6265 Box 5141 San Juan PR 00906.

CARIBBEAN MARINE SERVICES 809-742-3555   Divers: $50-50 D
Box 467 Culebra PR 00645. See: Flaminco Resort & Fishing Club.

CARIBBEAN SCHOOL OF AQUATICS, INC. 809-728-6606   Divers: $84-84 D
809-723-4270 809-723-4740 Box 4195 San Juan PR 00905. Located in the center of San Juan, they offer a convenient and unique alternative for your dive vacation. Their dive trip starts with an hour tour of Puerto Rico which will take you past the rain forest on the Innovation, a large party boat, to the small offshore islands for a day of adventure & diving. Lunch included on this full day trip. Instructors are NAUI and PADI certified. See: La Concha Hotel.

CARIBE AQUATIC ADVENTURES 809-721-0303
30 Divers: $70-70 DFOS

809-724-1307 Caribe Hilton Int'l, Box 1872 San Juan PR 00903. At the Caribe Hilton International. They offer the best diving in San Juan. NAUI and PADI instruction (resort course through Assist. Instructor), name brand equipment for sale, enclosed reef and cave dive areas (right at hotel), 4 dives daily. Deserted island day dive and snorkel trip available at least 3 times weekly. Three day liveaboard excursions on 60 foot Feadship, 6 in a group, starting summer 1989. NAUI PRO Facility located at a Dream Resort. See: Caribe Hilton International.

CASTILLO WATER SPORTS 809-791-6195
FOS

809-726-5752 Doncella 27, Punta Las Marias Sauturce PR 00913.

CORAL HEAD DIVERS 800-221-4874
71 Divers: $50-75 D

809-850-7208 Box CUHF Humacao PR 00601. A NAUI Pro-Facility with PADI instruction for the experienced and beginning diver. Located at the Palmas del Mar resort. They have three comfortable, motor vessels. Dive sites are 10-15 minute boat rides. They include virgin spots where the marine life is abundant and sociable, caves, walls and vibrant coral. Excursions and dives are available on a regular daily schedule all year long. See: Palmas Del Mar, Condado Plaza, El San Juan Hotel & Casino..

LA CUEVA SUBMARINA 809-872-3903
Divers: $45-45 D

Box 151 Isabela PR 00662. Offering excellent shore diving. La Cueva is a full service diving facility with packages at several nearby inns. They offer fresh and saltwater diving in magnificent caves, and in one of the longest underground rivers in the world. (NAUI & NASE). See: Parador Guajataca.

MARINE SPORTS & DIVE SHOP 809-844-6175
28 Divers: $50-70 D

Perla Del Sur Z-507, Box 7711 Ponce PR 00732. Dive the crystal clear, warm waters of Southern Puerto Rico. They will take you to CAJA DE MUERTO island where you can dive the drop-off or just enjoy the coral trail. Personal dive environment with an air of congenial informality catering to all levels of divers. Their highly qualified staff is ready to assist and advise. Small or large groups are accommodated easily. Full dive facility, sales, rental, repair. PADI & NASE. One day resort courses avail. See: Holiday Inn of Ponce & Melia Hotel.

MUNDO SUBMARINO 809-791-5764
Divers: $55-55 DO

809-768-6467 Laguna Gardens Shopping Center Isla Verde PR 00913. Full dive shop facility with air, repair service, rentals and sales. Beach diving trips to the east, south & west coasts. Packages include, air, tanks, bc and weights. Transportation available. Catering to divers of all experience levels and to snorkelers. For groups of 6 or more, special rates are available.

PARGUERA DIVERS 809-899-4171
12 Divers: $30-50 DO

809-899-3805 Box 514 Lajas PR 00667. Full service PADI/NAUI facility, with sales, repairs & rentals. Walking distance to shore and accommodations. They offer 1-on-1 instruction, from resort and certification courses up to instructor. A great place to complete your open-water dives, or work on your continuing education. Daily snorkel and two-tank dive trips. Some of the best wall diving in the Caribbean. One hour photo & overnight slides. Special packages from 2-days to 1 week inc. accom. See: Parador Villa Parguera.

SAN JUAN FISHING CHARTERS 809-725-0139
F

809-723-0415 Box 1698 Old San Juan Station PR 00903.

SCUBA SHOP 809-863-8465
Divers: $40-50 D

Villa Marina Shopping Center # 6 Fajardo PR 00648. Diving and snorkeling services are available. Night dives as well. This shop offers excursions to one of the most popular dive and boating destinations in Puerto Rico. PADI and NAUI affiliations. See: Family Guest House.

SPREAD EAGLE 809-863-1905
1 Boats S

809-723-0415 Box 445 Puerto Real PR 00740. Day trips to Icacos Island for snorkeling, beach combing, buffet lunches and lazing in the sun. This 40-foot catamaran is coastguard certified for up to 30-people.

Puerto Rico 16 (192)

Saba

Travel & Sports Guide

Saba

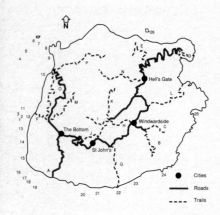

Useful Facts

• Airline Connections   Winair (tel. 2255) flies five times a day between Saba and Sint Maarten, daily to Statia. Cruise ships call on Saba occasionally, regularly scheduled stops are made by Windjammer's Barefoot Cruises, and Explorer Star Ship. The airport departure tax is US $1.00 to Windward Isles and US $4.00 per person elsewhere.

• Banking   The florin or guilder (currently 1NAf = US $.57) is the official currency, but US dollars are accepted everywhere. Credit cards are accepted at hotels and dive shops.

• Boat Trips   You can travel to Saba from Sint Maarten in Style, a 52-foot, high speed, luxury commuter craft that accommodates up to 50 passengers. Great for a day trip, this boat features an open bar, taped music and soft comfortable seating during the one-hour crossing. Tuesday through Saturday, 9am departure and 5pm arrival at Sint Maarten's Great Bay Marina. Round trip fare is $45. For reservations call Great Bay Marina at #5-22167 or Sint Maarten hotels.

• Courtesy & Dress   Formal clothes are never required on Saba. Summer sportswear is appropriate for daytime activities all year round. Bring a sweater or light wrap as evening temperatures can dip into the low 60's during the winter season.

• Customs & Immigration   No customs. The island is a free port. US citizens and Canadians need valid passport, birth certificate or voter's registration card (a driver's license isn't enough). You also need a return or onward ticket.

• Driving   On the right.

• Electricity   US standards.

• Events & Holidays   Good Friday; Easter; Easter Monday; Queen's Birthday (April 30); Labor Day; Ascension Day; Kingdom Day (Dec. 15); Christmas; Boxing Day (Dec. 26). Carnival is held in July and is celebrated with costumed dancing and Caribbean music; Saba Days are celebrated the first weekend in December with donkey races, dancing and parties.

• Languages   Dutch is the official language, but everyone speaks English.

• Taxes & Tipping   The 20% charge usually added to your hotel or restaurant bill is a combined government and service tax. You needn't tip beyond the service charge unless you're so inclined. For taxis, porters and guides, tip at your own discretion.

• Telephone   Most hotels have direct dialing worldwide. Otherwise, international calls may be placed from the wireless office at The Bottom.

• Time   Atlantic Standard (Eastern Standard +1 hour).

• Weather   The mountains create a temperate climate. Temperatures range from 78 to 82 degrees year round. In the evenings the air may cool to the mid 60's; with the trade winds you may actually need a light sweater or jacket. Minimum rainfall is 42 inches annually. While hiking, you'll find the temperature drops about one degree for each 330-foot gain in altitude.

History

Saba was discovered by Columbus on his second voyage to the New World in 1493 -- the same trip during which he discovered Statia and Sint Maarten. Sir Francis Drake sailed by more than 100 years later, in 1595. Pieter Schouten sighted Saba in 1624 and his fellow Dutchman, Piet Heyn, mentioned both Saba and Statia in 1626. In 1632 a handful of shipwrecked Englishmen landed, finding fruit trees but no people. Three years later, Pierre D'Esnambuc claimed the island for France.

But it was the Dutch who settled the island in the 1640's, building communities at Tent Bay and The Bottom. These settlements continued until August of 1665, when the English captured the island and sent the Dutch settlers to Sint Maarten. By October the Dutch were back. Seven years later the British regained control, and managed to hold sovereignty from 1672 to 1679.

Saba

To defend themselves against enemy attack, the Sabans constructed wooden platforms to hold large boulders which, by removing the supports, could be rolled down on invaders. Due to Western Europe's political climate, and the nearby fertile Saba Bank fishing grounds, tiny Saba was claimed by one country after another, in spite of its defenses.

Altogether, Saba changed hands 12 times and was claimed by the English, French, Spanish and Dutch. Finally, on February 21, 1816, peace prevailed under the gentle banner of The Netherlands.

Saba has a strong sea-going heritage. In the early days of navigation, boats were built at Tent Bay and Wells Bay, some as much as 60 gross tons in size. With an ingenuity born of their isolation, Sabans launched these large vessels on planks greased with cactus juice and other lubricating substances from local plants.

For the last two centuries Saba has been a quiet island, mostly devoted to farming. Until 50 years ago it was a secluded oasis, nearly inaccessible to the outside world, having neither an airport nor a sheltered harbor. There were just two sea approaches to the island. Entry into either required the assistance of expert local boatmen who knew just how to catch the crest of a wave and bring a small boat into the rocky beach at Fort Bay or at The Ladder -- a treacherous, hair-raising adventure, at best.

From sea level, there was a steep climb of 800 hand-hewn stone steps to the village of The Bottom. More steps -- lots of them -- led upward to Windwardside, Crispeen, St. John's and beyond.

Everything from pianos to provisions were hoisted up these stairs. Twelve men were needed to heft a Steinway from sea level to The Bottom. It took four men and a sedan chair to tote a visiting bishop up the steep stairs. Without roads, wheeled vehicles were useless. Everyone walked or rode on small donkeys.

Because of its remote location and difficult geography, Saba has only recently joined the 20th century. The concrete road from Fort Bay to The Bottom took five years to complete. However, it wasn't until 1947 that the first motor vehicle arrived. It was a second-hand jeep, heralded as a "donkey on wheels."

Four years later the road was extended to St. John's and Windwardside. The design and construction of the road is credited to Lambertus Has-

Saba Airport/Bourque

Saba's Transportation Team/Bourque

sell. He sent away for a correspondence school course in road construction, after engineers from Holland declared that the terrain made such a feat impossible.

The building of an airfield was the next step towards modernization. Juancho E. Yrausquin Airport was built in 1959 and regular air service from Sint Maarten began in the summer of 1963. That same year, electricity arrived on the island. At first, power was only available during the evenings, but service was extended to 24 hours a day in 1970.

Saba

Hikers/Bourque

The first television sets arrived on Saba in 1965. Will Johnson founded the Saba Herald, a monthly newspaper, in 1968, and in 1971 Max Nicholson signed on with the island's first radio station, The Voice of Saba.

The treacherous sea approach was eventually replaced by a more civilized landing at The Leo A. Chance Pier, built at Fort Bay in 1972. Fresh groceries and other supplies are still brought in each week from Sint Maarten via cargo boat.

Today, with a population of about 1,000, the island boasts a modern administration building and a new hospital, clinic and home for the aged. There's also a new library in The Bottom and at the annex in Windwardside.

Exploring

Twenty-eight miles south of Sint Maarten, Saba is the tip of an extinct volcanic range rising nearly 3,000 feet above the Caribbean. Instead of beaches, luxury hotels and nightlife, you will discover rugged scenery, a population of 1,000 friendly people and wall diving that is unsurpassed in the eastern Caribbean. Four picturesque villages -- Hell's Gate, Windwardside, St. John's and The Bottom -- decorate the hills and mountainsides of Saba. They are connected by the hair-raising six-and-one-half-mile road mentioned earlier and referred to by the Sabans as "the road that couldn't be built."

If you arrive in Saba by air, your Winair plane lands at Flat Point, one of the few level spots on the island. Be prepared for a dramatic approach as the plane heads for a shear cliff, only to turn sharply at the last moment for the drop onto a remarkably short runway. The airstrip is one of the shortest in the world, just 1,312 feet long, and is bracketed by cliffs at either end.

A 20-passenger DeHavilland Otter plane, called a STOL (short take off and landing), makes the landing five times a day from Sint Maarten. In this specially designed flying machine, the skillful Winair pilots use only half the length of the runway for landing. So relax. Winair has been providing safe inter-island transportation for 24 years. It has carried over 150,000 passengers to Saba alone.

Taxi drivers are your best guides. They proudly keep their vans in sparkling condition and will help you with every need. Your new friend on Saba can arrange lunch, diving, tours, nature walks or tell some interesting tales. Remember there are 90 minutes to every Caribbean hour, so

Saba

allow for understanding of the arrangements and... relax.

From the airport, the road rises to Hell's Gate and then continues on through banana plantations and tropical ferns to Windwardside, a tiny village on a ridge connecting Mount Scenery and Booby Hill, 1,800 feet above sea level. Windwardside is home to Saba's two largest inns and most of her shops. You will also find the Harry L. Johnson Memorial Museum in Windwardside. The former home of a Dutch sea captain, the museum is filled with restored antique furnishings and Johnson family memorabilia.

Step inside and you enter the Saba of the 1900's, when the antique organ was new, family members slept in a mahogany four-poster bed with pineapple carvings, and a Victorian couch, chairs and a (now) threadbare Oriental carpet graced the sitting room. In the kitchen, the visitor is invited to a plate of pork roasted in an original rock oven hearth. Throughout the museum, windows are bordered by crisp white curtains embroidered by island lace makers. While you're in Windwardside, stop at the Tourism Office (tel. 2231), around the corner from the post office. Glenn Holm, the Director of Tourism, will tell you

Director of Tourism/Jacobs

Carnival/Bourque

anything you wish to know about the island. He can also provide a list of rental apartments and houses for planning your next visit to Saba.

The road passes Kate's Hill, Peter Simon's Hill and Big Rendezvous on the way to St. John's, a tiny town featuring a spectacular view of St. Eustatius to the south. It then climbs over the mountain, descending sharply to The Bottom. This is the island's official capital, sitting 800 feet above the ocean on a plateau surrounded by volcanic domes.

For more information, order the Pfanstiehls' Saba, The First Guidebook, for $10 or the Saba Supplement for $5 from Vansteel Press, 11 Annandale Road, Newport, RI 02840.

Food

Most people staying on Saba for more than a day stay in one of the local guesthouses, which provide meals. The island also has 7 public restaurants, including the Captain's Quarters Hotel, originally the home of a Saban sea captain, now

Wahoo, Tuna & Barracuda/Bourque

Saba

The Bottom/Kelly

with an indoor/outdoor bar and an elegant dining room open for breakfast, lunch and dinner. Both American and West Indian dishes are beautifully prepared. Try barbecue spare ribs, peanut butter chicken or steak, but leave room for a desert such as fresh banana pie. The bar is a meeting place for guests as well as locals. Check the bulletin board or ask the bartender for special events including slide shows, parties, movies and night dives.

At Scout's Place check with Diana Medero for the day's menu. You'll walk away delightfully satisfied. After dinner, join in a card game or lively conversation. For Cantonese food try the Saba Chinese Restaurant. Cranston's Antique Inn serves native and Chinese dishes. And the new Chinese Family Restaurant serves Cantonese food as well as salads, steak and French fries. The bar's satellite TV brings in worldwide sports and shows. For pizza, burgers and sandwiches try Guido's Italian Restaurant. It's best to call ahead.

Sharon's Ocean View Bar and Restaurant in Hell's Gate offers a breath-taking view, fresh fish and indoor/outdoor dining. Owners Wilfred "Buddy" Hassell and his son Julian supply the daily catch and Buddy drives a taxi. A local steel band plays on occasion. In The Bottom are Lime Time and Queenie's Serving Spoon, serving such local specialties as callaloo soup, curried goat, breadfruit and soursop ice cream. Island fruits in-

clude mangos, papayas, figs, bananas and oranges.

Each restaurant is a neighborhood activity center. Weekends are active with live music and dancing. Remember Saba is small enough that everyone knows everyone, and strangers are always welcome. Chances are that if you stay more than a day or two, and are the friendly sort, you will be invited to dinner at someone's home. It's just that kind of place.

Nightlife

There are Friday and Saturday night dances at Guido's Lime Time and Saturday and Sunday movies at the Royal Theater. But generally evenings are quiet on Saba. Captain's Quarters, Scout's Place and Sharon's Ocean View have lively bars for friendly get-togethers, barbecues or slide shows.

Shopping

Most shops are open from 9am to noon and then from 2 to 6pm. Don't miss the Island Craft Shop in Windwardside or the Saba Artisan Foundation in The Bottom. The Artisan Foundation began in 1972 as a cooperative effort of the Dutch government and the United Nations' Development Program to create new employment opportunities and improve the economy. Here you can

Saba Deep/Jacobs

buy black coral jewelry, Saba Spice, dolls, books and silk-screened cloth and clothing.

The most famous local craft is Saban drawn threadwork, an intricate embroidery that resembles lace. The delicate threadwork creates airy designs on linen garments, napkins and kerchiefs. Designs are unique to villages and families. The technique, known as Saba Lace or Spanish Work, was originally brought to the island by Mary Gertrude Johnson in the 1870's, who learned the skill in a convent in Caracas, Venezuela. Today, excellent examples of this work are available at the shops in Windwardside as well as in many private homes. Another local specialty is Saba Spice, a sweet, spicy 150-proof rum. It is an acquired taste, but an exotic one, made by boiling anise seed, cinnamon, orange peel, cloves, nutmeg, spice bush and brown sugar in water. Add 151-proof rum, and flambe the mixture. The exact proportions of the ingredients and mixing techniques are an island secret you'll have to discover for yourself.

Stop to see Angela at the Island Craft for souvenirs and local news. And Velma at the Belle Isle Boutique loves to have visitors browse and chat. Down the road, Frieda makes Saba Lace at the Around the Bend gift shop. For local color -- as well as anything from tires and jewelry to rental cars -- visit Douglas Johnson at The Square Nickel. Ruth Buchanan and Anna Keene at the Weaver's Cottage Under the Hill in Windwardside offer handwoven garments and yardage as well as weaving workshops using large floor looms. In the Bottom, small shops are found

everywhere; just ask the locals. Colorful dresses and bags are available at the Lime Time bar. The shop behind the church in Hell's Gate has a special collection of hand made Saba Lace which can also be custom ordered. And Kiddie Book Corner offers toys and educational items for both young and old.

Sports

Organized sports are limited on Saba. If you're looking for tennis, there's a concrete court at Sunny Valley Youth Centre in The Bottom which is open to the public and another one in the planning stages. There's a swimming pool at The Captain's Quarters. Sunday afternoon at the museum grounds will find Scottish accented Dr. Buchanan, and his lovely wife Ruth, and many

Sea Saba/Jacobs

others in a tradition of Mimosa and Croquet. Newcomers are welcome. Wear your whites and watch your language as every profanity costs a gilder.

Also, the gentle Caribbean trade winds make flying a kite a breeze, windsurfing a challenge and summer nights a Saba delight.

• Hiking

Before "the road" was built, the only way to get from one village to the next was on foot or by donkey. The island terrain is laced with steep trails and thousands of stone steps linking villages and homes. Hiking is a popular activity for visitors as is relaxing afterwards! Some of the island's walks are strenuous enough for the hardiest, sure-footed hiker. Other trails are less steep and are perfect for casual strollers. The newly established Conservation Foundation of Saba is remarking and grooming trails for those of all abilities.

One rewarding hike follows the trail from Windwardside up the 1,064 steps to the crest of the central volcano, Mount Scenery. Others lead

Saba

/Bourque

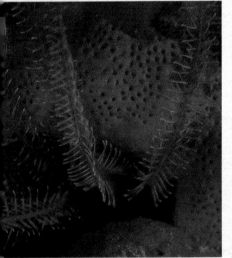

/Bourque

/Bourque

/Bourque

/Nick Fain

/Bourque

/Bourque

Saba

to an old village, an inactive sulphur mine or the most breathtaking vistas imaginable from Maskerhorne hill or Sandy Cruz. Catch the sunrise over St. Eustatius from Hell's Gate or the ocean sunset at Fort Bay.

Hikers can go on their own or with a guide. Bernard Johnson (you'll find him waiting tables in the evenings at the Chinese Family Restaurant) will lead you all the way around the island with first-hand knowledge of Saban lore.

Arrange a botanical hike with Anna Keene, an expatriate horticulturist, of Saba Botanico located at the Weaver's Cottage Under the Hill in Windwardside. Anne will guide you to some of nature's best kept secrets within habitats varying from dry bushlands to tropical rain forests. Pick a clear day for your hike to be assured of the best views. The estimated hiking time, round trip from Windwardside, is three hours, but allow extra time for photography, picnicking or just admiring the rain forest flowers: begonias, six-foot tall golden heliconias, as well as red ferns, mangoes and palms. Orchids bloom in the winter and philodendron climb to great heights.

An easier alternative is to go down The Ladder, the long pathway of stone steps leading to Ladder Bay. You may wish to pack a lunch and spend some time hiking along the shoreline. Comfortable shoes or sneakers are a must. To find The Ladder steps, go to The Gap, beyond Nicholson's supermarket. The steps begin near the large tree in the center of the road. Within a few yards, the passage becomes bordered with ferns and you lose sight of all signs of civilization. Relax at the base of the cliff before tackling the ascent -- it's much more strenuous than the descent, but be glad you aren't carrying a piano up the steps, as they did in the days before the road.

Check on the difficulty and length of your proposed hike or climb before setting out. Stop often to enjoy the spectacular views of village rooftops nestled into the mountains and of the neighboring islands of St. Eustatius, St. Kitts, St. Barthelemy and Sint Maarten.

If you get tired, just stick out your thumb and a passing car is bound to offer you a ride. Hitchhiking, a Saban tradition, is safe. It dates from the time of the first automobiles on the island. There are several standard spots where locals wait for rides. From The Bottom, sit on the wall opposite the Anglican Church. From Fort Bay, sit on the wall opposite Saba Deep. And look forward to meeting some new friends.

The named trails on Saba include: Tent Point, Booby Hill, The Level, The Boiling House, The Sulphur Mine, The Ladder, Giles Quarter, Rendezvous, Bottom Hill, Crispeen, Mount Scenery, Spring Bay, Troy, Sandy Cruz, Middle Island and Mary's Point.

• Diving

There are two words to describe diving on Saba, according to local experts: "variety" and "virginity." While other destinations claim these virtues, Saba delivers. It's the unexploited gem of the eastern Caribbean. Even better, it plans to stay that way.

So far, the pristine conditions underwater are due to the relatively small numbers of divers (under 1,000) that visit each year. Even if these numbers were to double or triple, Saba protects its waters from plunder and exploitation.

The Saba Marine Park officially opened November 1, 1987. Twenty-nine permanent mooring buoys are available for dive boats operating with permission from the Marine Park and the Saba Government. Tom Van't Hof, having also established other marine parks in Bonaire and Curacao, studies and monitors each dive site. His small office at Fort Bay welcomes visitors daily. Saban born Randall Thielman assists with slide shows, marine patrol, mooring maintenance and the information center. Park visitor fees are paid by dive operators. A dive site guide book and a snorkeling trail are in the works.

An excerpt from the Saba Marine Park proposal describes Saba's marine resources: "Diving tourism is a relatively new, but rapidly increasing use of the marine environment ... In view of the unaffected character of the marine resources, the enormous variation of the underwater environment and the spectacular nature of several dive sites, diving tourism is a potentially highly promising use. Diving tourism can be expanded without posing any threat to the resources, provided that the divers are made conscious of the fragile nature of coral reefs."

Diving is excellent on Saba all year round, with summertime visibility at 75 to 100 feet and water temperatures around 86 degrees. In the winter months, visibility increases to 125 feet and up. Temperatures drop to 75 degrees maximum.

Saba has no beaches, so diving is almost always done from boats. As you'd expect, there's less chop along the leeward shores. The southern and western sites are those most often visited. The north shore sites generally require longer boat rides (15 - 25 minutes versus 10 minutes to south shore sites) through rough water.

Few fishermen operate in these waters, so the numbers, varieties and sizes of fish are phenomenal. Seven to eight-foot tarpon and barracuda are common sights, as are giant sea turtles. And from February to April humpback whales migrate past the island on their way south. Great schools of porpoises numbering in the thousands have been sighted romping around the dive boats in the winter months.

There are plenty of shallow reefs, as well as towering walls and pinnacles for deeper experiences. Lava flows, sand spills, overhangs, caves, elkhorn coral forests and underwater mountains are among the dramatic reef structures awaiting discovery.

Week-long packages for groups, including accommodations and meals at Captain's Quarters, Juliana's Apartments and Scout's Place in Windwardside, are available.

• Liveaboards

There are three liveaboards plying the waters around Saba: the Sea Dancer, the Caribbean Explorer and the Coral Star. Each of these liveaboards has its own special ambience and schedule. When you are ready for a very intensive dive experience, you should check to see which one fits your needs best.

A typical week-long trip leaves from a nearby island, such as Sint Maarten, and then weaves its way through the Antilles touching islands such as St. Kitts, Nevis and St. Barths. You cover some of the best diving in the Caribbean, much of which is not dived by any land based operators. A major portion of the time is spent in the Saba Marine Park. Check the Directory for photographs of all the ships and an explanation of their facilities.

• Dive Shops

The island's two dive shops, Saba Deep and Sea Saba both have excellent facilities for novices and experienced divers.

Saba Deep is located at Fort Bay, near the pier. You can also buy beer, soft drinks, snacks, postcards and T-shirts here and relax on the shop's terrace to watch the harbor activities.

The staff, Carolyn, John, Antonio and Cecil, NAUI and PADI instructors and divemasters, offer a resort course that includes three hours of

Marguerite Hassell/Jacobs

instruction at the Captain's Quarters pool and a shallow, single-tank dive. A five-day certification course is also available with advance notice.

The three boats, one 18-foot and two 20-foot Privateers, take out small groups -- no more than eight to a trip -- and the service is always friendly and fun.

The Chinese Restaurant

Saba

In addition to diving, Saba Deep also offers sunset cruises, which circumnavigate the island in about an hour. Full day excursions to nearby islands can also be arranged.

Sea Saba, a full service dive shop in the picturesque village of Windwardside, is run by PADI instructors, Joan and Louis Bourque. The Bourques' shop is equipped with all the latest gear, including underwater cameras for photo buffs.

Their newly customized 36-foot cabin boat carries 14 divers for comfortable, dry rides to the island's numerous dive sites. Their 24-foot Privateer cabin boat carries eight divers. No crowded boats with Sea Saba. Both boats carry dive platforms, ladders, VHF radios, oxygen, dive refreshments, a dive instructor and a dive guide.

Weather permitting, lunch cruises to Statia can be arranged. Dive computers are available for rent. And there are never more than six divers per dive guide. Saban divemasters Martin Hasell, Greg Johnson and Esther Mommers assist divers before and after the dive. Introductory and five-day certification courses are always available.

The Sea Saba Team arranges dinners, lunches on the boat or a private beach and weekly cocktail parties and slide shows. Joan says, they offer a degree in RELAXATION and happy hour usually finds one of them involved in "buddy counseling."

Sea Saba's two dive shops are a five-minute walk from Windwardside Hotels (just outside Joan and Lou's home). One shop is exclusively for T-shirts, scuba accessories and the latest in Sherwood dive gear. Joan offers a weekly slide show; ask her about underwater photography and camera rentals. Week-long packages for groups, including accommodations, meals, dives, taxi, tips, taxes and all the extras are arranged with Captain's Quarters, Juliana's Apartments and Scout's Place. Call or write for special personal or group planning.

• Dive Sites

(1) Outer Limits, (2) Twilight Zone and (3) Third Encounter are adjacent anchorages on the same reef. Out of the "bottomless" depths rise three dramatic pinnacles. The first two peak at 90 feet, covered with bright red, orange, yellow and purple giant tube sponges, soft corals that appear to glow and huge schools of fish that obscure your view -- an eerie underwater experience you won't want to miss. The third pinnacle is more of a plateau at 100 feet, complete with rugged valleys and peaks. This is the home of friendly groupers and huge blackjacks -- even an occasional shark. This "extra-terrestrial" landscape is encrusted with colorful rare sponges and black coral trees.

(4) Shark Shoal, (5) Diamond Bank are off the northwest coast. At (6) Diamond Rock, an 80-foot sandy bottom is the base for this huge pinnacle, which breaks above the surface. It is encrusted with sponges, anemones, gorgonians and inhabited by a large, curious barracuda. The marine life here is similar to Man O' War Shoals, but on a larger scale. One cut in the rock reveals a veritable catalog of tropical fish: high hats, big-eyes, fairy basslets, bared hamlets, coneys, a great amberjack, jolthead porgy, spotted drum and several peacock flounders.

(7) Man O' War Shoals has a flat sandy bottom at 70 feet, with two giant hills reaching to within 15 feet of the surface. Between the hills are many crevices and caves where crustaceans hide. Along the sandy bottom dance yellow jawfish, goatfish and filefish. The shoal area is a colorful garden of sponges, anemones and tubeworms, always in bloom. Animal life includes large jacks, barracuda, stingrays and often a turtle. Bring your camera.

(8) Otto Limits is near Man O' War Shoals and just north of (9) Torrens Point, a dramatic dive beginning with an ancient elkhorn coral forest that leads into a tunnel streaming with blue light. Midway through the tunnel, schools of glassy sweepers greet you and swim past. At the far end of the tunnel you find an endless series of shallow caves to explore. So much to see, and all at about 20 feet but watch out for the fire coral.

(10) Wells Bay is a shallow dive -- 50-foot maximum -- with superb visibility. Lots of large sea fans and sea feathers, as well as hard and soft corals, sponges and schools of reef fish.

(11) Ladder Bay is a relatively small, deep patch reef structure sloping into a deep trench. Look for a black coral-encrusted anchor as well as other unique coral formations and large patches of yellow algae. Large pelagic fish swim here along with small reef tropicals. This site may be dived at many levels; its maximum depth is 90 feet.

(12) Lou's Ladder and Porites Point are characterized by giant rows of finger coral inhabited by schools of blue chromis, pairs of butterfly fish, often a turtle and usually a stingray. If you look hard enough you'll find Caribbean king crab here also.

Saba

(13) Babylon is a formation of boulders and mounds of brain coral lined up between sandy alleyways running perpendicular to the shore. Beautiful pillar coral, finger coral, sea fans, a friendly pair of marbled groupers and many crustaceans make their homes here.

(14) Ladder Labyrinth is named for its unusual seascape of giant coral mounds connected by a maze of alleyways. Look carefully in the dark crevices for shrimp and tiny lobster. There are plenty of pillar coral, big barrel sponges, an occasional scrawled filefish and schools of barracuda.

(15) Hot Springs is honeycombed with hot spring vents. It may be dived at various depths, from 40 to 60 feet. Large numbers of barrel sponges in numerous shapes and sizes are found here. Perhaps because of the warmer water, sea urchins, rare in the Caribbean since the algae blight of 1983, are reappearing in this location. Also schools of small reef fish abound.

(16) Tent Ran Reef is at the western edge of Tent Reef where the bottom drops off to 100 feet at (17) Tent Reef Wall. This wall has a rugged profile with colorful purple and yellow tube sponges, black coral and a myriad of small crevices to explore. Good for macrophotography.

There's always something new at (18) Tent Reef and (19) Tent Reef Deep, beginning with a quiet eel garden. Swim through a series of overhangs, schools of sergeant-majors, a few French angelfish and occasional turtles. Colorful gorgonians, sponges and pillar coral create a stately setting for schools of black bar soldierfish, parrotfish and Spanish hogfish.

Just five minutes from the pier is (20) Greer Gut where smaller varieties of spotted lobster live in the crevices among the elkhorn coral. Spotted eagle rays and schools of small tropicals cruise this reef.

(21) Giles Quarter Reef begins on a flat, sandy bottom then drops off to 100 feet at the seaward edge. Huge coral specimens abound with numerous cavities housing lobster and sleeping nurse sharks.

(22) Big Rock Market gives the illusion of an enchanted forest as light streams through the peaceful elkhorn coral. At (23) Giles Quarter drift past stands of elkhorn coral and boulder corals encrusted with sea fans. Encounter schools of creole wrasses, Bermuda chubs and French grunts. Look carefully for sea biscuits and starfish here.

(24) Hole in the Corner are adjacent sites featuring elkhorn coral, staghorn coral and many crustaceans, crabs and lobster. Plenty of overhangs and crevices to explore. Be on the lookout for pufferfish, queen trigger and schools of blue tang and doctorfish.

Saba Museum

A number of sites located on the windward northeastern coast are rarely visited by either dive operator. However, on exceptionally calm days both will take groups on special request. Highlights include undercuts, walls, a lava flow, caves, canyons and an abundance of plant and animal life. Check with your operator and you may be among the lucky few who have visited these sites.

(25) Core Gut is actually two sites. Weather permitting, both are well worth the 20-minute boat ride. The dive begins in a forest of healthy, dense elkhorn coral at 20 feet. Explore the forest and visit with the inhabitants: Bermuda chubs, midnight parrotfish and schools of small reef fish. At the far end of the forest enter an otherworldly village with giant boulder skyscrapers and dramatic overhangs housing families of fish of all kinds. To the left is a shear drop-off with a steep wall covered with iridescent tube sponges.

(26) Green Island, another windward site, is located northwest of the airport.

Saba

Coral Star

Caribbean Explorer

Sea Dancer

Key: The accommodations price range is based on the high season rate per night, double occupancy. The Liveaboard price range is per berth, high season. The dive price range is based on the cost of a two tank dive. Letter codes: Beach (or on the water), Diving, Fishing, Golf, Other watersports, Pool, Restaurant & Bar, Sailing, Tennis, Windsurfing.

Saba

Juliana's

Cranston's Antique Inn

Scout's Place

Captain's Quarters

Saba

Accommodations

CAPTAIN'S QUARTERS 800-328-5285   10 Units: $95-95 DFPR

011-599-42201 305-682-6000FX Windwardside Saba, N. A. Several restored buildings, combining old world charm with modern comfort. Spacious guest rooms (many with 4-poster beds), all with private bath, balcony and sweeping views of the sea and surrounding hills and valleys of mountainous greenery. Garden dining pavilion provides perfect setting for European, American and Saban cuisine. Relax by the sparkling freshwater swimming pool, adjacent covered terrace and bar, all overlooking Caribbean Sea 1,500' below. See: Sea Saba Dive Center.

CRANSTON'S ANTIQUE INN 011-599-43218   6 Units: $55-55 DR

011-599-43203 The Bottom Saba, N. A. A quaint 130-year-old inn which once housed visiting Dutch officials, including Queen Juliane. Each of the six rooms has original four-poster beds, antiques and hardwood floors. Our patio, outdoor bar and restaurant all overlook the garden. Breakfast, lunch and dinner are served, featuring local specialties.

JULIANA'S APARTMENTS 011-599-42269   9 Units: $65-75 DKOP

Windwardside Saba, N.A. Juliana and Franklin Johnson your hosts, own and operate a small group of charming guest rooms. Within an ambience of the oldworld, they offer new, modern and immaculate quarters that provide every comfort. Each spacious room provides a private bath and its own private balcony overlooking a spectacular view of the sea. All the facilities of Captain's Quarters are available to you. See: Sea Saba Dive Center.

SCOUT'S PLACE 011-599-42205   15 Units: $50-85 PR

Windwardside Saba, N. A. Their motto is "Bed and Board, Cheap and Cheerful." That sums up this small guesthouse located in the tiny village of Windwardside. All rooms have south-facing ocean views. The atmosphere is relaxed, and the food is very good. They are within walking distance of shops and Sea Saba Dive Center. Price includes breakfast. See: Sea Saba Dive Center.

SHARON'S OCEAN VIEW 011-599-42238   4 Units: $50-50 DR

Hells Gate Saba. The only guesthouse in Hells Gate. A commanding view of the airport and many neighboring islands. Presently 4 double rooms (two with twin beds). A pool is under construction along with four more rooms. Louise makes the best conch stew, and there is fresh fish daily. Buddy, the owner, drives a taxi too, so transportation will be at your doorstep. The price includes breakfast. See: Sea Saba Dive Center.

Information

SABA TOURIST OFFICE 011-599-42231

011-599-43274FX Windwardside Saba, N. A. Glen can provide you with a complete listing of houses and apartments that may be rented for long-term stays.

Liveaboards

CARIBBEAN EXPLORER 800-322-3577   16 Berths: $170-170 BDORW

203-259-9321 203-259-9896FX 10 Fencerow Drive Fairfield CT 06430. The 97' Explorer accommodates a maximum of 16 guests in 4 double and 2 quad airconditioned staterooms. She is equipped with E-6 processing, camera table, charging station, indoor dining salon and full-service galley, huge shaded sun deck with BBQ and bar, specialized audio-visual equipment, fresh water marker, rinse tanks, ships' stores and much more. All diving is done off the vessel itself. U/W photo, video & dive inst. Rent: Photo, gear, dive computer.

CORAL STAR 800-433-7262   9 Berths: $185-200 BDFORW

305-563-1711 17 Fort Royal Isle Ft. Lauderdale FL 33308. The luxury yacht Coral Star offers liveaboard diving at its very best! Dive sites vary around Saba (The unspoiled Queen of the Caribbean) from spectacular walls to world class pinnacle diving with 150 to 200' visibility. Coral Star welcomes non divers, there are amenities and diversions for all. Come and enjoy, just relax, dive, play, beach comb, watch videos, party or do blissfully nothing. The pleasures of the islands and Coral Star are beckoning.

SEA DANCER 800-367-3484   12 Berths: $157-185 BDRW

607-277-3484 54 Gunderman RD. Ithaca NY 14850. Catering to the serious diving enthusiast, Sea Dancer offers an all-inclusive package of first class accommodations, diving services, gourmet meals, plus photo and video services. The ship schedule revolves around 3-5 opportunities a day for wall diving, virgin reef exploration, and unsurpassed pelagic animal encounters. Eight-day 7-night trips feature diving in the warm, clear waters of Saba from Dec.-March. World renowned Peter Hughes Diving your host.

Sports

SABA DEEP 011-599-43347   24 Divers: $60-60 D

Box 22 Saba, N. A. Full service shop on the water at Fort Bay. Specializing in friendly, Caribbean-style service. The morning boat trip takes small groups (8 or less) to two sites, for a two-tank dive. You return to the pier at 2pm. Resort full certification, night dives and custom dives available. In addition to diving, Saba Deep offers sunset cruises, which circumnavigate the island in about an hour. Day trips to nearby islands can be arranged.

SEA SABA DIVE CENTER 011-599-42246   30 Divers: $60-60 DF

Windwardside Saba, N. A. More than a dive shop, Sea Saba is a recreation service. Louis and Joan Bourque plan a whole week of activities, including hiking, fishing, slide shows and custom-designed dives. Resort courses, full certification, open water and divemaster clinics are also offered. Two dives per day, at 10am and noon, visits two sites with two tanks. Special interest seminars on underwater photography, marine biology and other topics are available on request.

St. Vincent & the Grenadines

St. Vincent/Simpson, Grenadine Tours

Travel & Sports Guide

Carnival/Tr.Bd.

St. Vincent/Kelly

St. Vincent & the Grenadines

USEFUL FACTS

• Airline Connections   There are no direct flights from the US to St. Vincent. From Miami or New York, take BWIA, Eastern, American or Pan Am to Barbados, then connect with a LIAT flight to St. Vincent. Chartered planes may be hired through Air Mustique. Confirm your return or onward booking at least 72 hours before departure. Inter-Island Air Services flies from St. Vincent to Union and Canouan. Mustique Airways has regularly scheduled flights to Mustique, three times a week. Air Martinique stops over on St. Vincent on its way to Union and Canouan. There is a departure tax of EC$15/US$5.60.

• Banking   As of June 1988, the exchange rate is EC$2.67 / US $1.00. Most restaurants, shops and hotels will accept payment in American dollars or traveler's checks but you'll get a better rate at the bank. Banking hours: 8am to noon Monday to Thursday, and 8am to noon and 3-5pm on Friday. When shopping, check whether prices quoted are in American or EC dollars.

• Courtesy & Dress   Light, informal clothes. Lightweight cotton dresses, skirts, shorts and blouses for women; slacks, shorts and shirts for men. For hiking bring long-sleeved shirts, hiking boots and jeans. Evening attire is also informal, but bring a tie and jacket just in case. Bathing suits and short shorts are not appropriate on the streets or in stores.

• Customs & Immigration   Canadian and US citizens need a passport, birth certificate or voter's registration card plus an ongoing or return ticket.

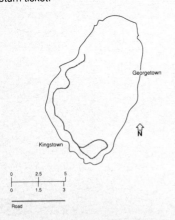

• Driving   On the left. The roads are narrow, twisting and hard to follow, with few signposts. Obtain a good map from the Tourist Office. Car rental agencies operate out of Kingstown on St. Vincent. A temporary driver's license is required, obtainable upon presentation of your US driver's license at the police station on Bay St. A fee of EC$10 will also be charged.

• Electricity   220 volts-50 cycles. Make sure to bring a converter/adaptor kit.

• Events & Holidays   New Year's Day; St. Vincent and the Grenadines Day (Jan. 22, also called Discovery Day); Good Friday; Easter Monday; Bequia Boat Races; Labour Day (May); Whitmonday; Caricom Day (July 3); Emancipation Day (Aug. 7); Independence Day (Oct. 27); Christmas; Boxing Day (Dec. 26).

• Events, Carnival   Starting the last week of June, St. Vincent hosts a 10-day long Carnival, otherwise known as "Vincy Mas." Originally a fairly small affair with folk dances, maypole and calypso bands, the event has expanded into an elaborate celebration. Incorporating the original festivities, the event also includes a beautiful pageant with dazzlingly costumed entrants. Designers begin work on the costumes up to a year ahead of time, and they reflect socially relevant themes like love, hate, African heritage and the human condition. Specially erected bars and cafes serve delicious cuisine to the revelers. Other events include athletic competitions, feasts and dancing, calypso and steel bands. Music plays a special part in Carnival. Renowned musicians like Shake Keane, Frankie McIntosh and Becket all call St. Vincent their home, and often return to contribute their talents to the festivities. Special packages are available to visitors planning to visit during this time of camaraderie and high spirits.

• Events, Bequia Easter Regatta   Taking place in March, this regatta is full of activities, both offshore and on. The event is open to all classes of boats, yachts, workboats and fishing boats, with a different course for each class. Prizes are awarded, and visitors and locals participate in the festive ongoings held at De Reef, a local establishment.

St. Vincent & the Grenadines

Bequia/Jacobs

• <u>Languages</u>   English.
• <u>Medical</u>   Three hospitals, two located in Kingstown, and a smaller one in Georgetown.
• <u>Off-Season Dates & Rates</u>   Rates drop 25 to 50% June - December 15.
• <u>Taxes & Tipping</u>   A 10%-15% service charge is added by most hotels and restaurants. Hotel tax is 5% of your bill. There's also a 5% government tax on international calls.
• <u>Taxi Fares</u>   Taxis are not metered but rates are fixed by the government. Usual rate for taxi tours is EC$30 per hour with a tip of 12% of the fare. At the time of publication, the 10 minute ride from the airport to Kingstown cost EC$12.
• <u>Telephone</u>   To dial direct from the US, dial the 809 area code + 45 for St. Vincent + the 5-digit local number. There is direct dialing from St. Vincent as well.
• <u>Time</u>   Atlantic Standard (Eastern Standard +1 hour).
• <u>Weather</u>   The trade winds cool the islands year round, keeping temperatures between 77 and 81 degrees. The rainy season is June through December, although a quick shower occurs most afternoons. There are occasional hurricanes July through September.

Introduction

Located in the East Caribbean between St. Lucia and Grenada are the more than 32 islands and cays that make up the archipelago of St. Vincent and the Grenadines. The quiet elegance and seclusion of these islands, coupled with the casual and simple lifestyle, have made the islands the favorite retreat of the rich and famous (as well as of travelers on a more limited budget), in search of uninhabited beaches, excellent diving and all around relaxation.

Sailors and yachtsmen have long known of the islands' many protected harbors, prevailing winds, pristine beaches and clear turquoise water. St. Vincent and its jewel-like Grenadines have become an internationally recognized yachting center, also acclaimed for spectacular scuba diving and warm and friendly inhabitants.

Ecology

These mountainous volcanic islands host a nutrient-rich soil and generous rainfall, perfect for the lush tropical flora, coconut, banana and arrowroot which grow here in abundance. Landscaped farmlands dot the interior valleys, while rugged cliffs meet the Caribbean ocean on the leeward and windward sides. Unspoiled

St. Vincent & the Grenadines

beaches of golden and black volcanic sand weave about the shoreline.

The islands are also home to a myriad of beautiful and captivating birds including: The Purplethroated Carib Hummingbird, the Lesser Antillean Bullfinch, boobies, and hooded tanagers. Patient birdwatchers may catch sight of the St. Vincent Parrot and the Whistling Warbler, both unique to the islands.

La Soufriere, the island's active volcano, last blew in 1979; but it's carefully monitored and too far from tourist areas to be a threat.

History

According to popular belief, Columbus discovered St. Vincent on his third voyage in 1498, but the Arawak and Carib Indians arrived first. The Arawaks, who migrated from South America, called themselves "Lokono," meaning "human beings." They were eventually conquered by the Carib (from Caraibes or Charibs, meaning rebellious) Indians, who killed all the men but saved the women. The race resulting from this mix of Carib men and Arawak women (the new race kept the name Carib) were the only residents of these islands until the arrival of European explorers in the late 15th century. In 1675, a passing Dutch ship, filled with settlers and their black slaves, sank off the coast of Bequia. The shipwrecked slaves, the only survivors, made the islands their home and added new blood to the original population. The blending of dark and golden skins resulted in a race known as "Yellow Caribs." Some of the descendants of this "Yellow Carib" race, now simply referred to as Carib Indians, live in Sandy Bay.

Inter-racial mixing continued with the arrival of slaves escaping from St. Lucia and Grenada. Making St. Vincent their home, they became firmly rooted, and as their numbers grew and strengthened, they became known as "Black Caribs." Feeling threatened by this new population, the Yellow Caribs asked assistance of the governor of Martinique; in 1700 the island of St. Vincent became divided, with the west going to the Yellow Caribs and the east to the Black. The French arrived, initially giving their support to the Yellow Caribs and eventually settling for a policy of non-involvement. They lived harmoniously with the two tribes, growing indigo, cotton, tobacco and sugar.

In 1722 the British tried to establish St. Vincent as a colony. The French and British squabbled over possession until 1763 when it was ceded to England; however, rule under the British did not take place without incident. Dissatisfied Black Caribs unsuccessfully attempted to oust the British in 1779 and later again in what became known as the Second Carib War (1775-1779). Aided by French radical Victor Hughes, chiefs Chatoyer and Duvalle attacked the British in Kingstown. In 1796 General Abercrombie squelched the revolt and shipped some 5,080 Black Caribs to British Honduras.

The mid and late 1800's saw the arrival of Portuguese and East Indian immigrants who further added to the growing cosmopolitan community. Over time, racial tensions ceased and tranquility prevailed as the races blended. Though the British and French influence exhibits itself in the islands' architecture and language, the population itself is mostly a mix of black, Indian and Portuguese.

Since gaining independence on October 27, 1979, life in St. Vincent and the Grenadines has remained quiet and peaceful. Part of the British Commonwealth, their government is based on a parliamentary government with 15 constituencies.

Exploring
• Kingstown and St. Vincent

Call the Tourist Office (457-1502) to arrange a sightseeing tour via mini bus or taxi or arrange for a guided tour through one of Kingstown's tour operators. Other options include hiring a taxi and driver (get one with the Taxi Driver's Association decal on the windshield) or renting a car and driving yourself. A quite inexpensive way to get around is in one of the small privately owned vans which leave from the market square in Kingstown every few minutes. Fares run from EC$1 to EC$4, depending on your destination. Be prepared, if you choose this method of transportation, to share the ride with other travelers and be surrounded by loud calypso music. It's a great way to meet locals and become immersed in the culture.

Kingstown is the capital of St. Vincent, and a busy port town. One of its biggest attractions is Fort Charlotte, on the north side. As you head up Grenville Street on the way to the fort, you'll pass a cluster of three churches: St. Mary's Roman Catholic Church, St. George's Anglican Cathedral and a Methodist Church. St. Mary's Church exhibits a fanciful mixture of architectural

St. Vincent & the Grenadines

/Jacobs

Botanical Gardens/Kelly

styles, with its Romanesque tower, Gothic spires and several Renaissance touches. The original church was built in 1823 and then embellished upon in the late 1930's by Benedictine monks.

St. George's Cathedral was built more than 150 years ago. Its Georgian style architecture sets the scene for a galleried nave dating from the 1820's, and some stunning stained-glass windows. Continuing north along Grenville Street, past the churches, will take you to Fort Charlotte. Perched on a bluff far above town, this fort was named after the wife of King George III, and housed English soldiers and armament for defense against the French. Interestingly, cannon used to defend the fort were pointed inland, in order to prevent the French from capturing the fort from the hills behind Kingstown (as opposed to from the sea). In what used to be the officers' quarters are Lindsay Prescott's paintings representing the Black Carib's history. The view of St. Vincent and the outlying Grenadines is spectacular, and on a clear day you can spot Grenada in the distance.

Traveling further north, visit the Botanical Gardens, established in 1765 by Governor George Melville. These gardens, the oldest in the Western Hemisphere, were originally established for the reproduction of herbs, spices and plants with medicinal properties. A techni-colored assortment of parrots live in the aviary found on the grounds. Botanists and visitors alike will be fascinated by the fragrant and colorful array of tropical flowers including frangipanis, jacarandas, bougainvillaea, wild orchids and several species of hibiscus. You'll also see a wide assortment of trees includ-

Comb & Brush/Jacobs

ing mahogany, banyan, rubber and teak. Of historical significance among this vast and varied tropical flora is a breadfruit tree grown from the original one planted by Captain Bligh in 1793. An important tropical staple, the breadfruit has many uses: the gum derived from the tree is used to caulk boats, a coarse cloth can be woven from its inner fibers, its edible fruit can be stored for a long time once cooked, and locals swear that the tea made from its leaves cures high blood pressure.

Next to the Gardens is the small National Museum containing various artifacts from the islands. Here you'll see, among other things, the curiously named "bathead potrest" with its threatening display of savagely carved teeth. The pre-Columbian artifacts are numerous, and especially interesting is the bust of a Negro with a flattened forehead carved by the Black Caribs. At one time, it was the practice of the Black Caribs to flatten their babies' foreheads between two progressively tightened boards in order to differentiate their race from that of the slaves brought in to work the fields.

Head north on the narrow, winding Leeward Coast Road to the Buccament Valley where nature trails thread through tropical rain forest. Various birds perch among the greenery, including the melodic Whistling Warbler. But a real treat is in store for the patient hiker who catches a glimpse of the beautiful Amazona Guildingii -- that's the St. Vincent Parrot to you and me. This bird, the national bird of St. Vincent and the Grenadines, is unique in the world. Serious efforts are being made to preserve this brightly plummaged and intelligent bird. Although the parrot population was fairly large not all that long ago, it is now an endangered species. Unfortunately, hunting, forestry and bird collectors have exacted their toll. Today, it is illegal to carry the bird off the islands. A parrot sanctuary is in the works, and will be located on some 600 acres in the upper Buccament Valley. Observing this bird in his natural habitat is a one of a kind experience.

There are pre-Columbian petroglyphs (ancient rock carvings by the Carib Indians, dating back 13 centuries) at Buccament Cave and at Layou. These petroglyphs reveal a wealth of historical data about the original Indian settlers of the Caribbean. Perhaps the most impressive are the carvings on the rock at Layou. These depictions can be divided into three groups. The topmost carving, not normally seen in the Caribbean, but

rather in ancient Cuban art, was made by a people known as the Siboneys, who lived in these islands from about 5000 BC to the time of Christ. The main figure, a toothy large-eyed face, is believed to be the representation of the god Yocalm, who provided the Indians with their main food and beverage substance: cassava. These ancient mementoes can be viewed at any time, but the best is before sunset in late December, when the lighting does them full justice.

Coming back to the 20th century, the Casino and the Aquaduct Golf Course are nearby.

Stop at Richmond Beach for a cooling dip in the Caribbean, or hike from there to the idyllic Falls of Baleine on the northern point. Approximately 60 feet high, the sparkling waters plunge into a swimmable rock enclosed pool.

To experience the more rugged Atlantic coast, take the Windward Highway from Kingstown. It's a scenic 24 miles to Georgetown. As you head up the coast, you'll pass the black sand beach at Rawacou, where you can go horseback riding or just enjoy the scenery, and the small towns of Biabou and Sans Souci.

Also worth a visit is the verdant Mesopotamia Valley. Follow the Vigie Highway east beyond the Arnos Vale Airport past rivers, streams and picturesque terraced farms to the town of Marriaqua. North of town lie the natural springs at Montreal Gardens. Surrounded by tropical flowers and plants, the view out over the valley and to the sea is magnificent. Paved walkways meander past fragrant orchids and vivid wild ginger lilies.

An expedition to the crater of the nearby volcano, Mt. Soufriere, takes all day and requires a guide, which costs about US $25-30. The volcano, 4,000 feet above sea level on the north coast, is still active, and experienced its last major eruption in 1979. Peering into the crater, which actually looks a moat with a rock island in its middle (the area is named Crater Lake and Rock Island), you'd never guess that it was the scene of so much activity not long ago. Today, volcanic activity is vigilantly monitored, and unless authorities warn you otherwise, a visit to the top is a safe and awesome venture.

The Rabaca Dry River, winding down the east side of Mt. Soufriere, is so named because of the gravel and ash which spewed forth, effectively halting water flow. At the foot of Soufriere, on the island's northernmost point, are the small towns of Owia and Sandy Bay. Owia is known for its large, naturally formed pool called Salt Pond, which is a splendid spot for sea-bathing.

Making a full circle back into Kingstown, stop at the St. Vincent Philatelic Services on Lower Bay Street, for a look at hundreds of beautiful and brightly colored stamps. As any avid stamp collector can tell you, St. Vincent and the Grenadines have long been noted for their

Whale Boat/Tr.Bd.

superior stamps with themes picturing fish, birds, tropical flowers, marine life and Caribbean street scenes and festivals. Their stamps have been in demand since 1861, the date of their first issue, and today's organization is responsible for meeting the demands of an international clientele.

Fishing Charter/Kelly

Young Island is a small private island almost within swimming distance from St. Vincent (it's 200 yards to the south). This edenic oasis is a favorite with honeymooners and is accessible by boat from Young Island Dock on St. Vincent. The Young Island Resort, features 29 quaint cottages scattered about the island's hills and beaches, and offers snorkeling, sailing, scuba and tennis. Fort Duvernette, on a spit of land neighboring the island, was built in the 1800's. Once used to defend Calliqua Bay, it is now the scene of festive Friday night cocktail parties.

• The Grenadines

The Grenadines are comprised of 100 islands and cays south of St. Vincent. This stretch of islands is considered one of the finest for yachting in the eastern Caribbean. Don't miss them if you've got the time, particularly Bequia, Mustique, Canouan and the Tobago Cays.

Bequia (pronounced Beck-wee) is accessible by boat from St. Vincent which land in Port Elizabeth, its largest town. Transportation is available on either the Bequia-built Friendship Rose, the Edwina, the Admiral, or by charter boat, dive boat or the yacht Carnival. This island gem has long been noted for its quality ship-building and its seaworthy sailors. With its perfect geographical setting (a wide harbor cooled by winds that come over the hills and fan gently over the waters without disturbing it), it is no wonder that visiting yachters find the deep, calm waters of Admiralty Bay a perfect spot for anchorage and any necessary repairs.

For about US$30, a taxi will take you around the island. Make arrangements with the Tourist

Feather Duster/Tewes

Anemone/Tewes
St. Vincent & the Grenadines 8 (216)

Bill Tewes/Jacobs

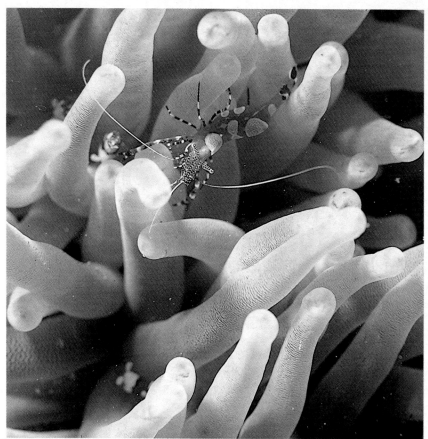

Anemone & Shrimp/Tewes

Porky/Tewes

Dive Bequia

St. Vincent & the Grenadines

Office to visit the cliffside dwellings of Moon Hole at the south end of the island. Featured in National Geographic, the original stone dwelling sits beneath a rocky arch, and swirling waters lap at its frontyard. On the north side of the island, catch the panoramic view back to St. Vincent from high atop the vista point.

Further west sits the village of Paget Farm, where harpooning whales is still practiced by the few surviving harpooners, all in their 60's and 70's. This ancient rite, the only killing of whales approved by Greenpeace, takes place every year from February to May. Unlike the large motor-powered commercial boats used in Russia and Japan, these whalers set out in two 26-foot long cedar boats. Their only means of locomotion comes in the form of oars, mainsail, sails and jib, and they utilize the same methods as Nantucket whalers two centuries ago. Sometimes years go by without a whale catch, so whaling in Bequia is really becoming more of a ritual practice.

In town, beautifully crafted ship and sailboat models can be purchased at the Sargent Brothers shop.

Mustique, 15 miles to the southeast of Bequia, is an exclusive island where the rich and famous come to escape the pressures of the hectic world. Privacy, service and a spectacular setting guarantee a restful and revitalizing visit.

Commercial and charter planes from Barbados and St. Vincent land visitors on this small island of elegant mansions and one posh hotel, the Cotton House, a beautifully refurbished cotton plantation. This beautiful inn is built of rock and coral and decorated with charming and curious antiques such as hammered leather screens and Spanish mirrors. Some mansions are available for rent, and although the prices are steep, they do include staff and a car!

With your driver's license, you can rent a moped for touring the island and sample the bathing at one of the white sand beaches which fringe the island, including secluded and lush Macaroni Beach. Then quench your thirst at Basil's Beach Bar, where the yachting and jet-set crowd gets together for seaside socializing.

Canouan is a petite crescent of an island, with three hotels and a small airstrip. Serene and unblemished, this island is also a favorite of visiting yachts. Anchorages exist all around the island. The main anchorage is Grand Bay. Corbay and Rameau are two picturesque and private spots, al-

though they have no shore access. Since the island is small (only 3.5 by 1.5 miles), its beautiful reef-protected beaches are within easy hiking distance and are perfect for snorkeling.

Mayreau's secluded population of less than 100 people live on 1.5 square miles of undulating green hills framed by pristine beaches. A charming little stone church sits atop a knoll looking out to Canouan, the Tobago Cays, Petit St. Vincent, Union and Grenada in the distance. Calm Salt Whistle Bay, popular with yachtsmen, has a quiet resort, the Salt Whistle Bay Resort, which provides outdoor dining, yacht charters and watersports all nestled in a South-Seas atmosphere. The beaches of Mayreau are reputed to be among the best in the world.

The Tobago Cays, well known to visiting yachtsmen, are a small collection of islets just off Mayreau. They are famous for their incredibly clear water and a technicolor array of fish swimming just below the water's surface. A horseshoe reef protects the cays from rough waters, making them an ideal snorkeling spot. Take one of the frequent day charters out of St. Vincent to this marine paradise.

Prune Island, also known as Palm Island, has only one resort, the Palm Island Hotel Company. Unassuming little bungalows are nestled among the whispering palms, planted by the Hotel's developer in 1966. The white sails of visiting boats moored off Casuarina Beach stand out sharply against the dazzling sapphire seas. To get to Palm Island, take the ferry from Union Island.

Union Island is only 3 miles by 1 mile long, yet it has two striking mountain ranges (Mt. Olympus and Mt. Parnassus) and such a riotous tropical flora that it has been compared to the much larger Tahiti. Scheduled commercial flights land at its well-appointed airport while its main port, Clifton Harbor, serves as the southern point of entry clearance for yachts. Its private resorts are noted for pampering their guests with rest, relaxation and outdoor activities like snorkeling, sunning and sailing. Union Islander's love for color is reflected in the bright blue of their church and the wildly decorated road signs which point the way to everything from the bar to the moon. The Snapper cruises to Union Island twice a week.

Petit St. Vincent, forty miles south of St. Vincent, is the southernmost island of the Grenadine archipelago. Those in the know refer to this unique, privately owned island as PSV. Twenty-two beautiful cottages of native "blue-bitch" stone and purple heart wood dot the island. Some sit perched high above the ocean, while others open directly onto a private stretch of beach -- privacy is the key word here. Pristine, deserted beaches ring the island, perfect for a solitary dip. Visiting yachts are the island's only other guests. Two small cays, Punaise and Morpion, are easily accessible by Sunfish or Hobie Cat, either of which can be rented from the resort.

Food

St. Vincent grows much of its own food, which helps keep prices down. Many of the hotels serve local West Indian cuisine. On St. Vincent, just opposite Young Island, is The French Restaurant, the island's most popular lunch and dinner spot. The CSY Yacht Club stages a well-attended happy hour from 5pm to 7pm each night, and features a different dinner special each night: pizza on Wednesday, barbecue on Thursday, seafood on Saturday and local cuisine for Sunday lunch.

Caribbean Beauty Contest/Jacobs

Basil's, one of Kingstown's finest restaurants, located in the famous Cobblestone Inn, features elegant lunches, seafood pasta, lobster and good French wines. Stilly's Aquatic Club has Friday night barbecues and music on Fridays, Saturdays and Wednesdays. Juliette's on Middle St. in Kingstown serves local cuisine, seafood and steak. The Bounty on Halifax St. serves inexpensive snacks. The nautical crowd flocks to the Dolphin for an impressive smorgasbord and fresh salad bar.

In the Grenadines, most resorts have some kind of beach barbecue at least once a week.

In Bequia, head to De Reef, The Harpoon Saloon, Daphnes or the Whaleboner (to name a few) for some local specialties. For straight forward American food, stop in at Mac's Pizzeria for pizza and the Harpoon Saloon for pizza, burgers, salads and live country music Saturday nights.

On Mustique, Basil's Beach Bar serves refreshing tropical drinks and their roast pig, available on Wednesday nights, is a mouth-watering treat.

Make sure to sample some of the tasty and uniquely flavored local specialties. Pastelles, for example, is a dish of banana leaves wrapped around a mixture of corn meal and spicy ground meat. One excellent soup, reminiscent of Thai cuisine, is pigeon-pie soup, made with coconut milk and bits of pork. Reservations at restaurants are recommended. Except for rum, alcohol and wine are expensive.

St. Vincent & the Grenadines

Nightlife

On St. Vincent, the Emerald Valley Hotel and Casino has roulette, black jack, poker and other games of chance, all in airconditioned, modern surroundings. The hotels host nighttime barbecues with dancing to steel bands. The locals frequent Mariner's Inn at Villa Beach or Stilly's Aquatic Club for dancing.

On Bequia, Thursday night barbecues at The Frangipani Hotel are a great way to meet new people and sample some delicious island cuisine. On Thursday nights, guests of Young Island Resort can take the shuttleboat to 18th century Fort Duvernette for a special cocktail party (non-guests may attend by making advance reservations). Basil's Beach Bar on Mustique has a show every other Friday.

Shopping

West Indian women's wear -- batik and tie-dyed sarongs, caftans and sundresses -- are beautiful buys. St. Vincent is also noted for its unique postage stamps, available at the Post Office. Saturdays, Kingstown is the scene of a lively outdoor market, with fresh fruit and local wares on display. If there's a cook on your gift list, bring home a bottle of St. Vincent hot sauce or a Caribbean cookbook. Noah's Arkade, the St. Vincent Craftsmen Center and Batik Carib all feature an excellent and reasonably-priced selection of locally made handicrafts.

On Bequia, the craftspeople at Sargent Brothers produce meticulously-built models of yachts and sailboats. On Mustique, Victorian linens and antiques as well as more contemporary beachwear and clothing gifts can be purchased at the Cotton House.

Sports

• Boating

With so much blue sea and white-sand beach to explore, it is, of course, boating that reigns supreme in these islands. Various pleasure crafts, from tiny Sunfish to skippered and bareboat charters, are available for hire out of St. Vincent, Young Island, Union Island and Bequia. Day sails, weekly crewed sails and dive packages can be arranged with most of the boat charter services (see our Directory for contacts).

Yacht races are popular and always colorful. Yachting events include the annual Whitsun Regatta in Kingstown and the Canoua Yacht Race on the (last) August Weekend.

In the spring, Bequia hosts the annual Easter Regatta. There's a different course set for each class of boat participating. Yachts of all styles and caliber race around the island in one direction, come back the other way and then head for the finish.

In the Fishing Boat Races, the various craft push off the shore into the waves and head downwind around the western cay, back up into Friendship and back down to the finish in Lower Bay. Even the kids get into the seafaring spirit, launching their model-sized gumboats made of lightweight wood and cotton sails.

• Fishing

No license is required to enjoy the variety of game fishing available including ballyhoo, mahi, bonito, kingfish, mackerel and red snapper. Charters are available at a number of local marinas. Lobster season starts in the Fall and lasts until April 1st. Spearfishing is illegal.

• Hiking

The lush tropical forests of these islands make St. Vincent and the Grenadines the perfect spot for scenic hiking, offering trails to appeal to every level of energy and physical condition.

On St. Vincent, the hike up Mt. Soufriere is definitely for the energetic, but the spectacular vegetation covering the slopes on the way up, plus the unbeatable view of the island makes it all worthwhile. You can explore Crater Lake with its Rock Island. Make sure to bring a sweater or windbreaker for the occasional chill on top. It takes a full day to hike up to volcano's crater and back, so plan on leaving in the morning. That way there will be plenty of light remaining for the trek back down.

Several routes are available: rent a sturdy vehicle for transportation along the 2.5 mile track through coconut groves and banana plantations to the start of the foot-trail. From there, it's about 3.25 miles to the top. If this route won't quite put that flush in your cheeks, then take the 10-12 mile trek from Chateaubelair or Richmond on the leeward (west) side (ask for directions or arrange for a guide).

Another enjoyable, and slightly less strenuous hike, is to the Falls of Baleine. You'll need to arrange for a boat ride to Richmond Beach. Dive St. Vincent makes weekly trips here. Or take an easy

St. Vincent & the Grenadines

/Grand View

Carnival/Tr.Bd.

tour of the Buccament Valley Nature Trail through the lush rain forest.

• Riding
Trailing riding can be arranged at the Cotton House on Mustique.

• Squash
Along with soccer, squash is very popular in the Caribbean, and St. Vincent is no exception. Their players are of international caliber. Squash courts are located at the Cecil Cyrus Squash Complex, the Grand View Beach Hotel and the Prospect Racquet Club.

• Tennis
There are two lighted courts at the Kingstown Tennis Club and others at the Emerald Valley Hotel, Young Island Resort, Prospect Racquet Club and the Grand View Beach Hotel. On Bequia, courts are located at the Plantation House, Spring on Bequia, Friendship Bay and Frangipani. More courts can be found in the resorts on Petit St. Vincent and Palm Island, at the Cotton House and Charlie's on Mustique, and the Canoua Beach Resort on Canoua.

• Windsurfing
Rentals for windsurfing and other watersports are available at the Windsurfing Center Villa, at Young Island and at several other hotels. Instruc-

tion and rentals are available at the Windsurfing International School at the Mariner's Inn. Ask for instructor Liston Phillips.

• Diving
Located across the water from Young Island is Bill Tewes' Dive St. Vincent. Bill offers one and two-tank dives from his 27-foot, closed-cabin inboard. Night dives, day trips to Bequia and the Falls of Baleine, resort courses and full certification are offered. Bill uses a depth-sensitive computer, THE EDGE, to extend bottom times on his dives.

Dive Bequia run by Bob Sachs, is a well-equipped shop with a helpful crew of instructors and divemasters to make your dive a memorable experience. Bob has another dive operation on Mustique. If you are boating in the area, the dive operations can be raised on VHF 68 for air and diving.

Every dive destination description includes the phrase "abundant marine life," or "large schools of reef fish." But to give an accurate and fair description of diving in St. Vincent one must say, "Fish, fish, fish, fish and more fish." They're lurking in caves, snooping under rocks, hanging out in basket coral, peeking from behind sea fans, feeding in frenzies and cruising in schools. There's also lots of pillar coral, deep sea fans, tall gorgonians and black coral.

• St. Vincent dive sites
St. Vincent reefs are relatively deep, 55 to 90 feet, so most sites are better suited to scuba than snorkeling. See the beautiful wall decorated with a rainbow assortment of coral bushes, including both white and black. Large French angels, snappers and schools of squid can be seen here, as well as a large number of invertebrates. There are also

=7
>7

several wrecks to dive, and even an underwater cave. The Indian Bay area on the southern end of the island is one of St. Vincent's best spots. In the Grenadines, Bequia is considered an excellent dive destination. Great snorkeling can be found at Tobago Cays and Palm Island.

New Guinea Reef is a black coral-watcher's dream. All three types of black coral proliferate here in six different colors. A profusion of soft corals decorate the entire area and sea horses drift lazily through the scene.

Bottle Reef is a combination wall and coral garden dive site, with a touch of St. Vincent history for spice. Uncountable fish watch over a collection of antique gin and rum bottles tossed down from the English Fort overlooking the site.

At The Forest, divers swim amid giant gorgonians, 6 to 10 feet tall. The effect is like flying through a forest of trees inhabited by fish instead of birds.

The Garden is an idyllic spot where thousands of fish "grow" in every conceivable color. A beautiful array of small corals and black coral make this site perfect for photography.

The Wall starts at 20 feet and drops steeply to oblivion. Encrusted with black coral and heavily populated with fish, the area offers unlimited variety. The dive is finished up in the shallows to explore a pristine coral garden. Maximum depth is 100 feet.

The Drift is for advanced divers only, as the current can sometimes exceed 3 knots. Huge groupers and a large number of bigger reef fish call the location home. In charge of it all is a resident rainbow parrot fish weighing in excess of 100 pounds. Big midnight parrots sometimes visit, as well. Due to the strange currents, the exhaust bubbles go sideways rather than up, so at the end of a dive the diver must monitor his depth gauge to assure that ascent is taking place.

The Coral Castle features one of the most magnificent stands of healthy, hard corals in the Caribbean. Standing on the edge of a super wall,

brain corals as large as volkswagons and pillar corals offer an unbelievable alternative to the normal dive sites found elsewhere.

Turtle Bay is the perfect spot for the first dive of the season or for checking out the seaworthiness of your underwater camera. With schools of reef fish, loads of corals and a host of large king crabs, there is something for everyone here.

The Seimstrand is an intact 120-foot long coastal freighter lying in 85 feet of water in Kingstown harbor. Sunk in 1984, she is fast becoming a refuge for fish of all types. Off her stern lies an ancient wreck of unknown origins, marked only by its ballast stones and anchors.

• Bequia dive sites

Bequia, just a 15 minute boat ride from St. Vincent, offers seven miles of undived reefs, vast numbers of fish and an abundance of soft corals. The deep channel running between Bequia and St. Vincent brings up vital nutrients supporting huge schools of tropicals and unexpected numbers of large pelagics, including rays, eels barracuda, and sharks.

There's more good news. Bequia has a leeward wall, meaning that all the sites are protected from the wind. Also, the entire wall is a designated marine park. No spearfishing, no traps, no nets and no anchors are allowed. And no site is more than 8 minutes away by boat.

West Cay, at the island's southernmost point, offers dramatic contrasts in coral and fish life as two different currents meet. On the Atlantic side of the point, large pelagics hunt in packs. On the Caribbean side, gentle reef fish loiter among the corals and sponges.

Devil's Tables, another popular site, is a pristine shallow reef with an added feature, an interesting sailboat wreck at 90 feet.

Key: The accommodations price range is based on the high season rate per night, double occupancy. The Liveaboard price range is per berth, high season. The dive price range is based on the cost of a two tank dive. Letter codes: Beach (or on the water), Diving, Fishing, Golf, Other watersports, Pool, Restaurant & Bar, Sailing, Tennis, Windsurfing.

St. Vincent & the Grenadines

Sunny Caribbee

Grand View

Dive Bequia

Young Island

Dive St. Vincent

Anchorage Yacht Club

St. Vincent & the Grenadines

Accommodations

ANCHORAGE YACHT CLUB 809-458-8221   14 Units: $125-180 BDFKORSW
    809-458-4848 809-458-8244 Union Island St. Vincent. The true center of the wonderful Grenadines Islands, the Anchorage Yacht Club Hotel is the meeting point of the international sailing and diving world in the Southern Caribbean. Surrounded by coral reefs, white beaches, crystal clear waters and over 40 small islands of unsurpassed, unspoiled beauty, they feature all airconditioned, beach located rooms and the best French Caribbean Restaurant. Scuba, fishing, windsurfing, sailing and air tours.

COTTON HOUSE HOTEL 809-456-4777   22 Units: $384-400 BDRTW
    Box 349 Mustique Island, St. Vincent. See: Dive Mustique.

CSY (CARIBBEAN SAILING YACHTS) 800-631-1593   19 Units: $40-65 BOPRSW
    800-237-1131 201-568-1726FX Box 491 Tenafly NJ 07670. See: Dive St. Vincent, Ltd..

GRAND VIEW 800-223-6510   12 Units: $125-165 BDFOPRSTW
    212-832-2277 809-458-4811 Box 173 St. Vincent NY 10022. Situated on Villa Point, just 10 min. from town and 5 min. from the airport, they are a delightful resort hotel featuring 12 guest rooms set amidst 8 acres of lush tropical gardens. The oceanview dining room, with a panoramic view of neighbor islands, offers a fine cuisine. Also on the premises are tennis and squash courts and a freshwater pool. Grand View offers an informal vacation in a truly lovely setting. All watersports & hiking, cheerfully arranged.

HADDON HOTEL 809-456-1897   18 Units: $30-52 R
    Box 144 Kingstown, St. Vincent.

INDIAN BAY BEACH HOTEL 809-458-4001   8 Units: $40-55 BDFKORSTW
    TX:7557 Box 538 St. Vincent. See: Dive St. Vincent, Ltd..

SUNNY CARIBBEE PLANTATION HOUSE 809-458-3425   24 Units: $120-180 BDPRSTW
    FAX 809-458-3621 Belmont Box 16, Admiralty Bay Bequia Island, St. Vincent. Secluded, comfortable and hospitable. A great place to relax and enjoy diving and all watersports. Comfortable cabanas scattered throughout the luxuriant flower scented gardens, offering a double bedroom, modern bathroom and charming veranda. Delightful open-air restaurant, clean private beach. Bequia has the clearest water in the Caribbean. Diving equal to the Maldives. Excellent dive shop on the grounds for novices and experienced divers. See: Dive Bequia.

SUNSET SHORE BEACH HOTEL 800-223-6510   19 Units: $105-180 BDRSW
    212-832-2277 809-458-4411 Box 849, Villa St. Vincent.

UMBRELLA BEACH HOTEL 809-458-4651   9 Units: $38-38 BDFKORSW
    Box 530 St. Vincent. See: Dive St. Vincent, Ltd..

VILLA LODGE HOTEL 809-458-4641   10 Units: $95-95 BDFKOPRSTW
    809-458-4018 Box 1191 Indian Bay, St. Vincent.

YOUNG ISLAND RESORT 800-223-1108   29 Units: $300-485 BDFOPRSTW
    914-763-5526 809-458-4826 Box 211, The Grenadines St. Vincent. A 35-acre fantasy island Caribbean hideaway, just 200 yards south of St. Vincent. All accommodations are private cottages with king-size beds, oceanview terraces and hot outdoor showers. Complimentary welcome drink and daily fruit basket. Windsurfing, snorkeling, tennis, day yacht charters, canoes, Sunfish and a resident scuba pro. Dive shop located just across the channel via water taxi. ROOM PRICES INCLUDE MEALS (MAP). See: Dive St. Vincent, Ltd..

Information

GRENADINE TOURS & ANCHOR TRAVEL 800-526-4789
    201-569-5464 Box 1098 St. Vincent, W.I. Complete dive packages with special low air fares with BWIA are available through Anchor Travel Service. They also arrange inexpensive shared charters to all the Grenadines, as well as packaged or individual day tours using the service of Grenadine Tours. Anchor Travel is also the agent for the AMIZADE an 82 foot trimaran with live aboard facilities for 16 divers at $180 a day P.P.including meals, drinks and 2 dives daily. Combination packages available. See: Dive St. Vincent, Ltd..

ST. VINCENT & THE GRENADINES TOURISM 212-687-4981
    212-949-5496FX 809-457-1502 801 2nd St., 21st Floor New York NY 10017.

Sports

BIMINI YACHT CHARTER & BAREFOOT HOLIDAYS 716-855-2774   1 Boats: $600-600 S
    809-456-9324 Box 39 St. Vincent.

DIVE BEQUIA 809-458-3425   20 Divers: $65-65 D
    809-458-3612FX Box 16 St. Vincent. Dive Bequia offers NAUI instruction and professional guide services to the visiting diver. Their boats never take more than 4 divers per instructor, and the diver never has to carry gear. This is unhurried, uncrowded diving in some of the world's most beautiful waters south of friendly St.Vincent. Explore spectacular walls, wrecks and reefs populated by rays, lobster, barracuda, squid & giant angels. For personal service contact Bob or Julie. See: Sunny Caribbee Plantation House.

DIVE MUSTIQUE 809-458-3504   10 Divers: $65-65 D
    809-458-3612FX Box 16 St. Vincent. See: Cotton House Hotel.

DIVE ST. VINCENT, LTD. 809-457-4714   8 Divers: $50-50 BD
    809-457-4409 Box 864 St. Vincent. Dive the unspoiled, uncrowded reefs with the oldest established dive shop in St. Vincent. Two fast dive boats take divers to the sites in 10 minutes or less. Offering all instruction from resort courses to assistant instructor. Dive St. Vincent has the latest equipment available. Maximum dive time is encouraged with the use of the Orca EDGE on all dives. Day tours for the non diver. Dive packages with most hotels on the island. Join them in Paradise. See: Young Island Resort.

Turks & Caicos

Travel & Sports Guide

Turks & Caicos

Useful Facts

• **Airline Connections**   Pan Am operates the only scheduled service between the US and the Turks & Caicos Islands (four times per week to Providenciales and twice a week into Grand Turk). All the flights originate in Miami and offer easy connections from other locations in the PAN AM world-wide system. The inter-island airline, Turks and Caicos National Airlines (TCNA), provides frequent connections between the islands of Grand Turk, Salt Cay, South Caicos, Middle Caicos, North Caicos and Providenciales. Flights may be chartered to the uninhabited island of West Caicos. There is a $10 departure tax, payable upon leaving the islands.

• **Banking**   The US dollar is used throughout the islands. International banking facilities are available at Grand Turk, South Caicos and Providenciales. Traveler's checks are accepted throughout. Some hotels and other facilities accept Visa, MasterCard and American Express credit cards, but not all. Banking hours are 8:30am -2:30pm Monday through Thursday and 8:30am-5:00pm on Friday.

• **Courtesy & Dress**   Dress is casual and suitable for warm weather: light cotton dresses and separates for women, cotton shirts and slacks or shorts for men. Light sweaters or jackets are recommended for breezy evenings. Beach wear should be reserved for the beach only. The hotels and restaurants do not require jackets or ties. Since water is precious on the islands, particularly in the south, it is a matter of courtesy to the residents to help conserve water and be sparing in its use. Island residents are proud of the beauty and abundance of their beaches, reefs and marine life and enlist the cooperation of visitors in preserving the islands' natural state.

• **Customs & Immigration**   Proof of citizenship, in the form of a passport, birth certificate or voter's registration card is required of American and Canadian citizens, plus a round-trip or onward ticket. Visitors may stay up to 30 days. Longer stays are allowed only with government permission. The usual cigarette and bottle restrictions apply, but there are no restrictions on the import of cameras, film or sports equipment. The importation or possession of illegal drugs or firearms, including spearguns (without previously obtaining a police permit), is strictly prohibited.

• **Driving**   On the left. Car and/or scooter rentals can be arranged through any hotel.

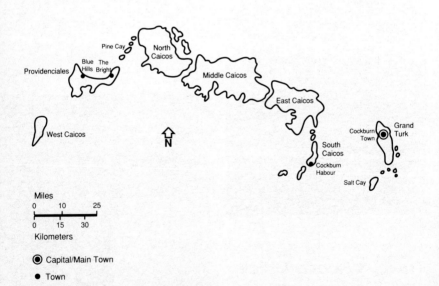

Turks & Caicos

Provo/Jacobs

Bicycles are available for rent by the hour or day.

• Electricity   US standards.

• Events & Holidays   New Year's Day; Good Friday; Easter Monday; Commonwealth Day (late May); the last weekend in May heralds the start of the South Caicos Regatta, commemorating the visit of Queen Elizabeth II; the Queen's birthday (mid-June); Annual Turks & Caicos Billfish Tournament (July); Emancipation Day, celebrating the freeing of the islands' slaves, takes place the first Monday in August, followed by the week long Carnival at the end of the month and into the beginning of September; Columbus Day; International Human Rights Day (October); Christmas Day; Boxing Day (Dec. 26).

• Languages   English.

• Medical   A fully equipped hospital is located on Grand Turk. There are also clinics on South Caicos, Middle Caicos, North Caicos, Salt Cay and Providenciales. Bring insect repellent as the mosquito population on some islands can be annoying. Conserve water and inquire before drinking tap water. There's a recompression chamber in Provo.

• Taxes & Tipping   Resorts add a 10% - 15% service charge instead of a gratuity. There is also a 5% government tax on accommodations. Tipping 15% at restaurants and bars is customary where gratuities are not already added to the bill.

• Taxi Fares   Fares from the island airports to the local hotels usually run between $3.00 and $6.00.

• Telephone   To reach the Turks and Caicos by phone from the US dial area code 809 + 946 + the appropriate four-digit number. For operator assistance, ask for "160 plus 105." Cable and Wireless (West Indies) Ltd. operates domestic and international telex, telegraph services and FAX.

• Time   Eastern Standard.

• Weather   Warm, sunny and arid all year long. Temperatures range from 60 to 90 degrees. The trade winds provide frequent ocean breezes. The southern islands of Grand Turk, Salt Cay and South Caicos have considerable sun and very little rain, with rainfall averaging 22 inches each year. For this reason, water is often in short supply on these islands during the summer months. The northern islands are less arid, averaging 44 to 50 inches per year.

Introduction

Considerably closer to the US than either Puerto Rico or the Virgin Islands lie the small cluster of unspoiled islands known as the Turks and Caicos Islands. In the Atlantic about 30 miles

Turks & Caicos

southeast from the Bahamas and half-way between Miami and Puerto Rico, the group consists of 8 large islands and 40 smaller cays. The Turks Islands (Grand Turk and Salt Cay) are separated from the six Caicos Islands to the northeast by the deep channel of the Turks Island Passage.

Two-hundred-thirty miles of pristine and often uninhabited, beaches as well as spectacular diving and snorkeling await the visitor to this virtually undiscovered archipelago. The contrast in color where the land, sky and sea meet, is dazzling. The sand is pure white or gold. The beach grasses are green and the water is bright turquoise, with up to 200 feet of visibility underwater, particularly in the summer months.

History

According to local legend, the Turks Islands were named for a red cactus with red blossoms which reminded one creative settler of a Turkish fez. The Caicos Islands probably were named for cayos, the Spanish word for small island.

The Lucayan or Arawak Indians were evidently the first people to inhabit the Turks and Caicos Islands, as evidenced by a small village unearthed in Middle Caicos. These early settlers may have established a salt industry in the Caicos Islands in pre-Columbian times.

It is unclear whether Christopher Columbus actually landed in the islands during his world travels in 1492, although recent evidence supports this theory. Ponce de Leon officially sighted the island of Grand Turk in 1512, during his quest for Bimini, the legendary island possessing the Fountain of Youth.

During the 16th and 17th centuries, the islands were used as hideouts for some of the world's most notorious pirates, including Rackam the Red. Small, flat Parrot Cay was the occasional home of a band of women pirates known as the "Bloody Sisters," otherwise known as Mary Reid and Anne Bonny. Mary Reid started her career in this predominantly male world early in life. As a child, she disguised herself as a boy and served on various ships as a footboy, sailor, soldier and finally pirate. During one raid, she was captured by an enemy pirate ship, captained by "Calico Jack" Rackman. There she met and became firm friends with Anne Bonny, Rackman's lover and one of his fearless crew members to boot. Their illustrious career as sea robbers came to an end when they were captured by British authorities. Mary was

sentenced to hang, but died of fever before it could be carried out. Anne pleaded pregnancy and her sentence was commuted. Eventually she met and married a rich aristocrat.

The first post-Indian settlement was founded in 1678 when salt rakers from Bermuda arrived with their slaves to establish a salt industry on the islands of Salt Cay, Grand Turk and South Caicos. The harvested salt, known as "white gold" for its important use as a means of food preservation, was carried back to Bermuda for use and sale. The Bahamas tried unsuccessfully to annex the islands in 1700 and during the next century both the Turks and Caicos were invaded, first by Spanish and then by the French.

British Loyalists arrived on Caicos in 1780 to establish cotton plantations. Driven from the United States after the War of Independence, they were repaid by King George with large land settlements. Plantations were built which rivaled the size and opulence of those in Georgia. They used slave labor to help supply the large demand for cotton in England, enjoying thirty years of prosperity until weather, insects, soil exhaustion and war depleted the resources. Today, the only physical evidence that remains are the Cheshire Hall ruins on Providenciales and remnants of stone walls scattered about the islands.

The Bahamas gained administrative control of the islands and governed them from 1799 to 1848. The Turks and Caicos separated from the Bahamas in 1848 and were governed by their own president and council for over twenty years. In 1874, Jamaica annexed the islands. They remained a Jamaican colony until Jamaica became independent in 1962, leaving the Turks and Caicos a separate colony. In 1972, the islands acquired their own governor (appointed by the Queen of England) and soon afterwards held elections. Today the islands remain a British colony with a ministerial government and an 11 member Legislative Council.

Of the 12,000 people currently inhabiting the Turks and Caicos islands, most of them reside on Grand Turk and Providenciales, which is regarded by many visitors as the most beautiful island. South and North Caicos are also relatively populous. While there are small settlements on Middle Caicos (also known as Grand Caicos) and Salt Cay, East and West Caicos remain uninhabited.

Turks & Caicos

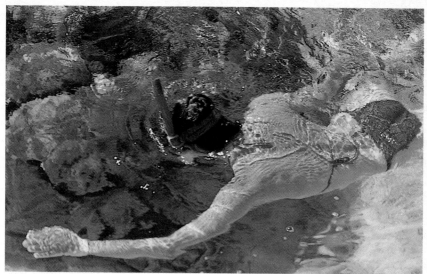

Snorkeling/Island Photo

Ecology

The islands' land surface is actually the top of a limestone platform rising from the sea. Windward (east) sides are sculpted with sand dunes and limestone cliffs, while leeward sides support more vegetation. The southern islands of Grand Turk, Salt Cay and South Caicos have considerable sun with very little rain. These islands, covered mostly by cactus, thorny scrub and crabgrass, have few tall trees since most of the high vegetation was cut down by early salt rakers attempting to thwart unwanted rain. In contrast, the northern Caicos islands receive much more rain and are relatively fertile. However, very little of the land is suitable for agriculture.

Dense scrub and low trees tend to cover the higher northern grounds, while eastern and southern shores give way to exposed sand beaches, cactus, meandering creeks and red mangrove swamps. For their daily diet, local residents depend on an ample supply of fish, crustaceans and mollusks. Some fish, lobster and conch are harvested for export, but tourism is the major source of revenue for the islands today.

An extensive reef system with steep wall drop-offs surrounds the island and is patrolled by friendly dolphins, Atlantic mantas and schools of colorful fish. Topside, shy iguanas sunbathe in the warm sands.

Exploring

The easiest way to explore the towns is on foot, but getting to more remote places will require a car. Rental agencies operate on Grand Turk, South Caicos and Provo. Local taxis can be hired for island tours at about $20 or $25 an hour, but it's advisable to establish the price with the driver before setting out.

Grand Turk is a 7-square-mile island of somewhat rocky eastern coast countered by undulating dunes on its western coast. It is encircled by an

Windward beach, East Cay/Coit

Turks & Caicos

offshore reef which provides crystalline shallow waters close to shore. A quarter-mile-off the western shore however, the waters deepen to 7,000 feet as they approach the Turks Islands Passage.

Grand Turk is the home of Cockburn Town, the government seat and the financial and business center of the islands. Buildings, particularly along Duke Street and Front Street, reflect the Bermudian style of architecture. On Front Street, which overlooks both the sea and saline, visit The Victoria Library, the institution most nearly resembling a museum on the islands. Donkey carts still traverse the town, transporting water and freight, while wild horses and donkeys roam the island.

On the road running from the town to the northern end of the island is an old lighthouse and the missile tracking station where John Glenn was debriefed after his space mission in 1962. Along the north-west shore lies beautiful Pillary Beach. Taking the same road to the south, the traveler will encounter Governor's Beach. Boat trips are available from Grand Turk to the cays east and south of the island. Gibbs Cay and Round Cay, two miles to the east of Grand Turk and Pennington Cay, three miles to the south, have been designated as nature reserves. Especially beautiful beaches stretch along Long Cay, Pear Cay, East Cay and Cotton Cay, all lying to the south of Grand Turk.

Salt Cay lies six miles south of Grand Turk and is accessible by the local airlines. Balfour Town is the major settlement, also noted for its Bermuda-style buildings. Old windmills, salt sheds and sluices dating from the late 1700's still stand. Also in Balfour Town is the White House, formerly the home of the salt proprietor and today a private residence whose owners are prepared to show visitors the collection of antique furniture built in Jamaica and Bermuda. While there are no scuba facilities around Salt Cay, snorkeling and swimming are excellent in the quiet little inlets and coves on east side of island and off the beautiful beaches on the north shore.

South Caicos, twenty-two miles east of Grand Turk, was once an important salt-producing island and is now a fishing center for queen conch and bonefish. Cockburn Harbor, its only settlement, is a natural port and the site of the annual South Caicos regatta. On a ridge overlooking the Harbor, a herd of wild horses can sometimes be seen roaming in the vicinity of a nineteenth century house, The Highlands.

Construction of a new road has simplified access to points of interest on South Caicos. Driving north along the western shore from Cockburn Harbor, you'll encounter shallow banks where spiny lobster and conch are harvested for export. Inviting white sand beaches meet the azure waters further to the island's north, where the Caicos Bank extends north and west to Providenciales. Driving along the island's east coast will take you along the 6-mile long, 150-foot high limestone ridge with excellent views out to the sea. From Cockburn Harbor, boat trips are available to the island preserves of Long Cay and Six Hill Cay, which are noted for their rich underwater life. Several miles further to the south are two little islands known not only for their excellent diving and fishing, but for their caves: the beach encompassing Big Ambergris Cave and its companion Little Ambergris Cave.

Middle Caicos, also known as Grand Caicos, is the largest island in the archipelago. Fifteen miles long, its coastline is made dramatic by towering limestone cliffs along the north and by its numerous coves and beaches. The one guesthouse on the island, run by the government, is the little settlement of Conch Bar. Make sure to visit the limestone Conch Bar Caves on the north side of the island. These cathedral-sized caves are natural museums of stalactites, stalagmites and clear underground salt lakes.

Continuing west from these caves, between the towns of Bambarra and Lorimar, are the ruins

Out for the day's chores/Jacobs

Turks & Caicos

Windsurfer/Jacobs

of a cave settlement of Lucayan and Arawak Indians. Mined in the 1880's for guano, theses ancient caves and the ruins near the towns of Bambarra and Lucayan, are a source of fascination to archaeologists looking for artifacts of these original inhabitants. South from Lorimer is Big Pond, a natural reserve with varied plant and animal life.

East Caicos, now uninhabited, was once important for its sisal crop. The island's main attraction is its spectacular 17-mile north coast beach, accessible only by boat.

North Caicos, known for its abundant fruit trees and vegetable farms, is the garden center of the islands. Separated by a narrow channel from Middle Caicos, it is accessible by boat or plane. The resort area of Whitby is at the northernmost tip of the island. Driving south from Whitby, wild flamingos nest at Flamingo Pond. West from Whitby are the little settlements of Sandy Point and Kew, with their abundant fruit trees bearing crops of papayas, limes and custard apples. Some of the produce farmed on this island reaches local markets, but none is transported beyond the island itself. To the southeast of Whitby lies the town of Bottle Creek, where the inhabitants live mainly by catching fish, shellfish and crayfish. Take a boat from Whitby and visit the nature reserve of Three Mary Cays.

Pine Cay is one of a chain of small islands between North Caicos and "Provo." Privately owned, it has its own exclusive resort development, The Meridian Club, and reputedly the most beautiful two-and-one-half miles of beach in the islands. Electric carts are the usual form of transportation around the island, although the beautiful hiking trails and nature walks will tempt the traveler to forego four-wheels and lace up the sneakers instead.

Fort George Cay, off the north coast of Pine Cay, is a national park containing the remains of a British fort and the stone footings of the old palisade. Close to the shore and visible with snorkeling gear, are old barnacle-encrusted cannons of times gone by. With the assistance of local guides, traces of pre-Columbian settlements can reputedly be found on both Pine Cay and Fort George Cay. Water Cay and Little Water Cay, southwest of the island, are great spots for shell hunting.

Providenciales, of all the islands, has the most developed tourist industry. Several British and American firms are building homes, hotels and resorts here. Developed by a group of millionaires headed by Dick Du Pont, the island has changed from an unknown gem-in-the-rough to a modern and accessible bit of paradise. East of Pine Cay, many consider "Provo" to be the most beautiful island of all, with its rolling hills and unspoiled 12-mile beach along the northeast coast. Also along this coast is Grace Bay, the site of Club Med's

Turks & Caicos

/Felgate

/Felgate

/Felgate

Turks & Caicos

/Craig

/Craig

/Tsapis

Turks & Caicos

newest and most elegant resort, Club Med Turkoise, which opened in December 1984.

On the south coast of the island is Five Cays Settlement, a village which boasts both a small harbor and a modern airport. West of Five Cays Settlement is Chalk Sound, a land-locked lagoon which has been made into a national park. Dotting the coast north and east of the Blue Hills Settlement are villages which supply food for export as well as for local consumption. Provo is also home of the Caicos Conch Farm which, in addition to harvesting conch for commercial export, also houses a conch maricultural lab open to visitors in the afternoons. In keeping with the archipelago's concern for the environment, Provo is the seat of PRIDE (Society for the Protection of Reefs and Islands from Degradation and Exploitation).

West Caicos, southwest of Provo, is uninhabited and can be reached only by charter plane. The rugged island, once inhabited by pirates, is totally without facilities. However, it possesses a large saltwater lake, Lake Catherine, where flamingos nest and other wild birds and animals proliferate. Offshore the diving is possibly the most exotic in the islands and many treasure hunters come here seeking the wealth buried in these waters.

Food

Restaurant fare tends to be expensive because so much of the food is imported, although good inexpensive restaurants can be found. On Grand Turk try the Regal Beagle for fresh fish and chips, the Poop Deck for spicy chicken and chips or Pillary Beach for good local food, particularly their turtle stew. Other island delicacies, served in delectable abundance at Papillon's, Xavier's and Peanuts Snack Bar, include conch fritters (the closest thing to "fast food" on the islands), conch stew and salad, spiny lobster, grouper, snapper, turtle and wahoo. For local cuisine on Provo, try beachside Le Deck, the Banana Boat or Fast Eddie's. All the hotels have notable restaurants and there's a surprising selection of international cuisine as well: Chinese, French, Mexican and Italian. Supermarkets sell a variety of good quality food, also imported for the most part.

Nightlife

Discos exist on all the inhabited islands. Most of the islands have local musicians who play a combination of Caribbean tunes and calypso, together with reggae, some traditional Caicos music with a Haitian/African influence and renditions of popular American tunes.

The first real nightclub on the islands opened on Provo's Airport Road in 1984. Sporting strobe lights and an elevated dance floor, Disco Elite opens at 8pm nightly except Sundays. More dancing can be had at the Banana Boat. Grand Turk also keeps feet tapping at its three discos: The Uprising, the Members Club and the Lady at the old North Naval Base. You can enjoy amateur theatre through performances given by the local schools and churches. The recently formed Turks and Caicos Royal Police Force Marching Band adds real Turks Island flair to public functions.

Shopping

There are no duty-free shops on the islands; however, due to modest import duties, liquor is inexpensive. Provo offers the best selection of small boutiques and other specialty shops. Conch Closet, at Provo Plaza sells gold jewelry, island fashions and items made of shells. Local taxi drivers and hotel staff are probably the most knowledgeable about local shops carrying particular items of interest.

Sports

It is not surprising that the majority of sports on these ocean-surrounded islands are water-oriented. However, there are also spectator sports like cricket matches, played from June to November. Sightseeing boat trips can be arranged for the visitor who would rather watch than swim.

• Fishing

A number of sportfishing possibilities exist in the Turks and Caicos. Bottom fishing for reef dwellers can be scheduled through the Third Turtle Inn on Provo. Bonefishing is possible on South Caicos, Middle Caicos, North Caicos and Salt Cay, but Provo and Pine Cay reportedly have the best bonefishing sites. On Provo, bonefishing charter boats leave from the Third Turtle Inn.

Deep-sea fishing for tuna, sailfish, marlin and wahoo are booked though several Provo hotels. In July, Provo hosts the annual Turks and Caicos Islands International Billfish Tournament, which offers cash prizes to its winners. For more information, contact the tournament organizers at: PO Box 8409, Hialeah, FL, 33012.

Turks & Caicos

Provo/Jacobs

• Sailing

Sailing is available through the Third Turtle or the Island Princess Hotel on Provo. The Inn also rents Sunfish and Boston Whaler craft. Charter boats can also be hired. May is the month of the annual regatta, drawing participants from Jamaica, Miami and islands in the vicinity. Starting in South Caicos, the regatta also features beauty contests, fishing boat and donkey races and the Women's Federation Cake Stand.

• Tennis

If tennis is your game, you'll find courts on Grand Turk at South Base, Island Reef and Cedar Home. On Provo look up Turtle Cove Yacht and Tennis Club, Club Med, Leeward and Erebus and the Third Turtle. There's also tennis on South Caicos, North Caicos and Pine Cay.

• Windsurfing

Windsurfing is popular in Provo and can be arranged through the hotels there. Kittina in Grand Turk and Island Princess and Seatopia in Provo, offer waterskiing and windsurfing. Jetskiing rentals are available at Provo Jetski next to Club Med.

• Diving

We can't tell you exactly what to expect underwater in the Turks and Caicos. Nobody can, because this is wilderness diving at its best: thousands of reefs that no one has explored before, with walls that run for miles and plunge to unfathomable depths. There are hundreds of sites, never before charted and millions of fish undisturbed by nets, spears or even cameras. There are large fish here like shark, pompano, barracuda, snapper and eagle ray, as well as the jewel-like reef fish that adorn the shallower depths. In November and December, schools of humpback whales pass Grand Turk Passage, heading south to the Silver Banks breeding grounds.

The Society to Protect our Reefs from Degradation and Exploitation (PRIDE) was founded in 1976 to conserve marine resources and to encourage safe scuba exploration. The Society's motto is, "Take only pictures, kill only time, leave only bubbles."

Another organization dedicated to diving safety is SUDS, the Society of Underwater Diving Safety of the Turks and Caicos Islands. Through the efforts of SUDS, Provo now has a multi-lock, 60-inch recompression chamber. Dick Rukowski, who recently retired from the National Oceanic and Atmospheric Administration, owns the chamber and oversees a program of diving and diving-medical training programs on the island. The

Grand Turk/Jacobs

Turks & Caicos

chamber is housed at the Erebus Inn and is available for the treatment of diving accidents.

All divers must possess and present a valid certification card before they rent equipment. Not long ago, the guide-books advised divers to bring all their own equipment except tanks and weightbelts when visiting the islands. Today, the dive shops are fully stocked with the latest gear. Leave your speargun home. Spearfishing is illegal here and the taking of live corals, sea fans and other marine life is forbidden.

Most diving is done by boat, supervised by certified instructors or divemasters. Some sites can be reached by shore entry, but unless you're very familiar with the islands, a guide is recommended.

The best time for a dive vacation is April through November, although a rare hurricane can occur late in this period. Rough seas occasionally occur in February/March. Divers wishing more detailed information should write for Divers, Snorkelers and Visitors Guide to the Turks and Caicos Islands, c/o Palm Publications, PO Box 101, Grand Turk, Turks & Caicos Islands.

Providenciales

Provo offers variety: first-class walls, wrecks, pinnacles and a high concentration of exotic marine life. The wall is just 30-50 minutes away and the north shore sites are even closer, 10-15 minutes. This is a good spot for beginners, as well as experienced dive explorers, as there are no currents, year round visibility of 80-100 feet and water temperatures ranging from 75F in the winter to 84F in the summer.

The diving on Provo ranges from wall dives in West Caicos and North West Point to wreck dives on Molasses reef to coral garden reefs on the North Shore. The reefs boast pelagic fish, grouper, rays, turtle, shark and dolphin.

South Wind wreck rests in 50 feet on the edge of a sloping wall. The hull was broken up during a 1986 hurricane but the site offers plenty of diversity, including lots of tame Nassau groupers, snappers, jacks, trigger fish, eels, lobster and large schools of tropical fish.

The Pinnacles is a coral garden starting at 30 feet with a nearby coral wall, dropping to a sandy bottom at 100 feet. Between the towering pinnacles, which run along the wall for several hundred feet, are deep gullies and canyons, as well as several large chimneys to explore.

Shark Hole, a deep dive for experienced divers, starts at 60 feet and follows a vertical hole down to 100 feet. Here the tunnel slopes more gently to the left and emerges under an arch at 130 feet into a sandy meeting place for a group of sharks. This dive is not for the claustrophobic or timid.

The Wall at North West Point starts at 40-50 feet and drops to 6,000 feet. Its topography is unique for the numerous gullies and chimneys, and its marine life is no less dramatic. Sharks, eagle rays and turtles cruise the wall. Nurse sharks sleep under overhangs. And manta rays whirl within a plankton cloud.

Along the wall at Red Sponge/Black Coral Forest, there's a shallow cave scooped into the wall's face lined with giant red elephant ear sponges and spectacular black coral trees.

Molasses Reef and South West Reef are areas of old galleon wrecks, now sitting in pieces with a few intact cannon and anchors encrusted with coral.

Photographers will enjoy Aquarium West, a shallow reef with a series of healthy coral mounds inhabited by large schools of tropicals.

There are four excellent dive operations in Provo. Provo Underseas Adventures, a Neal Watson operation, managed by Tony Felgate, caters to certified divers wishing a truly unique diving experience. The shop is equipped with a full line of rental gear and accessories and is located next to Island Photo, the island's only professional E-6 lab.

Provo Aquatic Center, managed by Becky Aldrich, is the facility on the southwest end of the island. A full-service marina with sailboat rentals, bonefishing charters, windsurfing, waterskiing and motor boat rentals, this shop offers diving at the northwest point of Provo and the leeward wall of West Caicos.

Third Turtle Inn Diving, located on the beachfront of the hotel of the same name offers equipment rental, instruction and film processing, as well as PADI certification, resort courses and underwater photography.

Provo Turtle Divers is the only PADI instructor training facility on the island and the oldest dive operation in the Turks & Caicos. Owner Art Pickering and his staff offer resort courses, certifications, rentals, repairs and sales in a friendly family atmosphere. Four of the island's hotels are serviced by this shop.

West Caicos

Dolphin Dip is an unusually large dip in the wall which attracts schools of dolphin at most times of the year. The wall approaching the dip is encrusted with large sponges, hard and soft corals and attracts thousands of fish.

Rock Garden Interlude, another wall dive remarkable for its dramatic color scheme of red, yellow and lavender sponges. A diversity of out-croppings and small gullies adds to the site's topographical interest. Depths range from 70 to 100 feet.

South Caicos

South Caicos offers world-class wall diving just 10 minutes offshore, plus exciting encounters with bull and blacktip sharks, even an occasional hammerhead! Large green, hawksbill and logger-head turtles, African pompano, large barracuda and schools (four dozen at a time) of spotted eagle rays are often sighted in these warm, pristine waters.

Eagle's Nest is named for its resident com-munity of gentle southern stingrays. The unusual seascape of spur and groove coral, sand channels and ledges make this site a perfect domicile for bull sharks, a 250-pound jewfish and schools of horse-eyed jacks.

Plane Wreck, a Convair 340 sunk in 55 feet of water, is another spectacular site for wreck fans and fish enthusiasts alike.

/Johnston

Small dock/Kelly

North Caicos

Much of the underwater world off North Caicos' north coast remains unexplored. There are huge coral hills rising 30-40 feet, separated by small canyons and overgrown with soft corals. Much of the reef is truly virgin and most sites are within a mile offshore.

Grand Turk

The drop-off into the 7,000-foot Turks Island passage begins only 1/4 mile offshore, a ten-minute boat ride from the beach. Lots of lush, soft corals, colorful encrusting sponges, canyons and black coral as shallow as 60 feet. The leeward wall offers calm, protected wall diving starting in 30 feet of clear, warm water -- a rare treat for novices and experts alike.

The Library, just off the main street of town, is an excellent night dive for its proximity and

Turks & Caicos

shallow profile. It's also a favorite of photographers because it hosts a large population of marine invertebrates, including lobster, crab, octopi, eels, shrimp and the rare, nocturnal orange ball anemone.

McDonald's, named for its large coral arch, is a 50-foot dive. This lush, colorful site is home to 6 friendly groupers and schools of yellowtail snappers eager for a hand-out.

The Tunnels start inside the reef at 60 feet and emerge on the outside at 80 feet. Turning north, divers come suddenly upon a large outcropping bursting with purple tube sponges, huge elephant ear, barrel and vase sponges, gorgonians and schools of jack and spade fish.

Black Forest, a concave scoop in the wall, is home to three species of black coral in rare abundance at 40 to 100 feet. An excellent night dive.

Amphitheater begins with a sandy bottom at 40 feet, then slopes down to a dramatic cut in the wall, with ledges, overhangs, abundant sponge growth and a healthy fish population. Turning north and working along the wall, divers enter a large sand amphitheater surrounded by lush coral. Humpback whales have been sighted here in season.

Finbar's Reef has two legs, one shallow and one deep, perfect for all levels of experience.

Coral Canyons and Coral Gardens feature a stairstep terrain. The dive starts at 35 feet and drops to 60-80 feet to a series of sand lakes. Twelve distinct sand bowls, 100 feet across, dot the landscape, punctuated with small coral heads, each housing a small grouper and cleaning station.

Cecil's Reef is a wall dive starting at 35 feet with an abundance of soft coral on top, dropping-off steeply into vertical rows of deep water gorgonia. Large schools of reef fish, big groupers, occasional sharks, lobster, crab and angels inhabit this thriving reef system.

Those who come to Grand Turk for a dive vacation may choose from two excellent dive operators offering dive packages with several first-rate hotels and guesthouses, as well a two comfortable liveaboards. Right on the beach along Front Street in Cockburn Town is Blue Water Divers, managed by Mitch Rolling. Mitch's down-home service includes hotel pick-ups in his comfortable 23-foot boat for groups of 8 or less. They offer two dives daily plus night dives, equip-ment rentals and the largest selection of T-shirts on the island.

Omega Divers, located on the premises of the Hotel Kittina, offers PADI training, E-6 slide processing, equipment and camera rentals, sunset cruises, snorkeling trips and a charter boat service, as well as a complete range of professional dive services.

For those who like to immerse themselves in diving, Peter Hughes' Sea Dancer is the answer to a dive fanatic's dreams. Accommodations for 19 people, good food, full-production video and audio-visual services and as many as five dives a day are offered. Dive in Grand Turk, South Caicos and several uninhabited cays.

The Aquanaut, anchored just off the center of town sleeps 4 to 6 and offers great food, unlimited diving and a resident marine biologist as a guide. Weekly rates are $1,100, all inclusive except alcohol. Aquanaut spends 9 to 10 months diving Grand Turk and its nearby cays, then moves to West Caicos and Provo in August and September.

Cover Photography: J Stone, DIVI Hotels, Jacobs, Provo Undersea Adventures.

Sea Dancer Liveaboard

Key: The accommodations price range is based on the high season rate per night, double occupancy. The Liveaboard price range is per berth, high season. The dive price range is based on the cost of a two tank dive. Letter codes: Beach (or on the water), Diving, Fishing, Golf, Other watersports, Pool, Restaurant & Bar, Sailing, Tennis, Windsurfing.

Turks & Caicos Islands - Information

AND BOOKINGS: TURKS & CAICOS TOURIST BD. 800-441-4419
  809-946-2321/2 Grand Turk Turks & Caicos Islands.
INFORMATION: MEDHURST & ASSOCIATES 516-673-0150
  1208 Washington Drive Centerport NY 11721.

Grand Turk, Turks & Caicos Islands - Accommodations

COLUMBUS HOUSE 809-946-2798   10 Units: $35-50 DR
  305-667-0966 Box 97, Pond Street, Grand Turk Turks & Caicos Islands.
GUINEP TREE LODGE 809-946-2977   6 Units: $75-75 BD
  General Delivery, Grand Turk Turks & Caicos Islands. See: Blue Water Divers.
ISLAND REEF HOTEL 800-634-3483   21 Units: $95-135 BDKPRTW
  809-946-2055 305-667-0966 Box 10, Grand Turk Turks & Caicos Islands. See: Omega Diving of Grand Turk, LTD.
KIRK'S PLACE 809-946-2227   3 Units: $65-65 D
  Box 140, Grand Turk Turks & Caicos Islands.
KITTINA HOTEL 305-667-0966   43 Units: $75-125 BDFKRSW
  809-946-2232 Box 42, Grand Turk Turks & Caicos Islands. See: Omega Diving of Grand Turk, LTD.
PILLORY BEACH HOTEL 809-946-2630   16 Units: $90-100 BDFPRW
  305-667-0966 TX:8275 Box 2, Grand Turk Turks & Caicos Islands. See: Turks Island Aqua Sports.
SALT RAKER INN 809-946-2260   10 Units: $55-90 BOR
  305-667-0966 Box #1 Duke St., Grand Turk Turks & Caicos Islands.
TURKS HEAD INN 809-946-2466   12 Units: $35-50 BDR
  305-667-0966 TX:8237 Box 58, Grand Turk Turks & Caicos Islands. See: Blue Water Divers.

Grand Turk, Turks & Caicos Islands - Liveaboards

AQUANAUT 800-348-9778   6 Berths: $157-157 D
  415-434-3400 Box 101 Grand Turk, Turks & Caicos Islands.
SEA DANCER 800-367-3484   12 Berths: $157-185 BDRW
  607-277-3484 54 Gunderman Rd. Ithaca NY 14850. Catering to the serious diving enthusiast, the Sea Dancer offers all-inclusive packages of first class accommodations, diving services, gourmet meals and photo & video services. Expect 3 to 5 diving opportunities per day featuring walls, virgin reef exploration and unsurpassed pelagic encounters. 8-day, 7-night trips feature diving in Grand Turk, South Caicos and several uninhabited cays. Host: Peter Hughes Diving. Exclusive charters available.

Grand Turk, Turks & Caicos Islands - Sports

BLUE WATER DIVERS 809-946-2432   12 Divers: $50-50 D
  Box 124, Grand Turk Turks & Caicos Islands. See: Turks Head Inn.
OMEGA DIVING OF GRAND TURK, LTD 800-255-1966   70 Divers: $45-45 DFO
  305-385-0779 809-946-2232 8420 S. W. 133 Ave., Suite 319 Miami FL 33183. See: Kittina Hotel.

Middle Caicos, Turks & Caicos Islands - Accommodations

TAYLORS GUEST HOUSE 305-667-0966   4 Units: $35-35
  Middle Caicos Turks & Caicos Islands.

North Caicos, Turks & Caicos Islands - Accommodations

OCEAN BEACH HOTEL 800-223-6510   10 Units: $100-170 BDFKOPRST
  212-832-2277 809-946-4694 P.O. Box 1156 - Station B Burlington, Ontario.
PELICAN BEACH HOTEL 305-667-0966   6 Units: $150-150
  North Caicos Turks & Caicos Islands.
PROSPECT OF WHITBY HOTEL 800-346-4295   28 Units: $110-160 BDFOPRSTW
  203-355-8236 203-354-3566FX Box 157 New Milford CT 06776. See: Dolphin Cay.

North Caicos, Turks & Caicos Islands - Sports

DOLPHIN CAY 416-475-1620   Divers D
  305-667-0966 North Caicos Turks & Caicos Islands. See: Prospect of Whitby Hotel.

Turks & Caicos

Pine Cay, Turks & Caicos Islands - Accommodations
MERIDIAN CLUB, RESORTS MGT. INC. 800-225-4255   15 Units: $190-450 BDFRT
  212-696-4566 201 1/2 East 29 Street New York NY 10016.
SMITH'S COTTAGE 305-667-0966   6 Units: $89-89
  Pine Cay Turks & Caicos Islands.

Providenciales, Turks & Caicos Islands - Accommodations
ADMIRALS CLUB 809-946-4375   9 Units: $100-200 BDR
  305-667-0966 Turtle Cove, Providenciales Turks and Caicos Islands. See: Provo Turtle Divers.
CHALK SOUND VILLAS 404-351-2200   3 Units: $145-175 BDFKSW
  305-667-0966 809-946-4253 Providenciales Turks & Caicos Islands. See: Provo Aquatic Centre, LTD.
CLUB MED TURKOISE 800-258-2633   600 Units: $226-226 BDFORT
  809-846-4491 Providenciales Turks & Caicos Islands.
EREBUS INN 809-946-4240   27 Units: $70-130 DPRT
  305-667-0966 800-351-8261 Box 52-6002 Miami FL 33152. See: Provo Turtle Divers.
ISLAND PRINCESS 809-946-4260   80 Units: $75-136 BDFORSW
  305-667-0966 TX:8432 Providenciales Turks & Caicos Islands. See: Provo Turtle Divers.
MARINER HOTEL 809-946-4488   25 Units: $70-70 BPR
  305-667-0966 TX:8220 Sapodilla Point, Providenciales Turks & Caicos Islands. See: Provo Turtle Divers.
NAUTILUS VILLAS 800-351-8261   10 Units BK
  514-333-2913 Providenciales Turks & Caicos Islands.
THIRD TURTLE INN 800-323-7600   13 Units: $150-150 BDFORTW
  809-946-4230 312-573-1400 Providenciales Turks & Caicos Islands. See: Third Turtle Divers.
TREASURE BEACH VILLAS 809-946-4211   18 Units: $98-138 BK
  305-667-0966 The Bight Beach, Providenciales Turks & Caicos Islands.
TURTLE COVE YACHT & TENNIS RSRT 809-946-4203   32 Units: $85-175 BDFOPRSTW
  809-946-4141FX Turtle Cove, Providenciales Turks & Caicos Islands.

Providenciales, Turks & Caicos Islands - Sports
PROVO AQUATIC CENTRE, LTD 800-351-8261   55 Divers: $45-45
  809-946-4455 809-946-4605FX Providenciales Turks & Caicos Islands. See: Mariner, Treasure Beach, Admirals.
PROVO JETSKI HIRE 809-946-4644
  Providenciales Turks & Caicos Islands.
PROVO TURTLE DIVERS 800-328-5285   32 Divers: $45-50 D
  809-946-4232 809-946-4326FX Box 52-6002 Miami FL 33152. See: Island Princess.
PROVO UNDERSEA ADVENTURES 800-327-8150   16 Divers: $50-50 D
  305-763-2188 809-946-4203 Turtle Cove Yacht & Tennis Resort Providenciales, Turks & Caicos Islands.
SEATOPIA 305-665-0198   6 Divers: $150-150 DFOSW
  809-946-4553 Box 52-6002, #16 Miami FL 33152.
THIRD TURTLE DIVERS 800-323-7600   24 Divers: $50-50 D
  809-946-4230 312-655-5678 Providenciales Turks & Caicos Islands. See: Third Turtle Inn.

Salt Cay, Turks & Caicos Islands - Accommodations
AMERICAN HOUSE 809-946-2485   7 Units: $68-68 DF
  305-667-0966 Salt Cay Turks & Caicos Islands.
DIVI HOLIDAYS-WINDMILLS 800-333-3484   4 Units: $250-450 BDRW
  607-277-3484 305-667-0966 Salt Cay Turks & Caicos Islands.

South Caicos, Turks & Caicos Islands - Accommodations
HARBOUR VIEW 305-667-0966   16 Units: $43-50 BR
  809-946-3251 South Caicos Turks & Caicos Islands.

Anguilla

• **Airline Connections** Winair has three daily flights from Sint Maarten. Air Anguilla flies from Sint Maarten, St. Kitts, St. Thomas and Tortola. American Eagle flys direct from San Juan (daily). You can also fly into Sint Maarten and then take the ferry ($8 to $12-one way, every 40-min.). The ferry runs until 10:45pm. The airport departure tax is US $5.00.

• **Courtesy & Dress** Daytime dress is casual. Nighttime is dressier with slacks or skirts preferred for local restaurants.

• **Events & Holidays** Carnival is one of Anguilla's most lively and colorful annual festivals where the locals show off their culture, drama and creativity. Beginning on the Friday preceding the first Monday in August and ending a week later on the Constitution Day. Activities include Calypso competitions, Carnival Queen competition, Prince & Princess Show, early morning street dancing, house parties and beach barbecues.

• **Electricity** US standards.

• **Time** Atlantic Standard (Eastern Standard + 1 hour).

• **Weather** Arid and hot. Average temperature is 80 degrees. Hottest months are July through October; coolest, December through February.

History

First sighted by Columbus, Anguilla was eventually settled by British Protestants and Irish Catholics at the end of the 17th century. In the 1960's England gave independence to St. Kitts, Nevis and Anguilla, which had previously been governed as a unit. Feeling neglected by the St. Kitts' government, Anguillans decided to declare their own independence in 1969 and, after a short uprising, received it. Today, the island is a self-governing British Crown Colony and proud of its development over the past 15 years.

Exploring

With 35 square miles and a population of 7,500, Anguilla is one of the most beautiful and unspoiled islands in the Caribbean. Because tourism is relatively undeveloped as yet, there are few tourist attractions. Best bets for sightseers include Island Harbor, at the northeast end of the island with a bustling waterfront and Blowing Point Village, which sits on a gorgeous section of bay.

/Weisner

There are several smaller islands just off Anguilla which are accessible by boat. Sandy Island is a tourist hot spot about one-and-a-half miles off Road Bay, which has often been used as a site for shooting movies and commercials.

Food

The specialty here is local seafood served in West Indian style and there are several excellent restaurants on the island. But you'll have to pay for a good meal and Anguillan prices are on a par with nearby islands that charge top rates. It's difficult to find meals served a la carte on Anguilla; most hotels serve a full meal, including soup, salad and dessert for one price.

Nightlife

Anguilla is generally quiet at night but local music and entertainment are highlighted at the hotels on weekends. Mariner's in Sandy Ground often has a band on Thursdays and Fridays. The night's entertainment may be booked at the last minute; your best bet is to ask a local what's on tap in town during your visit.

Shopping

Souvenirs, T-shirts, beachwear and a limited number of local crafts are about all you'll find on Anguilla, which is not known for its international shopping. Small shops in towns and at individual hotels usually carry necessities.

Sports

Boat racing is a favorite Anguillian pastime. In fact, it's the national sport of Anguilla, and races occur on almost every holiday. All boats are locally built, are world-famous and are sought after by world competitors. The biggest races are on Anguilla Day, August Monday, August Thursday and New Year's Day.

Diving and snorkeling are the main tourist activities. Otherwise, tennis courts are available at some of the hotels along with putting greens for golfers.

• Diving

Possibly the best-kept diving secret in the Caribbean, Anguilla is known to cognoscenti for its miles of unexplored coral reef, an abundance of fish and water so clear you can almost see forever. The first clue to the island's uniqueness is its status as a favorite vacation site for divers who live on other islands. The second is that the operators of Anguilla's only dive shop won't even start their boat unless the visibility is at least 50 feet. And they start their boat nearly every day.

Virtually all diving on Anguilla is found on the northwest side of the island, the area with the most reefs. Only a quarter of the prospective sites have been explored, and dive operators say Anguilla coral and sea life is some of the richest in all the Caribbean. Elkhorn, staghorn, brain, star, cactus, pillar and other coral formations highlight diving on this island, along with an unusually large number of turtles.

Sandy Island is the tiny island off Road Bay most frequented by dive operators. Depths from 30 to 70 feet make it a terrific site, favored also with otherworldly beauty and visibility up to 150 feet on a good day. Little Bay is an easy drift dive running along the cliffs off the western shoreline. As a breeding site for small fish, this is a mecca for underwater photographers.

Commerce and Ida Maria are the only two wreck sites near Anguilla. Both freighters were abandoned offshore, and were then later scuttled upright. They now rest intact on the coral bottom. Commerce is the larger of the two, and sits 200 yards offshore at Road Bay. The Ida Maria lies in 60 feet of water, one-half-mile on the far side of Sandy Island.

• Fishing

Fishing activities are best arranged through Mariners (1-809-497-2671) as well as at Island Harbour and Neville Connor at Blowing Point.

• Sailing

You can enjoy a day-sail aboard Baccarat, a comfortable 52-foot racing yawl that can also be chartered for longer sails. It departs daily from Road Bay (1-809-497-2470). Ninja, anchored off Blowing Point (1-809-497-2592), is a comfortable, new 6-foot catamaran that is available for day sails or longer charters.

• Watersports

Waterskiing, windsurfing and sailing are offered by Tamariain Water Sports, at Malliouhana (1-809-497-2798). Island Water Sports, at Road Bay, also offers windsurfing, small sailboats and waterskiing.

Anguilla, B.W.I. - Accommodations

ANGUILLA GREAT HOUSE 809-497-6061   25 Units: $160-475 BDFOPRSW
     809-497-6019FX 809-497-2616 Lower South Hill Anguilla. See: Tamariain Water Sports Ltd..
CINNAMON REEF BEACH CLUB 800-223-1108   18 Units: $200-250 BDFKOPRSTW
     809-497-2727 Box 141 The Valley, Anguilla. See: Tamariain Water Sports Ltd..
YELLOW BANANA HOTEL 809-497-2626   12 Units: $25-40 R
     Box 63 Stoney Ground, Anguilla.

Anguilla, B.W.I. - Information

ANGUILLA TOURISM 212-682-0435
     212-697-4258 809-497-2451 20 East 46th St. New York NY 10017.

Anguilla, B.W.I. - Sports

TAMARIAIN WATER SPORTS LTD. 809-497-2020   10 Divers: $30-50 DO
     809-496-6011FX Box 247 The Valley, Anguilla. See: Anguilla Great House.

Antigua

- **Airline Connections** Direct flights from New York and Miami on American, Eastern and BWIA. Barbuda is accessible only by LIAT. The airport departure tax is US $6.00.
- **Banking** Antigua uses the EC dollar. Current exchange rate is EC$2.70 = US $1.00. American credit cards are widely accepted.
- **Courtesy & Dress** Casual clothing for daytime. Some nightclubs require coat and tie for men in the evening.
- **Customs & Immigration** Proof of citizenship, along with an outgoing airline ticket, is required to enter the country.
- **Driving** On the left.
- **Electricity** 220 volts is standard; bring a converter.
- **Events & Holidays** Labour Day; Queen's Birthday; Midsummer Carnival; Police Week (Sept.); Caribbean Trade Fair; Antigua Rock Week.
- **Languages** English.
- **Medical** Holborton Hospital in St. John's.
- **Off-Season Dates & Rates** 33% to 45% cheaper in summer and fall months.
- **Taxes & Tipping** A 6% government surcharge is added to all hotel bills. Most also add an automatic 10% service charge.
- **Taxi Fares** Set by government commission on a per-hour basis.
- **Telephone** Call direct by dialing 809 + 46 + local five digit number.
- **Time** Atlantic Standard (Eastern Standard Time + 1 hour).
- **Weather** Tropical and humid. Average temperatures range from 75 in January to 85 degrees in August. Annual rainfall is 46 inches.

History

Antigua has the most developed tourist economy of any island in the British Leewards. Over 160,000 tourists visit the island each year for its beautiful beaches and well-established watersports facilities.

Charted and named by Columbus in 1493, Antigua was settled as a British colony in 1632. It was held briefly (one year) by the French, but was returned to Britain under the Treaty of Breda.

Antigua, together with its sister island Barbuda, and a tiny uninhabited islet, Redonda, gained independence in 1981. For many years

Half Moon Bay/HMBH

Antigua's economy was dependent on sugar cane production, which displaced much of the natural flora, until the now booming tourist industry took over.

Exploring

The most populated city on Antigua is St. John's, also the island's capital. This busy tourist center is home to over 25,000 Antigua residents, most of whom are involved one way or another with the tourist trade. In the town of St. John's there are many sights to see including St. John's Cathedral, located between Long and Newgate Streets. The Cathedral, built in 1847, features carved figures of St. John the Baptist and St. John the Divine, thought to have come from one of Napoleon's ships.

From St. John's Cathedral visit the courthouse located between Long and Church Streets. Erected in about 1750, the courthouse is newly

restored after sustaining damage in an earthquake in 1974.

Other churches worth a visit include the octagonally shaped St. Peter's, located in Parham and St. Mary's in Old Road Village. The latter has the distinction of being the oldest English church in the Caribbean.

Meanwhile, philatelists will enjoy a visit to the St. John's post office to pick up an Antiguan stamp. Historians might check with the Antigua Archaeological Society about an excursion to ancient Arawak and Carib Indian sites.

Other popular Antiguan sights include Nelson's Dockyard on English Harbor, from where Admiral Nelson commanded the Royal Navy in 1784 and Shirley Heights, with spectacular views of neighboring Montserrat and Guadeloupe.

Barbuda

Antigua's sister island is known throughout the Caribbean as one of the most exciting, unexplored diving sites anywhere. Barbuda is surrounded by fantastic coral reefs. The island is also a bird sanctuary with 62 square miles of beach.

Birdwatching, picnicking and sunbathing are the three main landlubber activities here. Codrington is the main town.

Food

There are plenty of restaurants on Antigua ranging from the casual to gourmet. Hotels tend to serve high-priced food and are more formal in setting, forcing those looking for a bargain to check out the town establishments. West Indian is the favored style, with seafood or beef the primary main courses.

Nightlife

Most of the nightlife is found in the major hotels such as the Halcyon Cove in Dickenson and the St. James Club at Mamora Bay. The bigger hotels generally have casinos as well as live entertainment with dancing; some even feature a floorshow. Those who venture into St. John's will find discos like the 18 Carat and Casey's Quay.

Shopping

If shopping is one of your favorite activities, you are on the right island. Antigua has plenty of duty-free shopping along with a casual, relaxed atmosphere. Shops are mostly concentrated in the

/Weisner

St. John's area, particularly on St. Mary's and Market streets. Everything from jewelry to crystal can be found at terrific prices.

Sports

Antigua is an ideal island for the sports enthusiast. All watersports are offered at nearly every major island resort. Sailfishing, windsurfing and Sunfishing are generally available at no extra cost to hotel guests, along with masks and fins for snorkeling.

• Fishing

Fishing charters operate out of Falmouth Harbor, Nelson's Dockyard and Mamora Bay. Some suggestions are Runaway Watersports, located at the Long Bay Hotel, which offers both deep-sea and in-shore fishing and Seasports at the Blue Waters Hotel.

• Golf

There are a couple of golf courses on Antigua. Of particular interest is the 9-hole par 34, 2,410 yard course at the Half Moon Bay Hotel. As you can see from the photograph of the course, you play in a beautiful setting, right on the Caribbean. The Cedar Valley Golf Club (18-holes) is three miles north of St. John's and has a PGA rated par 70. Visitors can sign up for short-term memberships.

• Sailing

Antigua Sailing Week is a traditional focus for yachts converging from the US and the Caribbean. Held at the end of April or early in May, depending on Easter, the events center out of English Harbour.

There are a number of marinas and charter operators on Antigua. Nicholson Yacht Charters is at English Harbour (1-809-463-1530) and Son Yacht Charters operates out of Crabb's Slipway Marina in Parham (1-207-236-9611, in the US). There's also Catamaran Marina in Falmouth, the St. James Yacht Club at Mamora Bay and Nelson's Dockyard at English Harbour.

• Tennis

Tennis is one of the most popular sports on the island and almost every hotel has courts. Those without equipment can easily rent whatever they need. There are International Tennis Weeks in January (for men) at several of the hotels and in April (for women) at the Half Moon Bay Hotel. The Mixed Doubles Tennis Week Tournament takes place in November also at the Half Moon. If you're interested in squash, contact the Bucket Club's Squash Court at Dutchman's Bay (1-809-462-3060). Temo Sports offers two lighted grass tennis courts and two squash courts.

Antigua

Dive Runaway

Half Moon Bay Hotel

Siboney Beach Club

• Windsurfing

Given Antigua's trade winds, blowing every day of the year from the northeast, the island is superb for boardsailors of all abilities. Windsurfing Antigua has the fourth-ranking worldwide International Windsurfer Sailing School at the Jolly Beach Hotel, with 20 sailboards for novices and intermediates. The same outfit has another 20 boards for intermediates and experts at the Lord Nelson Beach Hotel.

Every year the island plays host to Windsurfing Antigua Week: nine days of sailing, long distance, free-style, olympic triangles and many parties. It immediately precedes Antigua Sailing Week in late April or early May. Another two-day regatta is staged each January by Antigua Village Watersports on Dickenson Bay and Seasports puts one on every March.

• Diving

There's plenty of diving around this island. A 10 to 15 mile shelf surrounds the island, creating shallow dives with spectacular coral reefs that link for miles on all sides of the island.

All Antigua diving is at least one or two miles off shore, but numerous dive operations cater to hotel guests on every bay and provide transportation and all equipment. Antigua dive operators prefer to handle smaller, intimate groups of six to twelve, allowing them to give personalized attention. If you have a group of more than 16, you may have to break up to find an operator willing to meet your needs.

Most diving on Antigua is found on the western and southern sides of the island, which face the Caribbean. These waters are filled with abundant coral reefs and plenty of fish life, but occasional ground swells will force divers to the south, particularly during winter months. The eastern or Atlantic waters are rougher, with heavy currents, but have plenty of coral reefs, wreck sites and big fish, making diving in this area favorable when the weather permits.

Divers who choose Antiguan waters will find a myriad of colors on the coral reefs, with sea life including parrot and angelfish, barracuda, jacks, snapper, mackerel, turtles and an occasional dolphin or two. Some of the sites are frequented by tame fish that swim over to say hello as soon as the boat anchors. Most are looking for hot dogs, provided as fish food by the operators. The more impatient species may take a nibble or two at your fingers.

If it's wrecks you're after, Antigua has scores of them on all sides of the island. There are a few that are still intact, but in many cases only anchors and fragments remain. One last note: although spearfishing is not illegal in Antigua, it is frowned upon by most dive operators, who will not allow it from their boats.

• Western Dive Sites

The names of these sites vary, on occasion, according to your particular dive operator. The best

way to be certain you are headed where you want to go is to point to the desired spot on a map and show it to the guide.

Salt Tail Reef is an underwater park with 10 to 15 miles of continuous coral reef, along the northwest corner of Antigua. It is an exceptionally beautiful area with tame fish and shallow, calm water.

Dive sites within Salt Tail Reef include Diamond Bank, Boon Reef, Horseshoe Reef, Kettle Bottom, Long Island and Bird Island. These sites are all located between one and two miles offshore at depths from 25 to 35 feet. Many stunning coral formations live in these waters; watch for brain, star, elkhorn, staghorn and pillar. The fish here resemble tame house pets.

The Alley is a thick coral reef site, about half the size of Salt Fish Tail and is known for the elkhorn, brain and staghorn coral that form an alley on the sandy bottom.

This site, located about 800 yards from Long Island, off the northeastern side of Antigua, is accessible only by boat. The coral reef runs all the way from Long Island to Bird Island, with depths ranging from 45 to 60 feet. Water clarity varies with the seasons; the best time to dive here is in the fall.

/Weisner

Sandy Island is a small coral island, about 300 feet in diameter, located two miles off the shore on the western side of the island. There are only a few bushes and a lighthouse on the island itself, but for outstanding coral reef diving, it's the best on Antigua. The tremendous variety of coral along with the many fish that inhabit the waters make this one of the prettiest dives on the island. Depths range from 10 to 55 feet and water is generally clear. Weymouth Reef lies one quarter of a mile southwest of Sandy Island. It is named for a missionary ship that hit the reef in 1700 and sank. Though little remains of that wreck, there are several others nearby that remain intact. Weymouth Reef, is easily located by the local cargo boat which ran aground in 1984 and which has been pushed further inland by ground swells. The boat rests in less than two feet of water. It is sometimes jokingly referred to as Antigua's wading dive.

Sandy Island and Weymouth Reef are both accessible from the beach at Runaway.

• Eastern Dive Sites

Beautiful but rough is the way to describe these sites, exposed as they are to the open Atlantic. As a result, dives here are limited to brief periods of the year when the wind is calm.

Green Island is one of the very few shore dives in Antigua. The tiny island lies five miles east of Half Moon Bay off the eastern side of Antigua. It features stretches of sand mingled with columns of coral and has a two-mile reef with varying depths. Unfortunately, the diving here is only suitable during very calm weather conditions.

Antigua, B.W.I. - Accommodations

ADMIRAL'S INN 800-223-5695   14 Units: $80-94 BORSW
809-463-1027 Box 713, Nelson's Dockyard St. John's, Antigua. Admiral Inn is a small attractive Inn at historic English Harbor inside Nelson's Dockyard overlooking the Harbor. Rooms have ceiling fans & some have airconditioning. Cozy Bar & Terrace Restaurant specializes in local seafood like red snapper & lobster, and serving many other delicacies from homemade pumpkin soup to juicy tenderloin steak. Half a mile to the beach. Free transp. Operated with Falmouth Harbour Beach Apartments, 28 studios on beach nearby.

BARRYMORE BEACH RESORT 800-223-9815   36 Units: $105-300 BOPR
809-462-4101 809-462-4140FX Runaway Beach Box 244 St John's, Antigua. See: Dive Runaway.

HALF MOON BAY HOTEL 800-223-6510   100 Units: $285-335 BGOPRSTW
212-832-2277 809-463-2101FX Half Moon Bay Box 144 St John's, Antigua. Half Moon Bay Hotel, the complete vacation spot in the finest location on the island. Features a picturesque 9-hole golf course, five tennis courts, a swimming pool, sailing, snorkeling, windsurfing, seven nights a week enter tainment, complemented by excellent food and service. You won't want to go home. (Prices include breakfast and dinner).

JOLLY BEACH 800-321-1055   478 Units: $90-160 BDORSTW
809-462-0061 TX:2126 Box 744 St. John's, Antigua. See: Jolly Dive.

RUNAWAY BEACH CLUB 809-462-1318   56 Units: $75-295 BDKOR
703-450-6620 703-450-6659FX 1329 Shepard Drive Sterling VA 22170. See: Dive Runaway.

SIBONEY BEACH CLUB 809-462-3356   12 Units: $170-225 BDFKOPRSW
809-462-0806 TX:2172AK Box 222 St. John's, Antigua. An all suite hotel, charming and intimate, set in a luxuriant tropical garden on the milelong beach of sheltered Dickenson Bay. Our highly praised Coconut Grove Restaurant sits amongst the palms at the water's edge. Our fresh water swimming pool, the availability of all watersports coupled with nearby tennis courts, golf course, casino, discotheque and other restaurants means that we can cater for all discerning travelers : individualist, romantic or sportsman. See: Dive Antigua.

YEPTON BEACH RESORT C/O YEPTON LEISURE 800-327-6511   22 Units: $140-395 BORTW
514-284-0688 809-462-2520 869 Viger E., Ste 208 Montreal, Canada H2l2P5. See: Dive Runaway.

Antigua, B.W.I. - Information

ANTIGUA AND BARBUDA TOURIST BOARD 212-541-4117
212-757-1607 809-462-0029 610 Fifth Ave., Suite 311 New York NY 10020.

Antigua, B.W.I. - Sports

DIVE ANTIGUA, HAWKSBILL DIVERS 809-462-0256   24 Divers: $60-60 D
TX:2132 Box 251 St. John's, Antigua. See: Siboney Beach Club.

DIVE RUNAWAY 809-462-2626   24 Divers: $50-50 D
TX:2172 Box 1370 St. John's, Antigua. PADI training facility offering courses from beginners to dive masters. New SCUBAPRO & DACOR equipment includes octopus, pressure & depth gauge, power inflator and BC jacket. Specializing in service and professionalism, the fast, well-equipped boats leave on time and get you to spectacular diving in minutes. Diversified wrecks & reefs, with abundant tropical marine life create a photographer's paradise. Special Packages available at three hotels. See: Runaway Beach, Barrymore Beach, Yeptons.

JOLLY DIVE 809-462-0061   14 Divers: $50-50 BD
TX:2126 Box 744 St. John's, Antigua. See: Jolly Beach.

/Weisner

Barbados

• Airline Connections   Pan Am flies to Barbados from NY, Boston and Miami; BWIA flies from NY and Miami. American flies daily from NY, Raleigh-Durham and San Juan. The airport departure tax is B$16.00 unless your stay is less than 24 hours.
• Banking   Barbados uses the Barbadian dollar. Current exchange rate is B$2.00 = US $1.00.
• Courtesy & Dress   Dress is conservative; no shorts in the city. Jackets and skirts in the evening.
• Driving   On the left.
• Electricity   US standards.
• Events & Holidays   The island's annual national folk festival, Crop Over, celebrates the end of the sugarcane harvest. The finale is Kadooment, a carnival-like celebration the first Monday in August.
• Off-Season Dates & Rates   Rates are reduced up to 45% from mid-April to mid-December.
• Time   Atlantic Standard (Eastern Standard + 1 hour).
• Weather   Average temperature is 75 to 80 degrees. The rainy season is July through November.

/Weisner

Barbados

/Weisner

Exploring

Barbados is a relatively small island, 21 miles long and 14 miles wide. But there is plenty to see, even for the most avid sightseer. There are 26 forts, amazing vegetation and very diverse animals including monkeys, mongoose and many species of tropical birds. There are also plenty of museums, statues and works of art to see in Barbadian cities.

Bridgetown, the capital, is full of old churches, cathedrals, museums and other tourist attractions. Check out Trafalgar Square, the Fountain and St. Michael's Cathedral in particular. Holetown, the oldest city on Barbados, is on the western side of the island, with the whaling town of Speightstown just beyond.

Other sights not to miss include the Flower Forest in St. Joseph; George Washington House which is believed to have housed the President of the US the first time he visited the island; Cherry Tree Hill east of Speightstown with outrageous views of the Scotland District; and Welchman Hall Gully in St. Thomas, a tropical garden with natural caves owned by the National Trust.

Food

A legion of restaurants serve local and international cuisine for all tastes. Seafood is always delicious. Barbados is particularly famous for its flying fish (the national dish), breadfruit, the Barbados sweet potato and jug-jug made with Indian corn flour and green peas.

Nightlife

If it's nightlife you're after, this is your island. Nightlife in Barbados is varied and plentiful. Most of the larger hotels offer weekend entertainment ranging from live bands to dancing and floor shows reflective of the island's culture. Be sure to check out a steel band.

Shopping

The best thing about shopping on Barbados is that everything delivered to the airport and taken from the country, is duty-free. As a result, it has become a real Caribbean shopping "hot spot."

Sports

Cricket is the national game in Barbados and though you may not play it yourself you can usually find a game or two to watch. Almost every other sport is also available on the island. There are plenty of tennis courts and golf courses. Horseback riding, squash and all the favorite watersports are popular here.

DIVI St. James Beach Resort

• Diving

Barbados diving is characterized by reef formations and wreck sites with slow drop-offs and lots of smaller marine life. Because the island's fishing industry is so well-developed, there are very few large fish, lobster or turtles living anywhere near the shore. What you will find in Barbadian waters are a number of wrecks with old ship artifacts and coral formations which run all along the southern and western coasts.

Spearfishing is legal, but the majority of Barbadian operators do not allow it off their boats. You are allowed to collect any antique bottles that lie near wreck sites (some date as far back as 1672) but it's absolutely hands-off the coral.

(1) Stavronikita is the most popular wreck site on the island. Located 400 yards off the shore at Fitts Village on the west coast, Stravro was a 365-foot Greek freighter that caught fire and sank in 1982. One half of the ship sits on a coral reef in 18 feet of water and the other half lies in 130 feet.

DIVI Southwinds Beach Resort

(2) Barracuda, (3) Asta, (4) Outer-Asta and (5) Snappers make up a popular four-mile section of linked coral reef bordering the southern tip of the island. The fish life is abundant in this area, but it's the coral formations that really catch the attention. Brain and coronation coral, gigantic sea fans, sponges and gorgonians loom on all sides, forming a gorgeous underwater garden.

Of the four sites, Asta is closest to shore at 150 feet. The others range from 200 to 400 feet off the south shore near St. Lawrence. Depths range from 30 to 80 feet in the inner reef and from 60 to 140 feet in the outer.

You might also want to ask about Pamir Wreck, Six Men's Reef, Bell Buoy Reef, Clarks Bank, Berwyn, Friar's Craig and Dottings Reef.

• Fishing

The fishing is excellent in the waters around Barbados where fishermen find plentiful dolphin, marlin, wahoo, barracuda and sailfish. The Dive Shop in St. Michael (1-809-426-9947) arranges half-day and whole-day charters. Other alternatives are Blue Jay Charters (1-809-422-2098) and Jolly Roger Water Sports (1-809-432-7090).

Spinnaker's
Peter Hughes Underwater Barbados

The Barbados Game Fishing Club, a well-established organization, sponsors an annual fishing contest during March/April. Visitors may enter the competition.

• Golf

Sandy Lane's superb 18-hole course is on the site of an old sugarcane plantation that offers

panoramas of the Caribbean and the surrounding countryside. There's a clubhouse, pro shop, driving range and practice putting green (1-809-432-1311). A nine-hole executive course is at the Rockley Resort Hotel in Christ Church (1-809-427-5890), and there's another one at the Heywoods Resort (1-809-422-4900).

Each year the Barbados Golf Association holds six tournaments, one every second month starting in February. The Barbados Open attracts overseas golfers as well as local members.

• Sailing

For information on yacht charters, contact the Barbados Cruising Club (1-809-426-4434) or the Barbados Yacht Club (1-809-427-1125). Willie's

Water Sports is also set up to assist you with small-boat sailing.

• Tennis

Aside from the hotel tennis courts, you can play at the Government Tennis Courts in St. Michael (1-809-427-5238) and the Paragon Tennis Club in Brittons Hill (1-809-427-2054).

• Windsurfing

Many say that windsurfing off Bentson Beach is on a par with Hawaii. The Barbados Windsurfing Club (1-809-428-9095) is set up right here and offers board rentals and lessons. Also try Willie's Water Sports (1-809-425-9238) and Windsurfing Barbados (1-809-429-8216).

Barbados - Accommodations

BARBADOS WINDSURFING RESORT 809-428-7277   15 Units: $80-80 BRW
TX: 2368-TOMARC Maxwell Christ Church, Barbados.

DIVI SOUTHWINDS BEACH RESORT 800-367-3484   166 Units: $225-290 BDGRTW
607-277-3484 809-428-7181 54 Gunderman Rd. Ithaca NY 14850. A DIVI Resort with full amenities for all desires. Situated on more than 20 lush acres along the South Coast, their stretch of white-powder-sand beach is one of the most beautiful on the island. Their luxurious, spacious accommodations feature airconditioning, telephones and private patios or balconies. Restaurants and bars serve gourmet island cuisine. They provide all the quality you expect from a DIVI resort with PADI 5-star facilities. See: Peter Hughes Underwater Barbados.

DIVI ST. JAMES RESORT 800-367-3484   131 Units: $170-410 BDFGKOPRSTW
607-277-3484 54 Gunderman Rd. Ithaca NY 14850. DIVI St. James Beach Resort is situated on Barbados exclusive Gold Coast. Providing the ultimate in a sophisticated, adult escape with beautifully furnished guestrooms affording lovely views from their own private balconies. Enjoy gourmet meals in the causually elegant beachside Sand Dollar Restaurant. There is a full watersports program along with Nautalis, squash and sauna. DIVI St.James(exclusively for adults over 16)is the perfect place to get away.

PIRATE'S INN 809-426-6273   25 Units: $58-58 BDFKOPRSTW
Brownes Gap Christ Church, Barbados. See: Scotch & Soda Divers.

SPINNAKER'S 809-428-7308   13 Units: $45-45 BDFKOPRSW
St. Lawrence Gap Christ Church, Barbados. An intimate beach hotel designed with Mediterranean architectural lines, set against the splendor of the Caribbean Sea. All eight rooms are airconditioned and tastefully furnished. Our friendly, warm staff makes dining by candlelight on the waterfront terrace a real treat. Our small size is great for those who enjoy more personalized care. Everything from casual relaxation to exciting nightlife can be found at the Spinnaker. See: Scotch & Soda Divers.

Barbados - Information

BARBADOS BOARD OF TOURISM 212-986-6516
212-573-9850FX 809-427-2626 800 Second Ave. (17th Floor) New York NY 10017.

Barbados - Sports

CLUB MISTRIAL, C/O WINDSURFING RESORT 800-635-1155   100 Divers: $40-40 W
809-428-9095 809-428-6001 Maxwell Christ Church, Barbados. See: Barbados Windsurfing Resort.

PETER HUGHES UNDERWATER BARBADOS 800-367-3484   23 Divers: $30-30 BDOSW
607-277-3484 809-428-3504 St. Lawrence Gap Christ Church, Barbados. One of the Peter Hughes' chain of diving operations. The full service dive shop offers instruction, equipment rental and a retail store for purchasing equipment. NAUI and PADI certified instructors provide a free introduction to scuba along with full certification courses and resort courses. Specialties of the house include night diving, drift diving and bottle collecting on Carlisle Bay artifact hunts. Experience Barbados underwater with them. See: DIVI Southwinds Beach Resort.

SCOTCH & SODA DIVERS 809-428-7308   10 Divers: $30-60 DO
St. Lawrence Gap Christ Church, Barbados.

Belize

- **Airline Connections** Taca and Tan Sahsa fly into Belize City. There are direct flights from Miami, New Orleans, Los Angeles and Houston. Maya Airways and Tropic Air fly between towns in Belize. Several companies offer domestic charter flights. The airport departure tax is US $10.00.
- **Courtesy & Dress** Casual. Rare and perhaps nonexistent is the restaurant that requires ties for men or skirts for women.
- **Driving** On the right. Most Belizean roads are unpaved.
- **Electricity** Same as the US.
- **Off-Season Dates & Rates** Off-season is April to November, when some hotels and restaurants close, especially from August through October.
- **Time** Central Standard Time. Belize does not observe Daylight Savings Time.
- **Weather** Belize is a subtropical country. In summer, trade winds generally keep coastal temperatures under 90 degrees; inland, however, it can soar over 100. From November to February, the coldest months, the temperature drops to the mid-60's on the coast. The water temperature here rarely drops below 75 degrees or goes above 86. May, August and September offer the best diving and visibility.

Introduction

Belize is the outdoor adventurer's delight. It features both excavated (such as Altun Ha and Xunantunich) and unexcavated Mayan ruins in the jungles, white water rivers for kayakers and rafters, uncharted limestone caves for spelunkers, 500 species of birds, plus ocelots, wild boar and the world's only jaguar preserve at Cockcomb.

This jungle paradise lies between the Yucatan Peninsula of Mexico and the Caribbean coast of Guatemala. It's a frontier country of dense jungle and beautiful offshore cayes.

Belize is a parliamentary democracy with a prime minister, an elected House of Representatives and an appointed Senate. It is a member of the British Commonwealth.

Ecology

Belize is a patchwork of habitats. The coast is a tropical lowland crisscrossed by marshes, mangrove swamps and lagoons; the movie Mosquito Coast was filmed here in 1986. To the

Dock at Ft. George/Hobby

/Hobby

east stretches the world's second largest Great Barrier Reef, comprising some 175 offshore cayes and three atolls.

Exploring

Your port of entry will no doubt be Belize City. Built on broken bottles and mahogany logs, Belize City is over 300 years old and serves as the main commercial area, seaport and cultural center. The country's biggest city boasts modern buildings, colonial architecture, historic cathedrals and shacks on stilts with tin roofs.

For 75% of foreign visitors, a visit to Belize means a stay on its cayes and reefs, reached by boat or plane. Ambergris Caye, the most popular vacation destination, is 36 miles north of Belize City. Hotels, restaurants and dive operators are plentiful. Diving and fishing are both spectacular and readily accessible. Spectacular, too, are Ambergris' white sand beaches, lined with swaying palms. The majority of visiting divers base their vacations here.

Playground for ancient pirates, Caye Caulker (also know as Caye Corker and Cayo Hicaco) has

Belize

a community of about 400 residents. Only nine miles from Belize City, St. George's Caye is steeped in history. Today, there is a dive resort, some private homes and a small tropical-fish exporting industry.

The crescent-shaped Half Moon Caye, located some 70 miles from Belize City, lies at the entrance to Lighthouse Reef atoll. Nearby is the Blue Hole which Jacques Cousteau made famous. The Belizean government has declared the entire caye a national park, so it is illegal to take anything from the land or sea here. The Bird Preserve is one of two places in the world where red-footed boobies nest (the other is the Galapagos Islands). Also found here is the magnificent frigate bird.

Food
The staple Belizean food is beans and rice. But with the incredible ethnic mixture in Belize, the cuisine available to tourists is as varied as that anywhere in the world.

Nightlife
Nightlife centers around the hotels, both in the city and on the cayes. But generally, it's lights out after dinner.

Shopping
Local crafts include carvings of mahogany, ziricote (the two-toned wood native to the area) and rosewood. Straw goods made from jipijapa straw in the Punta Gorda area, and jewelry made from black coral or agate are also of interest. It is illegal for unauthorized dealers to sell black coral, so get a receipt.

Sports
Both deep-sea and river fishing are major activities. River canoeing, kayaking and white water rafting can revive the spirit. Spelunkers will exult in the hundreds of unexplored limestone caves. For hunters, a license is required and you must be accompanied by a guide holding a government concession. The jaguar is a protected animal; no hunting permitted. You need a special permit if you plan to bring firearms into the country. Belize has limited tennis facilities at a few resorts, but no golf courses.

For hiking and nature enthusiasts, Carisearch Ltd. offers ecology hikes (three hours in duration) on Caye Caulker. You can go out in the morning or afternoon, but schedule 24 hours in advance (011-501-44307 ext. 104).

• Diving
Belize offers divers an almost 200-mile-long barrier reef that starts at an average of only 35 feet and drops to spectacular deep wall dives and visibility that in places exceeds 300 feet.

At Ambergris Caye, the Holchan Reef is the best known dive. The inner reef has a maximum depth of 30 feet, so bottom time is virtually unlimited. The wall side of the barrier reef drops 110 feet to a sand bottom.

Outside Belize's barrier reef lie three coral atolls which offer some of the best diving in the world. Turneffe and Glovers have small resorts, while Lighthouse houses only the lighthouse keeper and his family. These atolls have sheer walls that start at depths of 40 to 60 feet and drop straight down to the great deep blue. Deep-water sea fans, tube sponges, barrel sponges, black coral trees and pelagics proliferate.

Turneffe is the most accessible, but also the most likely to have bad visibility and weather. Lighthouse Reef is famous for the Half Moon Drop-Off.

Belize - Accommodations
BELLEVUE HOTEL 800-237-6339
   813-822-7245 Box 428 Belize City, Belize. 38 Units: $55-75 BDFRS
CORAL BEACH HOTEL & DIVE CLUB 800-348-9101
   026-2013 San Pedro Ambergris Caye Belize. 12 Units: $30-90 BDFORS
FORT GEORGE HOTEL 800-44U-TELL
   011-501-027400 800-448-8355 Box 321 Belize City, Belize. 44 Units: $70-90 BDFPRST
ST. GEORGE'S LODGE-DIVE BELIZE 800-854-9303
   011-501-44190 714-955-2774 Box 625 Belize City, Belize. 16 Units: $130-165 BD

Belize - Information
BELIZE EMBASSY 202-363-4505
   1575 I. St. N.W., Room 695 Washington DC 20005.

Bermuda

• **Airline Connections**   Pan American, American, Delta and Eastern.
• **Courtesy & Dress**   Daytime dress is informal but not too informal. Short shorts, bathing suits and bare feet are acceptable only on the beach. Evening wear is more formal, especially if you are staying in a hotel or cottage colony.
• **Driving**   You can't rent a car in Bermuda, but you can rent bicycles, mopeds and scooters.
• **Electricity**   US standards.
• **Events & Holidays**   Commonwealth Day (last week in May) with dinghy races in St. George's harbor and a foot race from Hamilton to Somerset; Cup Match and Somers Day (July 31 and August 1).
• **Off-Season Dates & Rates**   Up to 40% off regular rates December through February.
• **Weather**   Mild, subtropical climate. Bermuda has two seasons: summer and winter. Winters may be cool and windy. Summer temperatures are in the 70's and 80's through November.

History

Juan Bermudez generally gets the credit for discovering uninhabited Bermuda when he passed that way in 1503. But Bermuda was ignored until 1609, when the <u>Sea Venture</u>, on its way to the new Jamestown colony, became the first of many ships to wreck on the Bermuda reefs. The crew and passengers were so impressed with the island while building new ships to finish their voyage, that Bermuda was soon after colonized by the Virginia Company. The first meeting of the island Parliament was held in 1620.

Today, the 57,000 Bermudians living on this subtropical archipelago, which sits 570 miles east of the North Carolina coast in the Atlantic Ocean, are of European (60%), Native American and African descent (40%).

Ecology

The Bermuda government, with tourism its top priority, still jealously preserves the natural beauty of the islands from over-development. Paget Marsh, a 26-acre nature reserve, hasn't changed since the first colonists arrived. Spittal Pond and all of Nonsuch Island are bird sanctuaries. The Coral Reef preserve, Gilbert and Springfield Nature Preserve and North Nature

/Kelly

Reserve, protect much of the natural beauty Bermuda is noted for. Of the 150 islands and islets, only 20 are inhabited.

Exploring

You can explore the island by taxi, bus, bicycle or moped. Glass-bottom boat, scuba diving and snorkeling tours run frequently March through November. Sightseeing cruises include the Wreck and Reef Adventure and the St. George's cruise, which allows time for shopping in St. George.

You can't get lost in Bermuda, not for long anyway. The island is less than two miles wide at its widest point, and you're never far from one of the main roads that run east and west. Take along swim wear, snorkeling gear and a towel.

Food

Eating out in Bermuda is expensive, but restaurants featuring Bermudian cuisine and homestyle cooking can be very reasonable. Try the Green Lantern in Pembroke for fried wahoo,

/Kelly

pumpkin and Hoppin' John (blackeyed peas and rice). Or have a traditional Bermudian breakfast of codfish and potatoes at MacHerman's.

Nightlife

Most hotels have entertainment and many of the islands' pubs and bars have local bands and guitar players. Both the local and hotel nightspots have a cover charge ($5 to $7), but no minimum on drinks.

Shopping

The best buys in Bermuda are European imports, such as English bone china, Irish linens, Scottish tweeds and cashmere sweaters. Woolens, china and crystal are about 30% less than in the US--and no sales tax.

Sports

Bermuda has all types of sports activities to choose from, both active and spectator. Tennis court rentals and greens fees are less than in the US.

• Diving

Bermuda is surrounded by over 200-square-miles of coral reef, the most northerly in the world. Over 350 ships have wrecked on Bermuda's breaker reefs, creating an underwater museum of maritime history. On the other hand, the shallow ring of reefs protects divers from strong ocean currents, as well as from sharks and other predatory fish. There hasn't been a shark attack in Bermuda since 1957.

Most diving on Bermuda is boat diving. For one thing, it is impossible to rent a regulator on the island, except from a licensed, certified operator/instructor. It is also impractical to attempt beach diving from most locations.

• Fishing

Visitors are encouraged to enter their catches in the yearly Game Fishing Tournament with the Department of Tourism in Hamilton. No license is required and there's no entry fee. Awards are presented for top catches in 26 varieties of game fish found in local waters. There's also the International Light Tackle Tournament, a deep-sea fishing competition, held in July.

• Golf

Since the first course was laid out in 1922, golf has become one of Bermuda's most popular attractions. It is played year round on the island's eight courses. Tournaments are held throughout the year; for specific schedules contact the Bermuda Golf Association, P.O. Box HM 433, Hamilton HM BX.

• Running

From April to October joggers gather at the Botanical Garden in Paget on Tuesday evenings for one, two and four-mile runs for a 25 cent fee. The Tourism Department publishes a runner's map with 5 scenic routes (free).

• Sailing

Bermuda is the scene for many sailing races. There's an international sailing regatta in April and May, for example, where yachtspeople from the USA, the UK, Canada and Bermuda compete.

• Tennis

Eighty-five courts dot the island from end to end- both on and off hotel premises. Contact the Bermuda Lawn Tennis Association, PO Box HM 341, Hamilton HM BX, for details about tournaments held throughout the year.

• Windsurfing

Boards, information and lessons are available from Watlington's Windsurfing Bermuda (1-809-236-6218) or Sail-On (1-809-295-0808).

Bermuda - Accommodations

BELMONT HOTEL, GOLF & COUNTRY CLUB 800-2235672   151 Units: $130-140 BGRTW
  809-236-1301 809-2366867FX Box WK-251, Harbour Rd Warwick, Bermuda.
CHANCE IT COTTAGE HOLIDAY RETREAT 809-238-0372   6 Units: $80-80 BGPT
  809-238-1579 Granaway Hts., Box SN75 Southampton, SNBX, Bermuda.
SOUTHAMPTON PRINCESS HOTEL 800-442-8418   600 Units: $270-370 BDFGPRSTW
  212-986 4660 212-697-2085FX c/o Western Media, 551 5th Ave #1916 New York NY 10017. See: Nautilus Diving.

Bermuda - Information

BERMUDA DEPARTMENT OF TOURISM 800-223-6106
  212-818-9800 212-983-5289FX 310 Madison Ave., Suite 201 New York NY 10017.

Bermuda - Sports

NAUTILUS DIVING 809-238-2332   38 Divers: $60-60 D
  809-238-8000 809-238-8245FX Box 310 Hamilton, Bermuda. See: Southampton Princess Hotel.

British Virgin Islands

- **Airline Connections** There is no direct jet service from the States to the British Virgin Islands. Easiest route is to fly to San Juan (Puerto Rico) or St. Thomas (US Virgin Islands); then connect via Air BVI, Crown Air, American Eagle, Eastern Metro Express or the Sea Plane Shuttle to either Tortola (Beef Island) or Virgin Gorda.
- **Courtesy & Dress** There is no dressing-up here except at the very exclusive resorts. However, bathing suits and bare chests are not suitable on the street and nudity is punishable by law.
- **Driving** On the left.
- **Electricity** Compatible with the US.
- **Events & Holidays** BVI Carnival (week preceding first Monday in August on Tortola).
- **Off-Season Dates & Rates** Rates drop 20-50%, April 15 to December 15. Several BVI resorts offer mid-priced "shoulder" rates between the winter and summer seasons.
- **Time** Atlantic Standard (Eastern Standard + 1 hour).
- **Weather** The weather is near perfect, with daytime temperatures between 75 and 85 degrees year round, and about 5-10 degrees cooler at night. August and September are the hottest months.

Ecology

The BVI, as locally known, lie east and north of St. John (US Virgin Islands). Of the 40 or so cays that make up the country, only 16 are inhabited. The waters are unusually clear. The Virgins are strung in two nearly parallel chains in the Caribbean, with the Sir Francis Drake Passage protected between them, creating some of the most perfect sailing waters in the world.

Exploring

Tortola is the principal island of the BVI. Road Town, the capital, has a main street, a series of marinas with hundreds of boats, and an assortment of hotels and restaurants. Tiny Drake's Channel Museum displays, in an open-air setting, artifacts recovered from wrecks. There's a folk museum on the Main Square.

The best bathing spots are on the north coast. Cane Garden Bay, where the beach slopes from leaning palm trees into the sea, is considered one of the world's prettiest beaches.

/Hobby

Virgin Gorda has 16 beautiful white sand beaches, tempting the sun worshiper to spend a lifetime here. The island's highest point, 1,359-foot Gorda Peak, is located in a national park. A hike up its well-marked shady nature path brings you to an observation tower for a panoramic view of the Sir Francis Drake Channel.

Food

Islanders favor anything made with the locally abundant coconut. Fish is fresh and plentiful. The local specialty is kallaloo, a spicy soup made of pigs' tails and diced beef. The islands have their own seasoning and companies to produce it. The rum that kept the British Royal Navy fighting for 300 years -- Pusser's Rum -- has its origins in the BVI.

Nightlife

BVI vacationers enjoy sun, sand and water during the day, but nighttime entertainment is limited. There are no discos, nightclubs, music halls, cabarets or piano bars, but there are occasional weekend bands and resort special events.

Shopping

The atmosphere in the shops is relaxed and welcoming, but these islands are not a shopper's destination.

Sports

Several hundred yachts sail these waters, with a diverse collection of crews including first-timers, serious sailors and those who have chartered their crew. There are dozens of secluded beaches, anchorages and even islands.

Spectator sports include softball on Saturday and Sunday afternoons from March to July and

British Virgin Islands

basketball during August through November, weekend afternoons. Cricket, soccer and rugby are played on an unscheduled basis throughout the year, with the best matches at schools and clubs.

There's also horseback riding, jeeping, hiking, snorkeling, fishing, bicycling, windsurfing and birdwatching to help pass the time of day.

• Diving

With so many islands, and so many reefs, the diving opportunities are limitless. Currents are minimal, and most sites have no surge. No spearfishing or collecting of any marine life or artifacts is permitted in the BVI or in the National Parks' underwater system.

The most famous dive in the British Virgins is the Wreck of the Rhone, site of filming for the movie The Deep. The Rhone put BVI on the international dive map, gets visitors daily and is a national underwater park. This Royal Steam Mail Packet Company's luxury liner, an advanced ship of her day, went down in a hurricane on October 29, 1867. The stern sits in 30 feet of water off Salt Island.

• Hiking

It's a three or four-hour hike from Brewers Bay on Tortola to the trailhead which leads to the top of Mt. Sage (1,710 feet). A very attractive area awaits you with the remains of old houses and orchids peeking out from the primeval forest. The highest mountain in the entire Virgin Islands, it

has been declared a protected area under the administration of the National Park Trust.

• Sailing

If you're visiting the area on your own yacht, Tortola has a number of marinas. Nanny Cay Marina is near the village of West End; Village Cay Marina is at Prospect Reef; and Fort Burt Marina is in Road Town. They all provide finger piers, and many of the individual yachts are available for charter.

Tortola boasts a number of established charter operations. Caribbean Sailing Yachts (CSY) is located in Road Town (1-809-494-2741). The boating complex at Baughers bay gives you a couple of rooms for overnighting before and after cruising. The Moorings, at Wickham Cay II on the east shore of Road Harbour, specializes in 39 to 51-foot sloops as part of a fleet of about 90 yachts (1-809-494-2331). Tortola Yacht Charters, acting as agents for several small boats and owning a few of its own Heritage 38's, specializes in groups, often from US based yacht clubs (1-809-494-2124).

On Virgin Gorda, you'll find the North South Charter Ltd. (1-809-495-5433).

• Windsurfing

Windsurfing is quite popular here. Aside from the hotels, there is the Windsurfer Sailing School at Trellis Bay and at Nanny Cay, near West End, Tortola.

British Virgin Islands - Accommodations
BITTER END RESORT 800-872-2392   84 Units: $270-370 BDFKOPRSW
    809-494-2745 312-944-5855 875 N. Michigan Ave., Ste. 3707 Chicago IL 60611.
LITTLE DIX BAY 800-223-7637   102 Units: $525-525 BDFORST
    809-495-5555 809-494-5651FX Box 70, Little Dix Bay Virgin Gorda, British Virgin Islands. See: Dive BVI.
MARINA CAY HOTEL 809-494-2174   16 Units: $260-360 BDORSW
    Box 76, Road Town Tortola, British Virgin Islands.
NANNY CAY RESORT & MARINA 800-223-9815   41 Units: $135-165 BDFRSTW
    809-494-2512 Box 281, Road Town Tortola, British Virgin Islands.

British Virgin Islands - Information
BRITISH VIRGIN ISLANDS TOURISM 212-696-0400
    212-949-8254FX 809-494-3134 370 Lexington Ave. New York NY 10017.

British Virgin Islands - Sports
BLUE WATER DIVERS 809-494-2847   30 Divers: $190-190 BD
    809-494-2506FX Box 437, Roadtown Tortola, British Virgin Islands.
DIVE BVI 809-495-5513   24 Divers: $60-60 BDO
    Box 1040, Virgin Gorda Yacht Harbour Virgin Gorda, British Virgin Islands.
ISLAND DIVER LTD 809-494-3878   22 Divers: $70-70 BD
    Box 3023, Road Town Tortola, British Virgin Islands.
KILBRIDE UNDERWATER TOURS 809-496-0111   40 Divers: $60-70 BDO
    809-494-4756FX Box 40 Virgin Gorda, British Virgin Islands. See: Bitter End Yacht Club.
YACHT CHARTERS INTERNATIONAL 800-922-4876   200 Boats: $135-995 BDFKOSW
    800-922-4873CA 415-775-0344 1686 Union St., Suite 305 San Francisco CA 94123.

Roseau/Kelly

Dominica

- **Airline Connections** Dominica has two airports, neither of which is large enough for jets to land. There are no direct flights from North America. Connecting flights on LIAT may be made south from Antigua or Guadeloupe and north from Martinique or Barbados. Air Guadeloupe also has daily flights to Dominica. The airport departure tax is US $6.00.
- **Courtesy & Dress** Informal outdoor clothing, along with good hiking shoes for mountain treks. Bring a lightweight rain coat for occasional sudden downpours. For cool evenings pack a sweater.
- **Driving** Driving is on the left.
- **Events & Holidays** Carnival (Monday and Tuesday before Ash Wednesday).
- **Off-Season Dates & Rates** Some hotels lower their rates 10-20% May through November, but others do not.
- **Time** Atlantic Standard (Eastern Standard + 1 hour).
- **Weather** Tropical, tempered by trade winds that can turn into hurricanes between July and September. Daytime temperatures average between 70 to 90 degrees, but the nights are cooler, especially in the mountains. The coolest months are December through March. The rainy season is from June to October but brief showers occur all year round.

Ecology

Largest and most northerly of the Windward Islands, Dominica's central section is covered with a dense tropical rain forest, making the vegetation here unique to the West Indies. Its rain forests are the most diverse and luxuriant in the Americas.

Mile-high volcanic peaks split the island from north to south and their high slopes are covered with impenetrable jungle. Dominica has over 350 rivers crisscrossing the terrain, waterfalls, hot springs and even boiling lakes. Morne Diablotin (4,747 feet) is wreathed in clouds. The higher elevations receive a phenomenal amount of rain and mists rise from the lush green valleys. Roseau, on the other hand, is in the driest part of the island.

Over 135 species of native birds make their home on Dominica, but there are no poisonous snakes or insects. Rare plants and animals extinct on neighboring islands are still found here, including two rare parrots, the Imperial and the Red-necked.

Exploring

You have several options for exploring the island. Taxi tours cost about US $15.00 per person for each hour, maximum 4 passengers. Or use one of the local tour companies, which offer Land Rover safaris, boat trips, fishing expeditions and hiking guides.

Dominica

Continental Inn

It is possible to drive yourself, but this isn't recommended. The roads are rocky, gutted, weaving and generally difficult.

Food

There are several good restaurants, serving delicious creole specialties. Try at least some of the local dishes, which include: fried plantain (a type of banana), pumpkin soup, callaloo soup (similar to spinach), breadfruit (a potato-like vegetable served in a variety of ways) and crapaud (mountain chicken, actually a type of frog).

Nightlife

During special celebrations, whole villages turn out to celebrate in the street with live music.

Shopping

Tropicrafts in Roseau sells handmade grass rugs, bags, placemats and dolls. Caribbean Handcrafts sells come Carib Indian-made crafts. Pots N' Things has high-quality pottery. The really good buys are pineapple and grapefruit marmalade.

Sports

Local cricket, basketball and soccer matches in season. Fishing, waterskiing, sailing and motorboating can be arranged at several of Roseau's hotels. Dominica Tours features watersport tours and trips inland.

• Diving

The Dominicans like to refer to their island as "The Nature Island of the Caribbean." This description is as true of the seascape as it is of the landscape.

One of the most exciting sites is Hot Springs, a 450-square-foot area of underwater volcanic vents. Here the ocean floor is perforated by thousands of small holes releasing hot, fresh water into the sea and one large vent too hot to approach. Millions of small silvery bubbles, like balls of liquid mercury, rise from the black sandy bottom. Swimming through the bubbles is like experiencing the most exotic kind of spa treatment.

• Hiking

Serious hiking is a major sporting interest. The village of Laudat is a departure point for many of the attractions in Morne Trois Pitons National Park, including a challenging trail to the Valley of Desolation, an active fumarole area with a sulphuric environment at the foot of the hills that forms the basin of Boiling Lake (the second largest of its kind in the world, next to the one in New Zealand). The lake is about 70 yards wide with an unknown depth, and the water temperature is close to 200 degrees at the edge.

Wilderness Adventure Tours in Roseau (1-809-442-198) offers arduous hikes through the rugged interior of the island. They provide guides and lunch.

Dominica, B.W.I. - Accommodations

ANCHORAGE HOTEL 800-223-6510   36 Units: $50-60 BDFRSW
212-832-2277 809-448-2638 Box 34 Roseau, Castle Comfort Dominica.

CONTINENTAL INN 809-448-2214   12 Units: $27-36 RW
809-448-2215 TX:DO/8625 37 Queen Mary St. Rouseau, Dominica. This small hotel has the comfort and style of any large modern hotel complex. Situated in the heart of the capital city of Dominica, it is within walking distance from the main shopping centers and all government departments and offices and is therefore ideal for the holiday maker, the tourist and indeed for all business persons. The Continental Inn is your "Home away from home."

PORTSMOUTH BEACH HOTEL 800-223-6510   77 Units: $50-50 BFRW
212-832-2277 809-445-5142 Box 34 Roseau, Dominica.

Dominica, B.W.I. - Information

DOMINICA TOURISM 212-682-0435
809-449-2351 20 East 46th St. New York NY 10017.

Dominica, B.W.I. - Sports

DIVE DOMINICA 809-448-2188   8 Divers: $45-45 DSW
TX:8649 Box 63 Roseau, Dominica.

Dominican Republic

- **Airline Connections** American and Eastern fly daily from NY to Santa Domingo. Dominicana flies daily from Miami and NY to the same destination. Pan Am flies daily from Miami to Santa Domingo and three times a week to Puerto Plata. The airport departure tax is US $5.00.
- **Courtesy & Dress** Conservative. Shorts only on the beach. Coats, ties and dresses appropriate in the evenings.
- **Driving** On the right.
- **Languages** Spanish.
- **Off-Season Dates & Rates** Up to 60% off from mid-April to mid-December.
- **Time** Atlantic Standard (Eastern Standard + 1 hour).
- **Weather** Average temperature is about 77 degrees. December through April are the coolest months. Rainfall is between 12 and 75 inches per year depending upon your location.

History

The Dominican Republic was discovered by Christopher Columbus on his first voyage in 1492. It is said that when he first saw the island he proclaimed it "the most beautiful place human eyes have ever seen." In 1508 King Ferdinand of Spain named it Santo Domingo, but the natives of the island called it Quisqueya, meaning "mother of all lands."

Exploring

As the capital, and oldest city on the island, Santo Domingo has much to offer sightseers. One of the most interesting sites is the Cathedral of Santa Maria la Menor in the southeast section of the city. The cathedral was built in 1514 and is one of three places claiming to hold the grave of Christopher Columbus. Historians have fairly well determined that this is in fact the location where the famous explorer is buried.

Puerto Plata is located on the north coast, almost directly opposite Santo Domingo. In the 1500's it was a thriving pirate port and now houses the most luxurious resorts on the island. It is also a booming playground for jetsetters. Sights near this area include Fort San Felipe, the oldest European fort in the New World, now housing a museum, at the entrance of the Puerto Plata harbor; and Isabel de Torres, a fortress with wonderful views.

Ozama First Fortress/Weisner

Food

The Dominican Republic has Spanish-style dishes at their finest. Specialties include black bean soup, rice and beans, and goat meat. The national dish is Sancocho, a sort of meat and vegetable stew. Catibias, fritters stuffed with meat, is a favorite local dish.

Columbus Square/Weisner

Nightlife

Nightlife in Santa Domingo is the best on the island and with its casinos compares to anyplace in the Caribbean.

Shopping

Shopping is easily found in all areas of the Dominican Republic. Besides the usual perfume, watches, jewelry, cameras and radios, be sure to check the local artifacts. Then be prepared to barter for a good price. Amber (petrified resin from prehistoric pine trees) and mahogany furniture are specialties.

Sports

Tennis, golf, horseback riding, squash, polo and every watersport in the world are available in the Dominican Republic.

Polo is very popular and you can usually find a game in progress. Horse racing and cock fighting are also popular pastimes along with hunting and trapping for those with special permits.

• Diving

Unexplored reef diving is the main attraction of the Dominican Republic. The Dominican Republic is bordered by the Atlantic Ocean on the north and the Caribbean Sea on the south. The south can be dived year round, but the north is best in the summer and somewhat shaky in the winter, depending on the weather.

Spearfishing is legal in the Dominican Republic with the exception of protected areas and underwater parks. Some dive operators allow it from their boats and others don't. Check before departing.

La Caleta offers the best diving for those staying in the Dominican's capital city, Santa Domingo. La Caleta is a national park area located near the airport, with a small museum and burial ground. The site is an underwater park consisting of two reefs about one-half-mile from shore that run for seven miles parallel to the airport. There are two main dive sites within La Caleta:

Wreck of the Hickory, an old salvage boat purposely sunk several years ago. The 140-foot ship lies intact in 55 feet of water about one mile from the La Caleta shoreline.

Los Bajos is a series of eight or nine coral mountains that lie between the first and second coral reef in La Caleta Park. The mountains start at about 55 feet with drop-offs falling to over 170 feet.

Sosua is a virtually unexplored area in the north, near Puerto Plata. Because this site is closest to the largest tourist resorts, it is used mostly as a training ground for beginning divers.

• Fishing

The Dominican coast offers exciting moments for fishing fans. International tournaments are held annually in which blue marlin, dorado and bonito are caught. For information, contact Santo Domingo Nautical Club (1-809-566-1684), Andres Boca Chica (1-809-685-4940) and Haina Nautical Club (1-809-533-3961).

• Golf

Golf courses in the Dominican Republic can be found in Santo Domingo (the Santo Domingo Country Club), in La Romana (Los Cajuiles course) and in Puerto Plata. There's an international golf tournament in Puerto Plata in January.

• Tennis

The Marlboro Cup is an international tennis tournament held annually in November. Playing courts can be found at the Olympic Stadium and the hotels.

Dominican Republic - Accommodations

JACK TAR VILLAGE 800-527-9299   240 Units: $130-130 BGOPRTW
    809-586-3800 TLX: 2025 Box 368 Puerto Plata, Dominican Republic. See: Watersports.
VILLAGE CARAIBE 800-223-9862   160 Units: $85-160 BDGKOPRSTW
    809-586-4054 809-586-5301FX Box 589 Puerto Plata, Dominican Republic. See: Actividades Acuaticas.

Dominican Republic - Information

DOMINICAN REPUBLIC TOURIST INFO. CENTER 212-826-0750
    809-688-5537 485 Madison Ave. New York NY 10022.

Dominican Republic - Sports

ACTIVIDADES ACUATICAS 809-586-3988   100 Divers: $20-20 DS
    Box 274 Puerto Plata, Dominican Republic.
WATERSPORTS 809-586-3800   16 Divers: $30-30 DFOSW
    c/o Jack Tar Village Box 368 Puerto Plata, Dominican Republic. See: Jack Tar Village.

Grenada

- **Airline Connections**   From New York and Miami, BWIA operates frequent direct flights to Grenada. Air Grenada flies direct from Miami. Air Canada, American, Eastern and Pan Am have flights to Barbados connecting with LIAT flights to Grenada. There is a departure tax of approximately US $10.
- **Courtesy & Dress**   Lightweight, informal clothing in the day. Evening wear is just a bit more formal.
- **Driving**   On the left.
- **Electricity**   220 volts/50 cycles.
- **Events & Holidays**   The Carriacou Regatta is a three day celebration the first weekend in August. Carnival is a national holiday in mid-August lasting from Friday until Tuesday.
- **Off Season Dates & Rates**   Discounted by 20% May through November.
- **Time**   Atlantic Standard (Eastern Standard + 1 hour) except when we switch to Daylight Savings Time. Then it's the same.
- **Weather**   Daytime temperatures hover around 80F year round, with refreshing trade winds. Mountain temperatures are about 10 degrees lower. The season from June to December experiences daily hour-long shower activity, while January to May remains dry.

Ecology

For a comparatively small island, Grenada's terrain is amazingly varied. Divided diagonally by the central mountain range of Grand Etang, the island has cool jungle and hot desert, plunging waterfalls, serene lakes and pounding surf.

Exploring

Pastel-colored and picturesque, the island's capital of St. George's is surrounded by water: the outer harbour of St. George's Bay follows the blue Caribbean, while the water-filled crater of an extinct volcano serves as a land-locked inner harbour. The buildings, built mostly of brick brought over as ballast on British trading ships, are a mix of French and English architecture with a tropical touch. The streets wind cozily up the green hills behind.

A true tropical paradise exists only 30 minutes northeast of town at Concord Falls, where the water plummets into a swimmable green pool. Drive out north past numerous stretches of white-

St. George's/Jacobs

sand beach and the small village of Gouyave to Morne les Sauteurs (or Caribs' Leap) where, in the 17th century, the unfortunate Carib Indians leapt to their death rather than submit to the French.

The road south of St. George's takes you to the fantastic beaches and scattered resorts of L'Anse aux Epines and to the panoramic lookout at Richmond Hill.

If you get a chance, visit the islands of Carriacou and Petit St. Martinique just off the island's north coast.

Food

The excellent local dishes include fresh fish, conch and lobster prepared with fresh vegetables and tropical fruits. Specialties include pumpkin and callaloo soups, turtle steak, breadfruit salad and conch and onion pie. To cool off, try avocado or soursop ice cream. Or sip a tall, cold rum punch with fresh grated Grenadian nutmeg dusted on top.

Nightlife

Most of the island's nightlife is centered at the hotels and includes island shows, barbecues and dancing. Locals hang out at the Sugar Mill Disco and the Love Boat near the Lagoon/Grenada Yacht Services. The Boat Yard at the south end of the island in L'Anse aux Epines and Fantazia 2001 in Grand Anse offer a more sophisticated all night atmosphere.

Shopping

Imported crystal, jewelry, china, perfume and liquor can be bought at great savings from the duty-free shops. Among the best native purchases are Grenadian woven spice baskets, filled with fresh and zesty island grown cinnamon, nutmeg and cloves.

Grenada

Sports

Grenada offers almost everything for the sports enthusiast, including boating, windsurfing, snorkeling, scuba, sport fishing, hiking, golf, tennis and cricket. Both bareboat and crewed charters are available for hire, as well as Sunfish, Hobiecats and windsurfers for simple offshore fun.

The 9-hole Grenada Golf and Country Club sports spectacular seaside views. Cricket has an avid following and the Tourist Board will provide you with tournament itineraries.

• Diving

Grenada has it all: wreck dives, drift dives, wall dives, 200-foot visibility and nearly constant sunshine. The dive boats are never crowded, the coral perfectly intact and the density of fish life is stunning.

By far the best-known Grenadian site is the wreck of the 600-ft. Italian luxury liner, Bianca C. This is a dive for experienced divers, as the wreck rests in 105-110 feet of water and surface currents can be tricky. Both of the island's operators require a check-out dive (or several) before guiding you through the Bianca C's decks.

Grand Anse Reef is just a few hundred feet off one of Grenada's most beautiful stretches of sand. Molinaire Reef, a ten-minute boat trip from Grand Anse, is protected as an underwater sanctuary. Here, beside a remarkably healthy reef is the wreck of the Buccaneer, an old sailing schooner. Five minutes further north is the unspoiled reef of Halifax Harbor, noted for its prolific marine life and fish populations. Two other dramatic sites are the canyon of Grand Mal bay and the giant sponges of Flamingo Bay.

• Hiking

Hiking, both solo and guided, is a wonderful way to see the island's natural beauty up close. Trails range from ten minutes to three hours. Grenada has a new system of National Parks, the centerpiece of which is the Grand Etang National Park, including spectacular rain forests and hiking trails. The new Morne LaBaye trail sets out from the Park's Forest Centre, and a 15-minute hike opens up marvelous views of the 2,309-foot Mt. Sinai and the island's east coast. Not far away, other trails lead to the 2,373-foot summit of Mt. Qua Qua and to the Grand Etang crater lake (30 minutes).

• Sailing

The event of the year on peaceful Carriacou Island is the Carriacou Regatta which takes place the first weekend of August plus Monday and Tuesday. Started in 1964, the event involves several yachts racing from St. George's to Hillsborough.

As the "Gateway to the Grenadines," Grenada is one of the world's foremost sailing areas. The Spice Island Marina at Prickly Bay, and Stevens Yachts (1-809-440-4257) have complete marina facilities and charters for week-long or shorter excursions. Grenada Yacht Services (1-809-440-2508) can arrange yacht charters, windsurfing, off-shore fishing and waterskiing.

Grenada, W.I. - Accommodations

HORSE SHOE BEACH HOTEL 809-444-4410   18 Units: $95-110 BDOPRSW
809-444-4244 EX:117FX P.O.Box 174 St.George's, Grenada, W.I. Located on the beach at L'Anse aux Epines, this charming, small hotel comprises 12 villas with antique 4-poster beds and kitchenettes, plus six super-deluxe modern units. Secluded beach, freshwater pool, Sunfish, sailboats scuba diving and snorkeling are the activities available. Candlelight dinners, exotic local and foreign cuisine and 2 bars offer romance and elegance in a beautifully landscaped setting. See: Virgo Watersports.

Grenada, W.I. - Information

GRENADA DEPARTMENT OF TOURISM 809-440-3377
809-440-2279 809-440-2123FX The Carenage, P.O.Box 293 St.George's, Grenada, W.I.

Grenada, W.I. - Sports

VIRGO WATERSPORTS 809-444-4410
809-444-4244 Box 174 St. George's, Grenada W. I. See: Horse Shoe Beach Hotel.

Honduras

- Airline Connections   Tan Sahsa.
- Courtesy & Dress   On the Bay Islands, casual attire is appropriate everywhere.
- Driving   On the Bay Islands, there are only limited vehicles for rent. The roads are unpaved and often deeply rutted.
- Electricity   Electricity is provided on-site by diesel generators at each resort; they yield 110 and 220 current.
- Events & Holidays   The port city of La Ceiba celebrates a week of Carnival Nacional the third week of May.
- Medical   Make sure you are prepared against malaria if you go to the interior.
- Off-Season Dates & Rates   Generally mid-April to mid-December, from 25-50%. off.
- Time   Central Standard Time.
- Weather   The Bay Islands are a pleasant 80 degrees most of the year. Rainy months are October through March, with few storms or hurricanes.

Ecology

Rugged lush mountains make up over 80% of Honduras, and an extension of this volcanic system juts up from the ocean floor to form the Bay Islands. The Bays include three major islands -- Roatan, Guanaja and Utila; Roatan's sister islets of Helene, Morat and Barbareta; the so-called Hog (Cochinos) Cays; plus dozens of scattered little cays.

The main islands feature unspoiled dense jungles (real ones with boa constrictors and tarantulas) and hills and streams that plummet from 1,300-foot mountains into crystal clear lagoons. Abundant trees blossom with extraordinary flowers and edibles including cashew, coconut, mango, guava, mandarin orange, breadfruit and almond. There are also dense mangrove patches, alive with white egrets.

Exploring

Roatan, largest of the Bay Islands, offers the most developed tourist services. The port of entry is Coxen Hole, the largest town and capital of the Bay Islands. The town, which boasts the only pavement on the islands, is officially called Roatan. However, nobody calls it anything but Coxen Hole, a name mindful of its pirate past. Brightly colored stilt homes stand out against the lush green backdrop of palms and hills. Everybody in town seems to know everybody

Hotel Honduras Maya

Oak Ridge/Pinkston

else. It's the island's business and commercial center, and you'll find banks, a post office and the public telephone.

Most visitors will wish to limit their side trips to the mainland, what with malaria and such along the Mosquito Coast, and border skirmishes overflowing from conflicts in neighboring El Salvador and Nicaragua. However, there are some interesting stops you might consider.

The Copan Ruins are based in a 74,130-acre park. Copan was the major art, science and cultural center of the Mayans.

Those whose travel arrangements call for an overnight in La Ceiba will understand why it's known as "the Sweetheart of Honduras." Thirty-thousand inhabitants live in an incredibly beautiful setting, where high and mighty green mountains meet the turquoise sea at a narrow plain dotted with plantations.

Honduras

Food

Most accommodation charges include three nicely prepared meals (per day) featuring seafood, fresh vegetables and such locally grown fruits as cassava, papaya, mango, guava, pineapple and banana. The water is usually from pure mountain springs, but you can request bottled water at most hotels. Bottled water is a good idea on the mainland. Mainland cuisine reflects the culture of Central America, with foods like tortillas, enchiladas, corn tamales, tapado (vegetable and meat soup), mondongo (tripe soup) and a variety of tropical fruits. Cold cereal is served with warm milk, unless otherwise requested. Also, the refried beans are mixed with sour cream and cheese.

Nightlife

The Bay Islands are not especially noted for nightlife. What there is centers around a few of the resort hotels. La Ceiba is the country's nightspot with nightclubs and casinos.

Shopping

Each of the resort hotels has a shop where you can purchase casual island wear, some dive gear, souvenirs and sundries. There are also shops in Coxen Hole, Sandy Bay, French Harbour and Oak Ridge.

Sports

You can use or rent a sailboard at many resorts, arrange for a deep-sea fishing expedition or set sail in a craft large or small. There is hunting (with a guide only) for rabbit, deer and iguana. Soccer is the national sport; baseball is popular too.

• Diving

Bay Islands' diving is often described as "aquarium diving." There are abundant corals, fish, sponges and marine invertebrates in warm waters. The corals are among the most diverse and dense in the region; of the 62 known coral species in the Caribbean, 50 have been found in the Bay Islands. The fringing reefs start at 25 to 40-feet.

Honduras - Accommodations

ANTHONY'S KEY RESORT 800-227-3483 — 56 Units: $150-150 BDFORSW
   305-858-3483 800-336-7717 1385 Coral Way, Suite 401 Miami FL 33145.
CAYE VIEW HOTEL 800-336-7717 — 15 Units: $40-50 BDOR
   011-504-221460 Coxen Hole Bay Islands, Honduras.
COCO VIEW RESORT 800-282-8932 — 19 Units: $70-90 BDFORSW
   904-588-4131 800-336-7717 Box 877 San Antonio FL 33576.
HOTEL COPANTL 800-336-7717 — 180 Units: $75-125 PRT
   011-504-532108 011-504-534170 Carretera a Chamelecon San Pedro, Sula, Honduras.
HOTEL HONDURAS MAYA 800-44-U-TELL — 200 Units: $94-293 KR
   011-504-323191 800-336-7717 Tegucigalpa Colonial Palmira Honduras.
HOTEL PARIS - LA CIEBA 800-336-7717 — 40 Units: $25-55 OPR
   312-336-7717 c/o Adventure Connections, Box 8826 Waukegan IL 60079.
REEF HOUSE RESORT 504-467-2949 — 15 Units: $130-160 BDFOPRSW
   Box 640399 Kenner LA 70065.

Honduras - Information

HONDURAS EMBASSY 202-966-7700
   4301 Connecticut Ave. N.W., Suite 100 Washington DC 20008.

Honduras - Liveaboards

ISLA MIA 800-348-9778 — 8 Berths: $75-120 BDORS
   Sea & Sea, 50 Francisco St., Suite 205 San Francisco CA 94133.

Jamaica

- **Airline Connections**   Air   Jamaica, American, Eastern and Air Canada.
- **Courtesy & Dress**   Casual and relaxed.
- **Driving**   On the left.
- **Electricity**   110 volts/60 cycles is common; bring a converter and adapter to be safe.
- **Events & Holidays**   Bob Marley Day and Reggae Superjam.
- **Off-Season Dates & Rates**   Lower rates are generally in effect from April 15 to December 15.
- **Time**   Eastern Standard Time.
- **Weather**   Jamaica is tropically warm all year, with the average temperature ranging from 80 to 86 degrees. Brief but heavy showers are common in March, May, June, October and November.

Ecology

The third largest island in the Caribbean is a botanical wonderland. Jamaica has 200 types of orchids, 500 species of ferns, 80 kinds of wild pines, 20 varieties of coral and hosts of whistling frogs, iguanas and mongoose, plus 4 different species of hummingbirds. A tropical rain forest covers the Blue Mountains, rising to almost 7,500 feet. Rivers wind through the mountains, then plunge to the sea on the southern coast. Other areas of the island feature savannas, mangrove swamps and plains. Jamaica is considered by many to possess the world's most beautiful coastline.

Exploring

It's rumored that Jamaican drivers are reincarnated kamikaze pilots. With that caveat in mind, rest assured that roads and rental vehicles are generally in good shape. The country is only 146 miles long, so nothing is too far from anything else.

Apart from the motor, the horn is a Jamaican vehicle's most vital part. People honk to say they're there, they're passing, thanks and to wish you a nice day. The different lengths and sequences each mean something unique. After a while, you'll learn the language.

Located on Jamaica's legendary north coast, Montego Bay is a spectacular place to golf or enjoy a full range of watersports. You can also ride horses or take a hot-air balloon tour.

/Poseidon Nimrod Divers

Mountains and waterfalls meet beaches along the 42 miles from Discovery Bay to Port Maria; in fact Dunn's River Fall at Ocho Rios cascades directly onto the beach. It's a beautiful, 600-foot waterfall that's a cool, refreshing climb by day and glistens gold from the torches lining its banks at night.

Ocho Rios proper is a resort city where you can parasail, golf, play tennis, freshwater or deep-sea fish, ride horses through plantation grounds or enjoy just about any sport. The "Night on the White River" excursion offers entertainment similar to Montego Bay's Grand River trip. Ride or walk around working plantations here or explore the Runaway Bay Caves.

Food

Seafood is the specialty, with rock lobster especially common. Typical Jamaican dishes include codfish and ackee (salted fish with an eggy-tasting vegetable), escaveche (marinated fish), curried mutton and goat and pepperpot stew, all highly spicy.

Nightlife

Dancing galore awaits, as participant or spectator; anything from funky to glamorous, barefoot to coat and tie.

Sports

Watersports -- diving, fishing, river rafting, sailing, waterskiing, parasailing predominate, but there are also 9 golf courses and scores of tennis

Jamaica

courts. More solitary pursuits include horseback riding amid hills and plantations, hiking or birdwatching.

• Diving

Very few people are acquainted with Jamaica's magnificent underwater world. Although there are only a few wreck sites, there are many unique coral formations, caverns, holes and overhangs to explore. All of the island's dive operators are very close to dive sites.

The main dive areas are Montego Bay, Negril, Ocho Rios and Runaway Bay,

• Fishing

Twenty-seven years of tournament fishing have helped establish Jamaica as a premier sport fishing location. Two prominent blue marlin fishing tournaments are held in Jamaica in September and October. One is in Port Antonio, the other in Ocho Rios. Montego Bay and Falmouth also host tournaments. Aside from game fishing, reef fishing produces snapper and grouper.

Ninja Sportfishing, at the Ocho Rios Marina (1-809-974-2442), provides charter boats for deep-sea fishing, and the catches include blue marlin, sailfish, kingfish, dolphins, shark, tuna and barracuda.

• Sailing

Cornwall Beach Watersports, in Montego Bay (1-809-952-5796), offers Sunfishes, boardsailing and waterskiing. The Heave-Ho Watersports Center provides sailing cruises as well as windsurfing and waterskiing. Extensive marina facilities are found at Huntress Charter and Marine Services Ltd. in Port Antonio (1-809-993-3318).

Jamaica - Accommodations

DOCTORS CAVE BEACH HOTEL 800-223-6510   77 Units: $90-110 BR
    809-952-4355 809-952-5204 Box 94 Montego Bay, Jamaica.
EXCLUSIVE HOLIDAYS 809-952-1126   50 Units: $195-360 BDOSW
    809-952-2679FX Gloucester Avenue, Box 85 Montego Bay, Jamaica.
FANTASY RESORT 800-327-9595   130 Units: $140-170 BDFKOPRTW
    809-952-4150 2 Kent Avenue, Box 61 Montego Bay, Jamaica.
JACK TAR VILLAGE, MONTEGO 800-527-9299   128 Units: $145-145 BDKOPRSTW
    809-952-4340 214-670-9874 Box 144 Montego Bay, Jamaica.
PLANATION INN 800-237-3237   79 Units: $240-600 BKOPRTW
    809-974-5601 Box 2 Ocho Rios, Jamaica.
SANDALS MONTEGO BAY 800-327-1991   250 Units: $255-370 BDGPRSTW
    809-952-5510 809-952-0816FX Box 100 Montego Bay, Jamaica.
TRYALL GOLF & BEACH CLUB 800-336-4571   100 Units: $230-310 BGRTW
    809-952-5111 Box 2, Sandy Bay P.O. Montego Bay, Jamaica.

Jamaica - Information

JAMAICA TOURIST BOARD 800-421-8206
    213-384-1123 809-929-9200 3440 Wilshire Boulevard, Suite 1207 Los Angeles CA 90010.

Jamaica - Sports

AQUA NOVA WATERSPORTS 800-423-4095   Divers: $10-40 DFOSTW
    809-957-4420 Negril Beach Club, Negril P.O Negril, Jamaica.
FANTASEA DIVERS 809-974-5344   61 Divers: $50-50 BDSW
    809-974-2353 809-974-5732FX Box 103 Ocho Rios, Jamaica.
HEAVE - HO WATERSPORTS AND DIVE CENTER 809-974-5660   31 Divers: $57-60 DFOSW
    809-974-2755FX 11 A Pineapple Place Ocho Rios, Jamaica.
HONEY'S WATER SPORTS 809-957-4467   90 Divers: $35-60 BDFOSW
    809-957-4408 Negril Post Office Jamaica. Honey's is the place to go when you are in Jamaica for watersports fun and friendly people: don't forget, check Honey's first! You'll find everything you want: parasailing, diving, snorkeling, glass-bottom boat tours to the caves. If you prefer to sail to Booby Bay; a beautiful little island, "Honey" will take you on his 50 feet catamaran. Fishing trips, waterskiing, water Banana rides, sunset cruise, sailing trips, island picnics and private tours.
POSEIDON NEMROD DIVERS 809-952-3624   8 Divers: $45-45 BDK
    Box 152 Reading, St. James, Jamaica. PADI training facility offering personalized service, private certification courses and specialties. The best guided shore and boat diving in Jamaica in small groups. Nightdiving, Photo, Video and complete dive packages available. Situated at two locations: Chalet Caribe and Marguerites Resturant; servicing Tryall Golf Club, Round Hill with pickup from other Montego Bay Hotels.
STANLEY BAY MARINA 809-953-2244   12 Divers: $50-96 BDFRS
    Mahoe Bay, Box 362 Montego Bay, Jamaica.

Mexico

• Airline Connections   C o n t i n e n t a l, American, United, Eastern and Aeromexico fly to Cozumel and Cancun. Aero Cozumel, Aeromexico and Mexicana each have domestic flights linking Mexico City, Merida, Cancun and Cozumel.
• Courtesy & Dress   Informal, shorts and light shirts   except discos and top restaurants.
• Driving   On the right.
• Electricity   US standards.
• Events & Holidays   Cozumel holds a Fiesta on San Miguel Day (Sept. 20) and Isla Mujeres celebrates Fiesta on Dec. 1 and 2.
• Off-Season Dates & Rates   A p r i l through November prices drop by 30%.
• Time   Central Standard Time.
• Weather   The annual average temperature is around 80 degrees, rising to the low 90's in July and August, and going down to the mid-70's in the winter. In December and January the weather is occasionally windy, overcast and cold.

Introduction

The Yucatan Peninsula is a giant land mass that thrusts out from Mexico to divide the Gulf of Mexico and the Caribbean Sea. It includes the Mexican states of Campeche, Quintana Roo and of course, Yucatan. One of the most amazing areas of Mexico, the Yucatan is home to bustling tourist resorts, vast tracts of virgin rain forest and savannah and fascinating Mayan ruins.

Among the most interesting of the Mayan ruins are Chichen Itza and Tulum, both located on the Yucatan mainland and both an easy day trip from Merida, Cozumel or Cancun. Also on the mainland is the resort area of Akumal. Cozumel and Isla Mujeres are islands lying off the eastern coast of the Yucatan Peninsula. Each island is easily reached from the US mainland and from one another by plane or, in the case of Isla Mujeres, ferry from Cozumel.

Akumal

Akumal --which means turtle in Mayan-- sits in a quiet bay lined with white sands and swaying palms. Just south of Cancun, this deluxe resort area is also headquarters for underwater archaeology organizations. Ancient Mayan sites abound both above and below the water. Wreck remains

Snuba at the beach

Tulum/Dean

can also be seen in near-shore waters. Facilities for watersports include fishing, boat trips, snorkeling and diving. Freshwater from visible crevices in the sea floor mix with the sea. The varied fauna makes Akumal a divers' delight.

Cancun

One-quarter-mile wide and 12 long, L-shaped Cancun is Mexico's newest Caribbean coast

Mexico

resort. Planned as such and constructed in 1967, Cancun sits on the northeast tip of the Yucatan peninsula about 30 miles north of Cozumel.

The island links to the mainland by causeways at both ends. Thus, it encloses 18 square miles of Nichupte lagoon, which is ringed with white beaches and unique flora including wild orchids, red mangroves, Australian pines and a profusion of other colorful plants.

Nightlife

As well as ultra-modern hotels and vacation homes, the Cancun resort area boasts a Convention Center whose 2,000-capacity auditorium is also used for cultural events including traditional folk dances. Most hotels have discos, some live entertainment and relaxing bars.

Shopping

There are several large shopping complexes in Cancun, and shops display the wares of local artists and craftsmen. Traditional arts and crafts include native pottery, baskets of straw, sisal and palm leaves, embroidered blouses, gold filigree work, hand carved wooden articles and sombreros.

Sports

Cancun provides a wealth of sports activities. Most hotels offer tennis or squash, and there is a modern golf course. For those with a competitive spirit, there are often golf and tennis tournaments. All kinds of watersports are available. The numerous marinas provide charter fishing boats, waterskiing and scuba instruction. The adventurous can try parasailing. Touring off the island is made easy by the variety of cruise and sail boats which offer daily swimming, sunning and snorkeling tours.

Chichen Itza

Chichen Itza lies on the mainland about 120 miles west of Cozumel, half way to Merida and 100 miles from Cancun. The best way to get to Chichen Itza is to travel with a tour. If you are interested in the grandeur and complexity of ancient civilizations, this very interesting site is well worth the travel.

For over 700 years, Chichen Itza was an important religious sanctuary for the Mayas, and later for the Toltecs. Founded around 450 AD, it reached its height during the Mayan Renaissance,

between 1000 and 1200 AD. There was a strong Toltec influence at the time, so that most of the architecture is a mixture of Toltec and Mayan styles. The city declined precipitously after 1200. According to chronicles from that period, Chichen Itza's ruler, Chac-xib-chac, fell in love with and abducted a woman betrothed to the king of nearby Izamal. This, of course, resulted in a war that devastated both cities.

Cozumel

Cozumel may be readily toured in a day by car or moped. There are three publications that provide up-to-date information on the island and give detailed island tours: Insider's Guide Sheet to Cozumel Diving and Snorkeling, What to Do and Where to Go, and the Free Blue Guide to Cozumel. We suggest that you pick up one of the free guides and spend a day or at least an afternoon trekking around the island.

Cozumel epitomizes the Mexican Caribbean: the white beaches, azure blue water and lush green palm trees are typically Caribbean, but Cozumel is unmistakably Mexican in its charm and hospitality. The island has all the advantages of luxurious seashore resort hotels combined with the breathtaking beauty of a Caribbean island.

Cozumel is the largest of Mexico's Caribbean islands. 28 miles long and 11 miles wide, it lies 12 miles off the coast of the Yucatan Peninsula. In Mayan "ah Cuzamil" means land of the swallows, but this might be changed today to "ah tourista" since the island is now visited by large numbers of tourists.

Food

The major hotels all feature a wide variety of Mexican and international dishes. As you would expect, fish is the main dish.

Nightlife

No trip to Cozumel is complete without a stop at Carlos & Charlies.

Shopping

Cozumel is not the place to go for inexpensive, duty-free shopping.

Sports

Each spring there is a major billfishing tournament held out of Cozumel, and year round you will find a veritable fleet of boats for rent. There isn't much in the way of parasailing or waterski-ing, but there are windsurfers for rent as well as all the other sports equipment you normally find in a major resort area. Cozumel is really a diver's paradise and that's what they do best here.

• Diving

Most all of the diving in Cozumel is drift diving. Typically, operators take you out for a two-tank dive that includes a deep dive in the morning, a stop on the shore for lunch and then a shallower dive in the early afternoon. Major dive sites include:

(1) Paradise Reef is actually a series of three reefs running parallel to shore, about 200 yards out. This is the only major reef accessible to beach divers. Maximum depth is 47 feet and the reef is abundant with marine life.

(2) Chancanab Reef is just south of Parque Chancanab and 350 yards offshore, with a maxi-mum depth of 55 feet. The coral formations and marine life are similar too, but a little less popu-lated than Paradise. This and Paradise are good locations for night diving.

Beginning on the southern end of "La Playa": (3) San Francisco Reef is a one-quarter-mile long reef broken into two sections separated by about 80 yards of sand. This is Cozumel's shallowest wall dive with the best diving at depths between 40 and 60 feet.

(4) Palancar Reef, the reef most identified with Cozumel, is actually a conglomeration of many different coral formations, each with its own personality. Stretching over three-and-one-half miles, this gargantuan reef lies about a mile off-shore and tops a sloping wall which descends to a maximum depth of 3,000 feet. (5) Palancar Gar-dens, at the northernmost end, is frequently dived but is still beautiful and relatively shallow.

Cozumel's second most popular drift-diving drop-off is Santa Rosa Reef--"The Wall"--which begins at 50 feet and drops straight off. There is usually a brisk current, and it is a thrill to fly along the face and frolic with the groupers that gather to be fed by divers.

Isla Mujeres

Though the few Mayan ruins on this small, narrow island prove that it was inhabited during the 8th and 9th centuries, not much is known of its pre-Columbian history. It was thought to be dedi-cated to Ixchel, the goddess of fertility, and when

Calinda Cancun, Cancun

Fantasia Divers, Cozumel

the first Spanish explorers arrived in 1517, they discovered hundreds of terra-cotta figurines of women among the ruins. They named it Isla Mujeres (Island of Women) after the figurines.

Nightlife

The nightlife here is pretty much limited to the hotel bars, but a nighttime stroll along one of the quiet moonlit beaches, or sitting under the stars can make for a very pleasant evening.

Sports

Waterskiing and fishing are both available on the Isle Mujeres. To the northwest between Cabo Catoche and the Isla Holbox there are marlin, shark, sailfish, barracuda, sea bass and mackerel.

• Diving

Isles Mujeres is known for its diving. However, there is an inviting beach on the north-ern side of the island, just beyond Bojorquez Hotel, that is worth avoiding. Strong cross-cur-rents and an undertow here have lead to a number of accidents. To make sure you dive the best spots,

Mexico

check with the local operators. Prices tend to be lower than Cozumel.

Tulum

This Mayan ruin is easy to reach from Cozumel, and definitely worth a visit. From the island, you can take an early morning ferry and then a short bus ride to Tulum. A sightseer's package also includes lunch and snorkeling at the Xel-Ha Lagoon, and gets you back the same day.

Perhaps the best reason to visit Tulum is its beautiful location atop rugged but overgrown cliffs that overlook a white-sand beach and some of the finest waters of the Caribbean. As you stand at the observatory, it may strike you that this was the world's first five-star beach club for high priests.

Mexico - Information

MEXICAN NATIONAL TOURIST COUNCIL 213-203-8151
  10100 Santa Monica Blvd. Los Angeles CA 90067.

Mexico, Akumal - Accommodations

AKUMAL VILLAS MAYA 800-351-1622   56 Units: $55-80 BDFOPRTW
  915-584-3552 915-581-6709FX Box 1976 El Paso TX 79950.
CLUB AKUMAL CARIBE 800-351-1622   56 Units: $63-80 BDFOPRSW
  011-529-8840780 915-581-6709FX Box 984 Cancun, Q. Roo, Mexico 77500.

Mexico, Cozumel - Accommodations

EL PRESIDENTE 800-472-2427   189 Units: $96-96 BDFGOPRSTW
  011-529-8720322 Box 49 Cozumel, Q. Roo, Mexico 77600.   See: Fantasia Divers.
LA CEIBA 800-621-6830   119 Units: $100-110 BDOPRTW
  214-669-1991 011-529-8720065 Box 284 Cozumel, Q. Roo, Mexico 77600. See: Fantasia Divers.
SOL CARIBE 800-223-2633   220 Units: $110-138 BDOPRSTW
  212-683-0060 011-529-8720700 Box 259 Cozumel, Q. Roo, Mexico 77600. See: Fantasia Divers.

Mexico, Cozumel - Sports

FANTASIA DIVERS 800-336-3483   92 Divers: $40-40 DO
  713-558-9524 011-529-8721258 Box 79714 Houston TX 77279. Fantsia Divers, beachfront locations featuring 4 dive boats and 2 trimarans, 14 divers maximum per boat. Standard 2-tank trips with lunch on private beach. Certification courses by international English speaking divemasters & staff. Easy excellent shore diving, "C" cards mandatory. Affiliated with Underwater Safety Services. Commission to Travel Agents and complimentary spaces offered to groups. U.S. office: (Fantasia Destinations) Houston, Texas.
NEPTUNO DIVERS 011-529-8721097   48 Divers: $35-47 DFOW
  011-529-8720233 Box 136 Cozumel, Q. Roo, Mexico 77600.
SCUBA COZUMEL 800-847-5708   75 Divers: $35-35 DP
  713-783-3305 011-529-8720627 c/o Galapago Inn, Box 289 Cozumel, Q. Roo, Mexico 77600.

Mexico, Cancun - Accommodations

CALINDA CANCUN 011-529-8831600   280 Units: $100-130 BDFOPRSTW
  011-529-8831857FX Paseo Kukulcan Zona Hotelera Cancun, Q. Roo, Mexico 77500. Pyramidal building adjacent to the bridge of Nichupte Lagoon and sea channel, Calinda hotel features: rooms with double beds, satellite color TV, servibar, safety boxes and phones in airconditioned rooms facing the sea and the lagoon. Tennis courts available winter of '89, 2 miles to golf course and 5 km. to shopping. Live entertainment, bars, car rental & travel desk.
CANCUN BEACH CLUB 011-529-8831072   160 Units: $110-132 BDFOPRSTW
  011-529-8850439FX Box 1730 Cancun, Q. Roo, Mexico 77500.
EL PRESIDENTE 011-529-8830200   200 Units: $100-300 BDFGOPRSTW
  Blvd. Cancun Cancun Cancun, Q. Roo, Mexico 77500.
KRISTAL CANCUN 011-529-8831133   328 Units: $180-180 BDRT
  011-529-8831790FX Paseo Kukulcan Cancun, Q. Roo, Mexico 77500.

Mexico, Cancun - Sports

KRYSTAL DIVERS 011-529-8831133   15 Divers: $50-50 BDOSW
  011-529-8831790FX Paseo Kukulcan Cancun, Q. Roo, Mexico 77500. See: Kristal Cancun.
OCEAN SPORTS 011-529-8846034   12 Divers: $48-48 BDO
  Av. Coba S.M.4 Lote 19, Box 704 Cancun, Q. Roo, Mexico 77500.

Mexico, Isla Mujeres - Accommodations

CRISTALMAR 011-529-8820036   38 Units: $73-73 BDKOPRSW
  Av. Morelos 85, Box 85 Islas Mujeres, Q. Roo, Mexico.

Montserrat

- **Airline Connections**   Fly from the US to Antigua and take LIAT or Montserrat Air into Montserrat.
- **Courtesy & Dress**   Casual summer clothing. Skirts and slacks appropriate at night.
- **Driving**   On the left.
- **Electricity**   220 volts; bring a converter.
- **Events & Holidays**   W h i t m o n d a y; Queen's Birthday (second Saturday in June); August Monday (first Monday in August).
- **Off-Season Dates & Rates**   Discounts from 25% to 40% May through November.
- **Time**   Atlantic Standard.
- **Weather**   A v e r a g e   t e m p e r a t u r e 83 degrees. It receives about 62 inches of rain each year.

History

Like many Caribbean islands, Montserrat was charted and named by Christopher Columbus, but it has something of an unusual history. Settled by Irish Catholics looking for freedom from religious oppression on St. Kitts in the 1600's, it retains a distinctive Irish flavor today.

The Irish established numerous sugar plantations on the island, which have since become obsolete with the abolition of slavery. In 1834, a British Quaker introduced lime trees to Montserrat, and these are still a major factor in the island's economy. Montserrat is a British Crown Colony with a governor who represents the Queen.

Exploring

Sometimes known as "The Emerald Isle," Montserrat is extremely green with a proliferation of flowers and tropical growth. Plymouth is the capital of this 39-square-mile island with a population of 3,000.

To the north of the city, St. Anthony's Church is one of the most popular attractions. Built in 1623, it has been rebuilt several times and houses two silver communion chalices given to the church by freed slaves. In the hills, taxi drivers are always proud to point out a well-known recording facility, which brings musicians like Paul McCartney and Sting to the island to record.

The Montserrat Historical Society Museum is housed on the northeast side of the island, located in a renovated sugar mill. Other sights include old forts, beautiful waterfalls and a volcano or two.

/Weisner

Montserrat

Vue Pointe Hotel

Food

Most of the hotels on the island have fine restaurants serving West Indian style cuisine and the seafood is almost always very good. Otherwise there aren't a lot of restaurants on Montserrat. In Plymouth, the Iguana Restaurant and The Attic serve international and local cuisine at very reasonable prices.

Nightlife

Entertainment on Montserrat is, for the most part, spontaneous; the only music is at the Vue Pointe Hotel. In Plymouth, try La Cave or 747 Disco, but it's best to ask a local what is happening during the period of your stay.

Shopping

Locally produced textiles and handicrafts from Montserrat shops make terrific souvenirs, but there isn't a great deal of shopping to be found here. Montserrat is best known for its Sea Island cotton products.

Sports

There are plenty of activities on this island, including tennis at various hotels, and Sunfish races on Sundays from the Yacht Club. Boats are available for fishing, and horseback riding can be ar-

ranged. Snorkeling and ocean swimming are limited.

• Diving

Montserrat has not developed any diving operations to service its visitors. Those determined to seek out what limited diving there is might talk to Bruce Farara, the owner of the auto parts store, who is an avid diver and knows the most interesting sites around the island.

• Golf

Located at the foot of the Vue Pointe Hotel's hill, the Montserrat Golf Course offers 11 holes, arranged so as to be played as two 9-hole courses with different tees for each nine. Club and cart rentals as well as caddies are available.

• Hiking

The island is perhaps best thought of as a hiker's paradise. There are many trails on all sides leading to waterfalls and volcanic areas. The Chance's Peak climb is for the adventurous, hardy hiker. The summit is at 3,000 feet, and you'll have to contact the Tourism Department to make special arrangements. There's also Galway Soufriere, a rugged volcanic rock, located not far from Upper Galway in the middle of the southern half of Montserrat. It's a curiosity for those who have never experienced a sulphur vent, reached after a 20-minute walk, with bubbling vents, very hot water, strong-smelling sulphur fumes and loud rumbling. And if you enjoy waterfalls, it's a challenge to get to the 70-foot Great Alps Waterfalls. This is a hike to be appreciated at a leisurely pace; hiking shoes and a guide are recommended.

Bird lovers will enjoy a trek through the local bird sanctuary or the tropical rain forest.

Montserrat, B.W.I. - Accommodations

PAULINE'S REAL ESTATE 809-491-2434
  Box 180 Plymouth, Montserrat.

20 Units: $60-80 BFKOPW

VUE POINTE HOTEL 800-223-6510

40 Units: $110-145 BDGOPRSTW

  809-491-5210 809-491-3599FX Box 65 Montserrat. Montserrat's largest and poshest resort facility featuring 40 modern cottages and rooms with full amenities. Accommodations are spacious and comfortable. Dining and entertainment are some of the best on the island with lots of local flavor. Activities includes day and night tennis, golf, sailing, windsurfing and snorkeling. Water sports are arranged at the beach, just a short walk away. Mix business with pleasure with our multi-purpose meeting center.

Montserrat, B.W.I. - Information

MONTSERRAT TOURISM 212-682-0435
  212-697-4258FX 809-491-2230 40 E. 49th St. New York NY 10017.

St. Eustatius

- **Airlines Connections** Windward Islands Airways (Winair) flies daily from Sint Maarten. Also connects from Statia to Saba and St. Kitts.
- **Courtesy & Dress** Casual summer clothes are sufficient. Don't wear bathing suits in town.
- **Events & Holidays** Statia-America Day (Nov. 16) celebrates the island's salute to the American Flag in 1976.
- **Off-Season Dates & Rates** 30% off in summer. Accommodations close September 1-October 15.
- **Time** Atlantic Standard.
- **Weather** Perfect, dependable Caribbean weather. Temperatures between 78 and 82 degrees year round. Rainfall averages 45 inches per year.

History

Only four miles long by two miles wide, Statia is a tiny shelf of land anchored by two extinct volcanoes. It was first sighted by Columbus on his second voyage in 1493, and was claimed by the Dutch in 1640. For a time during the 18th century, Statia was the richest trading center in the New World, hosting over 3,000 ships a year and trading in slaves, tobacco, cotton, sugar cane and rum.

/Kelly

In succession the island was: conquered by the English, then the French, won back by the Dutch and reconquered by the English. It changed hands twenty-two times before The Netherlands settled in to rule.

/Jacobs

Sint Eustatius

Exploring

With such a rich past, it's no wonder there's so much to see on Statia. First thing, pick up a free copy of the <u>Walking Tour Guide</u>, published by the St. Eustatius Historical Foundation. The walking tour starts in Lower Town, the part of Oranjestad at sea level. This was the center of commerce 200 years ago. Today much of this area is in ruins, and most of the ruins are under water..

In addition to its historical landmarks, Statia has more than its share of natural beauty. The Quill, a perfectly shaped extinct volcano, rises up nearly 2,000 feet on the south side of the island. Since its last eruption, the crater has filled with an exotic rain forest. Take a taxi to the top or make a day hike of the trip.

It's only a short hop to Sint Maarten or St. Kitts. Also, one-day diving trips to Saba can be arranged through Surfside Statia.

Food

A good selection of local food is available at the new Talk of the Town, L'Etoile and Golden Era. The Old Gin House, one of the few five-star restaurants in the Caribbean, offers both local and international meals. For French cuisine, La Maison Sur La Plage is the only place in town. For Chinese there are two restaurants, both called Chinese Restaurant.

Nightlife

Dancing and cocktails are the fare every night at the Stone Oven. There are informal dances at Maison Sur La Plage on Fridays and Saturdays. On Sundays there's a happy hour at the Golden Era Hotel. Enjoy the sounds of The Hippy Band, a popular local band.

Shopping

One local specialty is "blue beads," found nowhere else in the Caribbean.

Sports

• Diving

Diving off Statia's coast is safe and comfortable. The excitement comes from the surprises that await the bottom-comber. There are seven known shipwrecks within a half-mile of Oranjestad Bay and an estimated 100-300 yet undiscovered. Numerous sea battles, an earthquake, at least one severe hurricane and an encroaching water-line have buried much of Statia's history, making it accessible only to the underwater explorer. Sorting out the relics from three centuries of marine history can be a fascinating task; few of the remains are intact, and artifacts dating 100 years apart can lie side-by-side.

Of Statia's 16 or so charted dive sites, the best known is The Supermarket -- named for its remarkable selection of artifacts from at least seven distinguishable wrecks. The Supermarket sea floor is strewn with ballast piles, pre-1820 anchors, bottles, muskets, pistons, barrel hoops, crystal, knives, cannon, blue Delft plate shards and glass beads.

Dive site depths around Statia range from 20 to 90 feet. Visibility often exceeds 100 feet with water temperatures averaging 80 degrees. In addition to the jumbled wreck sites, expect to see miles of elkhorn coral forests, lots of sea turtles, rays and flying gunards. For wall diving enthusiasts there are two excellent south shore sites.

• Hiking

Besides diving, the best sport on the island is hiking. It's a tough walk up to the top of The Quill, but you are rewarded by spectacular views and by the lush rain forest nestled inside the crater. Watersports include swimming and snorkeling. There is a concrete tennis court at the Community Center in Upper Town, lighted for night use and available to visitors for a nominal charge. Bring your own racquet.

St. Eustatius, N.A. - Accommodations
OLD GIN HOUSE 800-223-5581   20 Units: $130-130 BDPR
    416-283-2621 011-599-32319 Box 172 St. Eustatius, N.A. See: Dive Statia.

St. Eustatius, N.A. - Information
SINT EUSTATIUS TOURIST INFORMATION 212-242-0000
    c/o Mallory Factor, 275 7th Ave. New York NY 10001.

St. Eustatius, N.A. - Sports
DIVE STATIA 800-468-1708   26 Divers: $45-45 D
    011-599-32319 Box 172 St. Eustatius, N.A. See: Old Gin House.

/Weisner

St. Kitts & Nevis

• Airline Connections   Fly direct from New York on BWIA. Within the Caribbean, Fiat, Winair and Prinair connect to other islands. The airport departure tax is EC$13.00/ US $5.00.

• Banking   The islands use the Eastern Caribbean dollar (EC$). The current exchange rate is EC$2.70 = US $1.00. Larger hotels accept credit cards.

• Courtesy & Dress   Casual day and evening wear.

• Customs & Immigration   Must have proof of citizenship other than a driver's license and an ongoing plane ticket.

• Driving   On the left.

• Electricity   230 volts AC; bring a converter.

• Events & Holidays   Labour Day (first Monday in May); Queen's Birthday (second Saturday in June); Independence Day (Sept. 19).

• Information   See Directory.

• Languages   English.

• Medical   Government operated hospitals are located in Basseterre and at Sandy Point on St. Kitts, and in Charlestown on Nevis.

• Off-Season Dates & Rates   Hotels drop as much as 50% between mid-April and mid-December.

• Taxes & Tipping   Government tax of 7% added to hotel bill plus an additional 10% service charge.

• Taxi Fares   Set by the Taxi Union. Establish fare before departing.

• Telephone   For both islands call direct by dialing 809 + 465 + the local 4-digit number.

• Time   Atlantic Standard Time (Eastern Standard + 1 hour).

• Weather   Dry and warm from November to April. Hotter from May through October. Average temperature from 76 to 81 degrees.

History

St. Kitts and Nevis were charted by Columbus in 1493 and annexed by the British in 1623. Despite the fact that British sovereignty was disputed by the French and Spanish through the centuries, the British maintained control until modern times. In fact, St. Kitts was the first important British colony in the Caribbean, serving as both a major slave trade center and sugar producer.

Nevis is famous as the birthplace of Alexander Hamilton, George Washington's loyal aide. This is where Captain Horatio Nelson, the famed British commander, met his bride, Frances Nisbett.

St. Kitts & Nevis

/Weisner

In the 1960's St. Kitts and Nevis attained the status of "Associated Statehood" with England. The arrangement originally included Anguilla also; however it was not interested in the link to St. Kitts and split off almost immediately. It wasn't until 1983 that St. Kitts and Nevis gained full independence from the British.

St. Kitts

Exploring

Basseterre is the capital of St. Kitts and home to the majority of the island's 35,000 residents. In Basseterre, the best sightseeing is near St. John's Harbor. Be sure to visit the Thomas Berkeley Memorial, a tribute to a past president of the Legislature, and Pall Mall Square, best known as the site of a former slave market.

One of the most impressive sites in St. Kitts is Brimstone Hill, a large fortress offering spectacular views of the island. Built between 1690 and 1736, Brimstone Hill was the site of a major British/French battle in 1782. Those with energy to climb the long flight of stairs will enjoy the small museum at the top of the Hill.

Four miles west of the capital is Bloody Point, a site where there's not much scenery to speak of, but who's chilling history makes it a curiosity point. Here 2,000 Carib Indians were massacred, in one battle with the British and French. A river of blood flowed for days, giving the site its macabre title.

About six miles from Basseterre is Old Road Town, the location of the first British settlement in the Caribbean.

/Roessler

/Weisner

St. Kitts & Nevis

Brimstone Hill Fort, St. Kitts/Weisner

Food

Nearly all the food on St. Kitts is locally grown. Best bets for lunch and dinner include the Golden Lemon at Dieppe Bay, which has received raves from the critics; the Ocean Terrace Inn; Fisherman's Wharf on the waterside; and The Patio at Frigate Bay, known for its buffets.

Nightlife

Besides the local hotels, there is plenty of nightlife to be found in Basseterre. Check listings for local casinos. These are usually found only at larger resort hotels; some are open to the public. In town check to see what is happening at the Fisherman's Wharf. You should also find some live entertainment at the Lighthouse on Deep Water Port Road and at Club Prive on Fort Sheet.

Shopping

Shopping in St. Kitts is quickly becoming more accessible than in the past as duty-free shopping expands to meet the demands of increased tourism. Local crafts such as Kihitian embroidery, basket work and handmade furniture are found at the Crafts House. Boutiques sell sportswear, souvenirs, imported jewelry and perfume. A must is the Caribelle Batik factory which sells locally designed and painted clothing.

Sports

While watersports are obviously the center of sports interest on St. Kitts, tennis enthusiasts will find courts at the hotels and there are also private courts in Basseterre.

Equipment for watersports is offered through most hotels. Boats for fishing or touring are easy to rent. Windsurfing and sailing equipment are available at several watersport shops.

• Fishing

Spearfishing is legal in St. Kitts. St. Kitts Water Sports, at Frigate Bay, can arrange this activity on the reefs off the peninsula at the southern end of the island. At the Pelican Cove Marina, near the Ocean Terrace Inn, you can also make arrangements for deep-sea fishing and bottom fishing.

• Golf

At Frigate Bay, the Royal St. Kitts Golf Course offers an 18-hole championship course designed by Robert Trent Jones. The course and club facilities can be used by all visitors to St. Kitts and Nevis. An alternative is the 9-hole course at Golden Rock in St. Kitts, two miles from Basseterre, also open to all visitors.

• Hiking

If you're eager to climb, then St. Kitts' extinct volcano on Mt. Liamuiga (3,792 feet) is the place to go. It's a steady climb through virgin forest and wild orchids, and you can actually descend into the crater (elevation 2,600 feet) clinging to vines and roots for support. This is an all-day excursion, and the hotels can arrange transportation to Belmont or Harris' Estate, the two starting points.

Kriss Tours, in Basseterre (1-809-465-4042), organizes hikes through the lush tropical rain forests of St. Kitts which are typically high in the mountains. They have 8-hour and 5-hour trips which include lunch, drinks and hotel transportation.

• Sailing

Sailing can be arranged through St. Kitts Boatbuilding Company in Basseterre (1-809-465-2325) which operates a large, comfortable catamaran for day charters as well as Beachcomber Sailboats Rental, in Frigate Bay, which has Sunfish sailing.

• Windsurfing

This sport is catching on here, too, so you might want to visit Caribbean Island Windsurfing in Basseterre which provides boards for rent and lessons (1-809-465-2695).

Nevis

Exploring

Perhaps the best way to see the island is to hire a taxi driver to show you the sites. Most likely

Nevis/Wiesner

your driver was born on the island and can tell you all you'd like to know.

Though Nevis is a mere two miles from its sister island, St. Kitts, the two couldn't be more different. Nevis is extremely tropical with color-

Nevis/Weisner

ful flowers growing everywhere, giving a feeling of tranquillity. The capital of Nevis is Charlestown, home to 2,500 residents. It has a well-known bathhouse, which was built in 1778 and is still operating today.

Outside of Charlestown sits Nelson's Museum with plenty of mementos of the British commander and his Nevisian bride. Be sure to stop and view the inside of one of the many churches on the island. Most are a bit "worn," but they are all interesting with bits of history on display.

Continuing your drive you'll pass Ashby Fort and Eden Brown on the east. Be sure to ask your driver to stop at one of the old sugar mills or at the ruins of the mansions and slave houses, that dot the island.

Food

Nevis food is similar to that of St. Kitts, with plenty of delicious local seafood prepared and served in West Indian style. The Longstone Bar and Restaurant in Charlestown is one of the most popular restaurants on the island. You might also try the restaurant at the Oualie Beach Hotel with its fabulous and original West Indian and Continental cuisine.

Nevis is also known for its pepper sauce which makes Mexican hot sauce seem mild by comparison. Believe us when we say "a little dab will do ya."

Nightlife

Nevis is not known for its nightlife, so the best bet is to try the local hotels. Disk's Bar, Hide-a-way Disco and the Mariner's Pub in Charlestown also offer music and dancing.

Shopping

Local crafts, Caribee clothing and unique Nevis stamps are all available for sale on the island. Though this isn't exactly a shopper's mecca, you should be able to find some enjoyable souvenirs to take home.

Sports

Tennis and horseback riding facilities are located on the island, but watersports are the primary activity here. The Oualie Beach Club (1-809-465-5329) is the main place for renting windsurfing, sailing, waterskiing and diving equipment although some of the other hotels have limited equipment for their guests. For lessons or guides check with Oualie Beach.

• Diving St. Kitts & Nevis

These two islands afford some of the most exciting diving areas in the Caribbean. Almost completely unexplored, they offer diverse diving sites and coral reefs, shelves, mini-walls, canyons and caves with drift diving in some locations. Because there are so few divers on these islands, the coral reefs are untouched and intact. There are impressive staghorn, brain and other types of coral, huge tube sponges and sea fans the size of coconut trees.

The sheer number of fish is also startling. Fishermen on St. Kitts and Nevis use only nets and traps - no trawlers - so there are greater numbers and variety of fish. A special characteristic of the coral reefs here are what the locals call "white holes," huge drop-offs teeming with schools of tropical fish.

The most beautiful reefs are generally found on the Atlantic (eastern) side of the islands. However, this side of both islands is virtually unexplored since divers tend to stick to the Caribbean, or western side, where water is calmer. Those who brave the heavy currents and aggressive sharks found in the eastern waters will experience plenty of color. Starting at the northwest point of St. Kitts and running all the way along the east to the southernmost point of the island, there is incredible diving past miles of linked coral reefs and massive schools of fish.

Whichever side you choose to dive, you'll probably have to go a mile or two offshore. St. Kitts and Nevis are both volcanic islands and runoff from the rain turns the water close to shore murky. But, a mile out to sea, the water remains as crystal clear as any in the Caribbean. One last note: spearfishing is legal on both islands but is generally frowned upon by dive operators. Sometimes operators will let you keep a dead shell or piece of coral from the ocean bottom, but it's always a good idea to ask before taking.

• St. Kitts: Western Dive Sites

(1) Shoal Reef is off the shore at the settlement of Old Road Town. Leave from the pier in Basseterre and take a 30 minute boat ride to the site, one-and-a-half miles from shore. Once there you'll find a coral wall starting at 90 feet and dropping to unknown depths. Huge grouper, snapper, spanish mackerel, albacore and tuna live here along with dolphin and other large sea life, making this one of the most interesting dives on the island.

St. Kitts & Nevis

No wrecks have been spotted, but there have been reports of anchors in the area. Water is clear to over 100 feet on a normal day.

(2) The Edge is so named because the eastern end of the dive is a shallow 30 feet while the western end is seemingly bottomless. It lies in the channel of St. Kitts and St. Eustatius off the northwest point of St. Kitts. Great numbers of fish are the main attraction here along with grottos and shelves that house sea fans and sponges. However, the currents in this area are fairly strong.

(3) Red Cliff, (4) Corn Hill and (5) Ponds Bar are all sites located about one-half-mile off Frigate Bay. These are coral reef areas interspersed with sandy bottoms and have plenty of fish life. They are the favorite beginning diver sites on the island. Red Cliff is known for barracuda and small lobster; Corn Hill is near what used to a fort and has old cannons and anchors; while Ponds Bar is best known for its moray eels and queen and angel fish.

(6) Taleta Wreck lies one-quarter-mile from the shore at Basseterre. This steel hull ship broke a stopcock and sank in 60 feet of water in the middle of a coral reef only a couple of years ago. Unfortunately, since it is so close to shore, the water can be murky depending on the weather; check conditions before trying this dive.

(7) Monkees Shoal is undoubtedly one of the most spectacular sites on either island. Located two miles off the southern shore of St. Kitts, the site is a giant circular reef about one-half-mile in diameter that lies directly in the middle of the channel between St. Kitts and Nevis. The reef is basically a small island about 35 feet underwater, surrounded by bottomless drop-offs. It provides a perfect habitat for schools of fish, whose numbers and colors are spectacular. Water in this area is also very clear, with a wide range of depths.

Frigate Bay Beach Hotel/Gruttner

Fairview Inn

Fort Thomas Hotel
Timothy Beach Resort Unlimited

Pinney's Beach Hotel (Nevis)

St. Kitts & Nevis

• St. Kitts: Eastern Dive Sites

(1) The Grid Iron is an 11-mile stretch of coral reef which runs from the shore at Conaree Village all the way to Nevis. Depths vary but currents are strong. While coral is abundant, there aren't the large numbers of fish found elsewhere.

(2) Booby Island is a giant rock which lies in the channel between St. Kitts and Nevis. As one local put it, "If you blew the top off Booby Island you could build a great hotel on it." True or not, there is a gorgeous coral reef circling the tiny island with lots of brain coral and many smaller fish.

• Nevis Dive Sites

There is wonderful diving everywhere on Nevis except for the western side of the island, which is mostly sandy bottom. However, since it is almost completely unexplored, there are no specific dive sites to mention. The best place to dive is an area called Redonda Bank, which starts at the southernmost point of the island and runs for 10 miles to within five miles of Redonda Island, a deserted land mass near Montserrat.

St. Kitts & Nevis, B.W.I. - Accommodations

FAIRVIEW INN 800-223-9815   30 Units: $88-98 DGOPRT

809-465-2472 809-465-1056 Box 212 St. Kitts. On a hillside amidst tropical gardens with terraced lawns and panoramic views of the sea and Nevis. Our modern cottage complex is three miles west of the capital of Basseterre and five miles from the airport. All rooms have patios, radio and a private bath with hot and cold water. Our private beach is 1/4 mile away. Amenities include a freshwater swimming pool, golf and tennis at nearby clubs, along with watersports, mountain climbing and horseback riding.

FORT THOMAS HOTEL 800-223-9815   64 Units: $80-90 DFPRT

809-465-2695 809-465-7518FX Box 407 Basseterre, St. Kitts. High on rocky cliff overlooking Basse-Terre, the Fort Thomas Hotel offers some of the most beautiful panoramas imaginable. The very spacious, airconditioned rooms all have two double beds and a private balcony. From the Olympic-size freshwater pool and terrace bar, you have a clear view of our sister island of Nevis. The Hotel's superb restaurant, carvery & barbeques is noted for its relaxed atmosphere and excellent cuisine. Seasonal evening entertainment. See: Kenneth's Dive Center.

FRIGATE BAY BEACH HOTEL 800-223-9815   64 Units: $95-145 DFGOPRSTW

809-465-8935 212-840-6636FX Box 137 Basseterre Frigate Bay, St. Kitts. Frigate Bay Beach Club is uniquely positioned with a commanding view of both the Caribbean and Atlantic. One of the finest Caribbean beaches is located next to the property. Complete comfort in a perfect paradise. Sailing, snorke- ling, tennis, horseback riding and much more are all conveniently available. The lush fourth fairway of St. Kitts' championship 18-hole golf course adjoins Frigate Bay. Visit an unspoiled island and let Frigate Bay spoil you.

ON THE SQUARE GUEST HOUSE 800-621-1270   5 Units: $30-45 BR

312-296-2271 809-465-2485 Independence Sq. Box 81 St. Kitts PN. Idyllic setting and unspoiled beauty. On The Square Guest House enjoys a prime position on the western side of historic and picturesque Independence Square. Despite its proximity to St.Kitts, the Guest House itself is an immaculately modernized original old colonial style building is quite a haven of peace and tranquility, friendly relaxing place to stay where all the cares of a tightly scheduled business day or a busy sightseeing trip just ebb slowly away.

OUALIE BEACH HOTEL 809-469-9735   6 Units: $100-100 BDKOR

809-469-5706FX TX:03976818KC Oalie Beach, Nevis B.W.I. See: Scuba Safaris/ Nevis Water Sports Ltd..

PINNEYS BEACH HOTEL 800-621-1270   48 Units: $95-140 BDOPRT

809-469-5207 TX:6898 Box 61, Charlestown Nevis. Unwind on Famous Pinney's Beach with a spectacular Caribbean view at Pinney's Beach Hotel. 48 airconditioned rooms with phone, patio and private bath, the finest island specialties served in 2 restaurants, 2 bars for cool island cocktails, 2 tennis courts and a fresh-water pool. Meeting facilities accommodating up to 150. Tours and watersports arranged. Intimate and friendly atmosphere combined with moderate rates. Join us for a total island experience

TIMOTHY BEACH RESORT LIMITED 800-621-1270   24 Units: $100-210 BDGORSTW

312-296-2271 809-465-8597 Box 81, 14 Independence Square West Basseterre, St. Kitts. On the sandy beach of Frigate Bay on St Kitts, facing out over the calmness of the Caribbean Sea, is the all-new Timothy Beach Resort, just steps from the shore, and poised as though waiting for you. Besides St. Kitts' fabled climate, visitors can also enjoy horseback riding. Also available are a full range of watersports, scuba diving with licensed instructors, waterskiing, windsurfing and sailing in Hobie Cats. No other resort is sited like this one!

St. Kitts & Nevis, B.W.I. - Information

ST. KITTS AND NEVIS TOURIST BOARD 212-535-1234

212-879-4789 414 E. 75th St., 5th Floor New York NY 10021.

St. Kitts & Nevis, B.W.I. - Sports

KENNETH'S DIVE CENTER 809-465-2670   36 Divers: $40-60 BDR

809-465-1034FX New Town Bay Road Basseterre, St. Kitts.

SCUBA SAFARIS/ NEVIS WATER SPORTS LTD. 809-469-9518   10 Divers: $60-60 BDFOT

809-469-9735 809-469-9187 Ouali Beach Nevis. See: Oualie Beach Hotel.

St. Lucia

• Airline Connections   American Airlines flies daily via Puerto. BWIA flies Saturday from New York, via St. Kitts and Barbados. Both BWIA and Eastern airlines have direct daily flights from Miami. LIAT has connecting flights from Antigua and Barbados. The island has one international airport, Hewannora in the south, and one inter-caribbean airport, Vigie Field near Castries.

• Courtesy & Dress   Very casual. Some hotels require jackets for dinner.

• Driving   Driving is on the left. The Atlantic coast roads are good but not well-marked. Expect a bumpy road along the west coast. Pick up a temporary driver's license at the airport or at police headquarters on Bridge Street in Castries (EC $30/$12.00 US). Applicants must be at least 25 years old.

• Electricity   220 volts, 50 cycles AC. Most hotels will supply you with a 110 to 220 adapter.

• Events & Holidays   The biggest celebration of the year is Independence Day, which is celebrated on Feb. 22. Depending on dates, it can closely precede Carnival, making for an ongoing winter festival.

• Off-Season Dates & Rates   From mid-April through December hotel rates may drop as much as 50%.

• Time   Atlantic Standard.

• Weather   Comfortable; temperatures range from 70 to 90 degrees and are tempered by trade winds. Wet season is May through November with usually rare and brief hurricanes.

History

Columbus probably discovered St. Lucia ("Loo-sha") in 1502. Early attempts by the French and English to settle the island were successfully foiled by the ferocious Carib Indians for about a hundred years. After fourteen changes of power, the Napoleonic Wars left St. Lucia in British hands.

In 1967 St.Lucia was accorded full internal self-government, and in 1979 gained complete independence from Britain. It is now a member of the Commonwealth of Nations and CARICOM - - the Caribbean Common Market.

Ecology

Located between Martinique and St. Vincent, this football-shaped island is the second largest of the Windward Islands. It is 27 miles long and 18 miles wide, consisting mainly of volcanic rock with one dormant volcano (Soufriere) still bubbling in the north. The southern part of the island is a flat coastal plain with secluded coves, sheer cliffs and long sandy beaches. The Amazon Versicolor Parrot lives only on St. Lucia.

Agriculture is the basis of St. Lucia's economy. Most of the 125,000 inhabitants live in the cities and coastal settlements, while the highland regions are largely uninhabited.

Exploring

Soufriere - Gros Piton/Kelly

Taxi drivers specially trained as tour guides are available for about US $14 an hour. Sightseeing boats from Castries will give you a quick glimpse of the island's highlights.

Tour operators offer a variety of tours including plantation, village and volcano excursions. St. Lucia Representative Services and The Carib Touring Company are among the best and most reasonably-priced on the island. Make reservations through your hotel activities desk.

You can also rent a car and hire a driver. Or, if you like adventure, get a good map from the Tourist Bureau and drive yourself. Don't miss Morne Fortune, The Pitons, the banana plantations in Cul de Sac Valley, the boat builders at Anse La Ray, Mt. Soufriere, the Diamond Mineral Bath with its waterfall and pond, the town of

St. Lucia

Soufriere and two remarkable hotels, Dasheen and Anse Chastenet.

Food

On St. Lucia you'll find French, English, German, American and Creole cuisine, but the Creole is the best. Try these local island specialties: pumpkin souffle, breadfruit soup, lobster creole, pepperpot soup, accras, lambi (conch), langouste (lobster) and fresh-made banana cake. Rum is reasonably priced, as is the locally brewed Heineken beer.

Nightlife

Most of the nightlife is at the hotels, which offer nightly dancing, and entertainment like limbo and steel band jump-ups several times a week. Splash and the Green Parrot are worth investigating.

Shopping

Pointe Seraphine is a totally self-contained tourist shopping complex with 23 duty-free shops. In Castries look for hand-made batik wall hangings and clothing, jewelry and carvings. Shop the Castries Market on Saturday mornings for fruit, vegetables and craftwork, such as straw items, rugs and weavings.

Sports

Horseback riding, golf, deep-sea fishing, snorkeling, swimming, sailing, parasailing and diving are all found here. There are also cricket and soccer matches. "Aqua Action," usually held in May, is a watersports competition organized by the St. Lucia Tourist Board.

• Diving

The best diving in St. Lucia is at Soufriere Bay. There are about 10 regularly visited sites north and south of here, along the island's mountainous leeward coast. Each boat ride offers dramatic vistas of The Pitons, principal southern landmarks looming up into the clouds.

An underwater shelf off the beach at Anse Chastenet, 10 to 30 feet deep, drops to 200 feet on a sheer wall. This shelf is actually the underwater base of the mountain peaks on shore. The area is noted for its giant vase sponges, huge barrel sponges, rope sponges in every hue and tube sponges.

• Golf

Golf can be played at either of St. Lucia's two courses. Cap Estate Golf Club is at the northern end of the island near the Cariblue Hotel. It has 9 holes and a clubhouse. The other is the Hotel La Toc Golf Course, also with 9 holes, but larger than the Cap Estate. Clubs can be rented at both courses.

• Sailing

Sailing facilities are centered at Rodney Bay and at Marigot. The former is home port for Stevens Yachts, roughly five miles from Castries and Vigie Airport. There's a variety of yachts for charter, both bareboat and crewed (1-809-458-648). The Moorings Yacht Charters, in Marigot, enjoys some of the Caribbean's most picturesque surroundings. Their planned programs include crewed yachts with 7-night itineraries, combination crewed yacht and hotel accommodations, as well as bareboat and flotilla programs where several yachts cruise Morgan 46's with the lead boat a Morgan 60 (1-809-454-256). Another alternative is Aquasail Yacht Charters at the Vigie Marina (1-809-455-754).

Several independent yachts are available for day charters. To find out what's available call St. Lucia Yacht Services at the Vigie Marina (1-809-452-5057).

St. Lucia, B.W.I. - Accommodations

ANSE CHASTANET HOTEL & SCUBA CENTRE 809-454-7354 — 38 Units: $150-180 BDFORSTW
  809-454-7355 TX:0398/6370 Box 216 Soufriere, St. Lucia. See: Scuba St. Lucia.
CUNARD HOTEL LA TOC & LA TOC SUITES 800-222-0939 — 254 Units: $175-350 BFGOPRSTW
  809-452-3081 809-452-1012FX Box 399 Castries, St. Lucia.
ISLANDER HOTEL 800-223-9815 — 44 Units: $85-105 BD
  809-452-8757 809-452-0255 Box 907 Rodney Bay, St. Lucia.

St. Lucia, B.W.I. - Information

ST. LUCIA TOURIST OFFICE 212-867-2950
  212-370-7867FX 809-452-4089 41 East 42nd St., Suite 315 New York NY 10017.

St. Lucia, B.W.I. - Sports

SCUBA ST. LUCIA 809-454-7354 — 60 Divers: $50-50 DOSW
  Anse Chastanet Hotel, Box 216 Soufriere, St. Lucia. See: Anse Chastanet Hotel & Scuba Centre.

Sint Maarten

• **Airline Connections** ALM Antillean Airlines has connections from Aruba, Bonaire, Curacao and San Juan. ALM, Pan Am and American fly direct from New York. American also flies from Dallas/Ft. Worth. Eastern flies via Miami, Philadelphia, San Juan and Antigua. BWIA flies from Toronto weekly and from Trinidad, Tobago, Barbados and Jamaica twice a week. Winair has daily flights from St. Thomas, Statia, St. Kitts, St. Barts, Anguilla and Saba. Air Guadeloupe flies from St. Thomas and St. Croix. The airport departure tax is US $5.00, if you're going anywhere but Statia, Saba, Curacao or Bonaire. There is no charge for children under two.

• **Banking** The guilder or florin (currently NAf 1.77 = US $1.00) is the coin of the realm. The US dollar is the preferred currency. Many larger shops, restaurants and hotels will give you a discount for using US dollars. Traveler's checks and credit cards are widely accepted. Bank hours are: Monday-Thursday, 8:30am - 1:00pm; Friday 8:30am - 1:00pm and 4:00pm - 5:00pm.

• **Courtesy & Dress** Everyone wears casual summer clothes. Swimsuits and bikinis are not appropriate wear for town. Evening wear is still informal, but a sports jacket or sweater (for men) is right for the casinos.

• **Customs & Immigration** US citizens need a valid passport, birth certificate or voter's registration card and a return or onward ticket.

• **Electricity** Compatible with US on the Dutch side.

• **Events and Holidays** New Year's Day; Carnival (last two weeks of April); Good Friday; Easter Monday; Coronation Day; Labor Day; Ascension Day; Whitmonday; Sint Maarten's Day (Nov. 11); Christmas; Boxing Day (Dec. 26).

• **Information** See Directory.

• **Languages** Dutch is the official language. Everyone speaks English.

• **Medical** St. Rose Hospital is located in Philipsburg. Also a helicopter airlift to Puerto Rico is available for extreme emergencies.

• **Off-Season Dates & Rates** 30-50% off in summer season, mid April to mid December.

• **Taxes & Tipping** Hotels and restaurants generally add a 10-15% service charge.

Maho Watersports

• **Taxi Fares** From the airport take a taxi to your hotel. Rental cars are picked up at your hotel and left at the airport. Cabs display a card showing standard fares along the main routes. A ride from Philipsburg to Juliana Airport will cost about $8. Multiple passengers and evening rates are higher.

• **Telephone** To call Sint Maarten from the States dial 011 + 599 + 5 + the five digit local number.

• **Time** Atlantic Standard (Eastern Standard + 1 hour) year round. Daylight Savings Time is not observed.

• **Weather** Balmy and comfortable. 80 degrees with annual rainfall at 45 inches.

/Roessler

Sint Maarten

History

With only 37 square miles, Sint Maarten is the world's smallest territory shared by two states. The larger state, St. Martin, is part of the French West Indies. Sint Maarten is the Dutch side. Each has a distinct cultural flavor of its own, but rather than producing conflict, the close proximity has made for a casual and friendly vacation spot.

Columbus discovered the island in 1493 and claimed it for Spain. It remained uninhabited until 1630 when the Dutch established an outpost, only to be driven out two years later by the Spanish who reasserted their rights. The island changed hands several times, until 1648, when the Spanish decided to relinquish their bases in the Caribbean and the Dutch and French both laid claim to it.

There are competing legends as to how the actual split was achieved but it's generally agreed that the Dutch got the better deal. Their portion included salt pans so valuable that Sint Maarten became the most prized property of the Netherlands West India Company. The Dutch also got the better harbor, suited for shipping and cruise ship trade.

Philipsburg, the Dutch capital, was founded in 1763 by Commander John Philips. Today the city is a typical modern Caribbean free port, bustling with resorts, restaurants and shops.

Exploring

Because of Sint Maarten's relatively tranquil past, there are few historical sites. The courthouse in Philipsburg is one of the few monuments. Built in 1793 to house both a new jail and the weights and scales used to figure taxes, it was rebuilt in 1826 and restored in 1969. There are, however, many natural sites to visit, including 36 beautiful long white-sand beaches, scalloping one cove after another. Mountains surround Philipsburg and the bays. To the southwest of Philipsburg are the ruins of a 17th century fort, Fort Amsterdam. To the west is Simpson Bay Lagoon, a very large land-locked bay near the airport.

From a spot on the road outside Philipsburg you can see four islands -- Nevis, St. Kitts, Statia and Saba. On the high road between Oyster pond and Philipsburg, there's a spectacular view of St. Barthelemy.

Exploring

Take a day trip by sail, power boat or air to Saba, Statia, Anguilla, St. Barts or St. Kitts. Or try a sailing trip with a picnic stop on an offshore deserted island. Day trips are offered through Bobby's Marina (tel. 22366) and Great Bay Marina (tel. 22167) or ask at your hotel.

Food

You could eat out every night for months on Sint Maarten and never repeat a restaurant; at last count there were more than 150 eating establishments. The menus tend toward traditional French food, but there's also Creole, Chinese, Indian, Italian, Indonesian cooking and even good American-style burgers. Dinner tabs average $20 per person or more.

Many restaurants specialize in Indonesian and Dutch cuisine, which may seem a strange combination. Historically, however, there is a strong cultural connection between The Netherlands and Indonesia.

And don't forget the French side of the island for fine dining. See the French West Indies section of Travel & Sports Guide for details.

Nightlife

There are many nightclubs in Philipsburg, including Studio 7, Le Club, the Blue Note and Sam's Place. Caravanserai is the ideal place to have a drink and watch the sunset. There are eight casinos, all affiliated with major resort hotels. Most are open from 8pm to 3am and players must be 18 or older.

Shopping

The shops of Philipsburg and those in the French capital, Marigot, make this the best island in the Caribbean for high-fashion clothing. If you plan to shop, comparison shop at home so you will recognize the best bargains. Also, pick up copies of the publications Sint Maarten Holiday, Sint Maarten Events, What to Do and Sint Maarten Nights, all available free on the island. They're full of shopping, restaurant and entertainment suggestions.

Philipsburg's shops line the two main thoroughfares, called Front St. and Back St. These are connected by lanes called steegjes, also lined with even more shops. Because the island is a freeport and there are no local taxes, you're likely to find good deals on many items, from designer clothing and jewelry to cameras and Dutch cheeses. Also china, batik, sea salt, spices, linens, tableware, embroidered items, watches, porcelain and housewares. Shops are open from 8am till noon and then again from 2 to 6pm daily. Most major credit cards are accepted.

Sports

Virtually every vacation sport that doesn't require snow and ice is available on Sint Maarten. There's a championship golf course, tennis courts at many of the larger hotels and many watersport centers for swimming, snorkeling, waterskiing, jetskiing, windsurfing, sailing, parasailing and sport-fishing. There are excellent dive shops on both the Dutch and French sides of the island.

• Diving

There's so much to do here above the water that few people come just for the diving. Once they take the plunge, however, they're likely to move "scuba" to the top of their list. According to the dive shop operations on the island, many of their first time resort course customers return the following year to complete their open water certification -- then keep coming back, year after year. Little wonder since visibility averages 120 feet. The reefs are shallow, from 30 to 80 feet and the fish and plant life are abundant and unspoiled.

Diving is good here all year round, except during occasional storms. Water temperatures vary from 72 to 82 degrees; from December through April a wet suit is advisable. There are plenty of calm days with 200 foot visibility, all year long.

There's very little beach diving since most sites are offshore -- a quick 10 or 15 minute boat trip, but too far to swim. Anyway it's a good idea to go with a dive shop guide as many of the sites are difficult to find. There are no walls, but there are some spectacular breakers, caves to explore and several wrecks, including an intact tugboat purposely scuttled as a dive attraction.

Expect to see beautiful elkhorn coral, plentiful soft corals and sponges and bountiful fish life including schools of reef fish and barracuda, rays and an occasional nurse shark. Although there is no government-enforced reef protection policy, speargun fishing and the collection of live specimens are frowned upon and are not allowed on guided trips. Hunt with your camera instead.

Sea Dancer Liveaboard

DIVI Little Bay Beach Resort

There are 10 regularly visited sites in the Dutch waters off Sint Maarten. In addition there are five sites off the French side. For descriptions of the French sites refer to St. Martin in the French West Indies section of the Travel & Sports Guide.

(1) French Reef and (2) Cay Bay Reef are excellent shallow reef structures lying close to shore. These are perfect spots for close-up photography. Waters here are usually calm, even when sites further offshore are choppy. (3) The Maze and (4) Explorers Reef lie south of Great Bay Harbor. Here you find many fine soft and elkhorn corals, crinoids and anemones. Sightings of barracuda, ray, grouper, turtles, nurse sharks and large French angelfish are quite common. At The Maze there can be a strong current running over the top of the reef.

(5) Proselyte Reef is one of the most requested dive locations in Sint Maarten. Here lies the wreck of the British frigate, HMS. Proselyte, which went down in 1801. You will still find several 12 to 14-foot coral encrusted cannons, three 12-foot anchors and some miscellaneous fragments.

(6) The Alleys is a series of large rock formations rising from 45 to 25 feet with some very interesting caves at their base. A short swim south

brings you to (7) Cable Reef, easily identified by a long tug boat cable draped over the top of the reef. More caves may be found here with plentiful fish life such as schools of barracuda and other pelagic fish. Bring your camera.

On the windward side of Sint Maarten (the east coast) are three sites which should only be attempted on exceptionally calm days. (8) Hens and Chicks is a series of breakers approximately two miles off Pt. Blanche. This is a mini wall dive with beautiful elkhorn coral forests at the top of the reef at 20 feet, tumbling 75 feet to a sandy bowl. Underwater visibility is usually quite good here.

The second windward site (9) Molly B'Day, has a large breaker rising 100 feet above the water line. It's a real treasure on a calm day because of a dramatic boulder slide and striking coral formations. Look closely for lobster, large banded shrimp and arrow crabs. The site presents great macrophotography opportunities but is dived only on special request on calm days. (10) Pelican Rock features a towering breaker wall and schools of large fish, including 6 to 7-foot tarpons.

(11) Long Bay Reef is a shallow reef close to shore at Long Bay. On days when conditions are not suitable for diving elsewhere, this site is usually accessible. This area however is subject to currents.

• Fishing & Sailing

In mid-February, the Heineken Regatta is held at Boby Marina. Several bare boat sailing charter companies operate with boats ranging from 30 to 50 feet and they can be chartered with crew as well. For a very inexpensive taste of deep-sea fishing you might try the Wampum (also at the Boby Marina). A half day of fishing costs $35 per person; including all the gear.

• Riding

If you are interested in a ride that requires a swimsuit, how about an excursion through the hills and beaches? At the end of the ride, the saddles are stripped off and you bareback along the shoreline. Check with Linda Russel at Crazy Acres Riding School (011-599-522061).

St. Maarten, N. A. - Accommodations

DIVI LITTLE BAY BEACH RST & CASINO 800-367-3484 220 Units: $220-270 BDOPRTW
607-277-3484 54 Gunderman Rd. Ithaca NY 14850. The newest member of the DIVI family of fine Caribbean resorts is situated on a postcard-perfect, palm-fringed 1,000-foot beach just 15 minutes from duty free shopping in Philipsburg. All rooms airconditioned with private patios or balconies, beachfront or with lovely garden views. Satellite, TV, pool, sundeck, 3 tennis courts (lighted), and all the quality you would expect from a DIVI hotel. They offer full watersports. Check their special packages.

GREAT BAY MARINA 011-599-522167   7 Units: $60-60 BR
Phillipsburg Point Blanche, St. Maarten, N.A. See: Maho Watersports. .

MULLET BAY SUN RESORT & CASINO 800-468-5538   597 Units: $90-200 BDGKOPRT
011-599-542801 011-599-542801 Box 309 Philipsburg, St. Maarten, N.A. See: Maho Watersports.

St. Maarten, N. A. - Information

SINT MAARTEN TOURIST BOARD 212-242-0000
212-989-0000 212-627-1152 c/o Mallory Factor 275 7th Avenue New York NY 10001.

St. Maarten, N. A. - Liveaboards

SEA DANCER 800-367-3484   12 Berths: $157-185 BDRW
607-277-3484 54 Gunderman RD. Ithaca NY 14850. Catering to the serious diving enthusiast, Sea Dancer offers an all-inclusive package of first class accomodations, diving services, gourmet meals , plus photo and video services. The ship schedule revolves around 3-5 opportunities a day featuring wall diving, virgin reef exploration and unsurpassed pelagic animal encounters. Eight-day 7-night trips feature diving in the warm, clear waters of Saba and St. Maarten from Dec.-March. Excellent Peter Hughes Diving.

St. Maarten, N. A. - Sports

MAHO WATERSPORTS 011-599-544387   18 Divers: $70-70 D
FX599-542801X379 Box 520368 Miami FL 33152. A very accommodating operation catering to all experience levels, now at two locations: Maho Dive Center, on the beach at Mullet Bay Resort and Trade Winds Dive Center, at Great Bay Marina, in Philipsburg. Equipment rental and retail, single and double tank dives, NAUI and PADI certification courses, and resort courses are available and easily arranged. Mike and Adrienne specialize in teaching beginners, as well as expanding certified divers' skills & abilities. See: Mullet Bay Resort & Great Bay Marina.

OCEAN EXPLORERS 011-599-545252   12 Divers: $55-55 D
011-599-545252 011-599-542220 Simpson Bay St. Maarten, N.A.

/Weisner

Tobago

- **Airline Connections** Fly to Trinidad on American, Pan Am, Eastern or BWIA. There is an hourly BWIA commuter to Tobago.
- **Courtesy & Dress** Conservative. Shorts only for the beach; evening wear is more formal.
- **Driving** On the left.
- **Electricity** 115 or 230 volts. Bring a converter.
- **Events & Holidays** Carnival here claims to be the most colorful in the world. Culminating the two days prior to Ash Wednesday, it's definitely creative and the one after which all the other Carnivals of the Caribbean have been patterned.
- **Off-Season Dates & Rates** Up to 35% discount from mid-April to mid-December.
- **Time** Atlantic Standard.
- **Weather** Generally very pleasant. Average temperature is 74 to 84 degrees. Cooled by trade winds.

History

Though Trinidad, Tobago's "big sister," was discovered by Columbus in 1498, Tobago was somehow overlooked by the great explorer. Lying 20 miles northeast of Trinidad, the island was eventually discovered by the British in 1508.

However, through the centuries, it changed hands more often than any other Caribbean island, moving from the English to the Spanish to the Dutch and then the French. Finally, Tobago was declared neutral territory and became one of the most popular pirate haunts of the 1700's.

A gorgeous tropical island, Tobago has been a favorite vacation getaway for Trinidad residents for many years. It is now gradually gaining recognition around the world for its beauty. This is rumored to be the island where Robinson Crusoe was marooned in the popular fictional tale.

Exploring

Quiet and relaxed, Tobago is definitely the place to go to escape big-city life. You'll find little in the way of sophisticated tourist sights but for nature lovers it is one of the most stunning islands in all the Caribbean.

Scarborough is the largest town on the island. Sights to see include Gun Bridge with cannon and balustrades, and Fort King George, built in 1777, complete with a small museum and fantastic views of the sea and Trinidad.

Speyside, on the northeast end of the island, is the most beautiful section of Tobago, and also the least developed. It takes about 2 1/2 hours to reach from the airport but the trip is well worth the effort. This small fishing village offers spectacular views and thick tropical flora and fauna. You might enjoy taking a boat ride to Little Tobago, a small island off Speyside, and the only place outside New Guinea where birds of paradise live in their natural environment.

Food

One of the most popular native dishes is Roti, a large burrito stuffed with vegetables, beef, potatoes, chick peas, goat or chicken. These are served at any number of small stands situated around the island.

The Keriwak Village near the airport; serves a specialty of the house each evening and a buffet on Friday and Saturday nights.

Nightlife

Trinidad is the place to go for exciting nightlife. Tobago on the other hand is quiet and relaxed, with most of the live entertainment presented on the weekends, primarily at hotels. It's really a treat to find a local Indian dance performance, but those are usually reserved for holidays and special occasions. There's a disco or two in Scarborough, but check with the locals for the latest information.

Shopping

As part of the British Commonwealth there are some good shopping bargains on Tobago. Shopping is limited mostly to the Scarborough area and James Park where a variety of local handicrafts are displayed.

Sports

There's a myriad of sports available on Tobago, including the usual and the not so usual. Tennis and golf are reserved for guests of certain hotels, but watersports are available to anyone visiting the island. Hunters might enjoy alligator tracking or hunting wild hogs in the forest, but check with the Tourist Board first.

• Diving

Proximity to the mouths of two South American rivers, the Orinoco and the Amazon, has created some of the most unusual and interesting diving anywhere in the Caribbean right around Tobago. The fresh-water overflow from these two enormous rivers mixes with the salt water of the Caribbean, turning it green. The color is produced by nutrients that grow in the fresh water. These nutrients also provide excellent food for the marine life in the salt water. As a result, some of the largest fish and coral formations in all the Caribbean exist here.

Water around the island is often rough, but the drift diving is unbeatable. Remote Speyside, a two hour drive to the north, offers the greatest number of difficult dives and the most breathtaking scenery. Speyside is also where you'll find tiny offshore islands with the most outstanding diving. Pigeon Point on southern Tobago has attractive beaches, and the only beginner sites.

• Fishing

Whether you prefer deep-sea, on-shore or inland waters, you will enjoy good fishing year round. In the waters off Tobago swim schools of kingfish, Spanish mackerel, wahoo, bonito, mahi mahi and yellow tuna.

• Golf

At the Mt. Irvine Hotel, not far from the airport is one the Caribbean's most scenic 18-hole championship golf courses. This is a world-famous course of 6,500 yards designed by the late John Harris.

Tobago - Accommodations

BLUE WATERS INN 809-660-4341
    809-660-4341FX Batteaux Bay, Speyside Trinidad and Tobago.
SANDY POINT BEACH CLUB 800-223-6510
    212-832-2277 809-639-8533 Crown Point Trinidad and Tobago. See: Dive Tobago L.T.D..

15 Units: $55-55 BDFKORT

42 Units: $60-70 BDGKOPR

Tobago - Information

TRINIDAD AND TOBAGO TOURIST BOARD 718-575-3909
    FX-575-3518 400 Madison Avenue New York NY 10017.

Tobago - Sports

DIVE TOBAGO L.T.D. 809-639-2266
    809-639-3695 Pigeon Point Box 53 Scarborough, Trinidad and Tobago. See: Sandy Point Beach Club.

40 Divers: $60-60 D

St. Thomas/Dean

US Virgin Islands

• **Airline Connections** There are direct and connecting flights to St. Thomas and St. Croix from a host of stateside cities on Pan Am, American, Delta, Eastern, Midway and TWA. For island hoppers, call Aero Virgin, Air BVI, American Eagle, Crown Air, Eastern Metro Express, Executive Air, LIAT, Virgin Air and the always-fun Virgin Islands Seaplane Shuttle.

• **Courtesy & Dress** Appropriate casual attire throughout the islands is the key; several fancier resorts require classier attire. Nudity is illegal, so is the wearing of shorts or swim wear in some communities, and you can be fined for offenses.

• **Driving** On the left.

• **Electricity** Same as the US.

• **Events & Holidays** St. Croix Carnival (from Christmas through Jan. 6); Migration of the Humpback Whale celebrations (begin in Feb.); St. Thomas Carnival (last week of April); St. John Carnival (July 4); Christmas Second Day (Dec. 26).

• **Off-Season Dates & Rates** Prices are 15-30% lower April 15 to December 15. Some hotels have mid-priced "shoulder rates" between their summer and winter seasons.

• **Time** Atlantic Standard.

• **Weather** With temperatures hovering from the mid-70's to mid-80's, Virgin Islanders claim an ideal climate. There are tropical storms periodically during hurricane season, June through October, but otherwise these are the driest, warmest months. The rainiest are October and November.

History

In 1917, for the then-outrageously high price of $25 million, the US bought the Virgin Islands to defend the Panama Canal during World War I. The islands' free-port status was retained in the sale treaty, still in effect. Today the US Virgin Islands is an unincorporated territory, which means its citizens are US citizens who pay taxes but do not have the right to vote in national elections. Locally, there is a 15-member elected legislature and a governor.

Exploring & Ecology

The US Virgin Islands--50 mini-islets and cays in addition to the three larger ones--are a volcanic part of the arc of the Antilles that separates the Atlantic Ocean from the Caribbean Sea. St. Thomas and St. John are only 35 miles apart. Their north coasts face the Atlantic, their southern the Caribbean. St. Croix, the largest, is further south, placing it entirely in the Caribbean. The islands

US Virgin Islands

St. Thomas/Dean

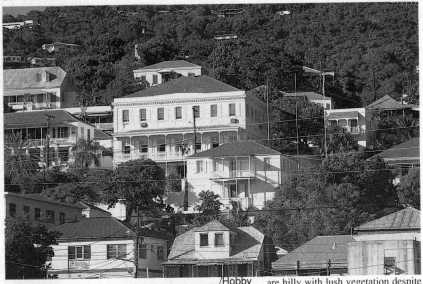

/Hobby

are hilly with lush vegetation despite scant rainfall and chronic water shortages. The three major islands all have spectacular expanses of soft white-sand beaches and warm turquoise waters.

St. Croix, nearly forty miles south of St. Thomas, is totally surrounded by the Caribbean. Its 50,000 unhurried inhabitants are Cruzans, pronounced and often spelled Crucians. This special tropical island of rolling countryside and satellite isles has a dreamy pace, with glorious scenery and Old World burgs. Unwinding, locally called limin', is the customary behavior.

The smallest and most beautiful of the major inhabited US Virgin Islands, St. John is a place where nature reigns. Two-thirds of the island is the Virgin Islands National Park. It's accessible by regularly scheduled ferries from St. Thomas and Tortola (in the British Virgin Islands) and by the Sea Plane Shuttles from St. Thomas, St. Croix and San Juan.

Busiest and best known of the US Virgin Islands, St. Thomas is famed as a shoppers' and honeymooners' paradise. But the island is also known for its wooded hills, mountaintop vistas, intimate beaches, historic houses and seascapes. The capital and only city is Charlotte Amalie. Here you'll find 2 to 14 cruise ships in port every day, unloading their passengers for some madcap spending and a tour of the sites. Downtown, is a short walk from the cruise line dock.

Food

Try gundy, a pate of salt cod or lobster smashed with olives and onions. Pumpkin soup and avocado purees are popular. Fresh fish is always a good choice. It's served with hush puppies, a fried corn meal concoction, or johnny cakes, an oven-baked dumpling. Kallaloo is a filling, pepperpot stew. Stewed goat is an island specialty. The drink is rum, which is cheap and plentiful; it is, in fact, cheaper than the mixers. Local guavaberry and sorrel wines are worth asking for.

Nightlife

The fancier the hotel, the more extensive the nightlife; that's the rule on these islands. Otherwise, dining is still the main form of evening entertainment.

Shopping

In St. Thomas, Dronningens Gade (Main Street) is a shopper's fantasy come true, offering luxurious merchandise, knowledgeable clerks, reduced prices and no tax. US residents may take home unlimited quantities of crafts and goods made in the Virgin Islands, including baskets, candles, dolls, fashions, food, jewelry, macrame, paintings, perfumes, sea shells, scrimshaw and sculpture.

Sports

You can do almost any warm-climate sport here: swimming, golf, fishing, windsurfing, waterskiing, horseback riding (including moonlight rides), tennis and sailing. There are international golf, tennis and fishing tournaments here; in the past 20 years, 23 world-record fish have been caught in these waters. If sailing is your sport, this is a great place to charter a boat or take some sailing lessons. Write for the Sail the Virgins brochure from the Virgin Islands Charter Yacht League, Homesport, St. Thomas, USVI 00801.

• Diving

The newest additions to this diving experience are the four wrecks off the west coast of Saint Croix, creating something like the world's first underwater wreck park at the Butler Bay artificial reef site. These wrecks are the perfect complement to St. Croix's north wall, beach and coral diving. The Suffolk Maid is a 120-foot trawler that sits upright on sand in 60 feet of water. The wreck was cleared and prepared for divers.

Underwater nature trails have been marked for snorkelers at Buck Island near St. Croix and at Trunk Bay on St. John. Visibility tends to run 75 to 120 feet (clearer offshore).

• Fishing

Caribbean Sea Adventures on St. Croix can arrange fishing expeditions on their 37-foot Striker. Marlin, tuna, wahoo and kingfish are the catches around here (1-809-773-6011).

• Golf

Renowned golf course architects George and Tom Fazio designed the Mahogany Run Golf Course in St. Thomas -a challenging championship masterpiece, famous for its 14th hole perched on cliffs above the Atlantic. The par 70 course stretches for 6,350 yards. There's a pro shop and equipment can be rented (1-809-775-5000).

There are a few courses on St. Croix: Carombola, designed by Robert Trent Jones, the Buccaneer (both 18 holes) and the nine-hole course at The Reef.

• Hiking

While on St. John, visit the Virgin Island National Park Visitor Center where you can obtain information on hiking trails (1-809-776-6201). Reef Bay Trail is the most popular on the island. The two-and-a-half mile, two-hour walk takes you through an abundance of nature: wet and dry forests, wild orchids and strangler figs, wild pigs, donkeys and remains of sugar estates. Other trails include Brown Bay, Caneel Hill and Johnny Horn.

• Tennis

In addition to several courts at various hotels, you can find public courts at Bordeaux (2), Long Bay (2), Sub Base (2), the Caribbean Tennis Club on St. Croix (7), La Grange Beach and Tennis Club on St. Croix (2), Cruz Bay on St. John (2) and the St. Thomas Yacht Club (3).

• Windsurfing

St. Thomas is host to the annual "HiHo" (Hook In and Hold On) open-ocean long distance sailing race.

US Virgin Islands

West Indies Management Co.   Divi St. Croix Beach Resort

US Virgin Islands - Information

US VIRGIN ISLANDS DIV. OF TOURISM 212-582-4520
212-581-3405FX 1270 Ave. of the Americas New York NY 10020.

US Virgin Islands, St. Croix - Accommodations

CARAVELLE HOTEL 800-524-0410   44 Units: $75-105 BDKRW
809-773-0687 800-773-2620 44A Queen Cross Street Christainsted, St. Croix VI 00820. See: V.I. Divers, LTD.

DIVI ST. CROIX BEACH RESORT 800-367-3484   86 Units: $180-230 BDFGOPRSTW
607-277-3484 809-778-9153FX 54 Gunderman Rd. Ithaca NY 14850. The newest addition to the DIVI family of fine Caribbean Resorts previously known as Grapetree Beach is nestled in the foothills along a spectacular beach on the islands eastern shore. Offering lots of really great watersports (including the largest freshwater pool in the islands),nearby golf courses and duty-free shopping for daytime enjoyment. DIVI St. Croix also offers a variety of excellent dining and cocktail venues with good nightly entertainment. See: Caribbean Sea & Reef Queen Charters.

REEF BEACH & GOLF RESORT 800-524-2026   101 Units: $114-171 BGKRTW
809-773-9250 809-773-9040 Teague Bay Christiansted, St Croix VI 00820.

WEST INDIES MANAGEMENT CO. 800-932-3222   313 Units: $70-500 BDFGKOPRSTW
401-849-8012 401-847-6290FX Box 1461 Newport RI 02840. West Indies Management Company (WIMCO) now represents villas and hotels on St. Croix, St. Thomas, St. John, Tortola, Virgin Gorda and Jost Van Dyke. Mc Laughlin Arguin, Newland-Moran, Island Villas and Rockview Holiday Homes have exclusive listings for the accommodations on these islands. Information about villas, hotels, restaurants, travel, best beaches, nightlife and activities can be obtained by calling 1-800-932-3222. VENDOME Guide available.

US Virgin Islands, St. Croix - Sports

CARIBBEAN SEA & REEF QUEEN CHARTERS 809-773-5922   120 Divers: $65-65 DFSW
809-778-7004FX TX: 3471097 Box 3881 Christiansted, St. Croix VI 00820. See: DIVI St. Croix Beach Resort.

V.I. DIVERS, LTD 809-773-6045   50 Divers: $55-55 D
Panam Pavilion St. Croix VI 00820. See: Caravelle Hotel.

US Virgin Islands, St. John - Accommodations

GALLOW'S POINT 800-223-9815   60 Units: $200-250 BDOPRSW
809-776-6435 Box 58 Cruz Bay, St. John VI 00830. See: Low Key Dive Tours.

US Virgin Islands, St. John - Sports

LOW KEY DIVE TOURS 809-776-6042   12 Divers: $65-65 BDOSW
Box 431 St. John VI 00830. See: Gallow's Point.

US Virgin Islands, St. Thomas - Accommodations

FRENCHMAN'S REEF BEACH RESORT 800-524-2096   519 Units: $240-375 BDOPRSTW
809-776-8500 EXT:249 FAX Box 7100 Charlotte Amalie, St. Thomas VI 00802. See: Sea Adventures.

SECRET HARBOR BEACH HOTEL 800-524-2250   60 Units: $175-230 BDKRSTW
809-775-6550 Box 7576 St. Thomas VI 00801. See: Aqua Action Watersports.

US Virgin Islands, St. Thomas - Sports

AQUA ACTION WATERSPORTS 809-775-6285   12 Divers: $65-75 DFOW
Box 12138 St. Thomas VI 00801. See: Secret Harbor Beach Hotel.

SEA ADVENTURES 800-524-2096   36 Divers: $70-70 DOSW
809-774-9652 809-776-8500FX Box 9531 St. Thomas VI 00801. See: Frenchman's Reef Beach Resort.

Kimo Fernie/Sunstar

Hawaii

Useful Facts

• <u>Airline Connections</u>   Most commercial and charter flights arrive in Hawaii at the Honolulu International Airport on Oahu. A few fly direct to the Big Island of Hawaii. Free stop-overs in Honolulu can be added to most plane tickets that cross the Pacific. Special "Common Fare" island-hopping packages are also available. Hawaiian Airlines has an extensive route system that includes most of the US west coast, major countries on the Pacific rim, and a number of smaller island groups in the Pacific. Hawaiian also flies an extensive inter-island route system. Hawaii's other main inter-island commercial airlines is Aloha Airlines.

• <u>Courtesy & Dress</u>   Casual.

• <u>Events & Holidays</u>   US, Japanese and Chinese holidays. Plus Kamehameha Day (June 11); Trans-Pacific Yacht Races (July); Honolulu Marathon (Dec.); Hula Bowl, College all-star football game (first Saturday in Jan.).

• <u>Languages</u>   English. Pigeon English: English and any combination of Hawaiian, Japanese, Chinese, Filipino or Portuguese.

• <u>Medical</u>   World-class medical facilities are readily available. Unlike most exotic destinations, your standard health insurance plans will cover you during your stay.

• <u>Off-Season Dates & Rates</u>   The high tourist season is from Dec. through March, July and Aug. Off-season discounts are available. The pricing is very competitive year round.

• <u>Weather</u>   Balmy 73-88 degrees from April through October. Wetter and cooler, 65-83 degrees, November to March. Trade winds cause rain on the windward sides of tall mountains and rough seas on the NE coasts, where steep cliffs, ledges, and drop-offs predominate. The west sides of the islands are always much drier than the east.

Introduction

"The loveliest fleet of islands that lies anchored in any ocean," noted American novelist Mark Twain in his "Letter from the Sandwich Islands." Although the awe inspiring beauty of the Hawaiian islands is undeniable, their supposed "anchorage" is more debatable. Adhered to the sliding Pacific Plate, these islands actually creep in a northwesterly direction two to three inches every year. This steady crawl across a standing vent in the earth's crust, which periodically spews forth lava, explains the birth of the entire Hawaiian island chain.

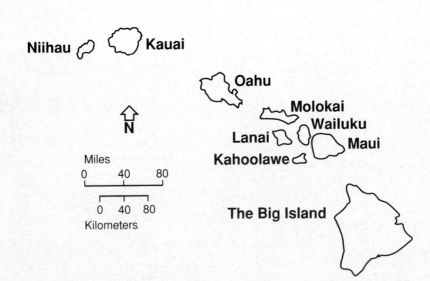

Niihau   Kauai

Oahu

Molokai

Wailuku

Lanai

Maui

Kahoolawe

N

Miles

0   40   80

0   40   80
Kilometers

The Big Island

Haleakala/Dean

Of the eight major islands, Kauai is the oldest and most weathered, with deep canyons and convoluted, jagged cliffs. Young and big, Hawaii is still growing, as evidenced by the "dancing curtains of fire" and "rivers of lava" from Kilauea and Mauna Loa. Through the millennium, new islands will continue to form southeast of the Big Island, and old ones will erode back into the sea.

Lost and weary birds, with seeds lodged in their bowels, were the first discoverers of the remote chain of islands. Beautiful, unique species evolved. Of the 2,500 native plant species still found in Hawaii, 95% don't exist anywhere else in the world. Most of the native birds and plants are now endangered species.

Exploring

Oahu, Maui, Kauai, Hawaii, Molokai and Lanai are the six major islands that have hotels. Kahoolawe and Niihau are off-limits to tourists. The islands are all easily accessible by inter-island commuter flights which travel to and from two-to-four times a day. Plan to see at least two or three islands; their uniqueness necessitates a visit. Oahu, Maui, Kauai and Hawaii have the most tourist facilities. Basically, only the bare necessities are available on Molokai and Lanai.

Food

Most restaurants, several of which are first-class, are found in major cities, resort complexes and hotels. You'll find a large variety of seafood, continental cuisine, and an array of international cuisine including Chinese, Japanese, Italian, and Thai. There are not many steak houses and few (if any) Hawaiian restaurants. Local specialties include: chicken luau, crackseed, haupia, kim chi, laulau, lomilomi salmon, mahi, malasadas, poi, saimin, sashimi, shave ice, sushi, tempura and teriyaki. If you can't find anything on this list, the burger barons will be there to help you out.

Nightlife

Oahu's Waikiki is the center of nightlife in Hawaii, but some live music, stage shows, dancing, Hawaiian melodies, commercial luaus, and easy-listening music are easily found in other cities, resort complexes and hotels. Most otaher areas and entire islands are pretty quiet at night.

Shopping

Except for a few local specialties, shopping does not vary much from island to island. However, Molokai and Lanai offer little more than the basics. On other islands you'll find lots of colorful aloha-wear, including muumuus, shirts

Hawaii

Philip Spalding III, Molokai/Dean

Conditions can be hazardous at different places and seasons. Be sure to check with local guides. Watch for riptide and undertow postings. For scuba diving, there are plenty of personal local dive guides and guide books available.

The State of Hawaii plans to make Hawaii an international center for recreational, spectator and Olympic sports. If you are interested in staging an event, contact the Sports Development Unit, BDED, Box 2359, Honolulu, Hawaii (808-548-8957).

Be sure to see the listings below for specific island sporting events. All of the sports events mentioned for each island are listed in the Directory at the end of this section.

The Big Island Sports

Amazing as it may seem, yes, you can ski on Mauna Kea from December through May. But there are no lifts. You can either rent a four-wheel drive vehicle and supply your own driver, or use the "ski lift" jeep which operates through Ski Shop Hawaii.

• Billfish Tournaments

One of Kailua's greatest features is its deep sea fishing. The Hawaii International Billfish Tournament is held here in late July or August, and 1988 marks its 30th year. The tournament includes two team events, The Kona Hawaiian Billfish Tournament and the Hawaiian International Billfish Tournament. The Pacific Gamefish Research Foundation Light Tackle Tag & Release is for individual competition. Marlin and ahi are the catches.

• Triathlon

1988 is the tenth anniversary of the Bud Light Ironman Triathlon World Cup Championship. Competitors have from 7 am to midnight to complete a 2.4 mile swim, a 112-mile bicycle race and a 26.2-mile running marathon. Approximately 1,250 starters are represented by about 44 countries and almost all the states. There's a $150 entry fee.

• Other Events

Other events include: the Kilauea Volcano Wilderness Marathon & Rim Run (Jan.), the Hawaii Ski Cup (March), Haili's Mens' Volleyball Tournament (March), the Paniolo Ski Meet (Apr.), the Green Goddess Ladies Fishing Tournament (May), the Kona Gold Jackpot Fishing Tournament (May), the Mauna Loa Hike (ex-

and wraps, as well as swimwear and T-shirts, woven hats, placemats, baskets and jewelry made of local shells, coral, maile leaves, seeds and feathers. Most of the kapa cloth is imported from other Pacific islands. Oriental jade, ivory, cloisonne and embroidery imports are also numerous. Crafts from local woodcarvers, scrimshaw artists, painters, and sculptures are also available. Visitors tend to stock up on macadamia nuts, pineapples, Maui potato chips, Kona coffee, and tropical jams and jellies from papaya, mango, guava, and passion fruit.

Sports

Outdoor activities abound in the Hawaiian islands. Terrestrial sports include golf, tennis, hiking, camping, horseback riding, hunting and even skiing. For water lovers there's swimming, snorkeling, diving, windsurfing, sailing, ocean kayak trips, outrigger canoe rides, yacht charters, deep sea fishing, river rafting and canoe rides.

Diamond Head & Waikiki/Jones

perts only, May), Keahou-Kona Triathlon Tournament (July), Big Island Marathon and Half-Marathon (July), Parker Ranch Rodeo and Horse Show (July), Kona Ahi-Marlin Jackpot Tournament (July), Hawaii Light Tackle Fishing Tournament (July), Parker Ranch Ranch Roundup (Aug.), Duke's Kona Classic Fishing Tournament (Aug.), Okoe Bay Rendezvous Marlin Tournament (Sept.), the Golden Marlin Fishing Tournament (Sept.), Church Machado's Luau Jackpot Fishing Tournament (Sept.), the Aloha Big Island Bike Trek (Oct.), and the Waikoloa Quarter Horse Show (Oct.).

Kauai Sports

Kauai has some of the best surfing in Hawaii, next to Oahu. There are dozens of beaches around the island for swimming and sunning; even the most popular aren't crowded. Sailing, windsurfing and snorkeling are available along the Na Pali coast from Hanalei Bay. Game fishing charters catch a huge variety of fish. Whale watching, waterskiing, rafting, kayaking, and canoeing are also available.

Campsites are available at Kokee State Park and Polihale Beach. There are miles of hiking trails through wild and remote areas, including: Kokee State Park, Waimea Canyon and Na Pali coast. There are also horseback riding, many tennis facilities and five golf courses.

• Golf

The annual LPGA Women's Kemper Open had a $300,000 purse in 1988. Nearly 150 professionals compete, and the event is free to spectators.

• Other Events

Additional events include: King Kong Ultraman (July), the Hanalei Stampede (Aug.) and the Kauai Loves You Triathlon.

Lanai Sports

Hulopeo Bay is one of Hawaii's best beaches for swimming, sunning and picnicking. Other beaches are dangerous or inaccesible. There is no surfing. Hulopeo Bay is the only place where camping is permitted.

Most Lanai visitors come to hunt the axis deer, Mouflon sheep and wild goats. Hiking is available, but restricted in many places. There is also a golf course and four public tennis courts in Lanai City. If you ask, the electric company will turn on the court night lights.

Aloha Classic/Sunstar

Maui Sports

Windsurfing is the big fad on Maui, particularly at Maalaea Bay. For surfing try Honolua Bay, Hookipa Beach Park, Kaanapali Beach, Haina Harbor and Maalaea Bay. Maui also offers hiking, camping, horseback riding, hunting, golf, tennis, deep sea fishing and boating.

• Golf

The Isuzu Kapalua International offers a $600,00 purse with $150,000 to the first-place finisher. This event is free to the public. The Kirin Cup World Championship of Golf has a $1,000,000 purse.

• Track

The Hana Relay features a six-person team relay of 54 miles. Eighty teams compete. There are no award monies and a $13.00 per person entry-fee is charged.

• Windsurfing

As the final event of the PBA world tour with a $40,000 purse, the annual Peter Stuyvesant Travel Aloha Classic is the wave sailing world championships. At Hookipa Beach competitors number near 100 men and 30 women, with roughly 4,000 spectators.

• Other Events

Other events include: the Maui Marathon (March), the Makawao Statewide Rodeo (July), the Hawaiian Pro-Am Windsurfing Tournament (Aug.) the Hawaiian Pro-Am Speed Slalom Windsurfing and Wailea Speed Crossing (Sept.), the Festival of Running (Nov.) and the Kapalua-Betsy Nagelson Pro-Am Tennis Invitation.

Molokai Sports

Molokai is not famous for its watersports. There are a few places to go swimming, snorkeling, boating or camping. While the west end beaches have lots of sun, but unpredictable conditions, the east end beaches have good swimming in isolated lagoons, but unpredictable sunshine. The best spot is at the western end of the north shore, but a four-wheel drive is needed to get there. There is good deep sea fishing from Penguid Bank and surfing at Halawa Bay and Kepuhi Beach.

The island's best sports are on land: golf, tennis, hiking and hunting. There are several tennis facilities and two golf courses on the island. The one next to the Sheraton is one of Hawaii's best and most beautiful. Horseback riding is also available.

Oahu Sports

• Basketball

The Rainbow Basketball Classic is an annual collegiate tournament. For tickets call the Neal Blaisdell Arena in Honolulu.

• Football

The Aloha Bowl, college bowl, is held on Christmas Day. Tickets are $15.00 (sidelines) and $12.50 (end zones).

The Hula Bowl is an annual college all-star football game with an estimated crowd between 20,000 and 40,000. Tickets go for $12.50 and $10. Contact the Aloha Stadium Box Office (see Aloha Bowl) for game times and tickets.

Each year since 1980, the National Football League all-stars have been playing the pro bowl in Aloha Stadium. It's consistently sold out (capacity 50,000). Check with the box office for game times and tickets.

• Golf

The PGA Hawaiian Open carries a $750,000 purse with 18% to the winner. The week-long event draws hundreds of pros and tens of thousands of spectators. Tickets are aviailable at the gate, airlines offices and various hotels.

The LPGA Hawaiian Ladies Open, carrying a $300,000 purse, is another immensely popular tournament. Tickets are available at the gate and Oahu golf shops.

• Honolulu Marathon

This annual event is held in December. There are entries from all over the world and almost every state, usually about 10,000 every year. The first ten finishers receive monetary prizes, and anyone can enter. It's "the people's marathon." Aid stations are situated every two miles. In conjuction with this event is the Wheelchair Marathon, typically held the day before.

• Sailing

The Kenwood Cup International Ocean Racing Series is a biennial two-week event which occurs in July or August. About 50 yachts from all over the world enter. They range from 40 to 85 feet, and races include the "Around the State of Hawaii" event as well as races in Waikiki.

• Surfing

Triple Crown of Surfing. There are three events on Oahu which are the culmination of the world surfing tour: The Hard Rock Cafe World Cup of Surfing at Sunset Beach, the Marui Pipeline Masters at Bonzai Pipeline and the Billabong Hawaiian Pro. Both men and women participate in the Billabong, and the average crowd of spectators (it's free!) numbers about 4,000.

• Other Events

Additional events include: The Great Aloha Run, Buffalo's Big Board Surfing Classic, Carole Kai International Bed Race and Parade, the Tin Man Biathlon, Kanaka Ikaika (Molokai to Oahu kayak race, May), Gotcha Pro Surfing Meet, Mud

Kona/Kelly

Bog, Waikiki Rough Water Swim, Na Wahine O Ke Kai (Women's Molokai to Oahu canoe race, Oct.), and the Hawaiian Canoe and Kayak Championships (Oct.).

Hawaii - Accommodations

ASTON HOTELS 800-92-ASTON
The Aston has beautiful properties located throughout the Hawaiian Islands. They offer a variety of price ranges and facilities including: resorts, hotels and condo's. They host Travel & Sports in Hawaii.

Hawaii - Information

DIVE HAWAII 808-922-0975
    Box 90295 Honolulu HI 96835.
HAWAII CANOE RACING ASSOCIATION 808-526-1969
    169 S. Kuki St. Hawaii HI 96813.
HAWAII INTERNATIONAL BILLFISH ASS. 808-922-9708
    2923 Makalei Pl. Honolulu HI 96815.
HAWAII VISITORS BUREAU 808-955-0956
    2270 Kalakaua Ave. # 801 Honolulu HI 96815.
HAWAII YACHT RACING ASSOCIATION 808-946-3361
    109 Poloke Place HONOLULU HI 96822.
HAWAIIAN ISLANDS WINDSURFING ASSOCIATION 800-231-6958
HAWAIIAN SURFING FEDERATION 808-671-6255
    Box 1707 Pearl City HI 96782.
KANAKA I KAI KA KAYAKING ASSOCIATION 808-235-8398
    46-018 Kuneki Pl. Kaneohe HI 96744.
WAKIKI SWIM CLUB 808-948-8370
    32 Kailua Road Kailua HI 96734.

The Big Island/Vaughn

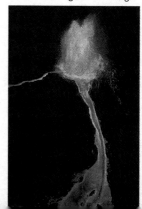

Hawaii

The Big Island, Hawaii - Sports
ALOHA BIG ISLAND BIKE TREK \OCT 808-537-5966
BIG ISLAND MARATHON & HALF-MARATHON \JUL 808-959-4848
BUD LITE IRONMAN TRIATHLON W.C.\SEP 808-528-2050
CHUCH MACHADO'S LUAU JACKPOT FISHING\SEP 808-836-0249
DUKES KONA CLASSIC FISHINGTOURNAMENT\AUG 808-325-5000
FIRECRACKER OPEN MARLIN TOURNAMENT\JUL 808-325-7275
GOLDEN MARLIN FISHING TOURNAMENT\SEP 808-322-3832
GREEN GODDESS LADIES FISHING TOURN.\MAY 808-322-3832
HAWAII LIGHT TACKLE FISHING TOURN.\JUL 808-325-5000
HAWAII SKI CUP\MAR 808-737-4394
KEAHOU-KONA TRIATHLON\MAY 808-325-6770
KILAUEA VOLCANO WILDERNESS MARATHON\JAN 808-967-7179
KONA AHI-MARLIN JACKPOT TOURNAMENT\JUL 808-322-2832
KONA GOLD JACKPOT FISHING TOURNAMENT\MAY 808-322-3832
OKOEBAY RENDEZVOUS MARLIN TOURNAMENT\SEP 808-325-7275
PANIOLO SKI MEET\APR 808-737-4394
PARKER RANCH RODEO AND HORSE SHOW\AUG 808-885-7655

Kauai, Hawaii - Accommodations
KOKEE LODGE 808-335-6061   12 Units
    Box 819 Waimea HI 96796. This is a moutain retreat at the end of Wiamea Canyon. A great place for dinner, or the weekend. Call ahead.

Kauai, Hawaii - Sports
HANALEI STAMPEDE\AUG 808-826-6777
KAUAI LOVES YOU TRIATHLON\OCT 808-826-9343
KING KONG ULTRAMAN\JUL 808-826-9343
LPGA WOMEN'S KEMPER OPEN\FEB 808-826-3580

Maui, Hawaii - Sports
ALOHA CLASSIC WORLD WAVE SAILING CHP\OCT 808-579-9765
CHAMINADE MAUI BASKETBALL CLASSIC\NOV 808-669-4844
GTE KAANAPALI GOLF CLASSIC\DEC 808-669-4844
HANA RELAY\SEP 808-877-5827
HAWAIIAN PRO-AM SLALOM WINDSURFING\SEP 808-579-9765
ISUZU KAPALUA INTERNATIONAL\NOV 808-669-4844
KAPALUA-BETSY NAGELSON PRO-AM TENNIS\NOV 808-669-5677
KIRIN CUP WORLD CHAMPIONSHIP OF GOLF\DEC 808-669-4844
MAKAWAO STATEWIDE RODEO\JUL 808-572-8102
MAUI MARATHON\ MAR 808-871-0777
O'NEILL INVITATIONAL WINDSURFING\MAR 808-579-9765

Oahu, Hawaii - Sports
ALOHA BOWL\DEC 808-488-7731
BUFFALO'S BIG BOARD SURFING CLASSIC\FEB 808-696-3878
CAROLE KAI INTERNATIONAL BED RACE\FEB 808-735-6092
GOTCHA PRO SURFING MEET\JUN 808-638-7266
GREAT ALOHA RUN\FEB 808-735-2835
HAWAIIAN CANOE & KAYAK CHAMPIONSHIPS\OCT 808-682-5233
HONOLULU MARATHON 808-734-7200
HULA BOWL\JAN 808-488-7731
KANAKA IKAIKA KAYAK RACE\MAY 808-326-1011
KENWOOD CUP INTRNL. OCEAN RACING\AUG 808-941-1273
LPGA HAWAIIAN LADIES OPEN\FEB 808-293-9294
MOLOKAI HOE CANOE RACE\OCT 808-525-5476
NA WAHINE O KE KAI CANOE RACE\SEP 808-525-5476
PGA HAWAIIAN OPEN\ FEB 808-247-6841
PRO BOWL\DEC 808-488-7731
RAINBOW BASKETBALL CLASSIC\ DEC 808-948-7523
TIN MAN BIATHLON 808-538-3991
TRIPLE CROWN OF SURFING\DEC 808-737-3313
WAIKIKI ROUGH WATER SWIM\SEP 808-537-5966

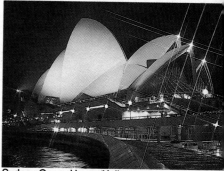

Australia

Koala/Jacobs

Sydney Opera House/Kelly

Surf Carnival QLD/ATC

**The DIVE
Travel & Sports Guide:**

**Australia
Fiji
Papau New Guinea
Solomon Islands
Vanuatu**

/Roessler

Useful Facts

• <u>Airline Connections</u>   Qantas is the primary international carrier to Australia. International passengers can travel on Qantas domestic sectors on special "Discover Australia" fares. Conditions for these fares are available from any international carrier. One of the key domestic carriers is Ansett. Ansett has an extensive domestic route system with good links to the Qantas international flights. The other main domestic carrier is Australian Airlines. Air New Zealand, Canadian Airline Int'l, United, UTA French Airlines, Hawaiian Airlines and Continental also offer flights from North America to Sydney, Melbourne, Brisbane and Cairns. Stopovers in Fiji or Tahiti may bump the price up a bit. Check with your travel agent for the best strategy as costs, schedules and travel packages change frequently. There is an airport departure tax of $AU 10 per person.

• <u>Banking & Currency</u>   The Australian dollar ($AU) is worth about $0.80 US. Traveler's checks are easily exchanged at banks (open 9:30-4 Monday-Thursday, 9:30-5pm Friday), but if you will be staying a while and/or in remote areas it's advisable to purchase Australian Traveler's checks. Most major credit cards are honored virtually everywhere and are required for auto rental.

• <u>Courtesy & Dress</u>   Manners and attire in resort areas are informal. For the cities, include formal and warmer wardrobe items, especially during the winter months (see Weather). For the Queensland coast, bring protection for feet, head and skin exposed to tropical sun and reef hazards.

• <u>Customs & Immigration</u>   All visitors need both a passport <u>and</u> a visa. To obtain a visa, visit your local Australian Embassy or

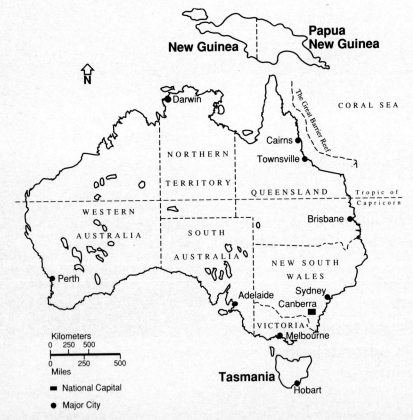

■ National Capital

● Major City

Outback/ATC

Consulate. You must also show an onward or return ticket, and the normal term is up to 6 months. The usual cigarette-and-bottle limitations apply. Photographic and diving gear will be waved through but the importation of any type of plant or animal material, or fresh or packaged food is <u>strictly</u> prohibited.

• Driving   On the left. Seatbelt laws are enforced. Overseas drivers' licenses are okay, but an international one is recommended. If you are a member of a North American automobile club, bring proof of membership along so that you can enjoy reciprocal privileges with the various Australian state auto clubs. The "Big 4" rental companies (Hertz, Avis, Budget, Thrifty) are widely represented, as are various local outfits. You may wish to hire a "moke," a vehicle that's stingy on fuel and generous with natural air-conditioning. You can also find four-wheel drives (the moke is <u>not</u> one), campers and motorcycles for off-road forays.

• Electricity   240-250. Bring an adaptor/converter kit with you as the necessary widgets are difficult to find in Australia.

• Events & Holidays   Remember that our winter is their summer and visa-versa. So, for example, our Christmas season falls during their summer. Holidays include New Years (Jan. 1); Australia Day (Jan. 26); Easter weekend (a moveable feast from Good

Friday to next Tues.); Anzac Day (April 25); Labour Day (May in Queensland and Northern Territory); Queen's B-Day (June 10); generic bank holiday (sometime in Aug.); and Christmas/Boxing Day (Dec. 25-26).

• Events, Down Under Celebrations   Celeb rations are frequent Down Under. In March, the Festival of Arts takes place in Adelaide in even numbered years, and there's the week-long Moomba in Melbourne. Every April, Hamilton Island Resort in the Whitsundays hosts "Hamilton Race Week," a week of nonstop parties and revelry. In the beginning of June, Townsville (Barrier Reef) puts on the Pacific Festival, a ten-day presentation of culture and exhibits. Nearby Heron Island hosts a scuba divers' rally in July, and the following month sees more yacht races in the Whitsunday archipelago. August also features the 14 km city to surf race in Sydney, with typically 25,000 entrants. Not to be outdone, Melbourne counters in September with the Sun Superrun and the final of Australian Rules Football. The same month, Queensland continues revelry with the Sunshine Coast Spring Festival. Cairns takes up the torch in October with Fun in the Sun events, but as the south warms up to summer in November the emphasis switches back to Sydney (Queen Street Festival in Paddington district) and Melbourne, with the Melbourne Cup,

Aboriginal Arts Festival/ATC

Australia's premier horse race and a public holiday in the state of Victoria. Summer surf competitions are weekend occurrences. And this is only a partial list!

• Information   The Australian Tourist Commission produces a 132-page book covering everything about travel to Australia. For a free copy call (800) 445-4400. The Commission has offices in North America at 2121 Avenue of the Stars, Los Angeles, 90087, phone (213) 552-1988; or 489 Fifth Avenue, 31st Floor, New York, NY 10017, phone (212) 687-6300; or 150 N. Michigan Ave., Suite 2130, Chicago, IL 60601, phone (312) 781-5150. Once in Australia , it's worthwhile to visit the tourist offices run by each state, as well as the excellent regional offices. They will provide you with handouts and will book transportation and accommodations for you.

• Languages   English. You'll hear a rich variety of local terms and slang, but even in the most remote regions of the outback you'll be greeted with a friendly "g'day."

• Medical   Medical care is excellent. Check to be sure your policy covers such expenses. If not, your travel agent can assist you with suitable coverage. Australia is well equipped to deal with diving emergencies. There are recompression chambers in Victoria, Sydney, Tasmania, Adelaide, Perth and two in Queensland (Townsville, Brisbane). There are also many physicians with special training in underwater/hyperbaric medicine. In addition, Australia has a dive emergency reporting hotline: (02) 9600321.

• Off-Season Dates & Rates   There is no off-season. You can, though, count on full bookings between Christmas and February most everywhere in the country.

• Taxes & Tipping   These are largely absent from Australian life. Porters are paid by the piece, bellhops are salaried and wait-persons might be offered 10% of the tab in the case of exceptionally good service. At any time tipping is your choice.

• Taxi Fares   Reasonable. Rates include a minimum "flag fall" and then a charge for distance traveled. Small additional charges are made for luggage. Taxi drivers do not expect to be tipped. Round off cab fares to the nearest dollar.

• Telephone   Australia has a modern automatic telephone system. Many hotel rooms have international direct-dial. Local calls are 30 cents from phone booths. To call the US or Canada from Australia, dial 00111 then area code and number. To call Australia from the US or Canada, just dial the number as listed in our Directory. When calling within Australia, just ignore the international dialing numbers at the beginning of each number in the directory.

• Time   Australia has three time zones: Western Time (WT), Central Standard Time (CST) and Eastern Standard Time (EST). WT is 2 hours behind EST. CST is one half-hour behind EST. Daylight Savings time does not apply in all states. Calculating the difference with US time zones is complicated by the fact the Australia is on the other side of the international dateline, and in the opposite hemisphere!

• Weather   Seasons in the temperate zones of Australia are the reverse of ours. Spring starts in September, summer in December, autumn in March and winter in June. But as you proceed further north, conventional seasonal variations disappear until, at Darwin, you have just two: monsoonally wet (Dec.-Mar.), and dry the rest of the time. In the Snowy Mountains in the south of New South Wales, there's a snow season with great skiing (starts around June). Real chill visits Melbourne, Tasmania and Canberra from June to August. In contrast, these months are the best times to visit areas (like Darwin, for example) that are often unbearably hot in the summer months. But with so many climactic belts, somewhere in "Oz" (as Australia is affectionately known) is ideal during any month you wish to visit.

Introduction

Australia is wild. And civilized. Lush. And dry. Flat. And mountainous. Ancient. And ultramodern. Its climate ranges from snowfields to deserts to rain forest. In fact, it is so huge and diverse that any attempt at description would be inaccurate at best. Australia, quite simply, must be experienced.

Thanks to Paul Hogan and the Australian Government's aggressive advertising and publicity campaign, Americans have discovered this island playground in droves. Once there, the visitor is awed by the number of choices which present themselves. In a typical two-week vacation, only a tiny fraction of Australia's attractions can be experienced. There's always more to see and do in Australia just around the next corner.

The Rock, Sydney/Jacobs

Here on the world's largest island, everything presents itself on a grand scale. The Great Barrier Reef is 2,000 miles long, Ayers Rock is the world's largest monolith. Seemingly endless miles of outback stretch out across central Australia. And the coastline with its pristine beaches, bays, coves and headlands extends for 23,021 sandy miles.

History

Australia was the last continental landmass to be discovered during the period of the European exploratory expeditions. Initial reports from Portuguese and Dutch navigators about this "Terra Australis Incognita," or Unknown South Land, were so disappointing that nobody bothered to return until Captain James Cook dropped anchor near the site of today's Sydney in 1770. Courageous, handsome, egalitarian, loyal to the Crown, but with no patience for clerics, Cook in many ways embodied the traits of modern-day Australia.

In 1788, Australia became a British colony, and as such, a harsh destination for thousands of convicts shipped there from England after America gained her independence. Matters did not improve until a growing number of free, voluntary colonists put an end to the worst abuses and opened up routes into the interior. In addition to charting the territory for mother England, these intrepid explorers were after tangible gains, specifically gold, which they discovered in abundance. As a result of this gold fever, Australia saw an instant doubling of the population.

As the fortune hunters moved in, the indigenous aborigines, who unlike the American Indians had never been particularly pleased to see outsiders, were progressively pushed back into more marginal lands, decimated by the white man's diseases and on Tasmania hunted down for sport.

On New Year's Eve 1901, Queen Victoria graciously proclaimed Australia's independence. A new capital, Canberra, was established midway between Melbourne and Sydney to avoid offending either of those bitter rivals.

But independence existed more in name than in fact as Australia dutifully answered calls by the Crown in both the Boer War and the First World War. Their casualties in both conflicts were phenomenally high. This cavalier expenditure of colonial fodder has long filled a reservoir of resentment, most recently reflected in the Australian films <u>Breaker Morant</u> and <u>Gallipoli</u>.

With the fall of Singapore and the Japanese bombings in the Northern Territory, it quickly became obvious that this war would affect Australia in a way that the previous two had not.

These wartime experiences gave Australia a bad scare. Determined not to be an Anglo nation of 7.5 million isolated near an Asia with a hundred times that number, the country opened her doors to immigrants. Over the next two decades, Australia was transformed from a staid, conservative, monoculture to a cosmopolitan, polyglot country. Today a quarter of the current population of 16.5 million is either immigrant or first-generation Australian. Most of them are Greeks, Italians, Yugoslavs, Germans, Jews, Turks and "pommies" (short for prisoner of mother of England), i.e. Brits.

Contemporary Australia is a country of relaxed and easy familiarity. The warm and inviting climate is equalled only by the friendliness of the Aussies themselves. These often irreverent and always fun-loving people enjoy life to the fullest and welcome visitors with open arms. So, bring your togs, a cobber or two and she'll be apples (or in Aussie that's: bring a swimsuit, a friend or two and everything'll be great).

Ecology

Australia is a living paleontological museum. Because of its isolation following the breakup of the original continental landmass (Australia, South America and Africa were joined at one time), it exhibits many unique species of plant and wildlife. For example, marsupials (mammals with an embryo pouch but without a proper womb) were able to flourish here where elsewhere they evolved into placental species. While such characters as kangaroos, wombats, Tasmanian devils, platypuses and koalas may seem exotic, they are merely the tenants of niches that would otherwise be occupied by (approximately) deer, badgers, martens, otters and sloths in the Northern Hemisphere.

Australian birdlife is a bit more familiar. The emu is an analogue to the ostrich, plus there are cassowaries, parrots, kookaburas, cockatoos and fairy (miniature) penguins. These penguins are among the few found in temperate waters.

The Great Barrier Reef off the Queensland coast is Australia's most renowned ecological wonder. Actually a collection of undersea shoals, reefs and coral cays, it stretches approximately 1,258 miles from the tip of Cape York Peninsula in the north to Gladstone in the south. Adorned with over 300 varieties of coral, 1,400 species of fish, as well as six types of sea turtles and some of the biggest black marlin to be found anywhere, the reef is definitely one of the natural wonders of the world.

Queensland

More than 50% of tourists to Australia are bound for the Sunshine State. With its tropical and sub-tropical climate, the enormous draw of its Great Barrier Reef, plus deserts, mountains and posh resorts, Queensland has something to offer everyone.

There are many ways to explore the reef. If you choose to stay on the mainland, excursions can be made via high-speed catamaran or luxury tour boats, many of which provide snorkeling,

Cairns/Kelly   /Kelly

scuba diving, reef walking or coral viewing in a semi-submersible sub. The coastal towns of Cairns, Townsville, Mackay, Gladstone, Proserpine and Hamilton Island have airport terminals which provide access to the offshore islands. Helicopter and sea plane tours can be arranged for speedy access to the reef. Or stay at one of the island resorts: Hayman, Hamilton, Heron, South Molle, Orpheus, Lindeman, Dunk, Lizard, Daydream, Fitzroy or Frazer, each of which provides daily trips to the reef, plus a host of other amenities.

/Kelly

Cairns

Cairns, Queensland's most northerly city, is a quaint tropical town with palm-lined streets situated along the azure waters of Trinity Bay. It's also important as the gateway to the reef resorts of Lizard, Orpheus, Dunk and Fitzroy.

Stroll along the Esplanade to Cairns Reef World, a living museum with a vivid exhibit of local fish and coral. Where the esplanade intersects Wharf Street is the old town, the former "Barbary Coast," with a number of fine old buildings to explore. Don't miss the Aboriginal artifacts exhibit at the Cairns Museum at the corner of Shields and Lake Streets.

For a scenic look at the inland regions and some spectacular panoramic views of the coast, take the Cairns to Kuranda Railway. Built 100 years ago, the railway makes a one-and-a-half hour journey through sugar cane fields, rocky mountains, lush jungle, over cavernous gorges and past waterfalls at Stony Creek and Barron Falls.

Although Cairns itself has no beaches, a number of gorgeous stretches lie to the north and south. To the north, try the scenic drive along the many white-sand beaches leading to Port Douglas, an hour away.

Townsville

No longer a town but a thriving port city, Townsville is Queenland's third largest city. Engaged in an intense rivalry with Cairns for dominance as the "Gateway to the Reef," the coastal city also serves as a departure point to Magnetic, Orpheus, Hinchinbrook and Dunk Islands.

Ask the Tourist Bureau (in Flinders Mall) about the city's old buildings, dating from the 19th century, located in the center of town. For a fascinating orientation to the reef offshore, visit the

nearby Great Barrier Reef Wonderland for a viewing of their dramatic Omnimax Theatre presentation and live coral reef aquarium.

The Strand, the main drive paralleling the beachfront, is a natural setting for banks of climbing bougainvillaea and waterside parks and gardens. Turning off of the Strand onto Gregory St., head inland to Castle Hill Road. You'll pass the Queen's Gardens along the way, as well as North Ward, the city's botanic gardens. The top of Castle Hill affords a panoramic view of the city, the port and the tropical landscape.

A short drive out of town will get you to Mt. Elliot, off the Bruce Highway. Tell the folks back home that you swam in Alligator Creek -- just don't tell them there's not a gator to be found in the refreshing waters. Or head further afield to Mt. Spec-Crystal National Park. Dramatic views of the country and coast make it worthwhile, and pleasant swimming holes make the summer heat bearable.

Mackay

Located on the Pioneer River, Mackay (pronounced McEye) is Australia's sugar capital, processing one-third of the nation's crop.

Start your jaunt at the tourist information center on the Bruce Highway. An attraction in itself, the center is housed in a Taiwanese fishing junk that was confiscated in 1976 for poaching clams in Aussie waters.

Gladstone

This fast growing port town, south of Mackay, sits on the shores of Port Curtis. In addition to its thriving mineral and agricultural exports, Gladstone is the gateway to Heron Island, via helicopter or boat.

Townsville/Kelly

Offshore Islands

Scattered along the reef are many small islands with excellent diving, snorkeling and other activities for the action traveler. Resorts range from casual to the most elegant. They can be reached by boat or plane from the major gateway towns.

From north to south, these include islands like Lizard Island, named for its monitor lizards and home of Blue Lagoon, a spectacular dive and snorkel spot. From September to November, the black marlin fishing is also five-star.

Dunk Island, about half-way between Cairns and Townsville is a well-designed and professionally run resort offering every imaginable activity. The hinterland is especially noted for its bird life and giant blue butterflies.

Enormous and lush, Hinchinbrook Island, the largest uninhabited island in the world, is a nature-lover's paradise where friendly kangaroos are a principal entertainment. Exclusive and small Orpheus Island (50 guest maximum) offers every possible amenity.

The Whitsunday archipelago is a group of some 74 islands. With its many deserted or barely inhabited white-sand islands fringed by inviting palm trees, this group is the special favorite of chartered and private yachts. Its elegant resort islands include bustling, modern Hamilton Island and the sedate and elegant Hayman Island. Both

offer everything in the way of recreational activity and world-class cuisine. South Molle and Daydream Island Resorts both offer mid-priced accommodations and a wide range of recreation.

Heron Island is considered among Australia's best dive spots, and is surrounded by kilometers of easily accessible coral reef. It is the host for the annual Diver's Rally in June/July, and the Skin Divers Festival each November.

One of the southernmost islands along the reef, Lady Elliot is a true coral cay, offering spectacular diving in pristine conditions. Fraser Island, just off the mainland, is covered with rain-forests, gurgling springs and crystal pools. Both are accessible from nearby Brisbane.

The Sunshine Coast is a longer, more low-key stretch of coastline to the north of Brisbane, where the main highway runs well inland. A secondary road skirts a tropical shore with some of the best surfing in Queensland. This area is home to some of the best of Australia's "big" kitsch, like the Big Bottle at Tewantia, the Big Cow at Nambour, and the Big Pineapple (welcome to the tropics). The Sugar Coast, a short stretch between Maryborough and Bondaberg, attracts visitors bound for Fraser Island and Lady Elliot Island. Noosa, at the coast's end and where you turn back to the blacktop, is an odd mix of surfers and wealthy retirees.

Brisbane

Brisbane, the state's capital, is the third largest city in Australia and a busy port town as well. This lovely metropolis of flowering trees, gardens and parklands is bisected by the Brisbane River which empties into Moreton Bay, about twenty miles away. Stop by the Queensland Government Travel Center, 196 Adelaide St. for a city map and a quick orientation.

Beautiful riverside parks and gardens, fostered by the sub-tropical climate, abound in this fair city. At the city's center, on the north bank of the Brisbane River, are the fragrant Botanic Gardens. Even larger is Victoria Park, extending over 193 acres. Included in the park are the Centenary Swimming Pool, and the Municipal Golf Links.

Brisbane's City Hall, an impressive building on the corner of Adelaide and Albert streets, is quite a showplace. Not only a museum for paintings and other historic treasures, it contains a grand organ said to be one of the finest in the Southern Hemisphere. Take the elevator to the ob-

Sydney/Kelly

servation tower for a panoramic view of the city and surrounding countryside.

Two top attractions await you just outside the city's center. A 15-minute car ride will take you to the Lone Pine Koala Sanctuary, the largest koala colony on display anywhere. Here, you can cuddle a koala and visit with the kangaroos, Tasmanian devils and wallabies.

Mt. Coot-tha Forest Park, 5 miles from the city center, is an oasis of tall eucalyptus trees and vista points. The view, especially beautiful at night, looks out towards the Glass Mountains to the north and down towards Brisbane with its glistening river snaking through.

Horse racing is the number one sport in Brisbane. The Stradbroke Handicap and The Brisbane Cup are held in June, and two other major races take place in July. Or, catch a greyhound race at Woolloongabba. On nearby Moreton Bay, yacht racing is quite popular, and on Moreton Island you can toboggan down the world's largest sanddunes, 300 meters high.

In late September, early October, Brisbane welcomes Spring with the Warana, a week-long celebration of parades, beauty contests, family activities and non-stop partying.

Gold Coast

This string of beachfront communities extends approximately 50 miles from Southport to Coolangatta. Consisting primarily of resort developments, the name of its largest high-rise development, Surfers' Paradise, says it all.

Diving, snorkeling, sunning, surfing, naturehikes, amusement parks, golf, tennis, deep-sea fishing, bushwalks, sailing, squash, waterskiing - - are just a few of the recreational options open to the active traveler. Add to this list a bustling nightlife complete with a casino and dozens of restaurants of every ethnic variety.

For a change of pace, visit one or more of the wildlife sanctuaries. Currumbin Sanctuary on the Gold Coast Highway is home to a variety of colorful Australian birds as well as a host of kangaroos, wallabies and koalas. Birdlife Park places it winged inhabitants in a natural setting.

In the mountains behind the Coast, Lamington National Park is an edenic garden of waterfalls, rain forests and lush scenery crisscrossed by graded walking paths. Take a picnic with you and stop at either Gwongorella or Warrie National Parks for some shaded relaxation and views of fern filled gorges and the coast below.

Australia

Snorkelers/Kelly

West of the Great Divide

Inland from the coastal cities, the Great Dividing Range runs north to south forming a barrier between the tropics and outback. Mount Isa in the northwest offers stunning rivers and remnants of ancient Aboriginal civilization, as well as rugged trekking in the granite hills nearby. Further south, sheep and cattle stations, few and far between, offer travelers working holidays jackarooing in the outback. Toowoomba to the south is a farming community in the heart of Australia's grain country. Each spring the Carnival of Flowers brings thousands of visitors to town.

New South Wales

When driving south from Brisbane into New South Wales, there are two completely different routes to choose from. The coastal Pacific Highway sweeps past numerous deserted beaches. Or, the inland route, the New England Highway, wends its way through some lovely and typically Australian pastoral scenery. The Highway also passes through Hunter Valley, one of Australia's premier wine regions, and a great place to wet your whistle on the way to Sydney.

Sydney

Sydney, the state's capital, is a thriving metropolitan city set on the sparkling waters of its busy and magnificent harbor. Originally named Port Jackson by Captain Cook in 1770, the city is the oldest in Australia.

The city is divided into two parts: the North Shore and Sydney proper. Located on either side of the Harbour, they are joined by the famous Harbour Bridge.

Since Sydney has so much to offer, from harbor to bridge, from old town to new, with shopping and site-seeing galore, it's definitely wise to stop in at the Tourist Center at 16 Spring St. (tel: 231-4444) for a map and orientation.

At the circular Quay, the primary departure point for ferries, catch an afternoon or evening meal cruise. As you glide about the harbor savoring the cuisine, you'll get an excellent waterside perspective of the city.

The Rocks, located at the south end of Harbour Bridge, is the original settlement of this now busy port metropolis. Once run down and decrepit, it has undergone cosmetic surgery, and has emerged resplendent. Colonial buildings grace winding cobblestone streets with gas lights. Here you'll find artisans, shops, restaurants and bars, all housed in the ancient dwellings.

The "inner city" of Paddington, or Paddo as it's locally known, has been renovated. One of the oldest sections of the city, it is an excellent example of unplanned urban restoration. Beautifully reconditioned houses terrace up the narrow streets. You'll find a whole host of shops and restaurants, and on Saturdays there's the Paddington Fair, an eccentric marketplace.

In addition to its historic buildings, cultural centers, lovely parks and big business, Sydney is a very outdoorsy city. Thirty-four golden beaches curve north and south about the harbor. Sydneysiders gather here from October to March for the best tanning rays, swimming and surfing. Protected by the harbor, these waters are calmer than the open-water beaches.

It's no wonder that, with its magnificent harbor, Sydney is a city devoted to watersports. Summer surf competitions are common on weekends between October and March. And in August, the city hosts the 14-km City to Surf running race. Bright white sails are a common sight any day of the week on the harbour. The yachting season lasts from September to May with regattas every weekend. To catch the intensely fought competition between the "18-footers," take the spectator ferry which departs from the Circular Quay at 2 pm. The famed Sydney-Hobart race takes place December 26. For your own sailing pleasure, you may charter boats at any number of resorts along the waterfront.

Just out of Coff's Harbour is an excellent location for deep-sea fishing. The Game Fishing Association in Sydney will set you up with charter

NSW/ATC

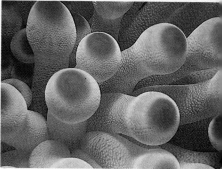

Polyps/Grayston

information. Or freshwater fishermen can cast their lines into the near-by streams and rivers of the Blue Mountains. Remember to obtain a license from the Department of Fisheries.

Landside sports are found in abundance as well, with public golf courses and tennis courts throughout the city. For a voyage into the bush, good trails are found not too far from the city. Try north at Ku-ring-gai Chase National Park, west in the Blue Mountains or south at the Royal National Park.

In the winter, football is the popular sport, with the most well-attended of the four varieties being Rugby League. The devoted and intense fans gather at Sydney Sports Ground at Moore Park to cheer their favorite teams on. In the summer months, cricket enjoys a large following. International and interstate matches are played at Sydney Cricket Ground, also in Moore Park.

Beyond Sydney

South from Sydney, the Prince's Highway is the scenic alternative to the Hume Highway which links the capital with Melbourne. The Princes's Highway tends to be a bit more scenic, weaving

east to the coastal beaches, and then turning inland to provide a glimpse of life in the interior towns.

Only 65 km west of Sydney, the Blue Mountains, featuring gorges, pinnacles and gum trees, are a mecca for bushwalkers. Katooma is the base of operations. White-water fans will find the upper reaches of the Murray and Richmond Rivers a challenge.

Lord Howe Island, 600 km NE of Sydney is the sight of the world's southernmost barrier reef. The coral strip, on Lord Howe's west coast, protects a lagoon perfect for snorkeling, diving and watersports. Also located due east of Sydney, never crowded, always relaxed Norfolk Island offers a variety of hotels, guest lodges and apartments for every budget. A full complement of sporting facilities is available, including golf, snorkeling, scuba diving, tennis, squash, horseback riding, fishing and just plain relaxing. Packages are available from US travel agents or Norfolk Airlines, including airfares, accommodations, transfers, insurance and a half-day tour.

Canberra

Australia's national capital is a planned city designed in 1912 by American architect Walter Burley Griffin. Here the business of government and administration is conducted in the setting of a landscaped masterpiece along the shores of Lake Burley Griffin. The effect is more like a huge, modern college campus than a city in the traditional sense.

To get a 360-degree view of its dramatic layout, visit the Telecom Tower on Black Mountain.

In the nearby satellite city of Belconnen is the Australian Institute for Sport, one of the world's most advanced sport training centers. Facilities

Sydney Harbour Race/ATC

for 10 olympic sports are housed here: basketball, gymnastics, volleyball, rowing, soccer, swimming, tennis, track and field, water polo and weightlifting.

Australia's bush country is right at Canberra's doorstep. Tours of nearby sheep stations, animal parks and reserves can be arranged, as can trips to the nearby Mount Stromlo Observatory and a space tracking station at Tidbinbilla, which is open to the public from 9 to 5.

Victoria

Despite its relatively small size (compared to the vast expanses of the other five states), Victoria has no shortage of natural and recreational wonders. The coast line, highlighted by the sculpted forms of the Twelve Apostles to the west, the popular Wilson's Promontory National Park to the south and the vast sandy expanses of Gippsland's 90-mile beach, is without exception, stunning.

The seaside towns of Lorne, Port Fairy and Portland are worth visiting for their fine architecture and their natural beauty. Inland, the Snowy Mountains are a year-round playground with hiking, fishing or skiing, depending on the season. In the far north, the Murray River provides a playground setting for boating, swimming, fishing and river cruises of all kinds.

The central highland is Victoria's gold country. Historic towns like Bendigo and Ballarat are packed with the history and flavor of gold rush days.

But Melbourne, the state capital, is very much the main attraction, especially for those interested in such cosmopolitan activities as world class cuisine, theater, art and shopping.

Melbourne

Melbourne is a graciously unhurried city of enormous charm and culture. Part of its charm is its remarkable diversity: Victorians reside with modern steel and glass structures, a vast selection of ethnic restaurants and weather that's as changeable as the street scenes.

Perhaps the best way to acquaint yourself with the city is to take the #8 tram, which connects the city on both sides of the Yarra river. Or for a quiet riverside approach, take the Princess Walk, which cruises the waterway daily from 11am to 4pm.

The city center, also known as the Golden Mile, is a compact area bounded on the south side by the Yarra and on the north by LaTrobe St. Here is the heart of business, commerce and the theatre arts. Most of Melbourne's best shopping is located in this area as well. Serious shoppers will be glad to know that Melbourne is considered Australia's fashion capital. Most of its exclusive stores reside on Collins Street, displaying top designs from both local and international designers.

Art and theater are alive and well in Melbourne. Don't miss the National Gallery of Victoria, The Victorian Arts Center, the Concert Hall and the city's many active theaters.

Another "must see" are the Royal Botanic Gardens in South Yarra. Highlights include massive oaks and river red gum trees, lakes, ponds and a miniature rain forest of lush ferns.

Drive or ferry to Phillips Island, about 90 miles away. Here you can watch the comical little Fairy Penguins stumble out of the water at Summerland Beach and waddle in their tuxedos to their burrows up the beach.

Melbourne provides plenty of diversions for the sports enthusiast. Port Phillips Bay is alive with summer water activities, including swimming, snorkeling, sailing, windsurfing and waterskiing. Check local resorts for boat and ski rentals. Melbournites are fierce "footy" fans, and their favorite brand is Australian Rules football, played each Saturday from April to September.

Two major festivities occur in Melbourne as well. The week long Spring Racing Carnival, in the beginning of November, heralds the much anticipated Melbourne Cup horse race. Then in late February/early March, the revelry really takes off at the Moomba, a week long celebration of watershows, fireworks and all around family fun.

South Australia

South Australia, the country's driest state, has surprisingly much to offer visitors: fine wines, brilliant opals, tasty crayfish, rolling green hills, lakes, pine forests, as well as some of the most arid, desolate outback in the country. Its Mediterranean climate, unpolluted air and unusual wildlife attract nature lovers, hikers, big game fishermen, campers and artists.

One of the state's prettiest towns is Clare. Located in the heart of South Australia's wine country, Clare hosts a vintage wine festival at Eastertime in even-numbered years.

Kangaroo Island, 113 kilometers southwest of Adelaide, is Australia's third largest island, and something of an all-around outdoorsmans's paradise. Flinders Chase National Park on the west end has thriving colonies of 'roos, wallabies and koalas. Seal Bay Conservation Park is home to around 10% of the world's sea lion population. These cold southern ocean waters, prolific in

Cairns/Kelly

marine life, are also the natural habitat of the Great White Shark. There are limited Great White viewing excursions which operate every year.

/Jacobs

Australia

On the mainland, just 18 kilometers south of Adelaide, the protected underwater reserve at Port Noarlunga offers dives at all difficulty levels. Mt. Gambier, close to the Victoria border, is famous for its sinkhole diving, reputedly the best in the world (most of the sinkholes require a cave-diving certificate).

Or you can sail or swim in the serene waters of St. Vincent Harbour. There's canoeing on the lower reaches of the mighty Murray, and cruising on the Torrens River in pedal boats.

Adelaide

Adelaide, the capital of South Australia, is a graciously planned river-bank city. Following its 1836 founding, the posh residential borough of North Adelaide and the central commerce district grew up on opposite sides of the Torrence River. Bordered on the east by the Mount Lofty Range, and on the west by long sandy beaches, Adelaide is a city of parks.

She is also a major festival center, hosting the biennial Adelaide Arts Festival. During the first 3 weeks of March in even-numbered years, performers, writers and artists of every kind from Australia and abroad come together at the Festival Center. The list of cultural and social activities includes international music, drama, opera and art. Another major international event is the Australian Formula One Grand Prix in October, considered to be one of the best events in the world.

Good shopping can be found at Rundle Mall. Best buys include South Australian opals, antiques and moleskin clothing. Local crafts are on display at Adelaide's Jam Factory and at the Central Market. Nightlife centers around the Hindley and King William Streets area.

Wine-tasting galore is to be sipped in the immediate environs of Adelaide. Even closer, 11 miles from town, sample the vintages at the Southern Wine District. Their Bushing Festival takes place in October.

Western Australia

Big, wild West Australia is a land of beaches, dry savanna, rugged mountain ranges and tropical wildlife. The operative word here is "big." The state occupies one-third of the Australian continent and is nearly four times the size of Texas. The coastline alone is 12,500 miles long! Because of the vast distances between towns and attractions, air travel is the quickest way to get around.

Perth

Perth is an ultramodern city full of energy, creativity and a unique pioneering spirit. Anything is possible in this casual open setting. The city straddles the broad, park-lined Swan River, named for the black swans which still grace its waters.

King's Park, sprawled over a hill at the end of St. George's Terrace, offers the best views of the city and river. Each January, musicians and performers from around the world gather in the outdoor Somerville Auditorium at the nearby University of Western Australia for the annual Festival of Perth, which involves other of Perth's entertainment venues as well.

Further along the riverfront is Claremont, an exclusive shopping area and home to the Claremont Fresh Markets which offer shoppers a vast selection of exotic produce, smoked meats, poultry, cheeses and breads.

An interesting suburb is Peppermint Grove, where the elite live in mansions perched along the face of the cliff to the river's edge.

Perth's sunsets are among the most spectacular in the world, but sun-up to sun-down is when Perth shines. The beaches, no fewer than 19 of them in Perth's immediate vicinity, are the playground for joggers, surfers, sailors, sun bathers and lay-abouts. Some beaches are topless, others more family oriented. Bring your tanning oil and enjoy the scenery.

Watersport activities are centered about the Indian Ocean, and on the Swan River where it widens out into an almost bay. You can rent just about any sort of boat you want on the banks of the Swan, from yachts to pedal boats. You'll find plenty of tennis, yachting, footy, golf, fishing, board and windsurfing as well.

Don't miss the Darling Ranges, a short 13 mile hop away, where in the Spring you can see a riotous and dazzling display of indigenous Australian wildflowers. Fremantle, 12 commuter train miles to the southeast, is the old convict-built port at the river's mouth, and in fact most of it predates the gold rush. With its characteristic architecture, the Esplanade Park along the fishing harbor (what better place for fish-and-chips), craft centers and market on South Terrace, it's a favorite with most Perth visitors.

Norfolk Island

Rottnest Island off Fremantle became famous as a landmark during the 1986-87 Cup Defense, but few outsiders realize that it's the best active daytrip or weekend escape from Perth, accessible by ferry or air. Once there, the island is just the right size for bicycle-touring to an assortment of beaches.

Geraldton, 428 kilometers north of Perth, is a popular beach resort featuring surfing and fishing, and also the site of four Dutch shipwrecks dating from 1629.

The Northern Territory

The "Top End," as it's familiarly known, is the home of the stereotypical outback, and the location for <u>Crocodile Dundee</u>, the "Red Center" (or Ayers Rock), its neighbors the Olgas, and the cliffs flanking the Katherine Gorge. But most of these wonders are some distance away from Darwin, the top of the Top End.

Only 150,000 or so people, less than 1% of Australia's population, occupy this vast territory, but the population is growing faster than any other state.

In the tropical Top End, temperatures range from 16C to 34C, and the precipitation ranges from "the Wet" from October to May, to "the Dry" from June to September. At the Red Centre, temperatures sometimes drop below freezing at night. The best time to visit is in the dry season, when sun worshipers are in their glory.

The main highway into the outback is the Stuart Highway, simply known as "the track," which heads south from Darwin through Katherine to Alice Springs, and beyond to Adelaide. Stop along the way at Katherine Gorge,

Gladstone

Australia

/Kelly

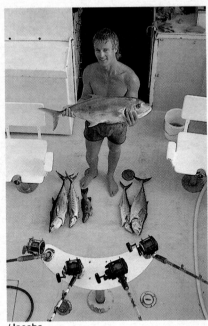

/Grayston /Jacobs

South Molle Golf/Kelly

Wonderland/Kelly

/Roessler

/Kelly

Australia

Tasmania backpacking/ATC

32 kilometers from Katherine, which during the dry season is a quiet haven with a gently flowing river, brightly colored parrots and relatively harmless freshwater crocodiles, but which is transformed into thundering mountain rapids during "the Wet."

For a good look at the local scene, try the Barunga Sports and Cultural Festival during Anzac weekend in April. The festival is held at the Beswick Aboriginal Reserve, 80 kilometers SE of Katherine. Aboriginal clans gather here from throughout the territory for football, rodeo, food and partying.

Along the Arnem Highway which heads east out of Darwin, there are several areas of scenic interest. Corroboree Billabong on the Mary River system is a great place to fish for the fighting barramundi, or just drift with the current. Further along the highway is Kakadu National Park. The park encompasses six regions, each with its own characteristic land forms, including rolling forests, tidal mudflats and tumbling waterfalls.

Darwin

Welcome to the beer drinking capital of the world (230 liter per person annually!) -- and with Darwin's hot and thirsty climate, it's no wonder.

But it's not all cowboys and jackaroos, by any means. Darwin's population is actually quite a melting pot of Chinese, Caucasian, Aboriginal, Greek, Italian, Timorese, Spanish, Indonesian and Scandinavian, among others. This intermingling of cultures, foods, languages and customs lends personality and flavor to Darwin that no other capital city has in such variety.

A tour of Darwin should include a visit to the pub at the Old Victoria Hotel in the Mall and the old Fannie Bay Jail with its hangman's noose and

iron walls, sitting in startling contrast to the bright sails and jet skis of the Sailing Club in the blue waters below.

Nearly every sport ever devised can be found in Darwin, including underwater hockey, rugby union and all watersports. The beaches surrounding Darwin are quite lovely and mostly deserted, but do check with local authorities before going in the water.

Tasmania

Separated from the mainland some 200 nautical miles south of Victoria, Tasmania is a jewel. It is graced with rich, rolling countryside in the north and east, and with one of the finest wildernesses in the world in the west and southwest.

Its isolation and rugged terrain are a large part of Tasmania's attraction, especially to naturelovers and hikers, known locally as "bush walkers." Along the southwest coastline are three popular hiking routes. The Port Davey track zigzags across miles of exposed coastline. The South West Track follows the coast from Cockle Creek to Melaleuca and connects with the Port Davey Track in the west. Another premier hike is the 83 kilometers, 5-day jaunt through Cradle Mountain/ Lake St. Claire National Park.

Trout fishing is excellent in Tasmania. Southwest of Launceston, at the Great Lake, it is especially plentiful. River rafting, mountain climbing, beach-combing and watersports are also a part of Tassie's charm.

Hobart

Ironically, it was to this fetching city that England's most hard-core criminals were sent. And although you can still get a feel for the past in the city's well-preserved buildings and relics, modern-day Hobart is engaging and unspoiled.

Sitting on the shores of the Derwent River, and backed by the majesty of snow-capped Mt. Wellington, Hobart is a cosmopolitan city with an interesting range of things to see and do. You won't want to by-pass Battery Point, the city's first settled area and so named for the gun battery protecting the harbour.

Constitution Dock, off of Morrison St. is important, both as the finishing line of the Sydney-Hobart Race in December and the site of February's Royal Hobart Regatta.

Catch the tour of Port Arthur Penal Colony, on the tip of the Tasman peninsula about one hour southeast of Hobart. This wretched and virtually escape-proof prison, closed in 1877, was reserved for the worst criminals.

Food

Australia's cuisine, particularly in the state capitals, can be ranked among the best in the world. Besides excellent Australian seafood and meat selections, there's a diversity of ethnic fare including: Greek, Italian, French, Middle Eastern, Baltic, Indian and Turkish. For a taste of a "traditional" Aussie dish, try the Colonial Goose, a highly seasoned and stuffed shoulder of lamb. Or sample the carpetbag steak, a rich dish consisting of a thick cut of beef stuffed with pockets of fresh oysters. But, aside from the vegemite, a brown yeast spread, only two other dishes can claim to be truly Australian: the Pavlova, a cream and meringue concoction, and the Lamington, a chocolate and coconut covered spongecake.

Queensland is especially noted for its mud crabs and its Moreton Bay Bugs. Although not particularly savory in name, these relatives of the crab and lobster are excellent in taste. For a sample of the local brew, sample a few Castelmaines.

Seafood lovers will be in their glory Down Under. The fare is superb and abundant all around Australia. Rock oysters, coral trout, prawns, barramundi, whiting, yabbies (a sort of salt-water crawdad), rock lobster and snapper are common selections. Local varieties include the Western Dhufish of Western Australia and the scallops in Tasmania.

Washing it all down poses no problem either. Distinctive local brews are strong and <u>cold</u>. A

Victoria/ATC

schooner of amber (that's a large glass of beer) will quench your thirst. In recent years, Australian wines have come to the forefront, even garnering worldwide recognition. When dining, you may spy the anagram "BYO" on your menu, meaning "bring your own bottle." These restaurants, which are not licensed to sell alcohol, will charge a small corkage fee.

Nightlife

In the larger cities, there's every conceivable entertainment from theatre and arts to rock, jazz and classical concerts to dancing. At the casinos, try your luck at the uniquely Australian game of "Two Up," where you place bets on whether two coins will land heads or tails. You'll find live entertainment and dancing in many nightclubs. Dinner shows are popular as well. In Brisbane, catch the nightly show at The Living Room. On the islands and in smaller resort towns, the resorts provide selected entertainment.

Shopping

Opal lovers, get your wallets ready. Opals are found in abundance here and at much lower prices than back home. New South Wales is famous for its black opals from Lightning Ridge. Other precious stones are available as well. Queensland's Anakie district is noted for its sapphires.

If you want to come home wearing more than just a great tan, sport the genuine Australian outback look: a Driza-bone rain coat, an Akubra hat and RM William boots. Other uniquely Australian buys include Aboriginal art, with its intricate bark paintings. Or how about a boomerang? Antique shoppers will want to browse in Melbourne and Adelaide.

Shute Harbour/Jacobs

Australia

Sports

Considering Australia's ideal climate and natural environment, it's no wonder that sports are a way of life Down Under. Most obviously, it's a watersport paradise, with diving, surfing, sailing, rafting and fishing topping the list. Not far behind come the land-lubber activities: golf, tennis, cycling, cricket, snow-skiing, horseback riding, camping --you name it.

• Boating

When in Australia, do as the Aussie's do: go boating. Opportunities exist for both independent and crewed charters. Crafts range from the sleekest of yachts to the most ordinary houseboats, and there are many lakes, rivers, bays and coastlines to explore. Crewed charters, both motored and sailing, offer first-class services and a crew with a good knowledge of the area. Some companies specialize in fishing, scuba diving or marine biology. Bareboat charters, in which you skipper your own craft, applies to yachts, motorboats and houseboats. Any way you go, it's an unbeatable opportunity for self-paced exploration and pure relaxation. The sunny Whitsunday group in Queensland is an idyllic spot to anchor and enjoy deserted cays and friendly sea life in complete privacy. New South Wales' myriad waterways offer different experiences from the beaches surrounding Sydney Harbor to the far reaches of the Parramatta River, which empties into the Harbour. Inland adventures abound on Victoria's icy Murray River which meanders west to the clear but cold Lake Alexandria in South Australia. In Western Australia, boaters can cruise the serene waters of Peel Inlet, Harvey Estuary and the Serpentine River.

• Bushwalking

A recreational day in the bush requires no more than sturdy shoes, clothing and a canteen of water. Serious walkers will, of course, need more equipment including tents, compasses and sleeping bags. Bushwalking clubs operate in all the states, offering information about bushcraft and organizing trips as well. Magnificent trails often exist just outside city limits. For example, the Gold Coast's Lamington National Park, Sydney's Blue Mountains and Melbourne's Dandenong Ranges offer awe-inspiring beauty within easy access to the cities.

With Australia's vast wildernesses, it would be difficult to list all the opportunities for bushwalking, but some of the best include: the New England and Dorrigo National Parks in New South Wales with its richly forested valleys and crashing waterfalls. In Victoria, the Grampians National Park displays vivid wildflowers, a wide assortment of plant and bird life and a large collection of Aboriginal rock paintings. The Overland Track in Tasmania's Cradle Mountain/ Lake St. Claire National Park is Australia's most famous trail. Queensland's Quinkan Reserve takes its name from the large human figures displayed on the ancient Aboriginal rock paintings found throughout the region.

• Golf

Enthusiasts will be pleased to know that, in the golfing world, Australia is ranked in the top five, and its greens are open year round. In October, Sydney hosts the internationally acclaimed NSW Open, and in November, pros and spectators flock to the Australian Open, held this year at the Royal Sydney Golf Club. A good way to sample the various courses is to participate in some of the clinics, "golf-weekends" and tours hosted by the various clubs. Golf tours usually include greenfees, transportation, 18 holes of golf, booked starting times, hole-by-hole information and occasionally an electric golf cart. Rental is available for clubs and shoes. With the exception of Brisbane, private clubs in capital cities accept only visitors with reciprocal memberships, though in rural areas private clubs tend to be more accommodating. Golfers visiting Queensland won't want to miss the world-class greens and assorted entertainment at Kooralbyn Championship Course. The 6,061-meter, par 70 course at Duntry League Country Club is quite a memorable challenge. Located 265 kilometers from Sydney, the Club offers guests overnight accommodations in a magnificent 19th century mansion. Melbourne, Australia's golf capital, contains many championship courses, some of which, Royal Melbourne Golf Club, for example, were designed by Dr. Alistair Mackenzie. Tasmania's Shearwater Country Club is an excellent spot for the complete holiday, with tennis and poolside activities in addition to its 9-hole course. Close to Perth the Joondalup Country Club in Western Australia sports a 6,275-meter, par 72 championship course designed by renowned architect Robert Trent. It is considered one of the best in Western Australia.

Coral Sea/Roessler

Cairns/Kelly

• Horseback Riding

Every state in Australia offers horseback riding, with organized tours to lead both the novice and the experienced rider through some of the country's most beautiful scenery. Both day and overnight expeditions are available.

In Victoria, ride through the mountainous and lake-spangled Great Dividing Range or take a flat-land ride about the state's agricultural region. For a different experience, check out the stark desert beauty in South Australia, Western Australia and the Northern Territory. In New South Wales' Koscuisko National Park, riders will traverse carpets of colorful and sweet smelling wildflowers, explore the Yarrangobilly Caves, fish in streams and relax in thermal pools. In Queensland, trails explore everything from sparkling coastal vistas to plush rain forests. In 1988, the Bicentennial National Horse Trail opened after 16 years of development. This superb trail traverses the entire eastern side of the continent, wending down from Cookstown in the north, through New South Wales and ending in Melbourne. The longest trail in the world, it follows many historic stock and pack-horse routes, and is designed so that water and campsites are no more than a day's walk or ride from each other.

• Rafting, Canoeing and Kayaking

White-water rafting, canoeing and kayaking fans will find that both smooth sailing and rough and tumble rapids await them on Australia's waterways. Hard-core, heart-pounding rafting enthusiasts will love the rapids of the Upper Murray River while the calmer reaches below are perfect for a more placid paddle. Between plunges down the boiling rapids of the Snowy River, rafters and canoeists will see some of the country's most beautiful and untouched wilderness. For the experienced, some of the most exciting rapids can be found on the Nymboida and Gwdyir Rivers of New South Wales, and novices will find exhilarating day tours as well. In South Australia's Red Centre, try uniquely Australian "desert canoeing" on Cooper's Creek, where the daring explorers Burke and Wills died in 1861 and where evidence still remains of their historic journey. Each August, in Western Australia, hundreds of rafters race down the difficult stretches of the Avon River in the famous Avon Descent. The area about Cairns in Queensland has top-notch rafting and canoeing on the warm tropical waters of the Tully, North Johnstone, Mulgrave, Herbert and Barron Rivers. This is deep gorge country, and both experts and beginners will find the scenery and the water immensely satisfying.

Australia has the perfect environment for kayaking as well. Sea-kayaking on the Great Barrier Reef is a unique experience to glide about the spectacular beaches and cays of this blue wonderland. Tours of Tasmania's Bathurst Harbour explore the area from Melaleuca Inlet to the Celery Top Islands and end in Port Davey on the edge of the cold Southern Ocean. Excitement is also to be found in Victoria's Wilson Point, while beginners will enjoy the serene waters at Gippsland Lakes.

• Rockclimbing

For the truly intrepid, Australia's ancient rocks provide the perfect place to rockclimb. Climbs are graded from simple walks (1) and scrambles (6-7) to the most difficult (32), and present the perfect opportunity for beginner and expert alike to explore the rocky summits. Climbing lessons are offered through clubs and commercial organizations to teach novices the safest techniques of this sport. Guides will take the more experienced on climbs of varying difficulty.

The sandstone cliffs of Mt. Arapiles, in Victoria, are Australia's climbing mecca, and are visited by famous international climbers like Chris Bonington. Equally famous Mt. Buffalo National Park offers both free-climbs and exhilarat-ing rope climbs in Buffalo Gorge. The delicate face climbs in the Blue Mountains of New South Wales, particularly on the cliffs of Cosmic County, have made the region famous. Crack climbers will enjoy the 40-meter-high Frog Buttress in Queensland.

• Spectator Sports

Popular spectator sports include horse racing, football (rugby and soccer) and cricket. Horse racing fans are numerous and passionate. Races are held throughout the year, typically on Saturdays.

To say that football has an enthusiastic following would be an understatement. Six-plus million fans follow the league games that are held each Saturday from April to September. The term "football" is a loose one encompassing four variations of the sport: Aussie Rules, League Rugby (professional), Union rugby (amateur) and soccer. The big meets, like the Melbourne Cup in October, are always sell-outs requiring advance purchase. See your travel agent for arrangements.

The cricket season lasts from October to March and has an avid audience as well. Competition is fierce between Australian and other Commonwealth country teams in particular.

Yacht racing is another popular passion, with a huge following and fierce competition. Among the major race events are the Sydney to Hobart Race on Boxing Day (a six-or-so-day ocean race for maxi yachts) and Hamilton Race Week in mid-April.

• Diving

Exploring Australia's 20,000 miles would take hundreds of lifetimes. But even a taste of these tropical and temperate waters will enchant even the most seasoned and worldly diver.

From the clear, balmy waters of the Great Barrier reef, to the shipwrecks of Bass Strait, to the freshwater sinkholes of Mt. Gambier, Australia downunder is a virtual supermarket of dive experiences.

Dive certification courses are offered in every major city, in most coastal towns and at many resorts and hotels. In fact, many of Australia's resorts offer certification, resort-course instruction and daily and/or nightly dives as part of their watersport offerings. Use this book as a guide to accredited dive operators. With as little as 5 days of instruction, you can become a certified openwater diver, all in the comfort and spectacular seascape of tropical Australian waters.

Kangaroo/ATC

Three professional dive organizations operate in Australia, the Federation of Australian Underwater Instructors (FAUI), the Professional Association of Diving Instructors (PADI) and the National Association of Underwater Instructors (NAUI). Most dive shops and dive charter operations will require an open-water certification card from one of these organizations, or from an overseas equivalent, before renting tanks.

Queensland

The best-known dive destination is, of course, Queensland's Great Barrier Reef. Extending from New Guinea down the Queensland coast to Lady Elliot Island, this vast system of coral reefs, coral cays and offshore islands fringes the coast 20 to 250 kilometers from the mainland.

This considerable distance is covered by boat, helicopter and sea plane by more than 100 dive operators, resorts and charter companies from all the major coastal centers, including Gladstone, Shute Harbour, Townsville, Cairns and Port Douglas. The island resorts can provide even quicker access than the coastal areas. For immediate access, the Four Seasons Floating Hotel, 74 kilometers off Townsville, is anchored right on the reef. If you're short on time and long on funds, a speedy helicopter flight from Hamilton Island, or an Air Whitsunday flight from Shute Harbour can bring you out for a two-tank dive after breakfast, and get you back for lunch. Most dive trips involving a boat, even a fast one, are full day excursions, but well worth the time. Bring your tanning lotion and a good book for sunning en route.

Visibility varies depending on the wind, tide, distance from the mainland (or an island) and your position relevant to the outside edge of the GBR. The Queensland Dive Tourism Association of Australia (ODTAA) is the safety monitor of the industry. Make sure you dive with a member.

Beyond the Reef itself, the reefs of the Coral Sea are a spectacular dive destination.

New South Wales

Because of its large population centers and tourist attractions, NSW has more resident divers and more facilities than the other states. Several sites close to Sydney offer excellent diving, including Lord Howe Island, with the southernmost coral reef in the world, and the Admiralty islets with excellent macro-photography subjects.

On the north coast, Byron Bay offers bommie diving (a bommie is a large coral head, also known as a bombora). Further south, the Solitary

Sydney Harbour/Jacobs

/Roessler

Aboriginal Art/ATC

Islands offers a good diversity of tropical and subtropical marine life.

Near Sydney proper, Port Hacking and Broken Bay offer good diving with generally good visibility.South of Sydney, Jervis Bay offers protected diving throughout most of the year. This is reputedly New South Wales best diving, in a gem of a setting with brilliant white beaches and crystal-clear water.

Victoria

The weather limits diving in some parts of Victoria. Many locals wait for a long, dry, calm spell, usually during April and May, before diving in, although many spots are protected from the elements and can be dived year round.

At Wilsons Promontory National Park, the visibility and the fish life are fantastic. Port Phillip Bay is one of Victoria's most popular areas, with a variety of unexplored reefs, several shipwrecks and diverse marine life. Beginners and night divers will enjoy Flinder's Jetty, accessible by beach or boat. Around San Remo, a series of volcanic pinnacles rise from 45 meters to within 10 meters of the surface. Visibility is limited, but the sea fans, zoanthids, sea whips and myriad fish make it worthwhile.

Port Phillip Bay, home to Melbourne and Geelong, is another popular dive center. No matter which way the wind is blowing, there are always protected sites to be found.

Tasmania

The water is cold, but several locations are worth exploring along the east and north coasts: Maria Island, the Tasman Peninsula, the D'Entrecasteaux, Channel and Bicheno.

South Australia

Most of South Australia's popular sites can be dived year round, although high winds in September present an obstacle. Visibility is generally best in early winter and summer. Popular sites include Port Noarlunga Reef near Adelaide; Port Lincoln on the Eyre Peninsula; Cape Wiles, a large lagoon offering sheltered, shallow diving; and the islands offshore, like Kangaroo, Wedge and the Sir Joseph Banks Group.

Freshwater diving is a popular challenge off Mt. Gambier, South Australia's second largest city. The water in Ewen's Ponds and Piccaninny Ponds is freezing cold, but the visibility is incredible. Divers at Piccaninny Ponds must hold a category 2 cave diver's certificate. Snorkelers must have a snorkeling permit from the National Parks and Wildlife Service.

Western Australia

Western Australia has plenty of good diving, but services and access in some areas may be limited. Check with local dive shops about weather conditions and visibility before venturing under.

Near Perth, Rottnest Island offers good visibility, caves, wrecks, reefs and schools of pelagics. The coast between Augusta and Esperance, including the Recherche Archipelago offers good deep diving opportunities for experienced divers. However, access and services are limited. North of Perth, the Abrohos Islands have some of Australia's finest coral gardens in a nature reserve setting.

Further north are Exmouth, the Rowley Shoals and excellent sites around Point Murat, Vlaming Head and Bundegi Reef. A unique and very special bonding between humans and mammals is exhibited at the small coastal village of Monkey Mia, located on the remote north-west coast. Here, a school of dolphins, who have befriended the townsfolk, come into the shallows every day to be fed.

Northern Territory

Diving is limited during the wet season, November to April. Much of the coastline is edged with mangrove forests, and the reefs closer to shore are swept with strong tides and currents. As protection from the jellyfish, always wear a lycra suit or lightweight wetsuit.

Darwin's waters offer a number of WWII wrecks and victims of Cyclone Tracey, including the <u>Megis</u>, a 15,000-ton freighter, and the <u>Peary</u>, a WWII destroyer. Butterfly fish, angelfish, sea fans and soft coral gardens inhabit the hot waters. Freshwater diving can be had during the dry season at Berry Springs, Edith Falls and Rum Jungle.

FIJI

Useful Facts
• <u>Airline Connections</u>   At the present no US carrier flies to Fiji. You can fly direct to Nadi via Qantas and Air New Zealand from the mainland US and from Honolulu on CP Air.

Sports
• Golf
Golfers will find 9-hole courses and putting greens on many of the resorts. There's a championship 18-hole course on Viti Levu and another in Suva.

• Fishing
Record-breaking sailfish and marlin are often caught during the international game fishing competition in Suva, held in late March. Game fishing season is September through January. Light tackle sport fishing is done all year round. Fiji's fish include mahi, coral trout, jacks, dogtooth tuna, barracuda and yellowfin tuna.

• Sailing
Fiji is the biggest sailing center in the Pacific. With 500 islands and plenty of facilities, it's no wonder that 95% of boats cruising the Pacific stop in Fiji. An active charter association rents crewed boats to visitors. At this time, no bareboat charters are available. Call Tony Philip, president of the Charter Boats Association for more information at: 361-788.

• Diving
There's a rule enforced by most of Fiji's dive operators: if you want to fish underwater you have to eat it underwater. In other words, nothing is to be taken from the sea, including shells.

The variety of dive sites is staggering, here on the world's second largest coral reef. There's something for every level of experience and every specific interest. Shallow lagoons, sheer walls, pinnacles, underwater canyons, wrecks, huge coral heads and everywhere thousands of fish and rainbows of coral. The diving is generally safe, the water warm and the sights spectacular. Best visibility can be had April through October.

Solomon Islands
• Airline Connections   There are no direct flights to the Solomon Islands from the US. Air Pacific flies twice a week from Brisbane, Australia, Nadi and Fiji. Air Niugini also services the islands. Solomon Airlines is responsible for all domestic flights, as well as flights to and from Papua New Guinea and Vanuatu.

• Weather   The Solomons experience a tropical climate all year round. Daytime temperatures hover at 86F, with evening temperatures occasionally dropping to 66F. The best months to visit are July to September.

Sports
There is tennis, squash and golf in Honiara. All sorts of watersports are available, including fishing, sailing, canoeing as well as particularly good snorkeling and diving.

• Diving
In Honiara the main attractions are the American and Japanese wrecks. The <u>Hirokawa Maru</u>, a 568-foot Japanese transport ship was beached November 14, 1942 after being hit by US bombers. Its hull is encrusted in hard and soft corals and the fish life is abundant. Depths range from 10 to 180 feet.

Just a few hundred yards away is the <u>Kinugawa Maru</u>, a 436-foot Japanese ship with its bow above water and its stern at 80 feet. Snorklers and divers alike enjoy this dive. The <u>Ruiniu</u>, another Japanese transport vessel, lies in 25 to 150 feet. Don't forget to bring a snack for the friendly fish who live here.

Fourteen miles from town, in 50 feet of water, is an intact B-17 American Flying Fortress plane, with an open cockpit to sit in and intact machine guns. Other interesting wrecks include the <u>Solsea</u>, a scuttled Island Trader and the <u>USS John Penn</u>, an American Troop/Cargo ship off Henderson Field, which lies at 120 to 180 feet. The Penn is swarming with large pelagic fish.

Other areas to check out include: Eastern Guadalcanal, Western Province, Anuha Island and Gizo.

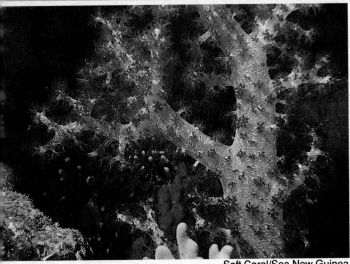

Soft Coral/Sea New Guinea

• Diving

Sea New Guinea handles all of the dive operators and operations in Papua New Guinea. If you are interested in diving anywhere in Papua New Guinea, they are the group to call.

Most of PNG's coastline has never before been dived. That which has been explored has yielded one of the richest underwater landscapes anywhere. Lush gardens of hard and soft corals, teeming with fish and punctuated with sudden drop-offs, caves, underwater volcanos and large pelagics, turtles and rays. Wreck diving fans and history buffs come here for the unlimited choices of WW II wrecks, both American and Japanese.

Port Moresby's excellent sites are just a short boat ride from the city front. Several wreck dives, including the SS Pruth, a sunken cargo ship, are outside of the barrier reef.

Another exciting dive is Shark Alley, 14 miles from the main wharf. Occasionally killer whales (Orcas) have been sighted here. Other good sites include Haidana Passage, Lolorua Island, The Beacon, The Caves and The Finger.

Simpson Harbor at Rabaul has 54 shipwrecks dating from the Japanese occupation. No fewer than 12 are accessible to divers. Great visibility enhance the experience, a big bonus to wreck fans too often forced to endure murky waters.

Madang has two areas to explore. The outer reef sites include spectacular Magic Passage, the Mitchell Bomber, Pig Island Reef, Barracuda Point and Planet Rock. Several excellent beach dives along the north coast are not to be missed, including The Quarry, The Waterhole and The Boston wreck, a fully intact US minesweeper.

Other PNG dive destinations include the many small islands and reefs in Milne Bay, hoards of reef and pelagic fish at Stettin Bay, dramatic caves and overhangs at Walindi and many remarkably intact Japanese wrecks at Hansa Bay.

Papua New Guinea

• Airline Connections   From either Los Angeles or San Francisco, fly Qantas to Port Moresby PNG via Cairns, Australia. Air Niugini is the domestic carrier with flights to Australia and Asia as well. There is a departure tax of K$10.

Ecology

The land of Papua New Guinea is lush, varied, mountainous and expansive. Its mountains, of which the Star Mountains form the principal range, are among the largest in the world. The wide, well-watered interior valleys support a sizable population and agriculture. The high rainfall makes rivers like the Fly and the Sepik, large, wide and fast. Volcanoes stretch along the northern coast, most notably Mt. Lamington, which last erupted in 1951. The mainland and several islands are surrounded by exceptional coral reefs and fringed by mangrove swamps.

Sports

Papua New Guinea offers a surprising variety of activities. Trekking, canoeing and rafting tours explore parts of the country off the beaten path. Guided bushwalking gives the opportunity for close-up enjoyment of the exotic flora and fauna. Yachting and football, both Australian Rules and League Rugby, are very popular. And off the coast of Port Moresby, Hiri Canoe races (motorized canoes with sails) are frequent, taking special importance during the Hiri Festival in September.

Vanuatu

• Airline Connections   Vanuatu is reached via Brisbane, Australia or Nadi, Fiji on Ansett Vila Services and Air Pacific. Air Melanesia is the inter-island airline. The departure tax is about US$10. Reconfirm your ticket upon arrival or at least 72 hours before departing.

Introduction

Situated at the southernmost end of the Melanesian archipelago, the islands of Vanuatu stretch 1,300 miles from the Solomon Islands in the north to New Caledonia in the south.

Ecology

Covered in dense tropical growth, these fertile islands are comprised of coral and ash. Vanuatu has five active volcanoes, most notably Lopevi, which erupted in the 1970's. Westward or leeward sides of islands get less rain and often support open savannas, while windward sides grow thick rain forests. Among the islands' tropical flora are the massive, gnarled giant banyan trees which dominate village meeting places. These trees rank among the world's largest living organisms.

Exploring

Efate's capital city of Port Vila, offers visitors 400 hotel rooms, duty-free shopping, dozens of good restaurants, dive shops, a fishing charter and even a disco. This bustling tropical town with its beautiful, protected harbor is the country's government and business center.

Espiritu Santo Island and its main city, Luganville is another popular destination. James A. Michener was stationed here during the war and it was this corner of the world which inspired his novel, South Pacific. Deep in the overgrown jungle, remnants of crashed airplanes, deserted air strips and other war reminders are still being discovered.

Sports

Soccer fans can usually catch a game at the stadium on Saturday afternoons. Big game and deep-sea fishing expeditions can be booked through Tour Vanuatu. There are two 9-hole and one 18-hole gold courses.

• Diving

Underwater, the Port Vila Harbor area is sheltered, clear and warm. Wet suits are usually unnecessary. The reefs, a one half-hour boat trip

President Cooldige/Roessler

from Port Vila's waterfront, are making a healthy come-back after the last cyclone. Friendly, colorful fish abound, cruising in great numbers, posing for underwater cameras or asking for handouts. One of the most popular Port Vila dive spots is the Star of Russia, the wreck of a steel clipper ship sitting upright and open on the sand in 36 meters of water, complete with masts, rigging and a huge anchor.

Just offshore of Efate, 5-1/2 miles from Port Vila, is Hideaway Island, a private holiday resort and marine sanctuary.

By far, the most famous Vanuatu dive location is Luganville, also known as "Santo Town," on the island of Espiritu Santo. Here lies the wreck of the President Coolidge, sunk on October 6, 1942, carrying American troops and thousands of tons of vehicles, ammunition and supplies to support the US war efforts in the South Pacific. Ironically, the Coolidge was felled by an American mine as it entered the harbor. All but two of the 2,000 troops escaped with their lives, just before the 21,939 ton liner sank into the sand, just 40 meters offshore.

A quarter mile from the Coolidge is another dramatic war memorial: Million Dollar Point. It's a man-made wall composed of discarded jeeps, bulldozers, trucks, cranes and other equipment dumped into the sea as US troops withdrew from Santo in 1945. The 2-acre pile of coral-encrusted surplus rises mysteriously from the bottom, a mountain of tumbled wreckage.

Four Seasons Barrier Reef Resort | Gold Coast International

Hamilton Island Resort | Hayman Island Resort

Heron Island Resort | Southern Spirit

Aviatour | Brisbane Dive Systems

Key: The accommodations price range is based on the high season rate per night, double occupancy. The Liveaboard price range is per berth, high season. The dive price range is based on the cost of a two tank dive. Letter codes: Beach (or on the water), Diving, Fishing, Golf, Other watersports, Pool, Restaurant & Bar, Sailing, Tennis, Windsurfing.

Australia - Accommodations

AUSTRALIAN RESORT COMPANIES 800-922-5122 495 Units: $105-378 BDFKOPRSTW
011-613-6663013 011-613-6663939FX 441 St. Kilda Rd, 3rd Floor. Melbourne, Victoria 3004, Australia. There are 5 resort islands operated by Australian Resort Companies: Bedarra Island, 32 Units: $340-378; Brampton Island, 120 Units: $135-150; Dunk Island, 153 Units: $117-188; Great Keppel Island, 160 Units: $105-139; Lizard Island, 30 Units: $270-320.

CAIRNS HILTON INTERNATIONAL 800-445-8667   264 Units: $148-407 BDR
011-6170-521599 011-6170-521370FX Wharf Street Cairns, QLD 4870, Australia.

FOUR SEASONS BARRIER REEF RST 800-654-9153 175 Units: $150-600 BDFOPRSTW
011-077-709111 011-077-709100 FX John Brewer Reef via Townsville Queensland Australia. The world's first floating hotel is set in a lagoon of the John Brewer Reef, 72 km. northeast of Townsville. Two excellent restaurants, a disco and numerous recreational activities are offered. A professionally staffed, well- equipped dive shop on the premises makes trips daily to the reef aboard Dive Bell, the resort's dive boat. Tennis, yacht cruises, helicopter sightseeing trips and a semi-submersible sub are also available. See: Dive Bell.

GOLD COAST INTERNATIONAL 800-421-0536   296 Units: $108-222 BDFGOPRSTW
011-6175-921200 011-6175-921180FX Box 976 Surfers Paradise, QLD 4217, Australia.

HAMILTON ISLAND RESORT 800-445-5505   400 Units: $119-888 BDFKOPRSTW
011-6179-469144 Private Mail Bag, Post Office Hamilton Island, QLD 4803, Australia. Hamilton Island is Australia's most popular island resort destination. Alone among the world's island resorts, it has its own commercial jet strip with direct flights from all major Australian cities. There is a choice of lodging styles, 8 restaurants, access to the Great Barrier Reef and a wide variety of activities including sailing, all watersports, fishing, tennis, health club, & a PADI dive operation. Dive trips by boat and by helicopter! See: H 2 O Watersports.

HAYMAN ISLAND RESORT 800-366-1300   230 Units: $163-552 BDFGKOPRSTW
011-6179-469100 011-6179-469410FX 3 Knox St. Double Bay, NSW, Australia. A member of the "Leading Hotels of the World," accommodation for 500 in luxury 6 restaurants, 24-hour room service. The Hayman Dive and Snorkel Center is full-service PADI facility offering complete learn-to-dive and resort course, sales, rental and repairs. Daily free snorkeling lessons. The 64-foot Reef Goddess is the most advanced day dive-boat in the world running daily to Bait Reef Marine Park and other nearby reefs with both divers and snorkelers. See: Barrier Reef Diving Services.

HERON ISLAND RESORT 714-786-0119   120 Units: $134-237 BDFOPRT
011-617-2688222 714-651-0139FX 4330 Barranca Pkwy, Suite 101-105 Irvine CA 92714. Located on a true coral island, 72 kilometers from Gladstone in Queensland. The Resort is situated in a Marine National Park and is acknowledged as the best diving and snorkeling on the Great Barrier Reef. Heron is the only international resort located on the reef and is surrounded by beautiful white sandy beaches. Accommodations range from suites with private facilities to lodges with shared facilities. Price includes 3 meals per day. Bookings in US.

LORD HOWE ISLAND GUEST-HOUSES 800-426-5888   55 Units: $46-140 BDFGKOTW
011-612-6656335 011-612-6642623FX 27 Alfreda Street Coogee, 2034 NSW, Australia.

ORPHEUS ISLAND RESORT 800-551-2012   125 Units: $188-188 BDFOPRSTW
011-612-32-3911 Private Mail Bag Ingham, 4850 QLD, Australia.

PARKROYAL BRISBANE 800-252-2155   191 Units: $111-289 DFGOPRST
011-6172213411 011-617-2299817FX Cnr. Alice & Albert Streets Brisbane, QLD 4000, Australia.

SHERATON BREAKWATER CASINO 011-6177-724066   190 Units: $78-370 BDFOPRST
011-6177-222333 011-6177-724741FX Sir Leslie Thiess Drive Townsville, QLD 4810, Australia.

SOUTH MOLLE ISLAND 011-6179-469433   202 Units: $170-222 BDFGOPRST
011-6179-469580FX P. M. B. 21, Mackay Whitsundays, QLD 4802, Australia.

SOUTHERN CROSS 011-613-6530221   426 Units: $110-628 DFGOPRST
011-613-6502119FX 131 Exhibition Street Melbourne, VIC 3000, Australia.

WHITSUNDAY TERRACE RESORT 011-6179-466788 124 Units: $71-78 DFGKOPRSTW
011-6179-467128FX Box 126 Arlie Beach, QLD 4802, Australia. The Whitsunday Terraces offers beautiful panoramic views over the Whitsunday Passage, two pools and a spa. The Terraces offer a free tropical breakfast daily, courtesy coach transportation to/from Proserpine Airport, free daily resort activities and nightly entertainment. Activities include aerobics, jazz ballet, archery, windsurfing, paddleskiing and volleyball. Golf, sailing, scuba diving, tennis and squash nearby. See: Whitsunday Diving Services.

Australia - Cruise Line

CORAL PRINCESS CRUISES 011-6177-724675   48 Berths: $134-148 D
011-6177-211335FX 78 Primrose Street Townsville, QLD 4810, Australia.

Australia - Information

ANSETT AIRLINES 800-366-1300
  213-642-7487 9841 Airport Blvd., Suite 418 Los Angeles CA 90045. Australia: 011-613-6681211, 011-613-6681114FX, 501 Swanston Street, Melbourne, VIC 3000, Australia.

AUSTRALIAN TOURIST COMMISSION 213-552-1988
  213-552-1215FX 2121 Avenue of The Stars, Suite 1200 Los Angeles CA 90067. Australia: 011-612-3601111, 011-613-3316469FX, 80 Williams St., Woolloomooloo Sydney, NSW, 2011, Australia.

BUNDABERG DISTRICT DEVELOPMENT BOARD 011-6171-722406
  Box 930 Bundaberg, QLD 4670, Australia.

GLADSTONE PROMOTION & DEVELOPEMNT BD. 011-6179-724000
  011-6179-725006FX Australia.

NORFOLK AIRLINES 011-617-2295872
  011-617-2297073FX Nat. Bank House, Cnr Creek & Adelade Sts Brisbane, 4000, QLD, Australia.

QANTAS AIRWAYS LTD. 800-227-4500
  415-981-1152FX 360 Post St. San Francisco CA 94106. Australia: 011-612-2363636, 011-612-2364016, Box 489 GPO, Sydney, 2001, NSW, Australia.

QUEENSLAND TOURIST & TRAVEL CO. 213-465-8418
  213-465-5815FX 611 North Larchmont Blvd. Los Angeles CA 90004. Australia: 011-617-8335400, 011-617-8335436FX, 123 Eagle St., Level 36, Riverside Ctr., Brisbane, 4000 QLD, Australia.

WHITSUNDAY TOURISM ASS. 011-6179-46673
  Box 83 Airlie Beach, QLD 4802, Australia.

Australia - Liveaboards

BARRIER REEF CRUISES - CORALITA 011-6170-537477   12 Berths: $134-182 D
  Box 6605, Cairns Mail Center Cairns, QLD 4870, Australia.

MIKE BALL WATERSPORTS 011-6177-723022   46 Berths: $82-200 D
  011-6177-212152FX 252-256 Walker Street Townsville, QLD 4810, Australia.

REEF EXPLORER 800-443-0799   12 Berths: $150-200 BDR
  011-612-9977151 011-612-992835FX 6 Konda Close Bayview, NSW 2104, Australia. 800-821-6670 800-247-3483 800-348-9778. This liveaboard is designed and built for divers. Twin compressors with air-banks combined with easy access to the water allows for unlimited diving. Based in Cairns, the Reef Explorer plies the Great Barrier Reef and far into the Coral Sea and Papua New Guinea, thus offering an immense diversity in localities and feature for divers and snorkelers.

SOUTHERN SPIRIT 619-225-0588   14 Berths: $325-700 DOSW
  011-612-4985622 011-612-4987804FX 4/33 Ryde Road Pymble, NSW 2073, Australia. Cruise the Great Barrier Reef and throughout the Whitsunday Islands. Operating set departure cruises out of Hamilton Island every Sunday for 7 nights, also special charters. Rates include French champagne and fine Australian wines, all watersports including windsurfing, waterskiing, snorkeling, boom netting and diving. Other diversions include trap shooting, beach-combing and deserted island picnics. Gourmet meals include local seafood and exotic fruits

Australia - Sports

AVALON GAME FISHING CHARTERS 011-6170-551731   13 Boats: $600-1000 F
  011-6170-581138FX Box 1385 Cairns 4870, Australia.

AVIATOUR AUSTRALIA 800-551-2012
  800-445-0190CA 011-612-9081584 98 Spencer Road Cremore NSW 2090, Australia. Individualized hand made designer tours of Australia by Limousine and Learjet. The President, Mr. Jonathan Campbell personally designs your tour and where possible will be the senior member of the flight crew. Travel in the ultimate of luxury, style and sophistication while experiencing the best geography, history, culture and cuisine that Australia has to offer.

BARRIER REEF DIVING SERVICES 011-6179-466204   25 Divers: $45-63 D
  011-6179-466252 Box 180 Arlie Beach, QLD 4802, Australia. Tony Fontes runs a 5-star PADI training facility in two locations. The Airlie Beach shop offers daily dives on The Whitsunday Diver, a comfortable, custom dive boat carrying 25 divers and/or snorkelers. Each month a week-long dive & sail charter takes divers around the Whitsunday Islands & outer reef. The shop on Hayman Island, uses the luxurious Reef Goddess to dive the outer reef. Full Certs. Reef dives, resort courses and snorkeling trips offered. See: Hayman Island Resort.

BRISBANE DIVE SYSTEMS 011-617-3593925   10 Divers: $40-85 D
  536 Rode Road Chermside, QLD 4032, Australia. This is a 5-Star PADI training facility and Brisbane's oldest total dive service. You can learn to dive, purchase or rent what you need at their full retail shop, and then join them for a day trip on their new dive boat the Poseidon. The Poseidon is a custom built 24' outboard 8-passenger boat. Their day trips include Moreton Island and other sites within 45 minutes by boat. They pickup from all the Brisbane hotels. Book in advance.

CAIRNS FUN BUS 800-551-2012
  800-445-0190CA 011-6170-514829 88 Lake St. Cairns, QLD 4870, Australia. This is a daily Cairns tour starting at your hotel. Less than 1 hour is spent on the bus. A typical trip includes a visit to Centenary lakes to feed the native birds, (and possibly a small crocodile), a walk through jungle on mangrove boardwalks and up to the lookout over Cairns. You will explore the Crystal Cascades with waterfalls, rock pools and natural water slides. Then you go to the northern beaches. An Aussie BBQ lunch of shrimp, steak & salad.

CORAL SEA DIVING SERVICES 800-821-6670 — 55 Divers: $80-180 D
011-6170-985254 011-6170-993384FX Port Douglas, QLD, Australia.
DEEP SEA DIVERS DEN 011-6170-521404 — 56 Divers: $63-63 D
011-6170-541413 011-6170-512223 319 Draper St. Parramatta Park, QLD 4870, Australia.
DIVE BELL 011-6177-211155 — 40 Divers: $50-100 D
011-6177-723119FX Shop 4, 141 Ingham Rd. West End Townsville, QLD 4812, Australia. See: Four Seasons Barrier Reef Rsrt.
DOWN UNDER DAY DIVE BOAT 011-6170-551724 — 40 Divers: $80-100 D
Box 3 Freshwater, Cairns, 4872, Australia.

DOWN UNDER DIVE TRAVEL 011-6170-311288 — 50 Divers: $37-74 D
011-6170-557102 011-6170-311373FX Cnr Esplanade & Aplin Sts. Cairns, QLD 4870, Australia. Located on the waterfront in the heart of the hotel, motel and hostel area of Cairns. Friendly competent staff to help you enjoy Cairns and the Great Barrier Reef on either a learn to dive course or an extended dive trip to the outer reef. They offer 5-day learn to dive packages, 1-day snorkel trips, 2 - 14 day extended trips, whole boat charters, full equipment sales, and lots of service. Bookings for spcl day dive boats inc: Tusa, Aquanaut and Down Under.
FITZROY ISLAND DIVE CENTER 011-6170-519588 — 20 Divers: $31-31 DO
011-6170-519588 011-6170-521335FX Box 2401 Cairns, QLD 4870, Australia.
H 2 O WATERSPORTS 011-617-9469144 — 25 Divers: $60-70 DO
EXT:8058 FAX Box 19 Hamilton Island, QLD 4803, Australia. See: Hamilton Island Resort.
JERVIS BAY SEA SPORTS 011-6144-415012 — 32 Divers: $25-40 DF
011-6144-416694FX 47 Owen Street Huskicson, NSW 2540, Australia.
PRO DIVING SERVICES 011-6170-519915 — 91 Divers: $72-72 D
011-6170-519955FX Marlin Parade, Box 5551 Cairns, QLD 4870, Australia.
QUEENSLAND YACHT CHARTERS 011-619-2250588 — 45 Boats: $250-5000 S
011-612-3311211 011-612-3316388FX Box 1485 Potts Point, 2011 NSW, Australia.
QUICKSILVER CONNECTION 011-6170-985373 — 40 Divers: $56-93 DS
011-6170-985772FX Marina Mirage, Box 171 Port Douglas, QLD 4871, Australia.
RAGING THUNDER WHITEWATER RAFTING 011-6170-514911
011-6170-514010FX 88 Lake St. Cairns, QLD 4870, Australia.
SCUBA WORLD 011-617-8709030 — 20 Divers: $56-56 D
011-617-3716453FX 538 Milton Road Toowong, QLD 48066, Australia.
SOUTHERN CROSS DIVERS 011-613-2991111 — 32 Divers: $28-40 D
011-613-293912FX 1368 Toorak Road Burwood, VIC 3125, Australia.

Fiji Islands - Accommodations
CASTAWAY NAVITI RESORT 011-679-50444 — 144 Units: $78-78 BDFGOPRSTW
011-679-50085FX Box 29 Korolevu, Fiji. See: Sea Sports Ltd.
FIJIAN RESORT 011-679-50155 — 364 Units BDFGOPRST
011-679-50676FX Private Mail Bag Nadi Airport, Fiji.
HIDEAWAY RESORT 011-679-50177 — 58 Units: $66-66 BDFOPR
011-679-50608FX Box 233 Sigatoka, Fiji. See: Sea Sports Ltd.
HYATT REGENCY FIJI 011-679-50555 — 249 Units: $119-134 BDFGOPRSTW
011-679-50163FX Box 100 Korolevu, Fiji. See: Sea Sports Ltd.
NA KORO RESORT 011-679-86188 — 40 Units: $90-90 BDFOPRSTW
Box 12 Savusavu, Fiji. See: H 2 O Sports.
PACIFIC HARBOUR INTERNATIONAL RESORT 011-679-45022 — 84 Units: $80-80 BDFGORST
Postal Agency Pacific Habour, Fiji. See: Scubahire Ltd. and Bequa Divers Fiji.
REEF RESORT 011-679-50044 — 72 Units: $80-80 BDGOPRT
Box 173 Sigatoka, Fiji. See: Sea Sports Ltd.
REGENT OF FIJI 011-679-70700 — 294 Units: $170-210 BDFGOPRSTW
011-679-70850FX Box 441 Nadi, Fiji.

Fiji Islands - Information
FIJI VISITORS BUREAU 800-621-9604
213-417-2234 6151 West Century Blvd Los Angeles CA 90045.

Fiji Islands - Sports
DIVE TRAVEUNI 011-679406M — 20 Divers: $65-65 D
Post Office, Matei Taveuni, Fiji.
H 2 O SPORTS 011-679-86188 — 10 Divers: $50-50 D
c/o Na Koro Resort, Box 12 Savusavu, Fiji. See: Na Koro Resort.
KINGFISHER SPORTS 011-679-71711 — 16 Divers: $10-11 D
011-679-70447FX Box 9010 Nadi Airport, Fiji.
MARAU 011-679-45347 — 1 Boats F
Postal Agency Pacific Harbour, Fiji. See: Pacific Harbour International Resort.
MATAGI ISLAND — 28 Divers: $60-65 DF
Box 83, Waiyevo Taveuni, Fiji.
PACIFIC NOMAD LIVEABOARD 415-434-3400 — Divers: $175-200 DF
011-679-312488 011-679-3122762 Eliza Street Wulu Bay, Suva, Fiji.

QAMEA BEACH CLUB 011-679-87220   15 Divers: $14-14 DFOSW
    c/o Post Office, Matei Taveuni, Fiji.
SCUBAHIRE LTD. AND BEQUA DIVERS FIJI 011-679-361088   42 Divers: $75-75 DO
    011-679-361241 Box 777 Suva, Fiji. See: Pacific Harbour International Resort.
SEA SPORTS LTD 011-679-50598   36 Divers: $70-70 DFOSW
    011-679-50155 011-679-50163FX Box 65 Korolevu, Fiji. See: Hyatt Regency Fiji.

Papua New Guinea - Accommodations
JAIS ABEN RESORT 800-443-0799   18 Units: $68-102 BDOR
    011-675-823311 011-675-823560FX Box 105 Medang, Papua New Guinea.
WALINDI PLANTATION & WUVULU RESORT 800-443-0799   14 Units: $70-120 BDFO
    011-612-2675563 011-612-2676118FX 100 Clarence St. Sydney, 2000 NSW, Australia.

Papua New Guinea - Information
AIR NUIGINI 714-752-5440
    5000 Birch St., Suite 3000, West Tower Newport Beach CA 92660. Air Nuigini is the national carrier of Papua New Guinea with regular services from Sydney, Brisbane and Cairns. Within Papua New Guinea they provide you with fast same day connections to your dive destination. Air Nuigini operates an international air bus service and F28 jet services to all major destinations in Papua New Guinea.

Papua New Guinea - Sports
MARINE WORLD PTY. LTD 800-443-0799   30 Divers: $35-35 DF
    011-675-217487 011-675-212363FX Box 6843 Bohoro, Papua New Guinea.
RABAUL DIVE & TOUR SERVICES 800-443-0799   16 Divers: $45-45 D
    011-675-922913 Box 1128 Rabaul, Papua New Guinea.
SEA NEW GUINEA 800-443-0799   Divers D
    011-612-2675563 011-612-2676118FX 100 Clarence St. Sydney, 2000, Australia. Sea New Guinea has over 10 years experience in providing some of the best diving in the world. They provide up-to-date information on all dive facilities, both land based and liveaboard. They can take you diving anywhere in New Guinea. Walindi, Wuvulu, Rabaul, Madang, Telita and Reef Explorer itineraries and travel arrangements or comprehensive information are no further away than a phone call.

Solomon Islands - Accommodations
ANUHA ISLAND RESORT 011-677-22794   31 Units: $63-200 BDFOPRST
    Box 133 Honiara, Solomon Islands. See: Island Dive Services Ltd..
MENDANA HOTEL 011-677-20071   101 Units: $53-80 BDOPR
    011-677-23942FX Box 384 Honiara, Solomon Islands. See: Island Dive Services Ltd..
TAMBEA VILLAGE 011-677-23639   24 Units: $27-34 BDFOR
    011-677-23639FX Box 506 Honiara, Solomon Islands. See: Island Dive Services Ltd..
UEPI ISLAND RESORT 011-618-3323733   13 Units: $45-60 BDFORS
    011-618-792896 Via Seghe Marovo Lagoon, Solomon Islands.

Solomon Islands - Sports
ISLAND DIVE SERVICES LTD. 011-677-22103   32 Divers: $28-29 D
    011-677-23897FX Box 414 Honiara, Solomon Islands. See: Mendana Hotel.

Vanuatu - Accommodations
BOKISSA ISLAND RESORT 855   8 Units: $56-56 BDOPR
    Box 261 Espiritu Santo Island, Vanuato. See: Santo Dive Tours.
HIDEAWAY ISLAND RESORT, LIMITED 2963   10 Units: $56-56 BOPR
    2699FX Box 875 Port Vila, Vanuatu. See: Scuba Holidays.
HOTEL SANTO 3250   22 Units: $68-69 BDPR
    Box 178, Luganville Espiritu Santo Island, Vanuatu. See: Santo Dive Tours.
IRIRIKI ISLAND RESORT 3388   70 Units: $80-80 BDOPRSW
    011-612-2901225 011-612-2903214FX Box 230 Port Vila, Vanuatu.

Vanuatu - Information
NATIONAL TOURISM OFFICE OF VANUATU 714-733-1744
    714-651-0139FX 4330 Barranca Pkwy. Suite 101 Irvine CA 92714.

Vanuatu - Sports
ISLAND DIVERS 2255   50 Divers: $15-30 DFOS
    Box 888 Port Vila, Vanuatu.
NAUTILUS SCUBA 2398   65 Divers: $40-40 DFS
    3710 Box 78 Port Vila, Vanuatu.
SANTO DIVE TOURS 822   Divers: $40-40 D
    Box 233 Espiritu Santo Island, Vanuatu.
SCUBA HOLIDAYS 2963   44 Divers: $42-42 DO
    Box 875 Port Vila, Vanuatu. See: Hideaway Island Resort, Limited.